MASTERING ALDUS FREEHAND™

October 1991

MASTERING ALDUS® FREEHAND™

MACINTOSH® 3.0 VERSION

BUSINESS ONE IRWIN
Desktop Publishing Library

Homewood, IL 60430

**Deke McClelland
& Craig Danuloff**

Sponsoring editor: Susan Stevens, Ph.D.
Project editor: Jane Lightell
Production manager: Ann Cassady
Printer: R. R. Donnelley & Sons Company

Library of Congress Cataloging-in-Publication Data

McClelland, Deke, 1962–
    Mastering Aldus FreeHand, Macintosh version 3.0 / Deke McClelland
& Craig Danuloff.
        p.   cm.
    Includes index.
    ISBN 1–55623–443–0
    1. Aldus Freehand (Computer program) I. Danuloff, Craig, 1963–
. II. Title.
T385.M37825   1991
006.6′86—dc20   91–17521

Printed in the United States of America

2 3 4 5 6 7 8 9 0 DOC 8 7 6 5 4 3 2 1

Acknowledgements

Thank you to the following people
for helping in the creation of this book:

Bill Gladstone and Susan Glinert

R.D., S.R., J.G., A.E., and J.M.

Kathi Townes of TechArts for copy editing

Scott Harmon and Robert Vernon for imagesetting

Jill Miller, Rachel Pitinga, and Freda Cook for product

Conrad Chavez for FreeHand technical support

Karyn Scott of VideoLogic for DVA-4000/Mac video board
with which book covers were captured

Elizabeth Pheasant for being so damn sweet!

Contents

Chapter 7:
Reshaping Existing Paths   185

Chapter 12:
Transforming and Duplicating Objects   405

Appendix B:

FreeHand and the PostScript Language 539

VOYAGER

a simulation of the space probe passing Jupiter

Mastering
Aldus
FreeHand

July 1985: Aldus Corporation changes the course of personal computing by introducing PageMaker. Though not the first page-layout package designed for a personal computer, the strength of the product and the strength of Aldus itself—in terms of marketing, engineering, and support—propels PageMaker to dominance in the desktop publishing arena.

Six months later: The small Texas-based Altsys Corporation releases Fontographer, a program that allows desktop publishers to design and execute their own PostScript-compatible typefaces.

March, 1987: Adobe releases Illustrator, the first fully functional PostScript drawing program. Not to be outdone, Altsys turns its attention to an advanced graphics program as well. The result is sufficiently impressive to attract Aldus' attention and eventual acquisition, increasing its predominance in the computer design field.

Now: Aldus FreeHand 3.0 provides you with precise control over the creation and alteration of high-resolution images. FreeHand is well suited to the creation of technical drawings, medical illustrations, logotypes, business graphics, fine art, product illustrations, and many other graphic forms using a relatively inexpensive personal computing system.

Your completed illustration may be printed on any PostScript-equipped output device or saved on disk and imported into another computer software, such as PageMaker or QuarkXPress. FreeHand graphics will print at the full resolution of any PostScript printer, such as the 300-dot-per-inch Apple LaserWriter or the 2540-dot-per-inch Linotronic 300 photo imagesetter. FreeHand also offers the capability to create automatic color separations for use in professional-quality color offset printing.

About this book

With the power of Aldus FreeHand 3.0 comes responsibility. Although the package adheres strictly to all the friendly interface guidelines required of a Macintosh application and is basically straightforward and easy to use, you will get the full benefit of this software only if you *master* it. This means becoming familiar with the drawing model on which FreeHand is based; understanding the tools, commands, and dialog box options that FreeHand provides; and gaining hands-on experience by completing a wide variety of quick but informative exercises. *Mastering Aldus FreeHand* is dedicated to the relentless, exhaustive delivery of this knowledge!

In the chapters that follow, you will find each of the concepts, features, and functions of FreeHand described completely, including functional descriptions required by novices, advice aimed at intermediate users, and advanced discussions demanded by power-users. Throughout, *Mastering Aldus FreeHand* adopts the viewpoint of the user. In addition to objective, technical details, FreeHand's strengths and weaknesses are considered—what to rely on and what to avoid. In every manner possible, this book captures the insights born from years of artistic and computing experience, with the hope that *Mastering Aldus FreeHand* will become your personal FreeHand 3.0 trainer, providing both bookwise details *and* street-smart tips and tricks.

Conventions

This book employs the following conventions to make it easier for you to understand Aldus FreeHand 3.0 and to glean useful information without slogging through a lot of words:

The *keyboard equivalent icon* calls out commands, options, and other features that can be accessed from the keyboard, allowing you to increase your speed and devote your mouse hand to the more important task of drawing.

The *power tips icon* calls out tips. Not "press this key to get this" tips, but real, honest-to-goodness thoughtful tips that will improve your drawing capability by leaps and bounds. If you didn't think it was possible to do something with FreeHand, we'll show you how.

We don't like everything about Aldus FreeHand, and the *gripe icon* allows us to share our complaints. Sometimes, our gripes come in the form of warnings or advice; sometimes, we're just plain upset. And for those of you who have access to more than one drawing program, we'll let you know if another program does a better job.

Chapter summaries

Mastering Aldus FreeHand is composed of 15 chapters, an appendix, and an index. The following is a summarization of the contents:

- **Chapter 1** looks at the concepts behind graphic creation in programs like Aldus FreeHand. In this discussion we provide a brief history of the development of computer graphics on the Mac using applications like MacPaint, MacDraw, Illustrator, and FreeHand.

- **Chapter 2** opens with a glossary of basic Macintosh terminology, followed by a comprehensive tour of the FreeHand toolbox and menu commands. This chapter is designed to familiarize you with FreeHand in case you want to begin using it immediately. If you are an experienced Macintosh user, you will probably be able to begin creating graphics after a brief survey of this chapter. If you are new to Macintosh or to this type of graphics application, this chapter will provide a thorough introduction to your new tools.

- **Chapter 3** discusses how to create a new illustration or open an existing illustration in FreeHand, including how to introduce, use, and change tracing templates. We take a brief tour through Free-Hand's on-screen environment, including view sizes and display modes. We also introduce the PREFERENCES and MORE PREFERENCES dialog boxes, FreeHand's central control stations. The chapter finishes by addressing the topics of saving your illustration and quitting the application.

- **Chapter 4** uses a conceptual tutorial to focus on the strategy used to draw complex graphics in FreeHand. Here, the creation of a sample illustration is approached from an entirely theoretical vantage; no specific commands or tools are discussed. Instead, this chapter addresses the thought process required to solve electronic drawing problems. This chapter will be beneficial to both the novice and the experienced graphic creator.

- **Chapter 5** examines how to draw geometric and free-form images from scratch using the rectangle, rounded-rectangle, and oval tools, the line and freehand tools, and the all-powerful point tools. Here's everything you ever wanted to know about point and path theory, but were afraid to ask.

- **Chapter 6** looks at tracing bitmapped and scanned images. If you can't draw, you can trace using the trace tool. We even compare this tool to stand-alone tracing utilities, like Adobe Streamline.

- **Chapter 7** focuses on the manipulation of existing lines and shapes. Everything in FreeHand can be molded and reshaped to your heart's desire. We look first at moving points and segments and measuring distances. We next turn our attention to three new tools for adding, subtracting, and converting points. Finally, you will learn all there is to know about Bézier control handles.

- **Chapter 8** explains how to use type in FreeHand. We describe how to create text objects, including text blocks and type on a path. We also explain the TEXT dialog box, which allows you to edit any character attribute. With version 3.0, you may convert type to a path and manipulate it until it doesn't even look like text any more.

- **Chapter 9** is about fills. The chapter starts out easy, but then we turn on the steam with exhaustive discussions of tile patterns, clipping paths, and composite paths. These last items, completely new to FreeHand 3.0, allow you to cut holes in objects so you can see the doily through the doughnut.

- **Chapter 10** is about the other side of the attribute coin—strokes. Everything's here: line weights, line caps, dash patterns, dash patterns with line caps, dash patterns and line caps with line weights layered on each other . . . well, you get the idea. We even show you how to add custom arrowheads to the ends of lines.

- **Chapter 11** colorizes your artwork. This chapter includes information on using the Pantone Colors library, as well as a theoretical introduction to the issues of color as it relates to working with computer-generated art and four-color process printing. We also explain the new COLORS and STYLES palettes.

- **Chapter 12** dwells on transformations and duplications. You will learn how to create a precision drawing environment using rulers and guides. Next we discuss the four transformation tools, with which you can scale, flip, rotate, and slant any graphic object or text block. The last half of the chapter covers duplication, layering, and blending.

- **Chapter 13** looks at the importing and exporting of graphic images. FreeHand imports images stored in the popular MacPaint, PICT, and TIFF formats used by most scanning software, drawing programs, and desktop publishing software available for the Macintosh computer. You may also export an illustration as an EPS graphic.

- **Chapter 14** focuses on printing your illustrations, including the creation and use of color separations. Printing problems and considerations are also examined in this chapter.

- **Appendix A** describes how to install Aldus FreeHand on your hard drive, just in case you need some help getting started. Even if you're already up and running, you may want to check out our description of the QuicKeys 2 macros included with FreeHand.

- **Appendix B** looks at how you can use the PostScript language to enhance your illustrations. We don't teach you PostScript, but we tell you what you need to know and where to learn. We also explain how to use the custom PostScript fills and strokes included with FreeHand, as well as those available from third-party distributors.

Each chapter contains practical tips and advice designed to increase your user potential. In addition, we provide essential warnings to minimize unforeseen problems and aggravation. From cover to cover, *Mastering Aldus FreeHand, Macintosh Version 3.0* is designed to provide you with all the information that you will need to get the most out of this powerful application.

Drawing
on the
Macintosh

The first image of a Macintosh computer that many users saw was a seemingly handwritten "Hello" scrawled across a tiny black-and-white screen. From this image alone, it was immediately apparent that the Mac was unlike everything computing had been before. Sure, the computer was a new shape, sort of a miniature arcade game, but that wasn't the giveaway. The scribbled "Hello" signaled something much more important.

Gone was the monotonous computer lettering that was a constant reminder of a computer's robotic nature. In its place was a free-form word, written at an angle in letters three inches high and looking distinctly friendly. The image on the screen, we'd later learn, was from a new piece of software called MacPaint.

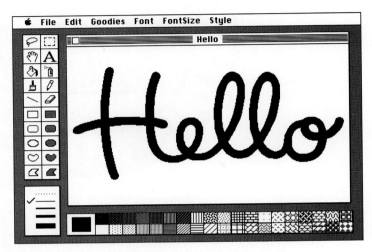

Figure 1.01: The debut of the friendly Macintosh computer.

MacPaint was as much of a revolution in applications software as the Macintosh itself was in hardware and the System/Finder was in operating systems. MacPaint was probably as much responsible for Mac's early success as were these other items. Looking back, it is easy to pinpoint MacPaint as a real turning point for personal computer graphics. All the promise held in that handwritten "Hello" unfolded as MacPaint became a familiar tool. Gone were the boxlike constrictions and programming tedium that had previously epitomized personal computer graphics. Instead, a diverse set of familiar drawing tools, such as the pencil, paintbrush, and spraypaint can were now *on-screen* drawing tools, adapted for computer use with an amazing similarity to their real-world counterparts.

The advent of MacPaint was important for two reasons. First, skilled artists were quickly able to produce tremendous works using MacPaint. The diversity of MacPaint's tools proved enough for the production of thousands of images that soon turned up in publications, art exhibits, and on clip-art disks and computer screens everywhere. The second important result of MacPaint was the effect the program had on "the rest of us," the non-artist masses who had never dreamed of lifting brush to canvas or stroking pen to paper in anything more elaborate than a telephone doodle. To this group, MacPaint provided freedom to try, forgiveness to correct, and tools to empower. Just as word processors had encouraged the writing process, MacPaint encouraged graphic creation and placed it within the grasp of every user.

While the inevitable wish list for additional MacPaint features grew, the more important limitation had already become apparent: its low-resolution bitmapped nature—which was in large part responsible for its power—was a limiting factor on the printed page. Many images require fluid curves, and MacPaint's stair-stepped approximations inhibited this new brand of computer art from establishing itself in the many areas where quality was the paramount concern.

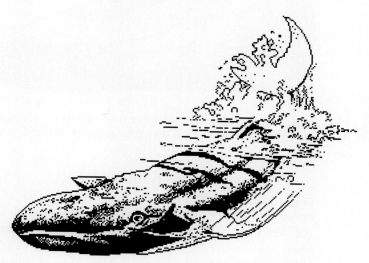

Figure 1.02: Soon after its introduction, MacPaint became synonymous with low-resolution graphics.

This limitation became more pronounced with the introduction of the LaserWriter printer. With the PostScript language built inside, this toner-based laser printer was actually capable of printing Macintosh-created words and pictures at 300 dots per inch—four times the resolution of the computer screen. The stair-steps that appeared on the screen were replaced with nearly perfect curves. The catch, however, was that only

PostScript-compatible typefaces and mathematically defined graphics utilized the full resolution of a PostScript printer. Alas, MacPaint was still MacPaint, cemented to the 72-dot-per-inch resolution of the software.

MacDraw, on the other hand, suddenly moved from its role as a technically oriented specialty application to the center stage of Macintosh graphics. This is because MacDraw took advantage of the full resolution of the LaserWriter. MacDraw's limitation—a limited set of tools useful for creating rather boxy images—was overlooked in favor of its sharp, smooth output. Computer graphics could now match the clarity of traditional graphics, but they were limited in their expressive range.

Figure 1.03: MacDraw took advantage of the LaserWriter's high resolution, but its output was typically stylized and simplistic.

As the abilities of the PostScript interpreter inside the LaserWriter became better understood, users began to search for an application powerful enough to drive its precise laser-printing engine. Held against this potential, MacPaint was seen as the toy its critics had always proclaimed it to be. Even MacDraw, utilizing only the most basic of PostScript's capabilities, was inadequate. It wasn't until Adobe released Illustrator and, later, Aldus released FreeHand, that the power of PostScript began to be tapped.

These new programs offered the resolution capabilities of MacDraw combined with drawing freedoms similar to MacPaint. Precise lines and shapes could be drawn in any weight, turning and curving limitlessly. Enclosed areas could be filled with any screen density or pattern that could be defined in the PostScript language. Not only were the vast quantity of PostScript typefaces useful for traditional writing tasks, but type itself became an object that could be manipulated to produce any graphic effect.

Figure 1.04: The new breed of PostScript drawing applications offered artistic freedom and high-resolution output.

By providing users with the ability to utilize the full power of the PostScript language, programs like Aldus FreeHand have shattered the distinction between computer art and traditional art. In the areas of graphic illustration, technical illustration, and for many other graphic forms, art finally enjoys the power of the personal computer.

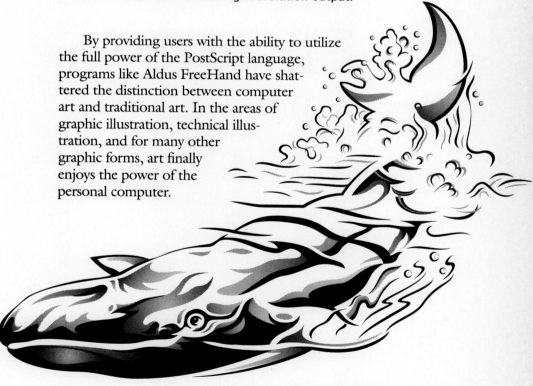

Figure 1.05: The field of graphic arts now enjoys the full power of the personal computer.

Terms, Tools, Menus, and Shortcuts

As a Macintosh application, Aldus FreeHand very closely follows the Macintosh interface. Your proficiency with FreeHand thus depends on how well you use your mouse and keyboard to interact with a collection of menus, tools, and dialog boxes. This chapter is an introduction to these fundamental aspects of FreeHand.

Each FreeHand tool and menu command, as well as many associated dialog boxes, will be discussed. After reading this chapter, you will have a good understanding of the range of capabilities provided by Aldus FreeHand. More experienced users—especially those familiar with previous versions of FreeHand—may find this information sufficient to allow them to begin their own experimentations with FreeHand 3.0. Less experienced users may find these summaries a bit overwhelming. In either case, remember that this is only a brief tour; the remainder of this book will provide all the details required to master the range of possibilities suggested in this chapter.

Before touring the menus and tools, however, we will take a moment to define the terms used throughout this book in describing the basic Macintosh interface. Terms like *select*, *choose*, *options*, and so on are defined here to remove ambiguity and to facilitate your learning experience. Because most of these terms are not universally defined, we recommend that even experienced Macintosh users review this section before going on to the other chapters of the book.

We will assume that you know how to perform a few functions required for the fundamental operation of your Macintosh. These include turning on your computer, inserting a disk, and copying files. You must also be familiar with the meaning of the terms *mouse*, *monitor*, *window*, *icon*, *cursor*, and *desktop*. If you are unfamiliar with these functions or terms, please consult your Macintosh operations manual.

Basic terminology

The terms defined in the following pages are ones with which you are probably familiar in a general sense. However, in the context of this book, they represent unique concepts that are applicable to operating a Macintosh computer. While they might have alternative meanings in other contexts, our use of these words throughout this book will be confined to the definitions contained in this chapter. Other terminology specifically applicable to using Aldus FreeHand will be introduced in later chapters. Whether defined in this chapter or later, all vocabulary words will appear in *italic type*.

Mouse operations

We will first review mouse operations. To *click* the mouse is to press the mouse button and immediately *release*. To *drag* is to press and hold down the mouse button, move your mouse to a new location, and release. To *double-click* is to press and release the mouse button twice in rapid succession. Each of these operations is demonstrated in Figure 2.01.

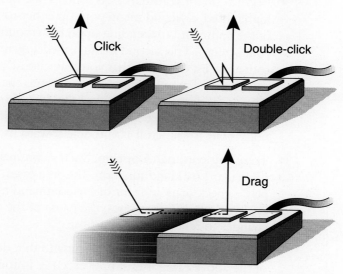

Figure 2.01: The three fundamental mouse operations.

Menus

Commands are organized into groups of related commands called *menus*. Each menu is assigned a name, which appears along the top of your screen in the *menu bar*. To *choose* a command is to pick it from a menu by clicking and holding your mouse button down on the menu name, then dragging down the list of commands. When the command you wish to choose is *highlighted*—displayed with white characters on a black background—release your mouse button.

Like other Macintosh applications, FreeHand offers four kinds of menu commands:

- **Command followed by ellipses**. Choosing a command whose name is followed by an ellipsis (…) causes a *dialog box* to appear. The dialog box FreeHand's way of requesting information before executing the command.

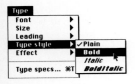

- **Pop-up menu command**. As soon as one of these commands is highlighted, a second menu pops up either to the right or to the left of the command (depending upon the amount of space available on your screen). This second menu, called a *hierarchical pop-up menu*, contains a list of *options* that you may choose much in the same way you choose a menu command. Drag onto the pop-up menu, then drag up or down the menu until the desired option is highlighted, and finally release the mouse button. If the entire pop-up menu is not visible, it will scroll as you drag toward its top or bottom.

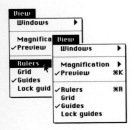

- **Toggling command option**. Such a command turns on and off a particular FreeHand function. In some cases, these commands display a check mark in front of the command name when the feature is turned on. In other cases, the name of the command itself changes to reflect its new purpose.

- **Executing command**. Any command that does not fall into one of the above categories simply executes immediately after you choose it.

Many menu commands may be chosen by simultaneously pressing two or more keys on your keyboard. Such a key sequence is called a *keyboard equivalent*. In most cases, the keyboard equivalent for a command is listed to the right of the command in its menu. Throughout this book, we will list applicable keyboard equivalents in parentheses each time a menu command is introduced. The cloverleaf symbol (⌘) represents the COMMAND key, the switch symbol (⌥) represents the OPTION key, and the up arrow (⇧) represents the SHIFT key.

Dialog boxes

A *dialog box* can present information to you, request information from you, or both. In most cases, dialog boxes appear in response either to a command that you have chosen or to some action that you have taken. When a dialog box requests information, it does so by presenting you with options, similar in function to those offered in hierarchical pop-up menus.

Four kinds of options may be found in dialog boxes:

```
Alignment
Align:  ◉ Elements   ○ To grid
  ◉ Top
  ○ Center
  ○ Bottom
  ○ Height
```

- **Radio buttons**. Within a group of options among which you may select only one, small round buttons appear before each option name. These are called *radio buttons*. To *select* or *deselect* a radio button option, click on the round button itself or on the name of the option following the button. Only one radio button option in a set may be selected at a time: selecting any one will deselect all others. A set of radio buttons are usually physically adjacent. Several sets of radio buttons may appear in a single dialog box, but only one from each set may be selected at any one time. A radio button indicates that an option is selected when the button is filled black and is deselected when the button is empty.

```
Preferences
Performance/display options:
  ☒ Draw object-by-object
  ☐ High-rez TIFF display
  ☒ Display text effects
  ☒ Better (slower) display
  ☐ Display curve levers
```

- **Check boxes**. Within a group of options among which you may select any number of alternatives, a small square button appears before each option name. This is a *check box*. To *select* or *deselect* a check box, click on the square before the option name or directly on the option name itself. If that option was previously deselected, it will become selected; if it was selected, the option will become deselected. Multiple check boxes within a set may be selected or deselected. A check box indicates that an option is selected when an × is displayed and is deselected when the box is empty.

```
Path/point
              Horizontal   Vertical
Point:        180          456
Handle 1:     186          468
Handle 2:     172          440
```

- **Option boxes**. An option for which you must enter data has one or more *option boxes*. Most option boxes contain default data when the dialog box first appears. When this default data is selected (highlighted with white characters on a black background), you can enter new values from the keyboard and the default data will be replaced. To *select* a value in an option box, double-click on a newly entered value or drag over the current value.

In a dialog box that contains several option boxes, you can move from one option box to the next by pressing the TAB key.

⬩ Pop-up menu. An option that is presented as a *pop-up menu* displays only the current option setting when its dialog box first appears. To view the list of alternatives for such an option, you must select the current option (or an icon in some cases) by pressing and holding down the mouse button on top of it. This will "pop up" a menu displaying the available options. An option is selected from the pop-up menu by dragging up or down the listing and releasing the mouse button when the name of the desired alternative is highlighted. If an option in a pop-up menu is followed by an ellipsis (…), choosing it will bring up yet another dialog box, which contains additional options.

Once you have finished entering, selecting, and choosing options, you may exit a dialog box by clicking on buttons. The most common buttons are the OK and Cancel buttons. Buttons may also serve as commands when they are placed within dialog boxes, where they are used to initiate an action or bring up another dialog box.

Dialog boxes that do not request information are known as *alert boxes*, since their purpose is to alert you to some fact. Some alert boxes warn you of the consequences of the action you are about to take and allow you to abort that action. Others inform you of some event that has already happened, allowing you only to acknowledge that you are aware of the event.

You will notice that an option, command, or menu is sometimes *dimmed*. A dimmed item indicates that it has no effect on a certain situation. Dimmed items cannot be chosen or selected.

Typographic conventions

Occasionally, this book will instruct you to press a key while performing a mouse operation. When not represented by symbols (⌘, ⇧, ⌥)—as in the case of keyboard equivalents—keys are listed in small caps (COMMAND, SHIFT, OPTION). Menus (FILE, EDIT), commands (SAVE, OPEN…), palettes (COLORS, LAYERS, STYLES), buttons (APPLY, CANCEL), and dialog box names (OPEN DOCUMENT, PREFERENCES, TEXT) are also listed in small caps to distinguish them from standard text. Option names are set apart with quotation marks, whether they appear in pop-up menus ("Helvetica," "Justify") or in dialog boxes ("Snap-to grid," "Corner radius").

The toolbox

The following are brief descriptions of the *tools* offered by Aldus Free-Hand 3.0 to create and manipulate the lines, shapes, and text that will make up your FreeHand documents. These are provided merely as a sample of the possibilities that exist. More thorough descriptions are presented in the following chapters.

A tool is chosen from the *toolbox*, or *tool palette*, by clicking on it. The chosen tool will become highlighted. A positive feature of the FreeHand toolbox is that it is entirely independent of a FreeHand drawing window. Therefore, if you reduce a drawing window, the toolbox remains unchanged so that all tools are visible and easily accessible. You may move the toolbox by dragging at its title bar, or hide the toolbox by clicking in its close box. To redisplay the toolbox, choose the WINDOWS command from the VIEW menu, then choose "Toolbox" from the resulting hierarchical pop-up menu. One toolbox serves, and is always positioned in front of, any and all open FreeHand windows.

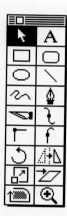

Figure 2.02: The FreeHand toolbox contains 18 drawing and manipulation tools.

The 18 tools included in the FreeHand toolbox are displayed in Figure 2.02 and each tool is described in the following text.

The arrow tool

The *arrow tool* (also called the *selection tool* or *pointer tool*) is the tool most commonly used in Aldus FreeHand. It is used to select, move, and duplicate existing objects in an illustration. The arrow tool may be used as follows:

- Click on a point or segment in any object to select the entire object and deselect the previous selection.

- Click the interior of a filled object or text block to select it and deselect the previous selection.

- Click on a point in a selected path to select that point independently of others in the path and deselect any previously selected point.

- Press OPTION and click a point or segment to select a path inside a group independently of other paths in the group.

- Press SHIFT and click a point or object to add it to the current selection.

- Drag on an empty portion of the screen to create a *marquee*. All points, groups, and text blocks surrounded by the marquee will become selected. Individual points of a group are not selected.

- Press OPTION and drag on an empty portion of the screen to select all points inside the marquee, including those that belong to a group.

- Press CONTROL and click a selected object to select the object located directly behind the selection and deselect the current selection.

- Press CONTROL and OPTION and click a selected object to select the path directly behind the current selection, even if that path belongs to a group, and deselect the current selection.

- Press CONTROL and SHIFT and click a selected object to add the object located directly behind the current selection to the current selection.

- Drag a selected object to move the current selection.

- Drag a selected object and press SHIFT before completing the drag to move the current selection in a 45° direction (horizontally, vertically, or diagonally).

- Drag any corner point of a selected group to enlarge or reduce the selection.

- Press SHIFT and drag any corner point of a selected group to enlarge or reduce the selection proportionally.

Press TAB to deselect all objects in the current illustration. Press the TILDE key (~) to deselect points while leaving their paths selected. This technique is commonly used after marqueeing, to avoid reshaping selected paths. Press TILDE a second time to select the entire group to which each selected path may belong.

The arrow tool affects selected text blocks differently than selected paths or groups. The following items describe how:

- Drag a corner handle to adjust the column width of a text block. The type inside the text block rewraps to fit the new column width.
- Drag the top or bottom handle to increase or decrease leading.
- Drag a side handle to adjust the letter spacing.
- Press OPTION and drag a side handle to adjust the word spacing.
- Press OPTION and drag a corner handle to enlarge or reduce the size of letters in a text block. Press SHIFT and OPTION to scale proportionally.

 To temporarily access the arrow tool at any time, press and hold the COMMAND key. Releasing the COMMAND key will return you to the previously selected tool.

The type tool

A Unlike type tools in other programs that allow you to both create and edit type, the FreeHand type tool serves for text creation only. The *type tool* may be used as follows:

- Click anywhere on the page to indicate the placement of the bottom left corner of the text block.
- Drag to draw a horizontal line representing the column width. Text entered into the TEXT dialog box will wrap to fit inside this column.

After you determine the placement of the text block, the TEXT dialog box will display, providing a text entry area for creating and editing type. Press ENTER to instruct FreeHand to display the type on the page inside a selected text block.

 Pressing the A key will select the type tool at any time, except when a dialog box is displayed. Pressing SHIFT-A will also select the type tool.

The rectangle tool

The *rectangle tool* is used to create a grouped rectangle with a center point, which appears as a small × when creating and manipulating the shape. The rectangle tool may be used as follows:

- Drag to draw a rectangle from corner to opposite corner.
- Press OPTION and drag to draw a rectangle from center point to corner.
- Press SHIFT and drag or SHIFT-OPTION-drag to draw a perfect square.

 Pressing the 1 key—either in the standard key set or on the keypad—will select the rectangle tool at any time, except when a dialog box is displayed.

The rounded-rectangle tool

The *rounded-rectangle tool* is used to create a grouped rectangle with rounded corners. The radius of the rounded corners may be specified by selecting the rectangle and choosing ELEMENT INFO… from the ELEMENT menu (⌘-I). The rounded-rectangle tool may be used as follows:

- Drag to draw a rounded rectangle from corner to opposite corner.
- Press OPTION and drag to draw from center point to corner.
- Press SHIFT and drag or SHIFT-OPTION-drag to draw a perfect square with rounded corners.

 Pressing the 2 key—either in the standard key set or on the keypad—will select the rounded-rectangle tool at any time, except when a dialog box is displayed.

The oval tool

The *oval tool* is used to create a grouped ellipse with a center point, which appears as a small × when creating and manipulating the shape. The oval tool may be used as follows:

- Drag to draw an ellipse from corner to opposite corner.
- Press OPTION and drag to draw an ellipse from center point to corner.
- Press SHIFT and drag or SHIFT-OPTION-drag to draw a perfect circle.

Pressing the 3 key—either in the standard key set or on the keypad—will select the oval tool at any time, except when a dialog box is displayed.

The line tool

 The *line tool* is used to create a straight segment at any angle. The line tool may be used as follows:

- Drag to draw a segment from one endpoint to the other.
- Press SHIFT and drag to constrain the line to an angle that is a multiple of 45° (horizontal, vertical, or diagonal).

 Pressing the 4 key—either in the standard key set or on the keypad—will select the line tool at any time, except when a dialog box is displayed.

The freehand tool

 The *freehand tool,* which appears as a squiggly line, is used to draw free-form paths. FreeHand automatically determines the placement and identity of the points required to define the free-form path. The freehand tool may be used as follows:

- Drag on an empty portion of the screen to create a free-form path.
- Press OPTION while dragging with the tool to draw a straight segment. Release OPTION to end the segment.
- Press SHIFT and OPTION while dragging with the tool to draw a straight segment at a 45° angle.
- Press COMMAND while dragging with the tool to erase portions of the path you have just drawn.
- Drag from either end of a selected open path to extend the length of the path.
- Drag from one end of a selected open path to the other end of the same path to close the path.

Pressing the 5 key—either in the standard key set or on the keypad—will select the freehand tool at any time, except when a dialog box is displayed.

Double-clicking the freehand tool icon in the toolbox displays the FREEHAND dialog box, which allows you to adjust the sensitivity of the freehand tool.

The pen tool

The *pen tool* is used to draw a path as a series of individual points. Although it appears nearly identical to the pen tool featured in the rival program Adobe Illustrator, this pen tool operates more similarly to its predecessor, the combination tool, familiar to users of previous versions of Aldus FreeHand.

Typically, you click or drag with the pen tool to establish the first point in a path. As you click or drag to create a second point, FreeHand draws a *segment* joining the two points. Another segment joins the second point to the third, the third to the fourth, and so on. Drawing with the pen tool is more laborious than drawing with the freehand tool, but the results are usually more accurate. The pen tool may be used as follows:

- Click on an empty portion of the screen to create a *corner point* and draw a segment between it and the previously selected endpoint.

- Press SHIFT and click to constrain the angle between the previous endpoint and the current corner point to a multiple of 45°.

- Drag on an empty portion of the screen to create a *curve point* with two symmetrical *Bézier control handles.*

- Drag and press OPTION before completing the drag to change the curve point in progress to a *cusp*; that is, a corner point with two independent Bézier control handles.

- Press OPTION and then drag to create a corner point with only one Bézier control handle.

- Double-click on an empty portion of the screen to create a deselected corner point, thus ending the path.

Pressing the 6 key—either in the standard key set or on the keypad—will select the pen tool at any time, except when a dialog box is displayed.

The knife tool

The *knife tool* is used to split segments in an existing path. FreeHand automatically determines the identity of the points based on the form of the path. The knife tool may be used as follows:

- Click on a segment to insert two endpoints, splitting the segment. This technique can be used to open a closed path or to divide an open path into two open paths.

- Click on a point to convert the point into two endpoints, thus opening a closed path or dividing an open path into two open paths.

KE Pressing the 7 key—either in the standard key set or on the keypad—will select the knife tool at any time, except when a dialog box is displayed.

The curve tool

The *curve tool*, which appears as a backward-S-shaped line running through a small square, is used to draw a path as a series of individual points, much like the pen tool. But unlike the pen tool, the curve tool creates only a curve point with two symmetrical Bézier control handles. While you may create paths from scratch with the curve tool, it is most useful for adding one or more curve points to an existing open path. After selecting an endpoint belonging to the path you want to extend, use the curve tool as follows:

- Click on an empty portion of the screen to create a curve point and draw a segment between it and the previously selected endpoint.

- Press SHIFT and click to constrain the angle between the previous endpoint and the current curve point to a multiple of 45°.

- Double-click on an empty portion of the screen to create a deselected curve point, thus ending the path.

KE Pressing the 8 key—either in the standard key set or on the keypad—will select the curve tool at any time, except when a dialog box is displayed.

The corner tool

The *corner tool*, which appears as a two straight segments meeting at a small square, is another specialized point-creation tool, used to create corner points only. The number of Bézier control handles associated with the point is determined automatically by FreeHand: none if the corner point is flanked only by other corner points, one if the corner point is connected to at least one curve point, two if the corner point is flanked by two curve points. Though you may create paths from scratch with the corner tool, it is most useful for adding one or more corner points to an existing open path. After selecting an endpoint belonging to the path you want to extend, use the corner tool as follows:

- Click on an empty portion of the screen to create a corner point and draw a segment between it and the previously selected endpoint.

- Press SHIFT and click to constrain the angle between the previous endpoint and the current corner point to a multiple of 45°.

- Double-click on an empty portion of the screen to create a de-selected corner point, thus ending the path.

KE Pressing the 9 key—either in the standard key set or on the key-pad—will select the corner tool at any time, except when a dialog box is displayed.

The connector tool

The *connector tool*, which appears as a hooked line running through a small square, is the third and final specialized point-creation tool, used to create *connector points* only. Each Bézier control handle associated with a connector point is locked into alignment with the point opposite the handle. The connector tool is most useful for creating a smooth transition between a straight segment and a curved one. The connector tool may be used as follows:

- Click on an empty portion of the screen to create a connector point and draw a segment between it and the previously selected endpoint.

- Press SHIFT and click to constrain the angle between the previous endpoint and the current connector point to a multiple of 45°.

- Double-click on an empty portion of the screen to create a de-selected connector point, thus ending the path.

Pressing the 0 key—either in the standard key set or on the keypad—will select the connector tool at any time, except when a dialog box is displayed.

The rotate tool

 The *rotate tool* is used to rotate one or more selected objects in your illustration around a single point, called the *rotation origin*. The rotate tool may be used as follows:

- Press the mouse button to establish the rotation origin; then, prior to releasing, drag around the origin to rotate the selected object.

- Press SHIFT while dragging to rotate the selected object by any angle that is a multiple of 45°.

- Press OPTION and click to display a dialog box that will allow you to enter the exact angle by which you want to rotate the selected object.

The reflect tool

 The *reflect tool* is used to flip one or more selected objects in your illustration across a *reflection axis*, which may be oriented horizontally, vertically, or at some angle. The reflect tool may be used as follows:

- Press the mouse button to secure one end of the reflection axis; then, prior to releasing, drag to determine the location of the other end of the axis. FreeHand then flips the selected object across the axis.

- Press SHIFT while dragging to constrain the angle of the reflection axis to any angle that is a multiple of 45°.

- Press OPTION and click to display a dialog box that will allow you to enter the orientation (in degrees) of the reflection axis.

The scale tool

The *scale tool* is used to reduce or enlarge one or more selected objects in your illustration. An object is resized with respect to a single point, called the *scale origin*. The scale tool may be used as follows:

- Press the mouse button to establish the scale origin; then, prior to releasing, drag up and to the right to enlarge the selected object.

- Drag down and to the left from the scale origin to reduce the selected object.

- Drag up and to the left from the scale origin to make the selected object taller and narrower.

- Drag down and to the right from the scale origin to make the selected object shorter and wider.

- Press SHIFT while dragging to enlarge or reduce the selected object proportionally.

- Press OPTION and click to display a dialog box that will allow you to enter the exact percentage by which you want to reduce or enlarge the selected object.

The skew tool

The *skew tool* is used to slant one or more selected objects in your illustration. An object is skewed with respect to a single point, called a *skewing origin*. The skew tool may be used as follows:

- Press the mouse button to establish the skewing origin; then, prior to releasing, drag with respect to the origin to skew the selected object.

- Press SHIFT while dragging to constrain the angle of the skew to a multiple of 45°.

- Press OPTION and click to display a dialog box that will allow you to enter the exact angle by which you want to skew the selected object and the exact angle of the *skewing axis*.

The trace tool

The *trace tool*, which appears as a line surrounding a gray area, is used to convert imported *bitmaps* into smooth object-oriented graphics by tracing the outline of an image with a closed path. To use the trace tool, drag to create a marquee around the portion of the bitmap you want to trace. Every image inside the marquee will be surrounded by a closed path.

Double-clicking the trace tool icon in the toolbox displays the TRACE dialog box, which allows you to adjust the sensitivity of the trace tool and to specify the images to be traced.

The zoom tool

The *zoom tool*, which appears as a magnifying glass with an inset plus sign, is used to expand or contract the *view size* of the current illustration. The image itself is not affected by this tool. Rather, it allows you to zoom in on a detail or zoom out to take in the big picture. The zoom tool may be used as follows:

- Click anywhere in the drawing area to expand a portion of your illustration to twice its previous level of magnification.

- Press OPTION and click anywhere in the drawing area to contract a portion of your illustration to half its previous level of magnification.

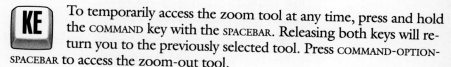

To temporarily access the zoom tool at any time, press and hold the COMMAND key with the SPACEBAR. Releasing both keys will return you to the previously selected tool. Press COMMAND-OPTION-SPACEBAR to access the zoom-out tool.

The hand tool

FreeHand provides an additional tool that is not displayed in the toolbox. This is the *hand tool* (or *grabber hand*), which is used to *scroll* the illustration; that is, to move it with respect to the FreeHand window boundaries. Dragging with the hand tool scrolls the illustration in 4-pixel increments.

To temporarily access the hand tool, press and hold the SPACEBAR at any time, except when a dialog box is displayed. Releasing the SPACEBAR will return you to the previously selected tool.

Menus and commands

The following are brief descriptions of the menus and commands offered by Aldus FreeHand 3.0. Again, these descriptions are provided simply as brief introductions to the commands. More thorough descriptions are presented in later chapters. Keyboard equivalents are listed in parentheses whenever applicable.

The Apple (🍎) menu

The APPLE menu behaves exactly as it does within all other Macintosh applications and at the Finder. You have access to all desk accessories currently available to your System file. When operating under MultiFinder, your APPLE menu also contains a list of other application currently running. Choosing any one of these applications will bring it forward as the active program and send FreeHand to the background. Return to FreeHand by choosing the Aldus FreeHand 3.0 icon (🐢) from the list of running applications in the APPLE menu or by clicking in the upper right corner of your Macintosh screen until the FreeHand toolbox reappears. (The toolbox is always hidden when FreeHand is running in the background.)

ABOUT FREEHAND… Choose this command to display the same startup screen that is displayed when launching the program. This time, however, the screen displays two buttons. Click OK or press RETURN to close the startup screen. Click HELP… to access FreeHand's on-line help system, which is described below.

HELP… (⌘-⇧-/ or HELP) Choose this command to access FreeHand's on-line help system, which allows you to access information about tools and commands without leaving the program. If FreeHand cannot find the FH3 Help file, an alert box will display, requesting you to locate it. If the file is unavailable, it may not have been installed properly. For more information, refer to Appendix A, *Installing Aldus FreeHand*.

The File menu

As in most Macintosh applications, the Aldus FreeHand FILE menu controls broad document-level activities, including the opening, closing, printing, and saving of illustrations. Additionally, the FILE menu controls the importation of graphic images and the exportation of EPS (*Encapsulated PostScript*) files.

```
┌─ File ──────────┐
│ New...        ⌘N │
│ Open...       ⌘O │
│                  │
│ Close            │
│ Save          ⌘S │
│ Save as...       │
│ Revert           │
│                  │
│ Document setup...│
│ Preferences...   │
│                  │
│ Page Setup...    │
│ Print...      ⌘P │
│                  │
│ Place...         │
│ Export...        │
│                  │
│ Quit          ⌘Q │
└──────────────────┘
```

NEW... (⌘-N) brings up the DOCUMENT SETUP dialog box, which allows you to specify the size of your illustration, the unit of measure, the grid size, and the resolution of your output device.

OPEN... (⌘-O) brings up the OPEN DOCUMENT dialog box, which allows you to open any available FreeHand 1.0, 2.0, 2.02, or 3.0 file or any object-oriented drawing saved in the Adobe Illustrator 1.1 or PICT format. A file originating from a program other than FreeHand 3.0 is opened as an untitled document.

CLOSE closes the current illustration, but does not quit the FreeHand application. If any changes have been made to a document before it is closed, a SAVE CHANGES alert box will appear, allowing you to save your changes, confirm the loss of your changes, or cancel the close operation.

SAVE (⌘-S) updates the disk file of your current illustration to include all changes made since it was last saved. If the current illustration already has a name, you are given no opportunity to confirm the save or to change the location or name of the file. If the current name of the illustration is "Untitled" followed by a number, the SAVE DOCUMENT AS dialog box will appear, allowing you the opportunity to enter a name for the illustration and to determine on which drive and in which folder you would like to save your file. The SAVE command will be dimmed if no changes have been made to the current document since it was last saved.

SAVE AS... brings up the SAVE DOCUMENT AS dialog box, which allows you to change the name or location of the file you are saving.

REVERT disregards all changes that have been made to the current illustration since the last time it was saved. The REVERT alert box will display, allowing you to verify or cancel the command. The REVERT command will be dimmed if no changes have been made to the current document since it was last saved.

DOCUMENT SETUP... displays the same DOCUMENT SETUP dialog box that displays when you create a new illustration. Here you may change the size of the current illustration, the unit of measure, the grid size, and the resolution of your output device.

PREFERENCES... brings up the PREFERENCES dialog box, in which several basic attributes affecting the on-screen drawing environment are specified. The PREFERENCES dialog box allows you to control the manner in which small text is displayed; how the screen refreshes; the on-screen appearance of TIFF images, type effects, gradations, and Bézier control handles; whether objects on different layers may be selected simultaneously; the number of consecutive undos; how points snap together; the movement equivalent of cursor keystrokes; guide and grid colors; the fluctuation of default settings and palette positions; and the on-screen color display.

PAGE SETUP... brings up Apple's standard LASERWRITER PAGE SETUP dialog box, provided that you have selected a PostScript-compatible printer with your Chooser desk accessory. Since most of the options available in this dialog box are duplicated in FreeHand's DOCUMENT SETUP, LASERWRITER, and PRINT OPTIONS dialog boxes, this command is generally unnecessary for PostScript printing. However, if you are printing to a QuickDraw device, such as an ImageWriter or a LaserWriter SC, the PAGE SETUP... command becomes an important first step in the printing process.

PRINT... (⌘-P) brings up the LASERWRITER dialog box, provided that you have selected a PostScript-compatible printer with your Chooser desk accessory. The dialog box allows you to specify the number of copies, the paper source, the reduction or enlargement, and whether composites or separations are printed. Use the CHANGE... button to control the printer description file, the paper size, the printer resolution, the screen frequency, the printer markings, and various high-end output settings.

PLACE... brings up the PLACE DOCUMENT dialog box, which allows you to import a graphics file created in another program. FreeHand will accept bitmapped artwork stored in the MacPaint or TIFF format as well as object-oriented graphics saved as a PICT or Encapsulated PostScript document. Imported graphics may be used as tracing templates or as part of your final FreeHand illustration.

EXPORT... displays the EXPORT dialog box, which allows you to store your FreeHand illustration as an Encapsulated PostScript file with a Macintosh or IBM screen representation for importation into a page-layout program such as Aldus PageMaker, QuarkXPress, or Ventura Publisher. You may also select whether to include PostScript descriptions of imported TIFF files.

QUIT (⌘-Q) exits the FreeHand application, closing all open illustrations and returning control to the Macintosh Finder (or possibly to some other application if you are running under MultiFinder). A SAVE CHANGES dialog box will appear for every illustration that has unsaved changes. If an illustration is untitled, the SAVE DOCUMENT AS dialog will appear, prompting you to name the file and determine its location.

The Edit menu

Most of the commands in the EDIT menu will be familiar to you if you have worked in other Macintosh applications. The menu contains most of FreeHand's duplication commands, including those that rely on the Macintosh Clipboard. Two EDIT commands—CUT CONTENTS and PASTE INSIDE—are unique to FreeHand, although they conform to the EDIT menu tradition of working with the Clipboard.

UNDO (⌘-Z) steps backward, one operation at a time, through the recent operations performed in FreeHand. You may specify the number of consecutive undos in the MORE PREFERENCES dialog box. As an operation is undone, all effects relating to that operation are also undone; the file returns to the state in which it existed prior to the operation. To help you keep track of what those operations were, the UNDO command lists the command it will undo if chosen, such as UNDO MOVE. The UNDO command will be dimmed if the last operation cannot be undone or if it has exhausted the maximum number of operations that may be undone.

REDO (⌘-Y) steps forward through the operations that were undone using the UNDO command, reperforming one operation at a time. Like UNDO, the REDO command can work through the number of consecutive operations specified in the MORE PREFERENCES dialog box and lists the command it will redo if chosen. REDO will appear dimmed if the most recent operation was not UNDO or if it has exhausted all redoable operations.

CUT (⌘-X) deletes one or more selected objects from your illustration and stores them in the Macintosh Clipboard, replacing the Clipboard's previous contents. If no object is selected, the CUT command is dimmed.

COPY (⌘-C) makes a copy of one or more selected objects in your illustration and stores them in the Macintosh Clipboard, replacing the Clipboard's previous contents. If no object is selected, the COPY command is dimmed.

PASTE (⌘-V) makes a copy of the items in the Macintosh Clipboard and places them inside the current illustration. If the Clipboard is empty, the PASTE command is dimmed.

CLEAR (DELETE, BACKSPACE, or CLEAR) deletes one or more selected objects from your illustration, but does so without placing them in the Clipboard or disturbing the Clipboard's contents. The objects can be brought back immediately by choosing UNDO CLEAR; otherwise, they are lost for good. If no object is selected, the CLEAR command is dimmed.

CUT CONTENTS deletes the contents from inside the selected *clipping path* (masking object), but it does so without placing them in the Clipboard or disturbing the Clipboard's contents. Rather, the cut objects are placed in front of the clipping path, where they appear selected. Except when the selected object is a clipping path, CUT CONTENTS is dimmed.

PASTE INSIDE pastes the contents of the Clipboard inside the selected closed path at the exact location from which the Clipboard objects were cut or copied. Only those portions of the Clipboard objects that fit within the selected shape are visible. The command will seem not to work if the Clipboard objects were not aligned properly with the intended clipping path, or if the intended clipping path is open. This command is dimmed if the Clipboard is empty or if no object is selected.

SELECT ALL (⌘-A) selects every object (no points) in the current document, both on the page and in the *pasteboard* (the area around the page). The only exception occurs if the TEXT dialog box is displayed, in which case choosing SELECT ALL highlights all text in the current text block.

DUPLICATE (⌘-D) performs one of two tasks. Ordinarily, DUPLICATE creates a copy of the current selection, slightly offset from the original, without placing the selection in the Clipboard or disturbing the Clipboard's contents. However, if the most recent operations were a duplication (performed using DUPLICATE or CLONE) followed by one or more consecutive transformations, choosing DUPLICATE repeats these operations, creating another duplication, which is additionally transformed. The command may be performed over and over to produce cumulative results. If no object is selected, the DUPLICATE command is dimmed.

CLONE (⌘-=, COMMAND-EQUAL) creates a copy of the current selection, without placing the selection in the Clipboard or disturbing the Clipboard's contents. This copy is placed directly in front of the original. If no object is selected, the CLONE command is dimmed.

MOVE... (⌘-M) displays the MOVE ELEMENTS dialog box, which allows you to move the current selection a specified distance both horizontally and vertically. If no object is selected, the MOVE... command is dimmed.

TRANSFORM AGAIN (⌘-‚, COMMAND-COMMA) applies the most recent transformation to the current selection, regardless of how many operations have been implemented since the last transformation or whether it was originally applied to the current selection. TRANSFORM AGAIN is particularly useful for experimenting with slight transformations; you can nudge the transformation along until the object meets your exact requirement. If no object is selected, the TRANSFORM AGAIN command is dimmed.

The View menu

The commands in the VIEW menu determine how your illustration appears on screen. The first command affects the display of the information bar, the toolbox, and other palettes. The next two commands are used to alter the view size and the display mode. Other commands control the display and effect of rulers, grids, and guides.

WINDOWS displays a pop-up menu of options that control the on-screen display of palettes. Your choices are "Info bar," "Toolbox," "Colors" (⌘-9), "Layers" (⌘-6), and "Styles" (⌘-3). A check mark appears before each palette that is currently displayed. The COLORS, LAYERS, and STYLES palettes are discussed in the *Palette menus* section later in this chapter. Below the palette options are the names of all open illustrations. The current illustration is preceded by a check mark. Choosing any file name option will bring the corresponding illustration window to the forefront of your screen.

MAGNIFICATION displays a pop-up menu of view size options. "Fit in window" (⌘-W) reduces or enlarges the view size so that the entire page can be viewed in the illustration window. The exact size at which your illustration is displayed varies, depending on the size of the window. Each of the other MAGNIFICATION options—"12.5%," "25%," "50%" (⌘-5), "100%" (⌘-1), "200%" (⌘-2), "400%" (⌘-4), "800%" (⌘-8)—reduces or enlarges the view size to some percentage of the size the illustration appears when printed. A check mark appears before the current view size.

PREVIEW (⌘-K) toggles the *preview display mode*, which displays all objects in the current illustration as they will appear when printed, complete with fills, patterns, strokes, colors, and so on. A check mark indicates whether the command is active. When PREVIEW is turned off, FreeHand assumes the *keyline mode*, in which objects are displayed with transparent fills and black, hairline strokes. The only exception is type, which is filled black and not stroked. Elements may be created and manipulated in either the preview or keyline mode; however while the preview mode shows more detail, it slows down the screen refresh speed considerably.

RULERS (⌘-R) toggles the display of horizontal and vertical rulers on the top and left sides of the current FreeHand window. Rulers display in the current unit of measure specified in the DOCUMENT SETUP dialog box. A check mark precedes the command when the rulers are displayed.

GRID toggles the display of the *visible grid*, a network of dots used to visually align objects in the illustration window. Visible grid increments are specified in the DOCUMENT SETUP dialog box. A check mark precedes the command when the visible grid is displayed.

GUIDES toggles the display of *ruler guides*, which may be dragged into the illustration from the horizontal and vertical rulers. A check mark precedes the command when the guides are displayed.

LOCK GUIDES prevents all existing ruler guides from being moved immediately locks new guides as soon as you release your mouse button. A check mark precedes the command when the guides are locked. LOCK GUIDES is dimmed when the GUIDES command is inactive (not preceded by a check mark).

SNAP TO POINT (⌘-', COMMAND-QUOTE) toggles whether a dragged object moves sharply toward a stationary point when the arrow cursor comes within proximity of the point in the illustration window. This proximity is measured in screen pixels, as specified in the MORE PREFERENCES dialog box. A check mark precedes the command when snapping is in effect.

SNAP TO GUIDES toggles whether a dragged object moves sharply toward a ruler guide when the arrow cursor comes within proximity of the guide in the illustration window. This proximity is measured in screen pixels, as specified in the MORE PREFERENCES dialog box. A check mark precedes the command when snapping is in effect.

SNAP TO GRID (⌘-;, COMMAND-SEMICOLON) toggles whether a dragged object moves sharply toward the invisible *snap-to grid* when the arrow cursor comes within proximity of the grid in the illustration window. This proximity is measured in screen pixels, as specified in the MORE PREFERENCES dialog box. The snap-to grid increments are defined in the DOCUMENT SETUP dialog box. A check mark precedes the command when snapping is in effect.

The Element menu

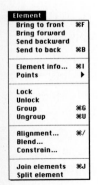

Commands in the ELEMENT menu affect relationships between selected objects. Although reorganized in FreeHand 3.0, all commands in the ELEMENT menu were available in previous versions of the program. Layering commands, once available in this menu and the VIEW menu, have been moved to the LAYERS palette, described later in this chapter.

BRING TO FRONT (⌘-F) moves any and all selected objects in front of all other objects in the current layer. If no object is selected, the BRING TO FRONT command is dimmed.

BRING FORWARD moves any and all selected objects one step forward in the current FreeHand layer, swapping the order of the selection and the object immediately in front of it. If no object is selected, the BRING FORWARD command is dimmed.

SEND BACKWARD moves any and all selected objects one step backward in the current FreeHand layer, swapping the order of the selection and the object immediately behind it. If no object is selected, the SEND BACKWARD command is dimmed.

SEND TO BACK (⌘-B) moves any and all selected objects in back of all other objects in the current layer. If no object is selected, the SEND TO BACK command is dimmed.

ELEMENT INFO… (⌘-I) brings up the customized element information dialog box that corresponds to the selected object. Examples are the RECTANGLE, ELLIPSE, PATH, GROUP, and TEXT dialog boxes. Each dialog box allows you to alter the placement of selected objects and elements. The ELEMENT INFO… command is dimmed when no object is selected, or when multiple objects are selected.

KE You may also initiate the ELEMENT INFO… command by OPTION-double-clicking a selected object with the arrow tool. In the case of text, it is not necessary to press OPTION; simply double-clicking a text block brings up the TEXT dialog box.

POINTS displays a pop-up menu of five options applicable to a selected point. The first option, "Remove point" (DELETE, BACKSPACE, or CLEAR), deletes the selected point from its path and draws a new segment between the remaining neighboring points. "Auto curvature" relocates Bézier control handles of the selected point to meet with FreeHand's built-in definition of the perfect curvature of a segment based on the location and identity (corner, connector, or curve) of each neighboring point. Moving a handle automatically deactivates this option. The "Corner point," "Connector point," and "Curve point" options change the identity of the selected point, adding or subtracting the required Bézier control handles. A check mark before one of these options indicates the current identity of the selected point. All five POINTS options are dimmed when no point is selected, or when multiple points are selected.

LOCK locks any and all selected objects so that they may not be moved. Locking one or more points in a single path locks the entire path. In Free-Hand, a locked object may be selected as well as subjected to commands that don't involve the movement of any of its points. This command is dimmed if no object is selected, or if the selected object is already locked.

UNLOCK unlocks a selected locked object so it may be moved. This command is dimmed if no object is selected, or if the selected object is not locked.

GROUP (⌘-G) combines all currently selected elements into a single object, which is assigned four corner handles, like a geometric shape drawn with the rectangle or oval tool. A single path may be grouped so that it cannot be reshaped except by first OPTION-clicking with the arrow tool. Grouping one or more points or segments in a single path groups the entire path. Multiple groups may also be grouped as a single object. The GROUP command changes the order of selected objects within a layer, bringing them forward to just behind the frontmost object in the group. If selected objects are on different layers, choosing GROUP moves them all to the current layer. This command is dimmed if no object is selected.

UNGROUP (⌘-U) separates a selected group into its original elements. Many images are created as groups. These include geometric shapes (rectangles and ovals) and blends. Ungrouping these objects allows you to edit them with the arrow tool; however, it will also prevent you from editing the object in other ways. For example, if you ungroup a geometric shape, you may no longer access the RECTANGLE or ELLIPSE dialog box. If you ungroup a blend, you may not change the number of steps. This command is dimmed if no object is selected, or if the selected object is not a group.

ALIGNMENT... (⌘-/, COMMAND-SLASH) brings up the ALIGNMENT dialog box, which allows you to align and distribute multiple selected objects with respect to their current locations. A small diagram inside the dialog box demonstrates the prospective results of your choices. This command is particularly useful when preparing graphs or schematic drawings. If no object is selected, the ALIGNMENT... command is dimmed.

BLEND... is used to create intermediate form, fill, and stroke manipulations between two selected open paths or between two selected closed paths with similar numbers of points. After selecting a single point in each of two paths, choose BLEND... to bring up the BLEND dialog box. Enter the number of steps desired and press RETURN. FreeHand creates the intermediary number of steps as instructed. This command is dimmed if fewer than two objects are selected.

CONSTRAIN… allows you to rotate the *constraint axes*, which control the angle at which elements are drawn and manipulated when pressing the SHIFT key. The orientation of the constraint axes also affects the creation of geometric shapes such as rectangles and ellipses, even when SHIFT is not pressed.

JOIN ELEMENTS (⌘-J) serves three purposes: First, it is used to join two selected endpoints—one positioned directly in front of the other—thereby connecting two open paths or closing a single open path. Second, the JOIN command may be used to join a line of type to a free-form path, which results in text on a curve. And third, in FreeHand 3.0, the JOIN command will combine two or more selected paths into a single *composite path*, in which the foremost objects cut holes in the fill of the rearmost object. Grouped objects cannot be joined into composite paths. If fewer than two elements are selected or if a group is selected, the JOIN ELEMENTS command is dimmed.

SPLIT ELEMENTS separates one or more selected points into two endpoints apiece, thereby opening a closed path or splitting an open path into two or more open paths. This command also serves to separate a line of type currently joined to a free-form path, or to split a composite path into its original paths. If no object is selected, the SPLIT ELEMENTS command is dimmed.

The Type menu

The TYPE menu contains commands used to edit and alter type in Free-Hand, particularly when the TEXT dialog box is displayed. The only new command to this menu is CONVERT TO PATHS, which converts a block of text into editable paths.

FONT displays a pop-up menu containing the names of every *font* (typeface) currently available to your System. Choosing a FONT option changes the highlighted characters in the TEXT dialog box, all characters in a text block selected with the arrow tool, or the default typeface setting if no text is currently selected. A check mark next to a font name indicates the typeface of the selected characters or the default setting. If the selected text is set in more than one typeface, no check mark will display.

SIZE displays a pop-up menu of type-size options (measured in points). These options represent the most common sizes, but any size from 0.1 point to 3000 points is permitted. To access an uncommon size, choose the "Other…" option to bring up the TYPE SIZE dialog box. Enter a size value and press RETURN. A check mark next to an option indicates the type size of the selected characters or the default setting. If the selected text is set in more than one type size, no check mark will display.

 You may change the size of all letters in a selected text block by SHIFT-OPTION-dragging a corner handle with the arrow tool. Drag inward to reduce the type size; drag outward to enlarge it.

LEADING displays a pop-up menu of *leading* options (the amount of vertical space between lines of type, measured in points). These options represent the most common leadings, but any size from 0 to 3000 points is permitted. To specify a leading value, choose the "Other…" option to bring up the LEADING dialog box. Enter a leading value and press RETURN. Other LEADING options include "Solid," which matches the leading to the current type size, and "Auto," which sets the leading at a value equal to 120% of the size of the selected type. A check mark next to an option indicates the leading of the selected characters or the default setting. If the selected text is not leaded uniformly, no check mark will display.

 You may change the leading between all lines in a selected text block by dragging the top or bottom handle with the arrow tool. Drag toward the text to reduce the leading; drag outward to increase the leading.

TYPE STYLE displays a pop-up menu listing four basic type styles— "Plain," "Bold," "Italic," and "BoldItalic"—that allow you to vary the basic appearance of a typeface. Some styles may not be available for a specific typeface, as determined by the available printer font styles. Unavailable style options will appear dimmed. A check mark next to an option indicates the style of the selected characters or the default setting. If the selected text is set in more than one style, no check mark will display.

EFFECT displays a pop-up menu filled with special effect options designed especially to be applied to type. Choose "None" to apply no special effect, displaying the current typeface as is. "Fill and stroke…" displays the FILL AND STROKE dialog box, which allows you to color the interiors and outlines of selected characters of type. "Heavy" makes text appear more bold, and is particularly useful if the current font offers no bold style. The "Inline…" option surrounds characters with up to 10 outlines. "Oblique" slants selected text, and is useful when a font offers no italic style. "Outline" creates type with a thin outline and a transparent interior. "Shadow" creates a 50% tint drop shadow behind the selected text.

Finally, the "Zoom text…" option applies a series of drop shadows behind the selected text, starting at a specified color and ending at another, creating the effect of letters leaping out from the page.

Type specs… (⌘-T) brings up the Type specifications dialog box, in which you may alter the font, type size, leading, type style, color, effect, letter spacing, word spacing, horizontal scaling, and baseline shift of the currently selected type or, if no text is selected, the next text entry. If a text block is selected with the arrow tool, the new formatting specifications affect the entire block. If type is highlighted in the Text dialog box, the formatting affects only the highlighted text. The Type specifications dialog box also controls alignment, which affects entire text blocks.

Spacing… brings up the Spacing dialog box, which controls the amount of horizontal space between selected letters and words. Both word spacing and letter spacing are measured in points. Positive values spread letters and words apart; negative values squeeze letters and words together.

 You may change the amount of space between letters in a selected text block by dragging a side handle with the arrow tool. Press OPTION and drag to change the amount of space between words. In either case, dragging inward reduces the spacing; dragging outward increases the spacing.

Horizontal scaling… brings up the Horizontal scaling dialog box, which controls the width of the selected type, measured as a percentage of its normal width. You may condense or expand type to any extent from 0.1% to 10,000% (100 times its normal width).

 You may horizontally scale a selected text block by OPTION-dragging a corner handle horizontally with the arrow tool. Drag inward to condense type; drag outward to expand it.

Baseline shift… brings up the Baseline shift dialog box, which determines the distance between the selected type and its baseline, measured in points. Baseline shift is especially useful for creating superscripts (positive shift values) and subscripts (negative shift values).

Convert to paths converts a block of text selected with the arrow tool into a collection of editable paths. For example, the letter A would be converted into a path that forms the outline of the letter A. This command is most useful for manipulating large type that you intend to use to create logos and other textual effects. The selected type may be set in either a Type 1 font—including those marketed by Adobe, Linotype, Bit-stream, and many other major distributors—or a Type 3 font—created using a utility such as Fontographer. Note that the CONVERT TO PATHS command functions only if the corresponding printer font is available on disk. This command is dimmed if no text block is selected, or if the TEXT dialog box is displayed.

ALIGNMENT displays a pop-up menu of alignment options for one or more selected text blocks. Your choices are "Left," "Centered," "Right," "Justify," and "Vertical," the last of which creates type that reads from top to bottom. A check mark next to an option indicates the alignment of the current text block. If the selected text blocks are aligned differently, no check mark will display.

The Attributes menu

Commands in the ATTRIBUTES menu are used to specify the strokes and fills of objects in your illustration. These commands also allow you to define and name new fills, strokes, and colors, and to edit existing ones.

FILL AND LINE... (⌘-E) brings up the FILL AND LINE dialog box, which allows you to specify the fill and line (also called the *stroke*) of one or more selected objects. Fill attributes include tint, color, gradation, and pattern. Stroke attributes also include tint, color, and pattern, as well as line weight, line cap, line join, miter limit, dash pattern, and arrowhead. This command is dimmed when type is selected.

HALFTONE SCREEN... brings up the HALFTONE SCREEN dialog box, which is used to alter the way in which the tints assigned to one or more selected objects print. You may alter the screen type (round dot or line), the angle of the screen on the page, and the number of dots or lines that print per linear inch.

SET NOTE... displays the SET NOTE dialog box, in which you may enter or access up to 255 characters of information about a selected object. The SET NOTE dialog box will always appear blank if more than one object is selected, even if all objects share a common notation. However, it may be used to apply notes to more than one object at a time.

REMOVE FILL makes the interior of one or more selected objects transparent, so that they appear hollow. This command is dimmed when type is selected.

REMOVE LINE makes the stroke of one or more selected objects transparent, so that they appear to have no outline. If this command is applied to an open path, the path will become invisible in the preview mode and it will not print. However, it may be viewed in the keyline mode. The REMOVE LINE command is dimmed when type is selected.

COLORS... brings up the COLORS dialog box, which is used to define and name a new color in FreeHand. The current color appears at the bottom of the dialog box, either in color or as a black-and-white composite, depending upon the color capabilities of your monitor. Spot colors may be defined based on one of three color models: red, green, and blue; hue, lightness, and saturation; or cyan, magenta, and yellow. Process colors are always defined as combinations of cyan, magenta, yellow, and black. Tints are lightened versions of existing colors. Colors defined in the COLORS dialog box may then be applied to the fill or stroke of an object by way of the FILL AND LINE dialog box or the COLORS palette.

STYLES... brings up the STYLES dialog box, which is used to define and name a new *attribute style* in FreeHand. Click the FILL AND LINE... button to display the FILL AND LINE dialog box; click HALFTONE... to display the HALFTONE SCREEN dialog box. Named attribute styles may be applied to objects by way of the STYLES palette.

Below these commands are the names of several line weights included with FreeHand. These commands affect only the stroke of a selected object and leave the fill unchanged. A check mark next to a command indicates the line weight of the selected object or the default setting. If all selected objects do not share a common stroke, no check mark will display. All line weight commands appear dimmed when type is selected.

Palette menus

In addition to the toolbox, FreeHand 3.0 provides three *palettes* that may be displayed at any time. Like the toolbox, all palettes are independent of the current illustration, and are positioned in front of any and all open FreeHand windows. The three palettes are displayed by choosing the "Colors" (⌘-9), "Layers" (⌘-6), and "Styles" (⌘-3) options, which are accessed by choosing WINDOWS from the VIEW menu. Each palette may be moved by dragging at its title bar and resized by dragging at its size box in the lower right corner. To hide a palette, click in its close box or press the keyboard equivalent used to display the palette.

Palettes offer options in a scrolling list. These options may be defined and manipulated using another set of options, made available by clicking and holding down your mouse button on the right-pointing arrowhead icon. The ▶ pop-up menu will display, as shown in Figure 2.03.

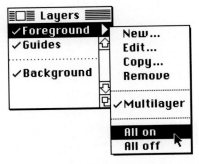

Figure 2.03: Choosing an option from a palette pop-up menu.

Each palette and its options are described in the following text.

The Colors palette

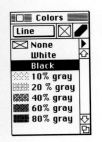

Displayed by choosing "Colors" from the WINDOWS pop-up in the VIEW menu (⌘-9), the COLORS palette allows you to define and access the colors used in the current illustration. Directly below the palette title bar is a pop-up menu that offers three options—"Fill," "Line," and "Both"— each of which is used respectively to view or alter the fill, the stroke, or both the fill and the stroke of a selection.

Clicking the fill icon (⊠ or ■) immediately to the right of the pop-up menu chooses the "Fill" option. Clicking the stroke option (✐ or ⊠) along the right side of the palette chooses "Line." To choose "Both," click one icon, then SHIFT-click the other.

When you select an object in the illustration window, the color name corresponding to its fill or stroke (depending on the chosen option) becomes highlighted in the scrolling list. Also, both the fill and stroke icons beneath the title bar will adopt the colors of the fill and the stroke of the selected object (⊠ if "None"). If the selected object contains a gradient fill, the highlighted fill color in the scrolling list represents the "From" or beginning color. (See Chapter 9, *Filling Type and Graphic Objects* for more information.) If all selected objects do not share a common fill or stroke color, no color option will be highlighted.

To change the color of one or more selected objects, choose the desired option—"Fill," "Line," or "Both"—then click on a color name in the scrolling list. Click "None" to make a selected fill and/or stroke transparent.

You may add, delete, or modify color names in the scrolling list by choosing options from the ▶ pop-up menu:

- **New**… performs the same function as choosing Colors… from the Attributes menu. The Colors dialog box will display, allowing you to define a new color that will appear in the scrolling list of the Colors palette.

- **Edit**… brings up the Colors dialog box, containing all settings applicable to the currently highlighted color. Adjusting the options in this dialog box will redefine the current color.

 Double-clicking a color name in the scrolling list of the Colors palette performs the same function as choosing "Edit…" from the ▶ pop-up menu.

- **Copy**… brings up the Colors dialog box, which contains all settings applicable to the currently highlighted color. However, the "Name" option will appear blank, so that you may create a new color based on the current color. The current color will not be affected by your alterations.

- **Remove** deletes the highlighted color from the Colors palette, provided that the color is not used in the current illustration. If at least one object is filled or stroked with this color, an error message will display and the operation will be canceled.

- **Library**… allows you to open colors contained in a color library (*clib*, pronounced see-lib) file on disk. A dialog box requests the location of the desired clib. Next, the Select library color(s) dialog box displays, containing a scrolling list of colors in the current clib. Select the desired colors from the scrolling list by clicking and shift-clicking, then press RETURN. The selected clib colors now appear in the scrolling list of the Colors palette.

Dragging a color name in the scrolling list changes the order of its appearance in the COLORS palette.

The Layers palette

Displayed by choosing "Layers" from the WINDOWS pop-up in the VIEW menu (⌘-6), the LAYERS palette allows you to define and access a series of invisible planes, called *layers*, on which objects may be organized in the current illustration. By default, FreeHand offers three layer names in the scrolling list: "Foreground," which contains the printing objects that make up your final illustration, "Guides," which contains the non-printing ruler guides used to align type and graphic objects, and "Background," which contains non-printing tracing templates and other images used in the creation of an illustration, but which will not appear in the finished artwork.

When you select an object in the illustration window, the name of the layer on which the object appears becomes highlighted in the scrolling list. If you select multiple objects from different layers, no layer option will be highlighted. If no object is selected, the highlighted layer is the default layer on which future objects will be created.

To move one or more selected objects to a different layer, simply click on a layer name in the scrolling list. Clicking a layer name when no object is selected changes the default layer.

Check marks indicate the layers that are currently displayed. To hide a layer, click its check mark; all objects on the layer will disappear from the illustration window. To display a hidden layer, click in the space before the layer name, and both check mark and all objects on the layer will reappear.

You may add, delete, or modify layer names in the scrolling list by choosing options from the ▶ pop-up menu:

- **New**… brings up the LAYERS dialog box, so that you may create a new layer, which will display at the top of the scrolling list in the LAYERS palette.

- **Edit**… brings up the LAYERS dialog box, allowing you to rename the currently highlighted layer.

Double-clicking a layer name in the scrolling list of the LAYERS palette performs the same function as choosing "Edit…" from the ▶ pop-up menu.

- **Copy**… brings up the L<small>AYERS</small> dialog box, allowing you to create a new layer based on the currently highlighted layer in the scrolling list of the L<small>AYERS</small> palette. All objects on the current layer will be duplicated to the new layer.

- **Remove** deletes the highlighted layer from the current illustration. If this layer contains one or more objects, an alert box will display, warning you that deleting the layer will also result in the loss of all objects on that layer.

- **Multilayer** is used to protect objects on certain layers in the current illustration. If a check mark appears before "Multilayer," you may manipulate objects on all layers of the current illustration. If no check mark appears, you may manipulate only those objects that exist on the default layer; objects on other layers are protected.

- **All on** displays all layers in the current illustration.

- **All off** hides all layers in the current illustration; no check mark will appear before any layer name in the scrolling list.

Dragging a layer name in the scrolling list changes its order in the L<small>AYERS</small> palette. Drag a layer below the dotted line to make it a non-printing background layer. Drag a layer above the dotted line to make it a printing foreground layer.

The Styles palette

Displayed by choosing "Styles" from the W<small>INDOWS</small> pop-up in the V<small>IEW</small> menu (⌘-3), the S<small>TYLES</small> palette allows you to define and access *attribute styles* used in the current illustration. Attribute styles affect the fill and the stroke of an object, as well as its halftone screen. By default, FreeHand offers one attribute style, "Normal," which may be modified but may not be deleted.

When you select an object in the illustration window, the corresponding attribute style becomes highlighted. If the selected object is based on a specific attribute style, but its fill, stroke, and/or halftone screen settings do not exactly match those of the style definition, a plus sign will appear before the style name, showing that some additional attributes are in effect. If you select multiple objects controlled by different attribute styles, no style name will be highlighted. If no object is selected, the highlighted style name is the default attribute style, which affects the fills and strokes of future objects.

To apply an attribute style to one or more selected objects, simply click on a style name in the scrolling list. Clicking a style name when no object is selected changes the default attribute style.

You may add, delete, or modify style names in the scrolling list by choosing options from the ▶ pop-up menu:

- **New**... performs the same function as choosing STYLES... from the ATTRIBUTES menu. The STYLES dialog box will display, allowing you to define a new attribute style that will appear in the scrolling list of the STYLES palette.

- **Edit**... brings up the STYLES dialog box, providing access to all settings applicable to the currently highlighted style. Adjusting the options in this dialog box will redefine the current style.

 Double-clicking a style name in the scrolling list of the STYLES palette performs the same function as choosing "Edit..." from the ▶ pop-up menu.

- **Copy**... brings up the STYLES dialog box, providing access to all settings applicable to the currently highlighted style. However, the "Name" option will appear blank, so that you may create a new attribute style based on the current style. The current style will not be affected by your alterations.

- **Remove** deletes the highlighted style from the STYLES palette. If the style has been assigned to one or more objects in the current illustration, the "Normal" style will be assigned in its place, although the previous attributes of the reassigned objects will remain unaffected. If "Normal" is the current style, "Remove" will appear dimmed.

Dragging a style name in the scrolling list changes the order of its appearance in the STYLES palette.

Shortcuts

As with any drawing program, most interaction with Aldus FreeHand must be performed using your mouse. However, many commands, options, and other operations can also be executed by way of the keyboard or by way of keyboard and mouse combinations. The charts in this section contain all keyboard equivalents applicable to FreeHand, categorized by function. The following is a list of commonly accepted Apple keyboard symbols used throughout our charts:

⌘	COMMAND (cloverleaf) or APPLE (🍎) key
⇧	SHIFT key
⌥	OPTION key
⌃	CONTROL key (not included on Mac Plus keyboards)
→|	TAB key
↵	RETURN key
⌤	ENTER key
⌫	DELETE or BACKSPACE key
▦	precedes characters that must be accessed from keypad
▦⌵	CLEAR key
⎵	SPACEBAR
↑	UP CURSOR ARROW key
←	LEFT CURSOR ARROW key
↓	DOWN CURSOR ARROW key
→	RIGHT CURSOR ARROW key

We also make use of the following mouse symbols:

▹	mouse click
▹▹	double-click
⋯▹	mouse drag

In each keyboard equivalent, keyboard symbols are separated by hyphens. This indicates that you should press and hold all keys displayed in the order displayed. For example, the shortcut for the SELECT ALL command is ⌘-A. This means that you should first press and hold the COMMAND key and then press the A key to perform the SELECT ALL command.

Mouse actions are a little more difficult. If one or more key symbols precede a mouse symbol, you should press the key(s), perform the mouse operation, and then release the key(s). For example, the shorthand for selecting multiple objects is ⇧-↖. This means to press SHIFT, click the object, and release the SHIFT key; the SHIFT key is held down throughout the completion of the mouse operation. On the other hand, if the key symbol appears *after* the mouse symbol, you must begin performing the mouse operation, *then* press the key, release the mouse button, and then release the key. To constrain the movement of one or more selected objects in a perpendicular direction, for example, you should perform the operation ⋯↖-⇧, which means to begin dragging the selected object before pressing the SHIFT key. When you are pleased with the new positioning, release the mouse button and then release the SHIFT key.

Menu commands

The following list shows how to access most of the menu commands included in Aldus FreeHand 3.0 using keystrokes and simple mouse operations. Any command that is not listed cannot be accessed from the keyboard and must be chosen from a menu.

Command or option	Keystroke and/or mouse action
Alignment…	⌘-/
Bring to front	⌘-F
Cancel screen refresh	⌘-. (COMMAND-PERIOD)
Clear	⌫ or ▦✎
Clone	⌘-= (COMMAND-EQUAL)
Close	↖ close box in illustration title bar
Colors (WINDOWS pop-up)	⌘-9
Copy	⌘-C
Copy (with PICT preview)	⌘-✑-C
Cut	⌘-X
Duplicate	⌘-D

Command or option	Keystroke and/or mouse action
Edit... (▶ pop-up menus)	↖↖ option name in scrolling list of palette
800% (MAGNIFICATION pop-up)	⌘-8
Element info...	⌘-I or ⬞-↖↖ object ⅋ arrow tool
50% (MAGNIFICATION pop-up)	⌘-5
Fill and line...	⌘-E
Fit in window	⌘-W
400% (MAGNIFICATION pop-up)	⌘-4
Group	⌘-G
Help... (context sensitive)	⌘-⇧-/ or HELP
Join elements...	⌘-J
Layers (WINDOWS pop-up)	⌘-6
Move...	⌘-M
New...	⌘-N
100% (MAGNIFICATION pop-up)	⌘-1
Open...	⌘-O
Paste	⌘-V
Paste (behind selection)	⌘-⇧-V
Preview	⌘-K
Print...	⌘-P
Quit	⌘-Q
Redo [operation]	⌘-Y
Remove point (POINTS pop-up)	⌫ or ⌨🗑
Rulers	⌘-R
Save	⌘-S
Select all	⌘-A
Send to back	⌘-B
Snap to grid	⌘-; (COMMAND-SEMICOLON)
Snap to point	⌘-' (COMMAND-QUOTE)
Split element (point only)	↖ point with knife tool
Styles (WINDOWS pop-up)	⌘-3
Transform again	⌘-, (COMMAND-COMMA)
Type specs...	⌘-T
200% (MAGNIFICATION pop-up)	⌘-2
Undo [operation]	⌘-Z
Ungroup	⌘-U

Tools

This list shows how to access many of the Aldus FreeHand tools. In some cases, a tool may be accessed only while a key is pressed; releasing the key returns you to the previously selected tool. Such equivalents are distinguished by the symbol ⚲ to indicate that the key or keys must be held down. Any tool that is not listed cannot be accessed from the keyboard and must be selected normally.

Tool	Keystroke
Arrow	⚲⌘
Connector	0 or ⌨0
Corner	9 or ⌨9
Curve	8 or ⌨8
Freehand	5 or ⌨5
Grabber hand	⚲ ⎵
Knife	7 or ⌨7
Line	4 or ⌨4
Oval	3 or ⌨3
Pen	6 or ⌨6
Rectangle	1 or ⌨1
Rounded-rectangle	2 or ⌨2
Type	A or ⇧-A
Zoom	⚲⌘-⎵
Zoom-out	⚲⌘-⌥-⎵ or ⚲⌥ when zoom tool is selected

Creating and manipulating type

This list explains how to create, select, delete, and replace type using the arrow and type tools.

Type manipulation	Keystroke and/or mouse action
Create type at origin point	↖ ᵂ/type tool, enter text, ↜
Create type in column	⋯↖ ᵂ/type tool, enter text, ↜
Insert type in text block	↖↖ block ᵂ/arrow, ↖ in text, enter text, ↜
Select type in text block	↖↖ block ᵂ/arrow, ⋯↖ over type
Select word	↖↖ block ᵂ/arrow, ↖↖ word
Select all type in text block	↖ block ᵂ/arrow or ↖↖ block ᵂ/arrow, ⌘-A
Delete type in text block	↖↖ block ᵂ/arrow, ⋯↖ over type, ⌫, ↜
Delete word	↖↖ block ᵂ/arrow, ↖↖ word, ⌫, ↜
Replace type in text block	↖↖ block ᵂ/arrow, ⋯↖ over type, enter text, ↜
Replace word	↖↖ block ᵂ/arrow, ↖↖ word, enter text, ↜
Join type to path	↖ block ᵂ/arrow, ⇧-↖ path, ⌘-J

Formatting type

Most text formatting in FreeHand must be accomplished by choosing commands and applying options. But a handful of formatting functions may be accessed from the keyboard or performed using mouse operations, as listed below.

Formatting function	Keystroke and/or mouse action
Adjust type size	⇧-↜-⋯↖ corner handle ᵂ/arrow
Adjust leading	⋯↖ top or bottom handle ᵂ/arrow
Adjust column width	⋯↖ corner handle ᵂ/arrow
Adjust horizontal scaling	↜-⋯↖ corner horizontally ᵂ/arrow
Adjust letter spacing	⋯↖ side handle ᵂ/arrow
Adjust word spacing	↜-⋯↖ side handle ᵂ/arrow
Kern together ¹⁄₁₀ em	↖↖ block ᵂ/arrow, ↖ in text, ⌘-⇧-←
Kern apart ¹⁄₁₀ em	↖↖ block ᵂ/arrow, ↖ in text, ⌘-⇧-→
Kern together ¹⁄₁₀₀ em	↖↖ block ᵂ/arrow, ↖ in text, ⌘-⌫ or ⌘-←
Kern apart ¹⁄₁₀₀ em	↖↖ block ᵂ/arrow, ↖ in text, ⌘-⇧-⌫ or ⌘-→

Creating and reshaping objects

The list below describes ways to create and edit various common elements in Aldus FreeHand. Each of these actions requires the use of a mouse in one way or another. Many require use of the keyboard as well.

Drawing operation	Keystroke and/or mouse operation
Circle, draw from corner	⇧-····▸ ʷ/oval tool
Circle, draw from center	⇧-⬲-····▸ ʷ/oval tool
Circle, adjust curvature	⌘-U, ····▸ Bézier control handle ʷ/arrow
Close open path	····▸ one endpoint onto the other ʷ/arrow
Connector point, create	▸ ʷ/connector tool
Connector point, add handle	⬲-····▸ point ʷ/arrow tool
Corner point, create	▸ ʷ/corner tool or ▸ ʷ/pen tool
Corner point, add handle	⬲-····▸ point ʷ/arrow tool
Curve point, create	▸ ʷ/curve tool or ····▸ ʷ/pen tool
Curved line, draw	▸, ▸, ▸ separate locations ʷ/curve tool or ····▸, ····▸ separate locations ʷ/pen tool
Curved segment, adjust	····▸ Bézier control handle ʷ/arrow tool
Cusp point, create	····▸-⬲ ʷ/pen tool
Delete point, break path	▸ point ʷ/knife tool, ⌫
Delete point, don't break path	▸ point ʷ/arrow tool, ⌫
Deselect all objects	➔⎮
Deselect all points, not paths	~ (TILDE)
Display Bézier control handle	▸ path, ▸ point ʷ/arrow tool
Display control handle in group	⬲-▸ path in group, ▸ point ʷ/arrow tool
Ellipse, draw from corner	····▸ ʷ/oval tool
Ellipse, draw from center	⬲-····▸ ʷ/oval tool
Ellipse, adjust curvature	⌘-U, ····▸ Bézier control handle ʷ/arrow
Erase while drawing ʷ/freehand tool	⌘-····▸ back over path ʷ/freehand tool
Extend open path	▸ endpoint ʷ/arrow, ▸ or ····▸ ʷ/pen, curve, corner, or connector tool or ····▸ endpoint ʷ/freehand tool

Drawing operation	Keystroke and/or mouse operation
Insert point in path	▶ segment w/pen, curve, corner, or connector tool
Insert two endpoints in path	▶ segment w/knife tool
Join coincident endpoints from two different paths	⋯▶ around points w/arrow tool, ⌘-J
Move point while creating	⋯▶-⌘ w/pen tool or ⋯▶ w/other point tool
Open closed path	▶ point or segment w/knife tool
Perpendicular line, draw	⇧-⋯▶ w/line tool or ⇧-⬳-⋯▶ w/freehand tool or ▶, ⇧-▶ separate locations w/pen or corner tool
Rectangle, draw from corner	⋯▶ w/rectangle tool
Rectangle, draw from center	⬳-⋯▶ w/rectangle tool
Rounded rect., from corner	⋯▶ w/rounded-rectangle tool
Rounded rect., from center	⬳-⋯▶ w/rounded-rectangle tool
Rounded rect., adjust corner	⌘-I, enter new "Corner radius" value, ↵
Rounded square, from corner	⇧-⋯▶ w/rounded-rectangle tool
Rounded square, from center	⇧-⬳-⋯▶ w/rounded-rectangle tool
Rounded square, adjust corner	⌘-I, enter new "Corner radius" value, ↵
Select object	▶ point or segment w/arrow tool
Select object behind selection	⌥-▶ point or segment w/arrow tool
Select single path in group	⬳-▶ point or segment w/arrow tool
Select group within group	⬳-▶ point or segment w/arrow, ~ (TILDE)
Select point	▶ path, ▶ point w/arrow tool
Select point in group	⬳-▶ path in group, ▶ point w/arrow tool
Select multiple points	⋯▶ around points w/arrow tool or ▶ one, ⇧-▶ another w/arrow tool
Select multiple points in group	⬳-⋯▶ around points w/arrow tool or ⬳-▶ path, ▶ one point, ⇧-▶ another
Split point into endpoints	▶ point w/knife tool
Square, draw from corner	⇧-⋯▶ with rectangle tool
Square, draw from center	⇧-⬳-⋯▶ with rectangle tool
Straight line, draw	⋯▶ w/line tool or ⬳-⋯▶ w/freehand tool or ▶, ▶ separate locations w/pen or corner tool

Manipulating objects

Manipulating elements in Aldus FreeHand also requires some use of a mouse as well as occasional keystrokes. The following are the most common transformations and duplications.

Manipulation	Keystroke and/or mouse operation
Enlarge selected object	⇢ up and right ʷ/scale tool
Enlarge object proportionally	⇧-⇢ up and right ʷ/scale tool
Move selected object	⇢ object ʷ/arrow tool
Move object perpendicularly	⇢-⇧ object ʷ/arrow tool
Move selection by increment	↑, ←, ↓, or →
Move path by point	⌥-⇢ object ʷ/arrow tool
Preview object in keyline mode	⇢-⌘ object ʷ/arrow tool
Reduce selected object	⇢ down and left ʷ/scale tool
Reduce object proportionally	⇧-⇢ down and left ʷ/scale tool
Reflect selected object	⇢ ʷ/reflect tool
Reflect object horizontally	↖ ʷ/reflect tool
Reflect object vertically	⇧-⇢ horizontally ʷ/reflect tool
Reflect object numerically	⌘-↖ ʷ/reflect tool
Rotate selected object	⇢ ʷ/rotate tool
Rotate object multiple of 45°	⇧-⇢ ʷ/rotate tool
Rotate object numerically	⌘-↖ ʷ/rotate tool
Scale selected object	⇢ ʷ/scale tool
Scale object proportionally	⇧-⇢ ʷ/scale tool
Scale selected group	⇢ corner handle ʷ/arrow tool
Scale group proportionally	⇧-⇢ corner handle ʷ/arrow tool
Scale geometric path horizontally or vertically	⇧-⇢-⌥ corner handle ʷ/arrow tool
Scale imported bitmap	⌘-⇢ corner handle ʷ/arrow tool
Scale bitmap proportionally	⇧-⌘-⇢ corner handle ʷ/arrow tool
Slant selected object	⇢ ʷ/skew tool
Slant object horizontally	⇧-⇢ horizontally ʷ/skew tool
Slant object vertically	⇧-⇢ vertically ʷ/skew tool

Accessing dialog boxes

Most dialog boxes are displayed by choosing menu commands or pop-up menu options followed by ellipses, such as the DOCUMENT SETUP... command and the "Zoom text..." option. Still more are accessed by clicking buttons in other dialog boxes. For example, the MORE PREFERENCES dialog box is displayed by clicking the MORE... button in the standard PREFERENCES dialog box. Only a few dialog boxes do not correspond to commands or buttons. These may be accessed using special mouse operations, as listed below.

Dialog box	Keystroke and/or mouse operation
Freehand dialog box	⬆⬆ freehand tool icon in toolbox
Trace dialog box	⬆⬆ trace tool icon in toolbox
Reflect dialog box	⬱-⬆ ⅋ reflect tool
Rotate dialog box	⬱-⬆ ⅋ rotate tool
Scale dialog box	⬱-⬆ ⅋ scale tool
Skew dialog box	⬱-⬆ ⅋ skew tool

Using dialog boxes

Keyboard equivalents can also be used to select options and activate buttons inside dialog boxes. The keystrokes listed below work inside all dialog boxes.

Dialog box function	Keystroke
Highlight next option box	➡|
Highlight previous option box	⇧-➡|
Cancel button	⌘-. (COMMAND-PERIOD)
OK button	↵ (except in TEXT dialog) or ⤱

A Brief Tour of Aldus FreeHand 3.0

Now that we have defined the terms we will use to discuss Aldus FreeHand 3.0 and have taken a look at the tools and menus of the application, it is time to start using FreeHand. This chapter will introduce the most basic activities you will perform when using FreeHand: starting the application, creating new files, opening existing files, altering the view size of your drawing area, changing the display mode, saving files, closing files, and quitting FreeHand.

Starting FreeHand

After you have installed Aldus FreeHand and its related utilities and documents as described in Appendix A, *Installing Aldus FreeHand*, you must *launch* the application before you can begin drawing. FreeHand may be launched in any of the following ways:

- **Double-click the FreeHand application icon.** The FreeHand application icon is shown with a FreeHand document in Figure 3.01 as it appears inside a folder at the Finder level. To launch the program, you may either double-click the icon or click the icon to select it and choose OPEN from the Finder FILE menu (⌘-O).

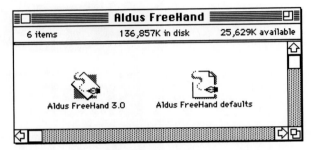

Figure 3.01: The FreeHand application (left) with an illustration file (right) as they appear at the Finder level.

- **Double-click a FreeHand 3.0 document.** Figure 3.01 displays a typical FreeHand 3.0 file, also called an *illustration*. Double-clicking this file icon will launch FreeHand and immediately open the file. Alternatively, you may select the file and choose OPEN from the Finder FILE menu.

 To open multiple illustrations at once, press SHIFT and click on each of the files you want to open. Then press the OPTION key and double-click any one of the selected files.

- **Use a launching utility.** If you own a launching utility such as OnCue, Disktop, or MasterJuggler, you may launch FreeHand by choosing it as a command from a menu of application names. Using a macro program like QuicKeys or Tempo, you may launch Free-Hand by pressing a sequence of keys, such as COMMAND-CONTROL-F.

Each time you launch FreeHand, the startup screen shown in Figure 3.02 will appear, featuring a line of text that lists the amount of free space currently available in the portion of your computer's RAM that is allocated to FreeHand (known as *application RAM*). To prevent a system error, which may crash your machine and result in the loss of your time and data, you should make sure that at least 300K of application RAM remains unused at all times.

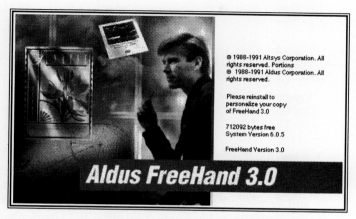

Figure 3.02: The Aldus FreeHand 3.0 startup screen contains copyright and memory information.

The startup screen provides an introduction to the FreeHand application. It will disappear after a few seconds. If you ever wish to see the startup screen again while in the application, choose ABOUT FREEHAND... from the APPLE (⌘) menu. This screen will include two buttons. Click OK or press RETURN to close the startup screen. Click HELP... (⌘-⇧-/ or HELP) to access FreeHand's on-line help system. The ALDUS ONLINE HELP dialog box will display, as shown in Figure 3.03 on the following page. This dialog box may also be displayed by choosing HELP... from the APPLE menu. The on-line help system provides a convenient source of information about utilizing commands and other features in FreeHand 3.0. To learn how to use the help system, click the USING HELP button and read the text presented in the scrolling field. If you are familiar with previous versions of FreeHand, click the TOPICS button, then double-click the " • NEW FEATURES" option at the top of the scrolling field to quickly acquaint yourself with the enhancements that distinguish version 3.0 from its predecessors. When you are finished browsing through the help system, click the QUIT HELP button to return to the FreeHand desktop.

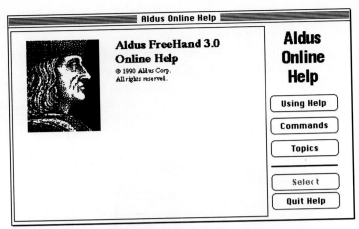

Figure 3.03: The Aldus Online Help dialog box offers access to the FreeHand help system.

While in the illustration window, press COMMAND-SHIFT-/ (SLASH) or HELP to access FreeHand's context-sensitive help feature. Your cursor will change to a question mark. Select a tool or command and FreeHand will automatically display the corresponding help screen. You may also access context-sensitive help from many dialog boxes.

After FreeHand finishes launching and the startup screen disappears, you will find yourself at the *FreeHand desktop*. Unless you are running under MultiFinder, the desktop is empty except for any open palettes and the menu bar at the top of the screen. For the present, most of Free-Hand's commands are dimmed. The only exceptions are WINDOWS under the VIEW menu, which allows you to open and close palettes, and the following commands from the FILE menu:

- **New**..., which allows you to create a new illustration.

- **Open**..., which allows you to open an existing illustration previously saved to disk.

- **Preferences**..., which allows you to adjust settings that control the performance of various tools and commands.

- **Quit**, which exits the FreeHand desktop and returns you to the Macintosh Finder (or another application if running under MultiFinder).

All of these commands are discussed in this chapter.

Creating a new illustration

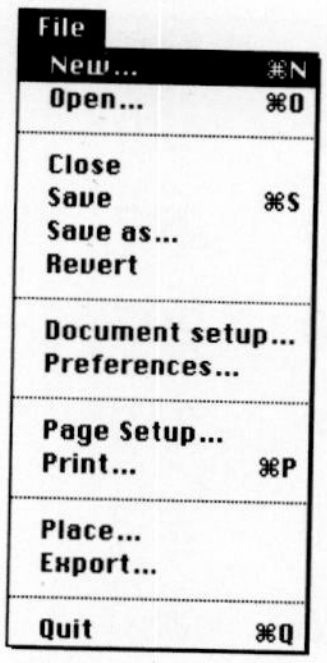

A new illustration is created by choosing the NEW... command under the FILE menu (⌘-N). Choosing NEW... displays the DOCUMENT SETUP dialog box, shown in Figure 3.04.

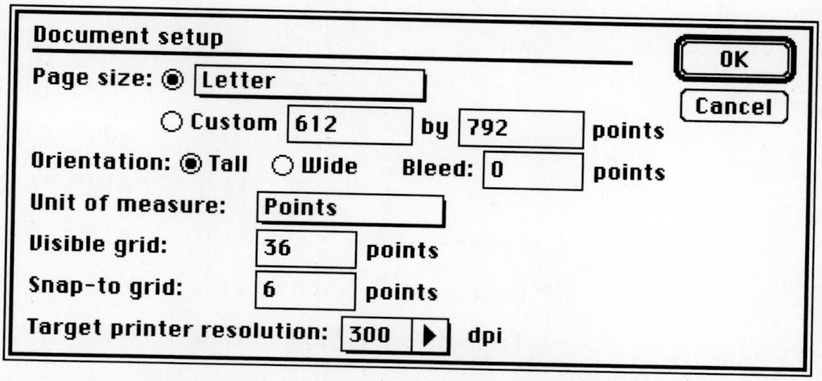

File menu:

New...	⌘N
Open...	⌘O
Close	
Save	⌘S
Save as...	
Revert	
Document setup...	
Preferences...	
Page Setup...	
Print...	⌘P
Place...	
Export...	
Quit	⌘Q

Document setup

Page size: ● Letter
○ Custom 612 by 792 points
Orientation: ● Tall ○ Wide   Bleed: 0 points
Unit of measure: Points
Visible grid: 36 points
Snap-to grid: 6 points
Target printer resolution: 300 ▶ dpi

[OK]
[Cancel]

Figure 3.04: The Document setup dialog box allows you to configure a new or existing illustration.

Setting up the illustration

The DOCUMENT SETUP dialog box is FreeHand's way of requesting information about your new illustration. Here you may indicate the size of the illustration, the unit of measurement, the grid increments, and so on. If you are unsure how to answer an option, don't worry. At any time, you may revisit the DOCUMENT SETUP dialog box and adjust the settings for the current illustration by choosing the DOCUMENT SETUP... command from the FILE menu.

The options in the DOCUMENT SETUP dialog box are as follows:

* **Page size**. Click and hold your mouse button on this option to display a pop-up menu offering several page size options. The option you choose will determine the size of the page that will display in the illustration window (see Figure 3.05 on page 67).

The measurements of each page-size option are listed below in inches, points, and millimeters:

Page size	Inches		Points		Millimeters	
NAME	WIDTH	HEIGHT	WIDTH	HEIGHT	WIDTH	HEIGHT
A3	11.7	16.5	842	1191	297	420
A4	8.3	11.7	595	842	210	297
A4small	8.3	11.7	595	842	210	297
A5	5.8	8.3	420	595	148	210
B4	9.8	13.9	709	1001	250	353
B5	6.9	9.8	499	709	176	250
Legal	8.5	14.0	612	1008	216	356
Letter	8.5	11.0	612	792	216	279
Lettersmall	8.5	11.0	612	792	216	279
Tabloid	11.0	17.0	792	1224	279	432

Note that the European page size "A4" is identical in width and height to "A4small." Likewise, "Letter" measures the same size as "Lettersmall." Both sets of options differ only in terms of *imageable area*; that is, the amount of the page on which objects may be printed to a laser printer or other toner-based output device. (Photo imagesetters, such as the Linotronic family of printers, will print the entire page size, regardless of imageable area.) The imageable area of the "A4" page size is 197 by 281 millimeters, or about 7¾ by 11 inches. The imageable area of the "A4small" page is slightly smaller, at 189 by 279 millimeters. Similarly, the imageable area of the "Letter" page size measures 576 by 776 points (about 8 by 10¾ inches), while the smaller "Lettersmall" imageable area measures 552 by 729 points (7⅔ by 10⅛ inches). Generally, you will only want to use "A4small" or "Lettersmall" if you encounter out-of-memory errors when printing. For more information, refer to Chapter 14, *Printing Your Illustration*.

Below the pop-up menu is the "Custom" option, which allows you to specify any page size from 2 inches square (51 millimeters square) to 40 inches square (1,016 millimeters square), as measured in the units displayed in the "Unit of measure" option. To use the "Custom" option, enter values into the "Custom" option boxes. (Notice that the "Custom" option boxes always display the dimensions of the current page size, regardless of whether the "Custom" or pop-up menu radio button is selected.)

● **Orientation**. Here, you may select either "Tall" to set your page upright (also known as the portrait setting) or "Wide" to set the page on its side (the landscape setting).

● **Bleed**. This option allows you to specify the *bleed*, an area beyond the perimeter of the page size that may be printed. In other words, if you choose "Letter" from the "Page size" pop-up and you enter 36 points (½ inch) for "Bleed," you enlarge the imageable area of your illustration to 9½ by 12 inches, because the bleed wraps around all four sides of the page. A bleed is most useful when creating a document that contains images which extend off one or more edges of the page. To successfully exploit the "Bleed" option, the paper that your printer outputs must be larger than the current page size. Although this option may be set as high as 32,000 points (over 37 feet!), the actual amount of bleed space available to you will depend on the width of the paper or film generated by the final output device. The bleed displays as a dotted (or gray) line surrounding the page in the illustration window.

● **Unit of measure**. Click and hold your mouse button down on this option to display a pop-up menu offering five systems of measurement options: "Points," "Picas," "Inches," "Decimal inches," and "Millimeters." A *pica* is almost exactly equal to ⅙ inch; a *point* is ½₂ pica, or about ¹⁄₇₂ inch. A *decimal inch* is identical in size to a standard inch; the only difference is that the standard inch is subdivided into 16 increments and the decimal inch is broken up into 10 increments. The option you choose determines the measurement system used in all dialog boxes (including this one) as well as on the horizontal and vertical rulers displayed by choosing the RULERS command from the VIEW menu (⌘-R).

✳ When entering measurements into a dialog box, you may override the selected "Unit of measure" option by adding the following abbreviations: *i* for inch, *m* for millimeter, and *p* for pica (with any value following *p* indicating points). For example, "3i" translates to 3 inches, "14m" means 14 millimeters, and 5p6 stands for 5 picas 6 points, or 5 ½ picas.

- **Visible grid**. This option determines the size, in the current unit of measure, of an increment of the *visible grid*, displayed by choosing Grid from the View menu. The visible grid is displayed as a network of dots in the current FreeHand window. It does not print and it does not affect the movement of your mouse. The latter is the job of the invisible *snap-to grid*, described next.

- **Snap-to grid**. This option determines the size, in the current unit of measure, of an increment of the invisible *snap-to grid*, activated by choosing Snap to grid from the View menu (⌘-;, command-semi-colon). The snap-to grid controls the positioning and manipulation of elements on the page. Generally, this option should be set to a value less than or equal to, as well as a factor of, the visible grid. The "Snap-to grid" option may be set to any value between 1 point and 864 points (12 inches).

- **Target printer resolution**. Click and hold your mouse button on this option to display a pop-up menu offering four options: "300," "600," "1270," and "2540," all measured in dots per inch. You may also enter any value between 72 and 5080. Choose the option that best reflects the *resolution* of the final output device (as discussed in Chapter 14, *Printing Your Illustrations*). This option controls the sizing of imported MacPaint and TIFF images. It also determines the degree to which FreeHand automatically breaks up long paths when printing and exporting illustrations, in order to avoid limitcheck errors and other printing problems. High resolutions allow for more potential limitcheck errors; therefore, more paths will be broken and into smaller pieces. To turn off the automatic path-breaking feature, enter 72 for the "Target printer resolution" option.

To escape the Document setup dialog box, click the OK button or the Cancel button. Clicking OK or pressing return executes the New… command and creates a new document according to your specifications. Clicking Cancel or pressing command-period returns you to the Free-Hand desktop without creating a new file.

The Document setup dialog box may be redisplayed at any time by choosing Document setup… from the File menu, thus allowing you to alter the page size, unit of measure, or grid increment for the current illustration.

The FreeHand desktop

Figure 3.05 shows the result of choosing NEW... and accepting many of the default settings in the DOCUMENT SETUP dialog box. Only the "Bleed" option was changed to make the bleed visible.

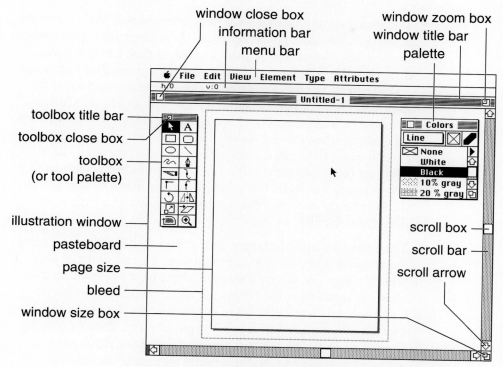

Figure 3.05: The FreeHand desktop, with all parts labeled.

This is the same FreeHand desktop that appears immediately after launching the FreeHand application, only now it contains an open *illustration window*. The desktop in Figure 3.05 is labeled with the following items (labeled items appear in bold type):

- **The menu bar** provides access to the nine menus discussed in the *Menus and commands* section of Chapter 2. Drag at a menu name to display a menu; release on a command name to choose a command.

- **The palettes** include the **toolbox** discussed in *The toolbox* section of Chapter 2 as well as the Colors, Layers, and Styles palettes discussed in the *Palette menus* section of Chapter 2. By default, only the toolbox and the Colors palette display after first launching FreeHand. Each palette includes its own title bar and close box. For example, you may drag the **toolbox title bar** to move the toolbox or click the **toolbox close box** to hide the toolbox.

- **The illustration window** is the large window that fills most of the desktop. A window appears for every open illustration. Like the toolbox, the illustration includes a **window title bar** and a **window close box** for moving and closing the current illustration window. The title bar lists the name of the current illustration. If the illustration has not been saved, the name will appear as "Untitled-" followed by a number. The title bar also includes a **window zoom box**, which when clicked slightly reduces the size of the window to make it easier to juggle multiple illustrations (although it has no effect on the illustration itself). Click the zoom box again to enlarge the window to fill the screen. Drag the **window size box** in the lower right corner of the window to manually enlarge or reduce the size of the window.

- **The page size** is the rectangle with a drop shadow in the center of the window. The page size represents the size and shape of your printed page. The dotted lines around the page size indicate the **bleed**, as specified in the Document setup dialog box, which defines the total imageable area of the illustration. The 44-inch-by-44-inch area outside the page is the **pasteboard**. Because objects positioned on the pasteboard are saved with your illustration but will not print, the pasteboard is useful for setting objects aside or storing them for later use. Together, page size and pasteboard are known as the *drawing area*, since this is the portion of the window in which all objects are created and manipulated.

- **The scroll bars** appear along the right and bottom edges of the illustration window, as they do in most Macintosh applications. They allow you to *scroll* the window; that is, move the window with respect to the drawing area. Click a **scroll arrow** to scroll the window ⅛ the current height or width of the illustration window. Click in the gray area of a scroll bar to scroll the window about seven times as far. Drag a **scroll box** to manually determine the distance to be scrolled.

- **The information bar** between the menu bar and the illustration window lists the coordinates of your cursor. It also lists details about the current transformation.

The cursor

The only desktop item not labeled in Figure 3.05 is the arrow-shaped *cursor*, the most important item in any drawing software. The cursor tracks the movement of your mouse as it relates to the Macintosh screen area. When positioned in any other part of the desktop other than the illustration window, the cursor appears as a black arrow. Inside the illustration window, the cursor changes to reflect the current tool or the current operation. Table 3.01 shows every cursor that may appear in Aldus FreeHand 3.0 and describes the action that it implies.

Table 3.01: Cursors that may appear in the illustration window and their meanings

▸	selecting objects with arrow tool
✛	dragging a selected object with arrow tool
↕	constraining a drag vertically by pressing shift
↔	constraining a drag horizontally by pressing shift
I	creating a text block with text tool; also displayed inside Text dialog box
+	drawing with rectangle, rounded-rectangle, oval, line, freehand, pen, curve, corner, connector, or trace tool; or using knife tool
✳	using any transformation tool (rotate, reflect, scale, or skew)
⊕	expanding view size to twice previous magnification
⊖	contracting view size to half previous magnification
○	view size has reached maximum level of expansion or contraction
✋	scrolling illustration window with hand tool

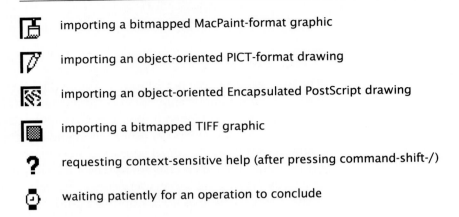

importing a bitmapped MacPaint-format graphic

importing an object-oriented PICT-format drawing

importing an object-oriented Encapsulated PostScript drawing

importing a bitmapped TIFF graphic

requesting context-sensitive help (after pressing command-shift-/)

waiting patiently for an operation to conclude

Opening an existing file

Existing illustrations can be opened from inside FreeHand or directly at
the Finder level. FreeHand 3.0 will also open files created in older versions of FreeHand and object-oriented drawings saved in the Adobe Illustrator 1.1 or PICT format. Both alternatives are discussed in the
following sections.

Opening illustrations at the Finder

If FreeHand is not already running, you can simultaneously open the
FreeHand 3.0 application and a specific illustration file by double-clicking
an illustration file icon at the Finder level. Figure 3.06 shows the various
kinds of icons associated with files that FreeHand 3.0 will open. Double-
clicking either of the files shown on the left side of the figure will launch
the FreeHand 3.0 application. The other files belong to FreeHand 2.02,
FreeHand 1.0, Adobe Illustrator 1.1, and Canvas 2.1. Double-clicking
any of these files will launch the respective application or display the message "Application not found" if the application does not reside on an
available disk or hard drive. Such illustrations must be opened from inside
FreeHand 3.0, as described in the next section.

Aldus FreeHand documents
9 items
141,780K in disk
20,706K available
FreeHand 3.0 file
FreeHand 2.0 file
FreeHand 1.0 file
3.0 template file
Illustrator 1.1 file
PICT
Canvas PICT file

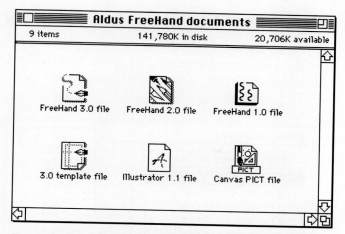

Figure 3.06: Six kinds of documents that may be opened by FreeHand 3.0, viewed by icon at the Finder level.

Figure 3.07 shows the files from Figure 3.06 when viewed by name. Be sure to double-click the small page icon rather than the file name when launching an illustration displayed in this manner.

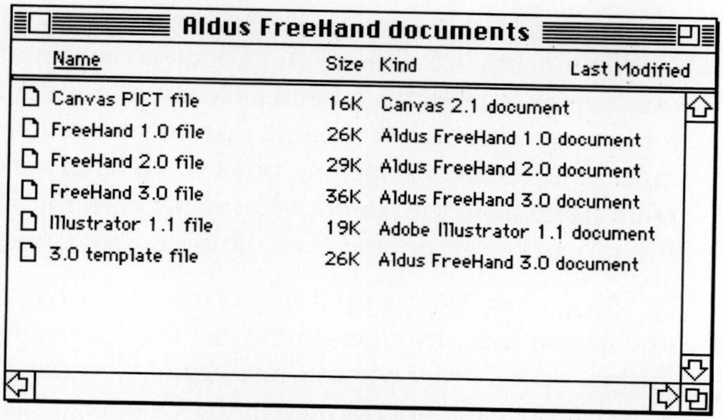

Aldus FreeHand documents
Name
Size
Kind
Last Modified
Canvas PICT file
16K
Canvas 2.1 document
FreeHand 1.0 file
26K
Aldus FreeHand 1.0 document
FreeHand 2.0 file
29K
Aldus FreeHand 2.0 document
FreeHand 3.0 file
36K
Aldus FreeHand 3.0 document
Illustrator 1.1 file
19K
Adobe Illustrator 1.1 document
3.0 template file
26K
Aldus FreeHand 3.0 document

Figure 3.07: The same illustration files viewed by name at the Finder level.

Note that none of these documents is saved in the Encapsulated PostScript format. FreeHand 3.0 cannot open the EPS files that it creates, nor those created by its predecessors or any other application.

Opening files inside FreeHand 3.0

To open an existing illustration while inside FreeHand 3.0, choose the OPEN… command from the FILE menu (⌘-O). The OPEN DOCUMENT dialog box will display, as shown in Figure 3.08.

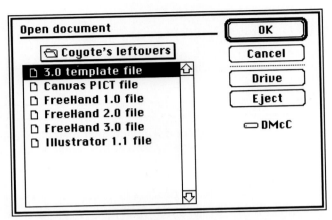

Figure 3.08: The Open document dialog box allows you to open FreeHand, Illustrator 1.1, and PICT files.

This dialog box allows you to open an illustration created in a previous version of FreeHand, open a file saved in the Adobe Illustrator 1.1 format, open an object-oriented document saved in the PICT format, or cancel the document opening process. To open a file, select the document name from the *scrolling file list* and click the OPEN button, or press the RETURN key, or double-click the document name.

As in most Macintosh dialog boxes of this type, you can quickly locate a specific file by entering the first few letters of its name. The first file in alphabetical order whose name begins with these letters will be selected. (Any typing performed in the OPEN DOCUMENT dialog does not appear on screen.) You may also press the ↑ and ↓ keys to move up and down the scrolling file list.

If the file that you wish to open is on a disk or hard drive volume other than the one containing your FreeHand application, use the DRIVE and EJECT buttons to move between available drives and remove disks so that other disks may be inserted. Double-clicking a folder name in the scrolling file list will open that folder and display the files it contains. Drag down on the *folder bar* above the scrolling file list to close a folder and display the contents of the drive or folder in which the given folder resides.

KE Press the TAB key to activate the DRIVE button. Press COMMAND-SHIFT-1 to eject a disk from the upper (or only) floppy drive, press COMMAND-SHIFT-2 to eject a disk from the lower drive. Press COMMAND-↓ to open the selected folder, press COMMAND-↑ to close the current folder. Press COMMAND-PERIOD to cancel.

After selecting the desired illustration, FreeHand creates an illustration window. If the file was created in FreeHand 3.0, the file name will appear in the title bar at the top of the window. If the illustration was created in a previous version of Freehand or in some other application, the window will be untitled.

You can open multiple files in Aldus FreeHand, provided that sufficient application RAM is available. Any opened illustration will display in a window similar to that shown in Figure 3.05.

Working in the illustration window

Once you have opened an illustration or created a new one, it is important to know how to use tools, commands, and scroll bars to move around inside the illustration window. In this section, we discuss how to change the view size, scroll the drawing area inside the window, and alter the display mode for your illustration.

Changing the view size

FreeHand provides seven *view sizes*; that is, levels of magnification at which the drawing area may be displayed in the illustration window. Expanded view sizes provide great detail, but allow only small portions of a page to be displayed at a time. Contracted view sizes allow you to look at a larger portion of the drawing area, but may provide insufficient detail for creating and manipulating objects. Because FreeHand makes it easy to quickly change between various view sizes, you can accurately edit your artwork and still maintain an overall design consistency.

When you first enter a new or existing illustration, the drawing area is displayed at *fit-in-window size*. At this view size, the drawing area is reduced to the extent that it can be displayed in the illustration window in its entirety. The actual magnification level required to produce the fit-in-window view size is dependent on the size and resolution of the illustration window, a calculation which FreeHand makes automatically.

Figure 3.09: An illustration viewed at fit-in-window size.

The view size may be changed using pop-up options displayed by choosing the MAGNIFICATION command from the VIEW menu. For example, to access the fit-in-window view size at a later point in time, choose the "Fit in window" option (⌘-W). To enlarge the drawing area so that the details of your illustration are displayed on screen at the size they will appear when printed, use *actual size*. This size generally provides the most natural visual feedback concerning the progress of your artwork. To access actual size at any time, choose "100%" from the MAGNIFICATION pop-up menu (⌘-1).

Figure 3.10: The same illustration viewed at actual size.

In addition to the actual and fit-in-window view sizes, FreeHand provides five other levels of magnification, each of which is expressed as a percentage of actual size. Any level may be accessed by choosing a MAGNIFICATION option or by using the *zoom tool*. When the zoom tool is selected, your cursor becomes a magnifying glass, displaying either a plus sign, a minus sign, or nothing in its center. The magnifying glass with inset plus sign functions as a *zoom-in tool*. Clicking in the drawing area with the zoom-in tool expands your view size to twice its previous level of magnification, thus displaying only half as much of your artwork. The magnifying glass with inset minus sign functions as a *zoom-out tool*. Clicking with the zoom-out tool contracts the view size to half its previous level of magnification, thus displaying twice as much of your artwork. The magnifying glass cursor appears empty when your current view size is at either the maximum (800%) or minimum (12.5%) level of magnification possible; you may therefore zoom in or out no further.

To access the zoom-in tool, select the zoom tool in the toolbox. To access the zoom-out tool, select the zoom tool and hold down the OPTION key.

KE To temporarily access the zoom tool when some other tool is selected, press and hold the COMMAND key and SPACEBAR. Releasing both keys will return the cursor to its previous appearance. Press COMMAND-OPTION-SPACEBAR to temporarily access the zoom-out tool.

Scrolling the drawing area inside the illustration window

Since most Macintosh screens are not as large as a full page, most users are not able to see their entire drawing when expanded to actual size or to a higher level of magnification. Therefore, FreeHand provides you with the ability to position your drawing area in reference to your illustration window, a technique known as *scrolling*.

The first method for scrolling the drawing area is to use the two *scroll bars*, which are located at the bottom and right sides of the window. (Refer to Figure 3.05 for their location in respect to the FreeHand desktop.) At both ends of each scroll bar are the *scroll arrows*. Clicking directly on a scroll arrow scrolls the illustration window slightly in that direction. The exact distance of the scroll is equal to ⅛ the current height or width of the illustration window. But because the window remains stationary in the FreeHand desktop, the drawing area appears to move in the opposite direction. For example, if you click the *up* scroll arrow, the drawing area and its objects will appear to move *down*. This is because your "window" into the drawing area has been raised.

To scroll the window more quickly, drag one of the two *scroll boxes* that move back and forth inside the scroll bars. Be sure to drag in small increments; if you drag a scroll bar all the way to one side of a scroll bar, you will scroll well outside the page size, into the pasteboard.

You may also click within the gray area of a scroll bar. This will cause the drawing area to move about 90% the current height or width of the illustration window (roughly seven times the result of clicking a scroll arrow) in one direction or another, depending on where you click in relation to the scroll box. If you click to the right of a horizontal scroll box, for example, the window scrolls to the right (so your drawing area appears to move to the left).

An easier way to move about your drawing area is to use the *hand tool*, which allows you to drag the drawing area in 4-pixel increments with respect to the illustration window. In most situations, dragging with the hand tool is more convenient and more accurate than clicking on a scroll arrow or dragging a scroll box.

 To temporarily access the hand tool when some other tool is selected, press and hold the SPACEBAR. Releasing the SPACEBAR will return the cursor to its previous appearance.

Using display modes

Display modes provide another way to control the way you see images in the drawing area. When you first create a new document or open an existing one, the screen display matches the printed appearance of the illustration as closely as the resolution of your monitor will allow. This display mode is called the *preview mode*. Figure 3.11 shows an illustration displayed in the preview mode. Figure 3.12 on the next page shows the same illustration when printed. Because the two are very similar, the preview mode is useful for assessing the appearance of your artwork.

Figure 3.11: An illustration viewed in the preview mode.

Figure 3.12: The same illustration as it appears when printed.

Unlike its closest competitor, Adobe Illustrator, FreeHand allows you to create and manipulate objects while in the preview mode. However, the preview mode can be slow. Complicated fill and stroke effects take time to process, creating a time lag between the moment you draw an element, and the moment it appears on screen.

If you become impatient with the speed of FreeHand's screen display, you may want to try out the *keyline mode*, the display mode of choice for many experienced illustrators. Rather than mimicking the printed appearance of an illustration, FreeHand displays objects with fine black outlines and transparent interiors. Only text displays as solid black, rather than outlined. No colors are shown. Imported artwork on a foreground layer is displayed as a large rectangle with inset diagonal lines. Figure 3.13 shows the flowers from Figure 3.11 displayed in the keyline mode. Though less exact, the keyline mode is very fast. FreeHand doesn't have to spend time displaying complicated visual effects. Admittedly, drawing in the keyline mode may take some getting used to. But if you spend the time necessary to become accustomed to it, you will increase your drawing speed and decrease much of your frustration with FreeHand's performance.

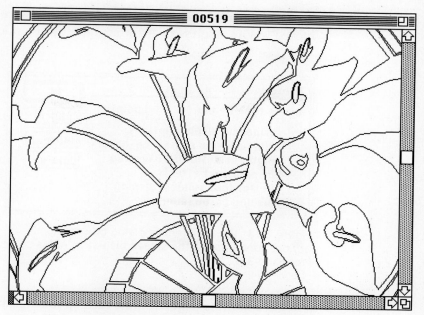

Figure 3.13: An illustration viewed in the keyline mode.

Both the preview and keyline display modes may be accessed by choosing the PREVIEW command from the VIEW menu (⌘-K). A check mark displays before the command in the preview mode. No check mark displays in the keyline mode.

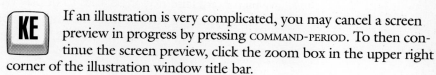

If an illustration is very complicated, you may cancel a screen preview in progress by pressing COMMAND-PERIOD. To then continue the screen preview, click the zoom box in the upper right corner of the illustration window title bar.

Setting preferences

Everyone does not draw alike. For those who draw to a different drummer (in other words, all of us), FreeHand provides the PREFERENCES… command, which allows you to edit a variety of settings that control the performance of Aldus FreeHand. Choosing PREFERENCES… from the FILE menu displays the PREFERENCES dialog box, shown in Figure 3.14 on the following page. Here you may control how various type and graphic objects in an illustration display on screen, the number of consecutive

UNDO commands, grid and guide colors, the distance a selected object is moved when you press an arrow key, plus much, much more.

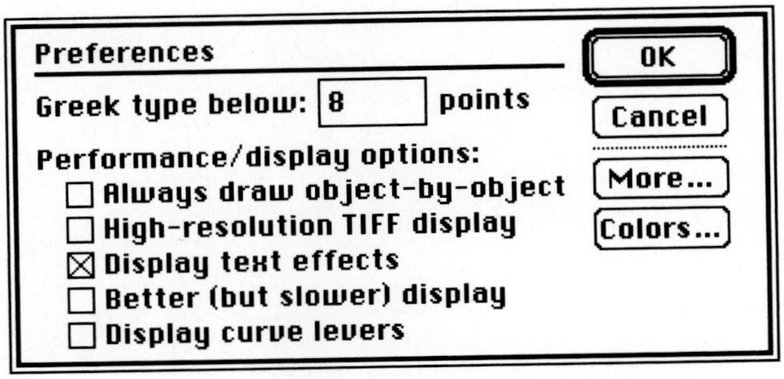

```
┌─────────────────────────────────────────────┐
│ ┌─────────────────────────────────────────┐ │
│ │ Preferences ─────────────    ┌──────────┐│ │
│ │                              │    OK    ││ │
│ │ Greek type below: │ 8 │  points ─────────│ │
│ │                              ┌──────────┐│ │
│ │ Performance/display options: │  Cancel  ││ │
│ │ ☐ Always draw object-by-object ──────────│ │
│ │ ☐ High-resolution TIFF display ┌────────┐│ │
│ │ ☒ Display text effects         │ More...││ │
│ │ ☐ Better (but slower) display  ┌────────┐│ │
│ │ ☐ Display curve levers         │Colors..││ │
│ └─────────────────────────────────────────┘ │
└─────────────────────────────────────────────┘
```

Figure 3.14: The Preferences dialog box contains options for adjusting the screen display in Aldus FreeHand 3.0.

The following pages describe each option available in this dialog, plus those available in the related dialog boxes, MORE PREFERENCES and DISPLAY COLOR SETUP. Much of the background required to fully understand these options has not been laid so far in this book. For this reason, many options are covered in greater detail in one or more later chapters.

The options available in the PREFERENCES dialog box are:

- **Greek type below___ points**. This option controls the size at which FreeHand no longer tries to display type accurately on the screen, replacing lines of text with thin gray bars. The size refers to the perceived type size of the text. For example, if you enter 6 for this option, text set to 6-point or smaller will appear gray at actual size, 12-point type and smaller will appear gray at 50% view size, 24-point type and smaller will appear gray at 25% view size, and so on. The benefit of *greeking* text is that FreeHand can display gray bars faster than is can generate individual characters. To turn off the greeking feature completely, enter 0 for this option.

All of the following "Performance/display options" affect on-screen display only; they do not affect the quality of your printed illustrations.

- **Always draw object-by-object**. This option controls the manner in which the screen refreshes both in the preview and keyline display modes. When checked, objects appear one at a time in the drawing area, according to their layering order, each time you change the view size or display mode or open a document. If you deselect this option, FreeHand redraws all objects one by one off screen, and then displays the entire illustration at once when the redraw is complete. This latter method is faster, but it requires more application RAM. If insufficient memory is available, Free-Hand will refresh the screen as if this option were selected.

- **High-resolution TIFF display.** This option controls the on-screen appearance of imported TIFF graphics in both the preview and keyline display modes if the image resides on a background layer. When checked, TIFF images are displayed in full resolution. When this option is deselected, FreeHand simplifies the TIFF image, which greatly speeds up the screen refresh time but diminishes the clarity of the image.

Figure 3.15: A TIFF image displayed with the "High-resolution TIFF display" option selected.

Figure 3.16: The same image displayed after deselecting the "High-resolution TIFF display" option.

- **Display text effects**. This option controls the appearance of type enhanced with options accessed by choosing the Effect command from the Type menu. It affects the preview display mode only, since type effects are never displayed in the keyline mode. When selected, effects display much as they will appear when printed (although stroking effects are slightly inaccurate). If you deselect this option, type will appear unchanged regardless of the effect applied. Once again, selecting this option slows down the screen refresh speed but results in a more precise on-screen display.

- **Better (but slower) display**. This option controls the display of linear, logarithmic, and radial gradations in the preview mode only. When selected, gradations appear to contain up to 256 steps on a 24-bit monitor, and 33 dithered steps on an 8-bit monitor or lower. If the option is deselected, only nine steps are assigned to a gradient fill, which increases the screen refresh speed.

Figure 3.17: A radial gradation as it appears on a 24-bit monitor when the "Better (but slower) display" option is selected (left) and deselected (right).

- **Display curve levers**. This option controls the appearance of Bézier control handles in both the preview and keyline display modes. When selected, lines (called *levers*) connect a selected point to its cross-shaped control handles. When "Display curve levers" is deselected, the handles appear to float in the vicinity of the selected point. Neither option affects the screen refresh speed. This option is entirely a matter of personal preference; however, we recommend that you leave it selected, since otherwise you may have problems determining which control handle goes to which point.

The PREFERENCES dialog box also includes two buttons used to access related dialog boxes. The first, MORE..., displays the MORE PREFERENCES dialog box shown in Figure 3.18.

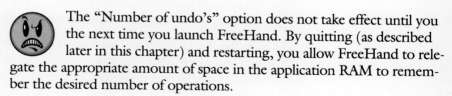

Figure 3.18: The More preferences dialog box allows you to change a variety of settings that affect FreeHand's performance.

The options in this dialog box include the following:

● **Number of undo's.** FreeHand's versatile UNDO command allows you to undo several consecutive operations. You may determine the maximum number of consecutive undos by entering any value between 1 and 99 for this option. Keep in mind that by increasing this value, you decrease the amount of free application RAM available while using FreeHand.

The "Number of undo's" option does not take effect until you the next time you launch FreeHand. By quitting (as described later in this chapter) and restarting, you allow FreeHand to relegate the appropriate amount of space in the application RAM to remember the desired number of operations.

- **Snap-to distance**. This option controls the distance at which a dragged object moves sharply toward a stationary point, snap-to grid, or guide, as measured in *pixels* (screen dots). For example, if the "Snap-to distance" option is set to 3, a dragged object will move sharply toward a guideline any time you move your cursor within three pixels of the guide. Called *snapping*, this sharp movement aids in the alignment of objects. This option also affects how close endpoints must be to be joined using the JOIN ELEMENTS command from the ELEMENT menu (⌘-J) and how accurately you must click or drag to select and modify points and handles.

- **Cursor key distance**. FreeHand allows you to move any selected object by pressing one of the four arrow keys (↑, ←, ↓, →). Each keystroke moves the selection the distance specified in this option box, as measured in the current unit of measure specified in the DOCUMENT SETUP dialog box.

- **Guides color**. If you are using a color monitor, you may adjust the color of all guides displayed in the illustration window. Click the color to the right of this option to display the Apple COLOR WHEEL dialog box, which allows you to select from any color your monitor may display. Guides display only when the GUIDES command in the VIEW menu is active (preceded by a check mark).

- **Grid color**. If you are using a color monitor, you may adjust the color of the visible grid displayed in the illustration window. Click the color to the right of this option to display the Apple COLOR WHEEL dialog box, which allows you to select from any color your monitor may display. The visible grid displays only when the GRID command in the VIEW menu is active (preceded by a check mark).

- **Changing elements changes defaults**. This option controls the default attributes assigned to all objects in the current illustration. When selected, changing the fill or stroke of a selected object also changes the default setting, so that the next object you create will be filled and stroked identically. If you deselect this option, the default attribute settings will remain unchanged.

- **Save palette positions**. This option controls which palettes are open and where they appear each time you start FreeHand. If this option is deselected, only the COLORS palette will display in the upper right corner of the window. When selected, each palette that was open when you last quit FreeHand will open the next time you start FreeHand, and in the same position as before.

The other button in the PREFERENCES dialog box is the COLORS... button. It displays the DISPLAY COLOR SETUP dialog box, shown in Figure 3.19. Compare the displayed color to the corresponding color on the special color card included in the Aldus FreeHand 3.0 package. If the color does not quite match, click it to display the Apple COLOR WHEEL dialog box and choose a more accurate screen color. For more information, refer to Chapter 11, *Assigning Colors and Styles.*

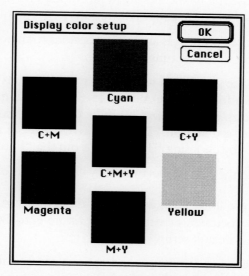

Figure 3.19: The Display color setup dialog box allows you to adjust the screen display for process colors and process-color combinations.

All settings specified in the PREFERENCES, MORE PREFERENCES, and DISPLAY COLOR SETUP dialog boxes are saved to a file called FreeHandPrefs in the same folder that contains the FreeHand application or in the Aldus folder (if such a folder exists) in your System folder. Your settings will therefore affect every file that you create or modify from this moment on.

To reset the PREFERENCES and related dialog boxes to their original default settings (as shown in Figures 3.14 and 3.18), quit FreeHand and drag the FreeHandPrefs file into the Trash icon at the Finder level. Choose the EMPTY TRASH command from the SPECIAL menu and relaunch FreeHand 3.0.

Changing defaults

In addition to the PREFERENCES dialog box options, FreeHand offers means for changing various default settings that affect everything from how a new illustration is created to the way the illustration prints. To permanently change the default settings, so that the new settings will apply to every new illustration, follows these steps:

1. Choose the NEW... command from the FILE menu (⌘-N) and press RETURN to create a new illustration.

2. Choose commands and adjust options to match your idea of the perfect default settings.

3. Save the illustration to the folder that contains the FreeHand 3.0 application or in the Aldus folder in the System folder under the name *Aldus FreeHand Defaults*. (Saving an illustration is described in the next section.) Be sure to save the file as an application template (by choosing "Template" from the "Format" option).

4. Close the default illustration by clicking in the close box.

Every new illustration will assume the settings of your defaults document. New documents created during future FreeHand sessions will also assume these default settings.

The following commands and options will be affected by settings saved to the Aldus FreeHand Defaults file:

- All options in the DOCUMENT SETUP dialog box, displayed by choosing NEW... (⌘-N) or DOCUMENT SETUP from the FILE menu.

- All options in the LASERWRITER dialog box, displayed by choosing PRINT... from the FILE menu (⌘-P).

- All options in the PRINT OPTIONS dialog box, displayed by clicking the CHANGE... button in the LASERWRITER dialog box.

- Settings for the PREVIEW (⌘-K), RULERS (⌘-R), GRID, GUIDES, LOCK GUIDES, SNAP TO POINT (⌘-', COMMAND-QUOTE), SNAP TO GUIDES, and SNAP TO GRID (⌘-;, COMMAND-SEMICOLON) commands in the VIEW menu.

- Settings for the FONT, SIZE, LEADING, TYPE STYLE, EFFECT, and ALIGNMENT commands in the TYPE menu.

- All options in the TYPE SPECIFICATIONS dialog box, displayed by choosing TYPE SPECS... from the TYPE menu (⌘-T).

- All options in the SPACING, HORIZONTAL SCALING, and BASELINE SHIFT dialog boxes, displayed by choosing the corresponding commands from the TYPE menu.

- All options in the FILL AND LINE and HALFTONE SCREEN dialog boxes, displayed by choosing the FILL AND LINE...(⌘-E) and HALFTONE SCREEN... commands from the ATTRIBUTES menu.

- Settings and options inside the COLORS, LAYERS, and STYLES palettes.

- Type and graphic objects created in the drawing area.

To reset all commands and options to their original settings, quit FreeHand and drag the Aldus FreeHand Defaults file into the Trash icon at the Finder level. Choose the EMPTY TRASH command from the SPECIAL menu and relaunch FreeHand 3.0.

Saving an illustration

Your computer is not immune to external forces. In the event that your computer crashes due to a system error or a power fluctuation or failure, it is possible to lose much of the work that you have performed on the current illustration. To prevent as much wasted time and effort as possible, you should frequently save your illustration to disk by choosing the SAVE or SAVE AS... command from the FILE menu.

These two file-saving commands work as follows:

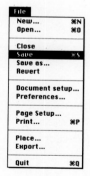

- SAVE. If an illustration is titled, the SAVE command (⌘-S) updates the disk version of the file to reflect the current contents of the file, including not only text and graphic objects, but also typefaces, custom colors, and tile patterns. If the document is untitled, the SAVE command invokes the SAVE AS... command, described below. It is possible to receive a "Disk Full" error message during the save operation, in which case the SAVE AS... command must be used to change the drive or volume on which the illustration is to be saved.

● SAVE AS.... Use this command to determine the name and location of an illustration before it is saved. Choosing the SAVE AS... command from the FILE menu brings up the SAVE DOCUMENT AS dialog box, shown in Figure 3.20.

The SAVE AS... command provides security. By saving multiple versions of an illustration in various locations, you dramatically reduce your chance of losing a substantial amount of work due to file corruption or a system crash.

If your illustration is titled, the current file name appears in the option box directly below the scrolling file list. If your illustration is untitled, the name appears as "Untitled-" followed by a number. Enter or edit the file name as you wish, using up to 32 characters.

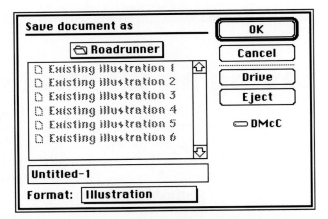

Figure 3.20: The Save document as dialog box appears when you choose the Save as... command or when you choose the Save command for an untitled illustration.

Use the DRIVE and EJECT buttons and the folder bar to determine a location for the file in the same way as described for the OPEN DOCUMENT dialog box. (See the section *Opening files inside FreeHand 3.0* earlier in this chapter.)

FreeHand offers a "Format" option at the bottom of the Save docu-MENT AS dialog box. Clicking and holding on this option produces a pop-up menu with two alternatives. "Illustration," the default setting, saves the current document as a standard illustration file. This is the option you will generally use. Choose "Template" to save the current document as an *application template*, which may serve as a starting point for future illustrations. Template files always open as untitled, but they contain all the information and settings stored with the document. After you make changes and attempt to save the file, FreeHand will display the Save docu-MENT AS dialog box, just as if this were a new untitled document. In this way, you may derive all the benefits of opening an existing document without worrying about saving over it and destroying the original file.

When you have selected a name, location, and "Format" option for your current illustration, click the OK button or press RETURN to complete the Save as… command. You may also click the Cancel button or press COMMAND-PERIOD to return to the illustration window without initiating the save operation.

Replacing an existing file

If you try to save an illustration with the same name as an existing illustration in the current drive and folder, FreeHand will present the Replace existing alert box, shown in Figure 3.21, asking you to confirm that you wish to replace the existing file. Click Yes to save over the existing file; click No or press RETURN to return to the Save document as dialog box, where you may change the name or location of the current illustration.

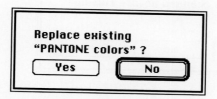

Figure 3.21: The Replace existing alert box.

If the disk that you have selected does not have enough room for the file being saved, a "Disk Full" error message will appear. Click the Con-TINUE button to return to the Save document as dialog box so that you may select another drive or volume and reinitiate the save operation.

Finishing an illustration

When you have finished working on an illustration, you can close the illustration window. Then you may begin a new illustration, open a different illustration, work on a different illustration that is already open, or quit the Aldus FreeHand application altogether.

Closing an illustration

To close the current illustration, choose the CLOSE command from the FILE menu, or click the close box in the upper left corner of the illustration window. If you have made any changes to the illustration since it was last changed, a SAVE CHANGES? dialog box will appear, as shown in Figure 3.22, asking if you would like to save the illustration before closing it. Clicking the YES button or pressing RETURN will perform a SAVE operation (or display the SAVE DOCUMENT AS dialog box if the illustration is untitled) and then close the file; clicking the No button will close the illustration without saving the changes; and clicking CANCEL or pressing COMMAND-PERIOD will return you to the illustration window without saving the file or closing it. Cancelling is useful if you want to choose the SAVE AS... command in order to change the name or location of the file, or if you would like to continue working on the publication.

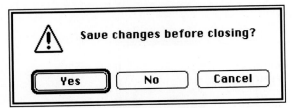

Figure 3.22: The Save changes? dialog box.

If more than one illustration is currently open, closing an illustration will bring one of the remaining illustration windows to the front of the desktop. If only one illustration is open, the contents of all palettes except the toolbox will disappear along with the illustration window when you choose the CLOSE command. Your options will be the same as they were when you first launched FreeHand: you will be able to create a new illustration, open an existing illustration, alter the PREFERENCES dialog box settings, or quit FreeHand and return to the Macintosh Finder.

This final operation is discussed below.

Quitting FreeHand

When you have finished your work in the FreeHand application, choose the QUIT command from the FILE menu (⌘-Q) to close any and all open illustrations and return control of your Macintosh to the Finder. Like the CLOSE command, the QUIT command prompts the appearance of a SAVE CHANGES? dialog box for every open illustration to which changes have been made since it was last saved. Clicking the YES button or pressing RE-TURN will perform a SAVE operation (or display the SAVE DOCUMENT AS dialog box if the illustration is untitled) and then close the file; clicking the No button will close the illustration without saving the changes; and clicking CANCEL or pressing COMMAND-PERIOD will return you to the illustration window without saving the file or closing it. If no illustration window is open or if no changes have been made to any open window since the last time it was saved, FreeHand will quit without presenting an alert box.

The Graphic
Creation
Process

In Chapter 1 we looked at the differences between bitmapped painting software and object-oriented drawing software. In this chapter we examine the actual process of creating a graphic using a drawing application like Aldus Free-Hand 3.0. This chapter will prove most helpful to beginning users, because drawing with FreeHand relies on concepts and approaches different from those required to draw with painting software or with pen or pencil.

93

As we did in Chapter 2, we begin this chapter by defining the terms and concepts on which ensuing discussions rely. Terms such as *point*, *segment*, *path*, and *element* are the focus of our attention here. Once these are explained, we will undertake the creation of a moderately complex graphic.

A step-by-step description of the process of creating a graphic is provided so that you can share in the thought process of creating such a graphic—not so that you can follow along and actually create the illustration. Few of the specific FreeHand tools or commands required to produce this graphic have been properly introduced yet—they are the focus of the remainder of this book. Perhaps later, after reading the following chapters, you will want to return to this chapter and complete this graphic along with us. This first time, however, we recommend that you just read along, paying specific attention to the manner in which we approach each aspect of the creation process.

Drawing with objects

No matter what type of drawing you wish to create, its production in FreeHand must be approached as a combination of *objects* belonging to two simple categories: *lines* and *shapes*.

Suppose that you want to create a collage. FreeHand provides an inexhaustible stack of lines and another stack of shapes. Each line or shape may be stretched, bent, and otherwise *reshaped* to any extent that you choose, as if it were made of putty. Its color may be changed. You can then lay each of these manipulated lines and shapes on your collage in the location and order that you decide is best. Because it exists on a computer, this collage is impermanent—any line or shape may be picked up and placed in a new position, slipped between two other objects, or discarded altogether. An element may be exactly duplicated, manipulated in a new way, or left as is.

Every drawing, no matter how complicated or how simple, can be expressed as an interacting collection of lines and shapes. The trick is to start simple and work toward complexity. In this manner, you may successfully evaluate an illustration by analyzing its most basic parts. The first step in learning to identify the parts of a prospective illustration is to learn about lines and shapes themselves.

The line

Conceptually, lines in FreeHand are the same as lines drawn with a pencil on a piece of paper. Any line starts at one location and ends at another. A line may be any length. It may be a mere scratch mark or it may stretch from the top of a page to the bottom and loop around like a roller coaster.

Lines in FreeHand are made up of the most basic building blocks—*points*. The simplest line is created as a combination of only two points, one at each end. Anyone familiar with a little geometry will recognize this principle: two points make a line.

But in FreeHand, the concept of a line has been broadened to incorporate many points. A *segment* is drawn between two points to connect them. A segment may be straight, as if it were drawn against the edge of a ruler. A straight segment is created directly from one point to another in any direction. A segment may also curve, like the outline of a circle. Such a segment is drawn in an indirect manner between two points.

Segments may be linked together so that neighboring segments share a common point. In this way, you may think of a line in FreeHand as a dot-to-dot puzzle. Each point is a dot. One segment is drawn from dot A to dot B, a second segment is drawn from dot B to dot C, a third segment is drawn from dot C to dot D, and so on. The completed dot-to-dot image is called a *path*. A path may be composed of only one segment or one hundred.

Figure 4.01 on the next page shows two separate dot-to-dot images. Each dot is a point. A segment is drawn from one point to the next sequential point. The points of one image are numbered; the points of the other are labeled with letters. No segment is drawn from a numbered point to a lettered point, or vice versa. The numbered and lettered images are therefore separate paths.

Obviously, the form of each straight and curved segment in a path determines an image's overall appearance. The appearance of a path is also affected by the manner in which one segment meets another segment at a point. Segments may meet at a point in one of two ways. First, the two segments may curve symmetrically on either side of the point. For example, each of the four segments in the numbered path in Figure 4.01 meets its neighbor to form a seamless *arc* about their shared point. Second, two segments may meet to form a *corner*. A straight segment may meet another straight segment to form a corner, such as at point D in the figure. Or a straight segment and a curved segment may meet at a corner like the one at point E. Two curved segments may also meet to form a corner like the one at point F.

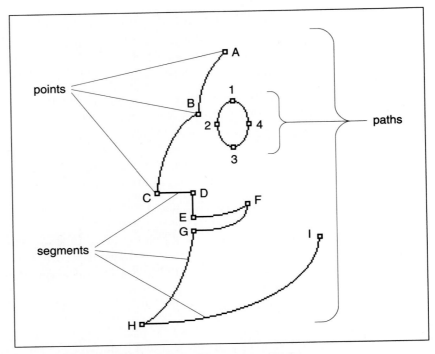

Figure 4.01: Examples of a line (lettered) and a shape (numbered). Elements within both paths are labeled.

The shape

The lettered path in Figure 4.01 is an example of an *open path*, because no segment connects its last point I to its first point A. The numbered path is a *closed path*, because a segment does connect its last point 4 to its first point 1. An open path in FreeHand is what we have been calling a line; a closed path we will call a *shape*. Lines and shapes have various characteristics, as described in the following section.

Properties of lines and shapes

Unlike a line drawn with a pencil on a piece of paper, any path in Free-Hand must be consistent in thickness, or *weight*, throughout its entire length. For example, a line drawn with a very dull pencil will be heavier in weight than a line drawn with a newly sharpened pencil. But, because a graphite pencil is an imprecise tool, the weight of a pencil line will fluctuate, depending on how hard you press while drawing. This is not the case in FreeHand. Different lines may have different weights, but the weight of each line must be constant throughout its length.

Also, drawing a path in FreeHand is like having a countless number of differently colored pencils at your disposal. A line may be black, as it would be if drawn with pen and ink, or it may be light gray or dark gray. It may also be red, or green, or blue, or any one of a million other colors. A line may even be white or transparent.

Line weight and color combine to determine the *stroke* of a line or the outline of a shape. In addition, the area inside a path may be manipulated separately from the outline itself. This area is called the *fill*. The fill of a shape may be black or white, transparent or colored, just like a line. It may even be a combination of many colors interacting or fading into one another.

Determining a path

Before creating a path in FreeHand, you must evaluate each of its segments. This is done one point at a time. Each point indicates 1) where a corner occurs, 2) where a path begins to curve or stops curving, or 3) where a path changes its curve. Each segment ends at a point at which another segment begins.

To fully understand the point/segment/path relationship, suppose that you are driving on a winding mountain road. You will see many yellow, diamond-shaped street signs indicating what kind of path lies ahead. In Figure 4.02 on the next page, the center sign indicates that the path of the road curves gradually to the right. The sign on the left indicates that the road turns dramatically to the left, forming a corner. The sign on the right indicates that the road curves all the way around so that your car will eventually face a direction opposite your initial position.

Figure 4.02: Points guide segments in a path just as street signs interpret a road.

There is one sign for every change in the path of the road. For example, you will never see a sign like the one shown in Figure 4.03. If a road were actually to curve about, following the path described on this sign, you as a driver would not be told about all of these turns at the same time. You would be warned at every change in direction.

Figure 4.03: Too much information for a single sign or point.

The course of a path must be defined at the beginning of every new segment—at the point. Think of each point as a road sign. The road sign of a point defines how one segment enters the point and how the next segment exits.

Conclusion: Points define segments. A path follows a number of segments, which determine the form of the line or shape. Strokes and fills are added to a line or shape to imitate real-life images. Finally, these images are brought together like a collage to represent the finished illustration.

A sample illustration

As the preceding discussion suggests, the first step in approaching any prospective drawing in FreeHand is to analyze its fundamental parts. As an example, suppose we want to create the cartoon image of Groucho Marx shown in Figure 4.04. For the remainder of this chapter we will explain the steps you would undertake to create this drawing in Aldus FreeHand. Remember, this discussion is intended to introduce the overall methods we use to approach such a project. It is not intended as a "how-to" lesson in FreeHand. Specific techniques will be introduced in the remaining chapters of the book.

Figure 4.04: A bitmapped sketch of Groucho Marx created in MacPaint.

We have created this sketch in MacPaint, and although we are pleased with its general appearance and form, the image is riddled with jagged edges. Since MacPaint images are limited to a 72-dpi resolution, they rarely meet professional standards. Our cartoon of Groucho is presently defined as a collection of pixels. We will now describe Groucho as a series of object-oriented shapes and lines. Our final FreeHand-version of Groucho will be identical in form to our MacPaint image, but it will be superior in resolution.

If you are not an artist, the idea of creating a cartoon of Groucho Marx may seem beyond your ability. However, as with most creative endeavors, creating an drawing in FreeHand has more to do with how you think than with your dexterity or experience. That is why this tutorial has been constructed entirely from a theoretical vantage. No menu commands are used; no tools are mentioned. By avoiding the details of the application, we are able to more fully concentrate on the intellectual process. An illustration must be created in your head before it can be created on paper or on a computer screen.

If it makes you more comfortable, imagine that you are tracing the cartoon of Groucho rather than creating it from scratch. In FreeHand, it is often more efficient to trace from a sketch or photographic scan that to draw from scratch. For the purposes of this example, it is not important that you feel confident that you can create the sketch of Groucho shown in Figure 4.04. It is only important that you understand how to trace it.

1: The eyes

We will begin by creating Groucho's eyes. Groucho's left eye is shown in Figure 4.05. The eye is *grayed* to show that it is part of the *tracing template*. In FreeHand, any image positioned on a background layer will appear grayed, which is FreeHand's way of showing that it is not a part of the actual drawing. However, the grayed image is still visible so that we may trace it easily.

In Figure 4.06, we have traced a perfect circle around the left eyeball. The circle and template are shown together to give you a perspective for the rest of the illustration. However, these are the only figures in this chapter where the underlying template will be shown. Hiding the template in following figures will help to avoid confusion and to present each portion of the drawing in sharp focus. Keep in mind, however, that the tracing template does exist and that every line and shape we create is traced over some part of it.

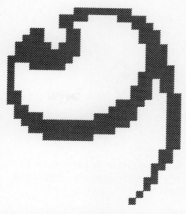

Figure 4.05: The left eye of the Groucho tracing template.

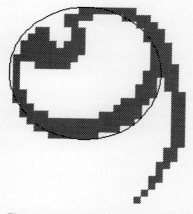

Figure 4.06: Create a circle that traces around the left eye.

The circle that we have created as Groucho's left eyeball is a shape composed of four points. Each of the four points helps to define the path that the outline of the circle follows. We mentioned before that making a line follow a path is like driving a car on a mountain road. Each point acts like a street sign, indicating where the line should go. In the case of our circle, all four points are identical. Suppose the outline of the circle follows its path in a counterclockwise direction. Each point would then act like the street sign shown in Figure 4.07 on the following page. As the outline progresses, the points tell the curve to continue to the left in a consistent manner.

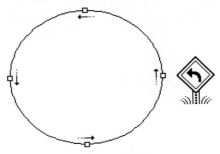

Figure 4.07: The points in the circle tell the path to continue in a consistent, counterclockwise direction.

The next few parts of Groucho's eye may be created from our present circle. We will do this by *cloning* and *scaling*. Cloning creates a copy of an object without using the Clipboard. This is useful any time that you are tracing several lines or shapes that are very similar in form. You need only create one original and then clone all objects from that. Cloned objects may then be manipulated separately, so that the finished object only vaguely resembles the original from which it was cloned.

After we clone our circle, we scale the resulting shape to 85% of its original size. Scaling makes an object larger or smaller. In this case we have two distinct circles; the size of the newest is 85% the size of the original. We situate the cloned shape so that the tops of both circles meet as shown in Figure 4.08.

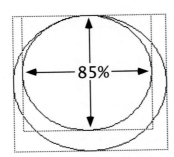

Figure 4.08: Clone the circle and scale the clone to 85% its original size.

Next we clone our newest circle and scale its clone to 55% of original. Then we clone that circle and scale this clone to 75%. We move each of these clones to the positions shown in Figure 4.09. We now have all shapes required for the left eyeball. We will next create the wrinkle under the eye.

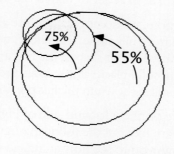

Figure 4.09: Scaling two additional clones.

The wrinkle is only slightly more difficult than the circles we have created thus far. Figure 4.10 shows how we create this shape. The wrinkle is simply a long, thin crescent made up of four points. Each point is labeled according to one of three analogous street signs. Each sign is shown as if you were approaching the point in the direction indicated by the small arrows on the path. Therefore, if you were driving counterclockwise along the outline of this shape, you would meet four signs, two notifying you of sharp corners in the path.

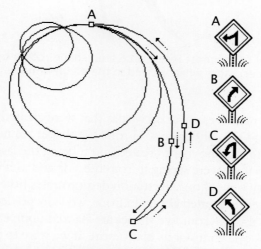

Figure 4.10: Each of the street signs on the right corresponds to a point in the crescent.

Every one of the five objects we have created so far is a shape. This means they all have the properties of both line and fill. So far, all of our shapes have very thin, black strokes and transparent fills. We will need to change their fills and strokes in order to match our template.

For our present purpose, we do not need to use any strokes. Groucho's eye can be easily created from fills alone. Therefore, we make all the strokes transparent. We will fill three of our shapes, the first and third circles and the crescent wrinkle, with solid black. The second and fourth circles will be filled with white. The result is shown in the left portion of Figure 4.11.

Note that the image on the left-hand side of Figure 4.11 is displayed in the *preview mode*, as are most of the following figures in this chapter. The preview mode allows you to see how an image will appear when printed.

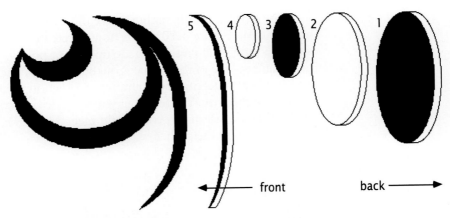

Figure 4.11: The most recently created shapes cover up their predecessors when viewed in the preview mode.

Recent shapes cover up shapes that were created before them. On the right-hand side of Figure 4.11, our five shapes are numbered 1 through 5, 1 being the first shape created and 5 being the last. Each shape is shown as if we were seeing it from the side and as if it had depth. This imaginary view of our illustration demonstrates how FreeHand places the most recently created object in front, while its predecessors remain in back. In this way, our five shapes are stacked upon each other so that they appear as one continuous black form. If we were to paint this version of

Groucho's eye onto a canvas, we might use a combination of three brush strokes. In FreeHand, we create it as five shapes. A computer may yield painterly results, but our approach often must be technical and carefully considered.

Now that we have created one of Groucho's eyes, it is very easy to create the other. First, we gather our five shapes and *group* them, so that they all become one object. Grouping protects the relative placement and size of line and shapes within the group.

Next, we clone the group. We then *reflect* the clone about a −70° *axis* as shown in Figure 4.12. To more fully understand this process, think of the axis as a double-sided mirror. Suppose that the mirror is mounted like an old cheval glass so that it is free to tilt within a support. Our mirror is normally situated horizontally, like a table top. But if we were to angle the mirror 70° downward (−70°, or 360°−70°=290°), we would see the exact reflection shown in Figure 4.12. That is what is meant by reflection about an axis. The axis simply acts like a mirror tilted at a prescribed angle.

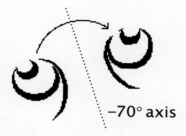

−70° axis

Figure 4.12: Clone the five shapes that make up the left eye and reflect them about a −70° axis.

Since the cartoon of Groucho faces slightly away from the viewer, it would not be appropriate for both eyes to be the same size. The right eye, which is farther away from us, should be smaller to give the illusion of distance. Therefore, we must scale the eye. However, if we wish to follow our template, we must reduce the eye so that it is proportionally narrower than it is tall. This is no problem, since FreeHand allows for separate vertical and horizontal percentages when scaling. Figure 4.13 on the next page shows how we scale the eye to 80% of its original width and 90% of its original height. The original size of the eye is shown as the larger, dotted box. Both of Groucho's eyes now match our template almost perfectly.

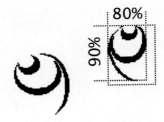

Figure 4.13: Scale the right eye to 80% horizontally and 90% vertically.

2: The eyebrows

Now it is time to create the eyebrows. We will begin with the left brow. This is a slightly more difficult shape than any we have created so far. The brow involves eight points, which are labeled A through H in Figure 4.14. Each point is analogous to the street sign that bears the same letter. Keep in mind that, for the purpose of this example, you are seeing these street signs as if you were traveling on the path in a counterclockwise direction.

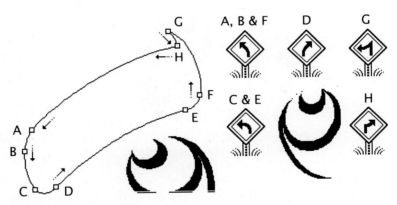

Figure 4.14: The left eyebrow is made up of eight points, each of which corresponds to one of the street signs shown above.

Once again, we make the stroke of this shape transparent. We fill the shape with solid black. Then we clone the eyebrow and reflect the clone about a –75° axis. Figure 4.15 shows the result.

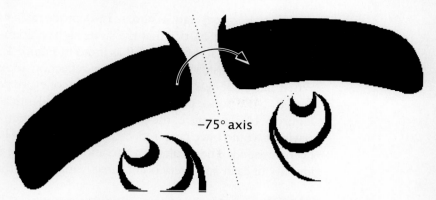

Figure 4.15: Clone the eyebrow shape and reflect it across a −75° axis.

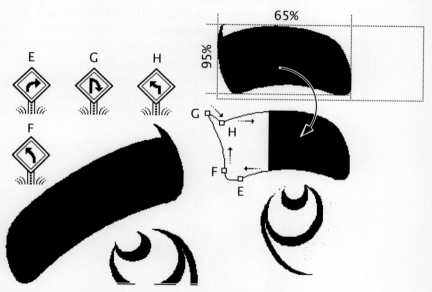

Figure 4.16: Reshape the right eyebrow by converting points F, G, and H.

The newly reflected right eyebrow is not the correct size, nor does its path correspond entirely to the form of the right eyebrow in our template. To remedy the first problem, we must scale the brow to 65% of its original width and 95% of its original height, as shown in the top part of Figure 4.16. To change the path of the shape, we must convert the identity of a few appropriate points. Converting a point's *identity* is like changing the street sign. Figure 4.16 demonstrates which points we change, and how. Notice that the street sign analogous to point E curves to the right instead of to the left as it did in Figure 4.14. This is not a change, but is instead the result of the reflection about the −75° axis. When the shape was reflected, the identity of every point was also reflected. Now notice point F. Its street sign is identical to that shown in Figure 4.14. Therefore, the point's identity has been changed, since otherwise it would have been reflected as well. Points G and H have also been changed. The result is an alteration in the path of the shape. The identity of each and every point directly influences the path.

3: The cigar

Next we will work on Groucho's prominent cigar. First we trace a circle around the lighted ashes at the tip of the cigar. Then we clone this circle and reduce the clone so that we have two concentric circles. We again clone the larger circle, and move its clone about one-quarter inch to the left. In Figure 4.17, each of the four points of the circle is shown along with the street sign that is analogous to all four. We will change the path of this shape not by changing the identity of its points, but by deleting and adding points.

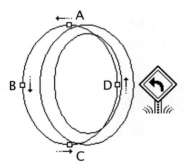

Figure 4.17: Drawing the tip of Groucho's cigar.

From the labeled shape in Figure 4.17, we delete point D and join points A and C with a single, straight segment. The result is shown in Figure 4.18. Notice that both of the street signs analogous to points A and C have been changed so that a corner occurs at each point. Points are thus directly influenced by the points that surround them.

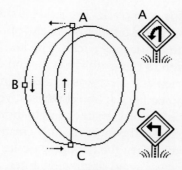

Figure 4.18: Deleting point D and adding a straight segment in its place changes the identities of neighboring points A and C.

Before we go any further, we need to *copy* our most recent shape. Copying an object places a copy of the selected object into the Macintosh Clipboard. We will need to recall this image in a few moments.

In Figure 4.19, we add two points D and E to our shape. The identities of points A and C update to fit in with their new neighbors. Since point B is nestled between points A and C, its identity remains constant.

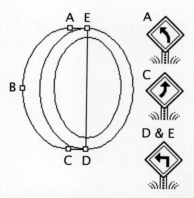

Figure 4.19: Adding points D and E further alters the identities of points A and C.

We have now created the very tip of Groucho's cigar, though one would hardly recognize it. We still need to define the line and fill of each of our three shapes. We will make all lines transparent. We fill our first circle with a dark gray and our second, smaller circle with a light gray. We

fill our most recent shape with black. The result is shown in Figure 4.20.
You may notice that we have a problem. Since the black shape is the most
recent, it covers up both of the gray circles. The black shape is in front of
both circles. The solution to our problem is to send the black shape to
the back. No matter when an object was created, it may be sent to back
or brought to front. By sending an object to back, you tell FreeHand to
assume that the object is the first created, and by bringing it to front, you
tell FreeHand to assume it is the most recently created. Now, FreeHand
first draws the black shape, then the dark gray circle, then the light gray
circle. The result is the cigar's end of glowing ashes.

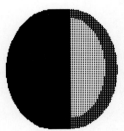

Figure 4.20: The most recent black shape covers up the
shapes behind it.

A moment ago, we copied an object to the Macintosh Clipboard. We
now need to retrieve that image. We do this by *pasting*, which takes a
copy of the image in the Clipboard and places it on our drawing area.
Once we have pasted the shape, we move it into position, as shown in
Figure 4.21, and open the path so that points A and C have no path segment linking them.

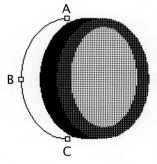

Figure 4.21: Paste the shape copied earlier and open it.

By opening our path, we convert the shape into a line. We now add the necessary points to this line to cause its path to trace the form of the cigar as it goes into Groucho's mouth. As we create the last point in the line, we reclose the line to form a shape.

This time, we stroke the outline of the shape with a heavy, black line weight. We fill the shape with white. By filling our shape with white rather than leaving it transparent, the shape will cover up any objects that we may create and send to back later in the drawing process. The finished cigar is shown in Figure 4.22.

Figure 4.22: A heavy, black stroke finishes the cigar.

4: The nose and mustache

Groucho's nose is created as a series of eight points, as shown in Figure 4.23. In this figure, we are no longer zoomed in as closely as in some of our other figures. We may see all of Groucho that we have created so far in one glance.

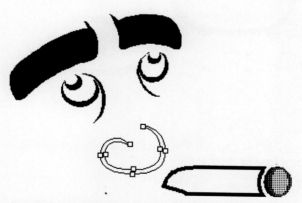

Figure 4.23: Because the outline of the nose tapers at both ends, it must be expressed as a filled shape.

We assign to the shape of Groucho's nose a transparent stroke and a black fill. Looking at the nose, you might wonder why we created it as a shape rather than as a line. It is, after all, very much a line in the traditional sense. The problem is that the weight of this line in not uniform. In fact, it is downright calligraphic. The line of the nose begins thin, becomes fatter as it sweeps around, and becomes thin again at its end. Lines in FreeHand cannot have this property. We said earlier that while the thickness of a stroke is determined by its line weight, the thickness of a fill is determined by the path that surrounds it. Therefore, to express a calligraphic line, we must create a path that surrounds both sides of the "line," then fill the resulting shape. This is what we have done to create the nose, and will do throughout the remainder of this illustration.

In setting out to create Groucho's mustache, the first thing that we notice is how similar it is to his eyebrows. Therefore, we clone the left eyebrow and move it into the position shown in Figure 4.24, between the nose and the cigar. Incidentally, you may notice that although we have cloned a shape that has no stroke and a black fill, our clone has a thin outline and no fill. We have purposely changed the stroke and fill of this shape to make it stand out from the shapes around it.

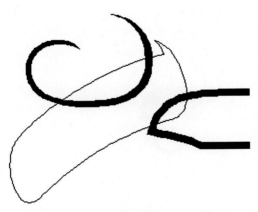

Figure 4.24: Clone the left eyebrow to serve as a starting point for the mustache.

We reflect the mustache shape about a 25° axis. This reflection is interesting because the axis runs directly through the shape as shown in Figure 4.25. The shape actually reflects upon itself. A reflection axis can be angled in any way you desire.

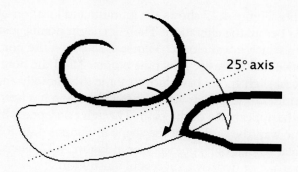

Figure 4.25: Reflect the eyebrow clone about a 25° axis.

The mustache is considerably larger than either of the eyebrows, therefore we enlarge the shape to 130% of its original size.

The next step is to *skew*, or slant, the shape. In this case, we wish to skew our shape –25° horizontally. Figure 4.26 shows how the skew is measured from the mean horizontal axis. Dotted lines show roughly the angle at which the shape sat before the skew and the resulting new angle of the shape.

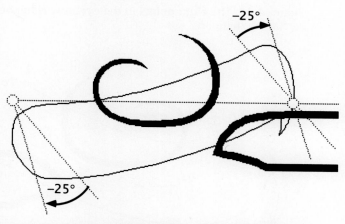

Figure 4.26: Skew the eyebrow clone –25° horizontally.

The basic form of the mustache is still not what it should be, so we must alter the path to match our template. We accomplish this as a combination of changing the identities of present points and adding new points. Figure 4.27 shows the amount and location of the points that existed before the alteration. There are eight points, just like the eyebrow from which it was cloned. Figure 4.28 shows the points after alteration. Notice that there are now nine points. All of the points have been moved at least slightly. We have moved some dramatically and have changed the identities of several as well. Yet our alteration has been subtle in its effect on the appearance of the path. Though every point has been changed in some way, the outline of the shape in Figures 4.28 follows a path very similar to that of its predecessor in Figure 4.27. The subtleties of a path can make or destroy a successful illustration.

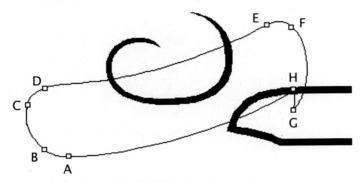

Figure 4.27: The eight points in the eyebrow clone before reshaping the path.

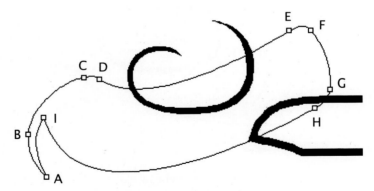

Figure 4.28: After reshaping, the path has nine points, many of which differ in identity or position from their predecessors.

Like the eyebrows, the mustache is assigned a transparent stroke and a black fill. We then send it to back. The result is shown in Figure 4.29. Because the cigar has a white fill, it effectively covers a portion of the mustache to appear as if jutting from Groucho's hidden mouth. Unfortunately, the same cannot be said for the nose. The nose appears to be behind the mustache, because the fill of the nose shape is acting like the outline of the nose. A second fill is needed to act as the flesh of the nose.

Figure 4.29: The black mustache obscures the shape of the nose, despite the fact that the mustache has been sent to back.

The fill of the shape that will act as the flesh of the nose must exactly fit into the shape that acts as the outline of the nose. Therefore, we must clone the existing shape. The fill of the cloned shape should cover the area enclosed by the original shape. A segment of the path must connect the points that represent the top of the nose and the tip of the nostril. This is easily accomplished by deleting all the points that form the inner rim of the nose and then closing the remaining path. The result is shown in Figure 4.30 on the following page.

Notice that this figure shows shapes with no fills and thin strokes. As we mentioned earlier, most of the figures in this chapter display images as they appear in the preview mode. However, for Figure 4.30, we show the paths in the *keyline mode*, in which all lines and outlines are shown with very thin, black strokes and all fills are shown as transparent. By viewing the paths in this figure in the keyline mode, we may more clearly view our most recent developments.

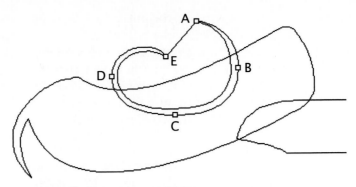

Figure 4.30: The nose and mustache shapes displayed in the keyline mode.

We fill the most recent shape with white and send it to the back so that it does not cover the shape that represents the outline of the nose. Then we send the mustache to the back again. We zoom out from our illustration in Figure 4.31. We can see the result of everything that we have done so far. Our illustration looks about half finished, but looks can be deceiving. We are actually much closer than that.

Figure 4.31: Our progress so far as viewed in the preview mode. Note that the nose now appears in front of the mustache.

5: Finishing the face

We are still missing many of Groucho's features. We have yet to draw his glasses, the bridge of his nose, his ear, his hair, the outline of his face, and a few wrinkles. But, if you will recall our template (refer to Figure 4.04), all of these features are more suggestive than those we have created so far. The subtle features in a template are often harder to approach than their more obvious or outstanding counterparts. The best advice we can offer is to dive right in. Create object after object in a rhythmic sequence, forging on with alacrity and grace. These are the incidental parts of an illustration that round it out, giving it a lucid appearance.

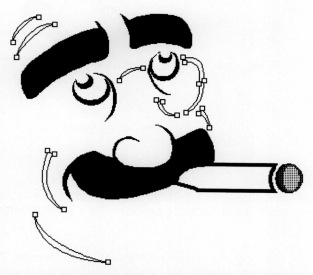

Figure 4.32: The wrinkles in the flesh and portions of the glasses are expressed as many small shapes, most of which comprise only two points apiece.

In Figure 4.32, we have created a series of small shapes that act as calligraphic swashes. The majority of the shapes are made up of only two points each. The identity of each point causes one path segment to curve more than another so that the fill creates a free-flowing stroke, simple but highly effective. The most complicated shape is constructed of only five points. All of these shapes are flourishing and playful, yet each must be approached intentionally and with care.

Figure 4.33: Most of the outline of the face as well as several incidental features can be expressed as a single complex shape.

The next shape that we create is very extensive. As Figure 4.33 shows, there are 48 points in this shape. With one shape, we have created the hair, most of his ear, lip, chin, neck, and part of his glasses. But the process itself is no more difficult than any other shape we have created. The most difficult step may be to recognize that such a large portion of the template can be expressed as a single shape. Such recognition comes with practice. Once you have seen the shape, you need only trace its outline point by point, carefully and patiently. The only difference between a simple line with two points and a complex shape with one hundred is that the latter takes longer to produce. Never be intimidated by a large shape.

After filling our complex shape with solid black, only two shapes remain to finish Groucho's face. These are the remainder of the ear and the bridge of the nose. The ear requires eleven points and the nose requires six, as shown in Figure 4.34. Always use points sparingly. If you find that you do not have enough points, you may always add more. But just one point too many means that someplace there are two path segments where there should be only one. The result is a needlessly complicated object, whose path is slightly clumsy and malformed.

Figure 4.34: Finish the face with two shapes, one representing the details of the ear and the other the bridge of the nose.

6: The collar

By now, you can probably easily imagine how to draw Groucho's collar. But there are a couple of stumbling blocks along the way. Figure 4.35 on the next page shows the points required to create the jacket lapel and the shirt collar—four shapes altogether. Each of the lapel shapes gets no line and a black fill. The collars get a medium-weight black line and a white fill. Figure 4.36 shows the results. Notice how we have matched up the line of the collars exactly with the fill of the shape that wraps around to form the throat. Here is a case where the fill of a shape and the weight of a line are designed to be identical.

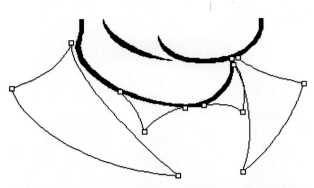

Figure 4.35: The four shapes required to create the collar and lapel.

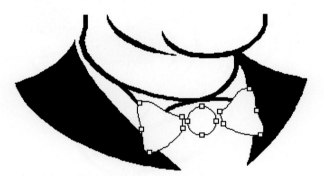

Figure 4.36: The three shapes that make up the bow tie.

Figure 4.36 also shows that the tie is made of three separate shapes. One is a simple circle and the other two have five points apiece. The tie must cover the lapels in an unusual manner, requiring that we consider the stroke as well as the fill of each shape. In the template, there is a white line between the black color of the tie and the black color of the jacket. Therefore, all three shapes of the tie get a medium-weight white stroke with a black fill. The white stroke provides the necessary definition between the tie and the jacket to distinguish the two as independent objects. Last, we bring both of the collar shapes to the front of the other objects so that the tie becomes nestled where it belongs, as shown in Figure 4.37.

Figure 4.37: The white strokes of the tie shapes distinguish them from the lapels.

7: Smoke from the cigar

Often a last detail will add spirit to a drawing. Our last detail will be smoke rising from Groucho's cigar. This is an unnecessary but friendly addition that gives our cartoon the small bit of realism that it needs.

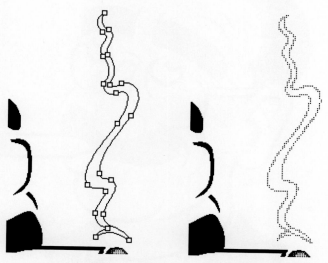

Figure 4.38: The points required to express the cigar smoke and the same path when stroked with a gray outline.

We trace the smoke with one shape containing 21 points. Figure 4.38 shows the path. We then assign the shape a thin, light gray stroke with no fill. The shape is simple, yet also elegant and functional.

The completed Groucho

Our illustration is finished. Figure 4.39 shows the completed Groucho as he appears when printed from Aldus FreeHand. Despite his large size, his resolution is far better than his MacPaint template. Every detail is crisp and accurate. His appearance is clean and smooth. All things said and done, we have created a highly professional product.

We have now laid a groundwork for creating almost any electronic illustration. The following chapters discuss the tools, commands, and dialog box options required to create such a drawing in FreeHand 3.0. However, the ultimate secret to achieving a professional illustration is not reliant on the specific environment provided by the application. Rather, it relies on your approach.

Figure 4.39: The completed Groucho cartoon printed from Aldus FreeHand 3.0.

Drawing Paths from Scratch

In the previous chapter, we demonstrated that an image drawn in Aldus FreeHand must be constructed as a network of lines and shapes called *paths*. This chapter demonstrates how to draw the paths themselves using each of Free-Hand's nine drawing tools.

We will begin with the most basic paths that you may create in FreeHand 3.0. These include rectangles, squares, ovals, and circles—a collection of objects known collectively as *geometric*

paths. If you are an experienced Macintosh user, you will probably recognize the tools used to create these paths. Each tool works similarly to tools in MacPaint, MacDraw, PageMaker, and other common Macintosh applications. If you have used any of these programs, there is little doubt that you can master the creation of any geometric path in FreeHand.

Geometric paths

FreeHand offers three tools for creating geometric paths. Each tool is operated by dragging from one location to another. The points at which you begin and end the drag signify the boundaries of the simple rectangle or oval. Although limited in utility, these geometric shapes are very easy to draw, because they involve no planning and little guesswork.

Drawing a rectangle

Consider the *rectangle tool,* second tool on the left side of the toolbox. After selecting this tool, drag inside the drawing area to create a rectangle. This is the same process used to create a rectangle in all graphics applications that run on the Macintosh. One corner of the rectangle is determined by the point at which you begin the drag; the opposite corner is determined by the point at which you release (see Figure 5.01). The two remaining corners line up vertically and horizontally with their neighboring corners. A fifth point, the *center point,* is also created at the center of the shape. The center point of a rectangle is always visible in the keyline mode, but is visible in the preview mode only when transforming the shape.

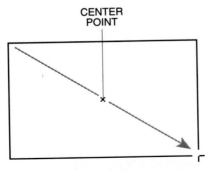

CENTER
POINT

Figure 5.01: Operate the rectangle tool by dragging from one corner to the opposite corner of the desired shape.

If you press the OPTION key while drawing with the rectangle tool, the beginning of your drag becomes the center point of the rectangle, as shown in Figure 5.02. As before, the release point becomes a corner point and also determines the distance and direction from the center that each of the three other corner points are located.

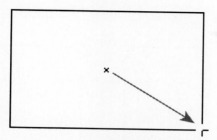

Figure 5.02: Option-drag with the rectangle tool to draw a rectangle from center point to corner point.

Pressing the SHIFT key while drawing with the rectangle tool *constrains* the resulting shape. To constrain the creation or manipulation of an element is to attach certain guidelines to the effects of your mouse movements. In this case, pressing SHIFT ensures that each corner of the rectangle is equidistant from both its neighbors, thereby creating a square. Pressing both SHIFT and OPTION while drawing with the rectangle tool creates a square from center to corner.

 Pressing the 1 key—either in the standard key set or on the keypad—will select the rectangle tool at any time, except when a dialog box is displayed.

Drawing a rectangle with rounded corners

In FreeHand, you may create rectangles with rounded corners using the *rounded-rectangle tool*, second tool on the right side of the toolbox. Unlike the horizontal and vertical segments of a standard rectangle, those of a rounded rectangle do not meet to form right-angle corners. Instead, perpendicular segments curve to meet one another. Figure 5.03 on the next page shows a standard rectangle with perpendicular corners and the same rectangle drawn with the rounded-rectangle tool.

 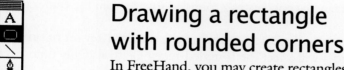

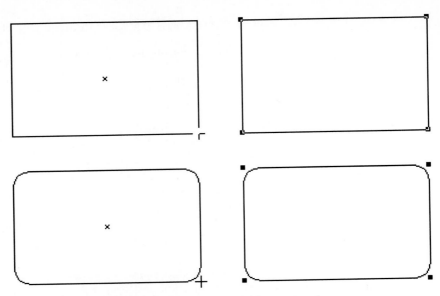

Figure 5.03: Drawing similar shapes with the rectangle
and rounded-rectangle tools (left) and the same shapes
shown when completed in the preview mode (right).

You may adjust the roundness of the corners of a rectangle
created with either the rectangle or rounded-rectangle tool by
OPTION-double-clicking the shape with the arrow tool and entering a new value for the "Corner radius" option. See Chapter 7, *Reshaping
Existing Paths*, for more information.

If you press OPTION while drawing with the rounded-rectangle tool,
the beginning of your drag becomes the center point of the rectangle.
Pressing SHIFT and dragging with the rounded-rectangle tool creates
a rounded square. Pressing both SHIFT and OPTION while drawing with the
rounded-rectangle tool creates a rounded square from the center point.

Pressing the 2 key—either in the standard key set or on the keypad—will select the rounded-rectangle tool at any time, except
when a dialog box is displayed.

Drawing an ellipse

The *oval tool*, third tool on the left side of the toolbox, is used very much like the rectangle tool. The difference, of course, is that the oval tool is used to create *ellipses* and circles rather than rectangles and squares.

As is the case with the click and release points created with the rounded-rectangle tool, those of the oval tool do not reside on the path of the ellipse. They are merely reference points. In this sense, you might think of an ellipse as a rectangle with so large a percentage of its path devoted to rounded corners that the vertical and horizontal segments altogether disappear. The ellipse drawn with the oval tool fits inside the invisible rectangle outlined by your drag. While you drag with the oval tool, it might help to imagine that a dotted bounding rectangle is formed, outlining the area of drag, as shown in Figure 5.04. The ellipse exists entirely within the boundaries of the dotted rectangle, as when drawing with an oval tool in most other Macintosh applications.

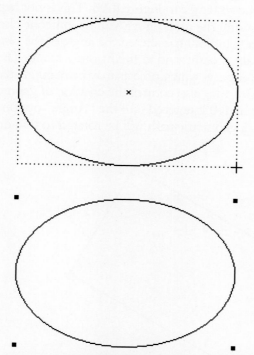

Figure 5.04: Drawing an ellipse from corner to opposite corner (with bounding rectangle, top) and the same ellipse shown when completed in the preview mode (bottom).

If you press OPTION while drawing with the oval tool, the beginning of your drag becomes the center point of the ellipse. As usual, the release point becomes the bounding corner, determining the size and shape of the ellipse.

Pressing SHIFT and dragging with the oval tool creates a perfect circle. Pressing both SHIFT and OPTION while drawing with the oval tool creates a circle from center point to corner.

 Pressing the 3 key—either in the standard key set or on the keypad—will select the oval tool at any time, except when a dialog box is displayed.

Geometric paths at an angle

Element	
Bring to front	⌘F
Bring forward	
Send backward	
Send to back	⌘B
Element info...	⌘I
Points	▶
Lock	
Unlock	
Group	⌘G
Ungroup	⌘U
Alignment...	⌘/
Blend...	
Constrain...	
Join elements	⌘J
Split element	

In the course of drawing a shape with one of the three geometric path tools, you may find that your path rotates at some odd angle, as demonstrated by the rectangle in Figure 5.05. This is not happening because you are misusing the tool; rather, you or someone else using this same copy of FreeHand 3.0 has altered the angle of the *constraint axes* using the CONSTRAIN... command in the ELEMENT menu. The constraint axes control the angle at which objects may be manipulated while the SHIFT key is pressed. But they also control the creation of geometric paths. If any value other than 0 is entered into the "Angle" option in the CONSTRAIN dialog box, a geometric path will be rotated to that degree as it is drawn.

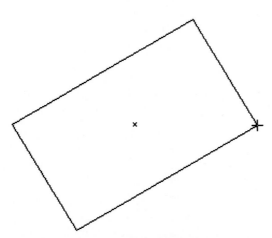

Figure 5.05: Drawing a rectangle when the constraint axes have been rotated by 30°.

To draw rectangle and ellipses that are not rotated, you must reset the constraint axes to the normal orientation. This may be accomplished using one of two methods:

- Choose the CONSTRAIN... command from the ELEMENT menu. Enter 0 for the "Angle" option or select the "Horizontal or vertical" radio button and press RETURN.

- Quit and restart the FreeHand application.

Any geometric paths that you draw will now be oriented normally.

Free-form paths

The geometric path tools allow you to create simple shapes quickly and easily. However, FreeHand's true drawing power is based in its ability to define free-form lines and shapes. Such a path may be simple, like a triangle or crescent. Or it may be an intricate polygon or naturalistic form that meets the most complex specifications.

The line tool

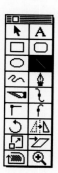

Due to its simplicity and limited utility, the straight line may seem like more of a geometric path than a free-form path. But in FreeHand 3.0, the straight line shares more similarities with paths drawn with the free-hand and pen tools than with rectangles or ellipses. Though simple to create, a straight line may be manipulated without ungrouping and it may also be easily integrated into a more complex path.

To draw a straight line, select the *line tool*, third tool on the right side of the toolbox, and drag in the drawing area. The distance and direction of your drag determine the length and angle of the line. The beginning of your drag marks the first point in the line; the release location marks the final point. Both points are called *endpoints*, because they appear at either end of the path, and both are associated with only one segment. Endpoints have special properties that we will explore later in this chapter.

Pressing SHIFT and dragging with the line tool constrains the line to a 45° angle; that is, a line that is horizontal, vertical, or diagonal. Keep in mind that the effect of pressing the SHIFT key may be altered by rotating the constraint axes using the CONSTRAIN... command from the ELEMENT menu, as described in the previous section.

Pressing the 4 key—either in the standard key set or on the keypad—will select the line tool at any time, except when a dialog box is displayed.

The freehand tool

The fourth tool on the left side of toolbox, the *freehand tool*, is used for real-time drawing. After selecting this tool, you may click and drag as if you were drawing with a pencil on a sheet of paper. FreeHand tracks the exact movement of your mouse on screen, creating a free-form line between the locations at which your drag begins and ends. After you release, FreeHand automatically determines the quantity and location of points and segments and creates the freehand path.

Consider the example of the apple shown in Figure 5.06. The figure shows the progression of the freehand tool cursor. We start by dragging with the tool from the upper right corner of the apple's stem down to the beginning of the leaf. We then drag up and back down in two opposite arcs to create the leaf. After dragging downward to finish the stem, we sweep around in a great rightward arc and down to the lower tip of the core, as shown in the third example of the figure. Finally, we drag back up and around to the left, eventually meeting the first point in a single continuous movement.

Figure 5.06: Drawing an apple with the freehand tool.

Notice that the outline of the final apple in Figure 5.06 has a few tiny jagged edges. These jagged edges exist for two reasons. First, we drew this figure with a mouse. The mouse is not a precise drawing instrument. When you move a mouse, a ball within its chamber rolls about against the surface of the table or mouse pad. This ball in turn causes two internal tracking wheels to move, one vertically and one horizontally. Based on the activity of these two wheels, the mouse conveys movement information to the computer. No matter how thoroughly you clean a mouse, there will be some interference between the ball and the wheels, even if it is only small particles of dust. For example, if you draw a 45° diagonal line, both the vertical and horizontal tracking wheels should move at exactly the same pace. If some interference comes between the ball and the horizontal wheel, causing the wheel to remain motionless for only a moment, the mouse will send purely vertical movement information to the computer until the interference has passed. The result is a momentary jag in an otherwise smooth diagonal line.

Second, most people—even skilled artists—are not very practiced in drawing with a mouse. It takes time to master this skill. You may find that your first drawing efforts look much different than you had planned—possibly far worse than Figure 5.06, for example. Luckily, the freehand tool is capable of smoothing out many imperfections.

If you're comfortable with drawing with a mouse, but you want to avoid some of the tracking problems associated with the standard Apple mouse, consider purchasing an *optical mouse*. Our favorite is the A+ Mouse ADB from Mouse Systems, (415) 656-1117. For about $100, this pointing device projects two lights that bounce off a reflective pad. Because it lacks moving parts, an optical mouse tends to last longer and perform more consistently than any track-ball device.

Once you release your mouse button, having completed the process of drawing a path, FreeHand makes calculations to determine how many points your path should be assigned, as well as their locations. Thus, drawing with the freehand tool is entirely automatic.

Pressing the 5 key—either in the standard key set or on the keypad—will select the freehand tool at any time, except when a dialog box is displayed.

Freehand curve fit

To fully understand the freehand tool, you must understand how Free-Hand assigns points to a freehand path. It makes its determinations based on three factors:

- **Consistency.** FreeHand assigns a point to every location at which your freehand drag changes direction. Thus, smooth, consistent mouse actions produce smooth, elegant paths; jerky or unsteady mouse actions produce overly complex lines.

- **Speed.** The speed at which you draw may also affect the appearance of a freehand path. If your mouse lingers at any location, FreeHand is more likely to assign a point there. However, if you draw too quickly, FreeHand will ignore many of the subtle changes in direction in your drag. A slow but steady technique is the most reliable.

- **Curve fit.** FreeHand allows you to control the sensitivity of the freehand tool using the "Tight" option in the FREEHAND dialog box. Selecting this option results in a tight *curve fit*, which results in a freehand path that more accurately matches your drag; deselecting this option results in a looser curve fit, with FreeHand smoothing over inaccuracies in your drag.

To access the "Tight" option, double-click the freehand tool icon in the toolbox. The FREEHAND dialog box, shown in Figure 5.07, will display. Select the "Tight" option to increase the sensitivity of the freehand tool; deselect the option to smooth out your freehand paths.

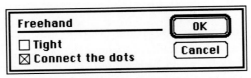

Figure 5.07: Double-click the freehand tool icon in the toolbox to access the Freehand dialog box.

Figure 5.08 shows how FreeHand interprets our apple path depending on the selection of the "Tight" option. The path on the left was created with "Tight" selected. The right path is the result of deselecting

"Tight." The two paths are similar; however, the indent at the bottom of the first apple is represented fairly accurately, but the loose curve fitting used to create the second apple completely eliminates the indent. We recommend that you select the "Tight" option unless you consider yourself very clumsy with a mouse or have little confidence in your overall drawing ability.

Figure 5.08: The points and segments assigned to the apple path when the "Tight" check box is selected (left) and deselected (right).

The curve fit for a path cannot be altered after the path is created, since FreeHand calculates the points for a path only once, after your release when dragging with the freehand tool. For each of the paths in Figures 5.08, we had to change the curve fit and then draw a new apple from scratch.

The other option in the Freehand dialog box, "Connect the dots," allows you to determine the manner in which FreeHand displays your freehand path while in the process of drawing with the tool. When this option is selected, your path is displayed as a solid line, as shown back in Figure 5.06. If you deselect "Connect the dots," your path will be displayed as a sketchy line, as shown in Figure 5.09 on the next page. Your selection is entirely a matter of preference; it will have no effect on the appearance of the finished freehand path.

Any changes to the options in the FREEHAND dialog box will be saved to the FreeHandPrefs file, introduced in the *Setting preferences* section of Chapter 3, and will therefore apply to all future illustrations until the next time you adjust these options.

Figure 5.09: Drawing the apple path when
"Connect the dots" is deselected.

Erasing with the freehand tool

Normally, a continuous path tracks every movement as you draw with the freehand tool. If you press the COMMAND key while drawing with the tool, however, you may erase a mistake. In the middle of a drag, press COMMAND and trace back over a portion of a path that you have just drawn. You will see it disappear. Therefore, you can draw a path with the freehand tool, immediately "undraw" part of it while pressing the COMMAND key, and then release COMMAND and continue drawing.

Drawing straight segments

Rather than COMMAND-dragging back over your path, COMMAND-drag away from it and then release the COMMAND key and continue to draw. Notice that FreeHand does not display your path between the point where the COMMAND key was pressed and the point where it was released. At the end of your drag, FreeHand calculates the quantity and position of the points necessary to represent your freehand path in the usual manner. The only difference is that any portion of your path that was created while the COMMAND key was pressed is represented by a single straight segment.

This feature is a fluke, but it's a fun fluke. The official way to create a straight segment with the freehand tool is to press OPTION while dragging. As when pressing COMMAND, a straight segment is created between the points at which you press and release the OPTION key. However, when pressing OPTION, you can see the straight segment between the two points as you draw.

To experiment with adding a single segment with the freehand tool, try the following exercise:

1. Drawing a squiggle with the freehand tool, as shown in Figure 5.10.

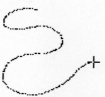

Figure 5.10: Draw a squiggle with the freehand tool.

2. Press the OPTION key and drag to the location represented by the cross-shaped cursor in Figure 5.11. For as long as the OPTION key remains pressed, a straight segment will follow the movements of your cursor. Notice in the figure that although the squiggle is sketchy (our "Connect the dots" option is deselected), the straight segment appears solid.

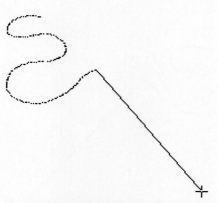

Figure 5.11: Press the option key and drag away from the squiggle.

3. Release the OPTION key, and draw another squiggle. Your movements are interpreted exactly as they were before you pressed OPTION, as shown in Figure 5.12 on the following page.

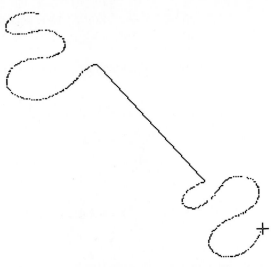

Figure 5.12: Continue to draw after releasing the option key.

4. Release your mouse button. Figure 5.13 shows the completed path, which contains a single, straight segment between the OPTION key press and release points.

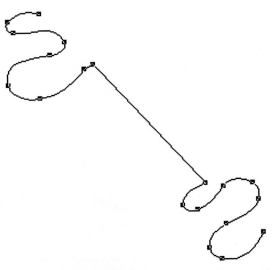

Figure 5.13: The completed path contains a straight segment between the points at which the option key was pressed and released.

In conjunction with the OPTION key, the freehand tool can serve as a polygon tool, similar to the one included in MacDraw. Press OPTION before beginning to drag with the freehand tool. When satisfied with your first segment, momentarily pause your freehand cursor (do *not* release the mouse button), then release and immediately repress the OPTION key and draw your next segment. Repeat this technique to create additional straight segments. After completing your final segment, release the mouse button, then release OPTION.

Pressing SHIFT and OPTION and dragging with the freehand tool constrains the straight segment to a 45° angle. Keep in mind that the effects of pressing the SHIFT key may be altered by rotating the constraint axes using the CONSTRAIN... command from the ELEMENT menu, as described in the *Geometric paths at an angle* section earlier in this chapter.

Extending a line

The freehand tool may also be used to *extend* an open path. For example, suppose that you have drawn a line with either the line tool or the freehand tool some time ago, but now you wish to make the line longer or close the path. Select the path with the arrow tool, then drag from an *endpoint*—that is, the point at either end of the line—with the freehand tool, as shown in Figure 5.14. The line created by dragging with the tool is treated as an extension of the existing open path. To extend a path, drag from an endpoint and end your drag when the line has become the desired length. To close the path, drag from one endpoint to the other.

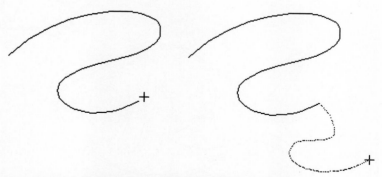

Figure 5.14: To extend an open path (left) with the freehand tool, drag from either of its endpoints (right).

Sketching complicated paths

The freehand tool can be used to sketch complicated objects, especially line drawings. If you are skilled in drawing with the mouse or tablet, you may find that the immediacy of producing high-resolution images in real time is very appealing. Drawing with the freehand tool can soften the computer-produced appearance of an illustration, and may convey a sense of immediacy to those who view or read the piece. However, regardless of your drawing ability or preferences, the freehand tool rarely renders images that may be considered professional in quality.

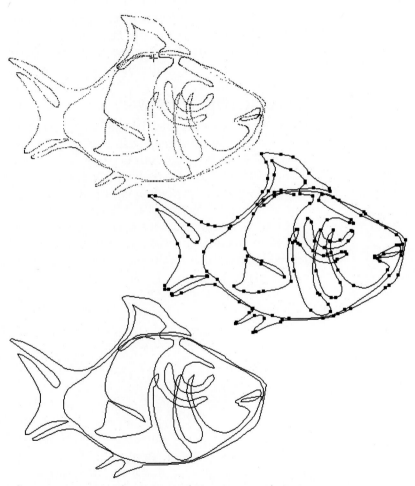

Figure 5.15: Three steps in the process of sketching a fish with the freehand tool.

Suppose that we draw a fish as a single line with the freehand tool. The first example in Figure 5.15 shows the path as we originally draw it, before FreeHand calculates the quantity and location of points and segments. The second example shows the points that FreeHand has assigned to our fish. The third example shows the fish as a deselected path.

It is amazing how accurately the finished product resembles the original movement of the freehand tool. This is primarily due to the fact that we selected the "Tight" option in the FREEHAND dialog box. The final path is by no means perfect, mostly because the original drawing lacks perfection, but it is a very good place to start.

Most illustrations created with the freehand tool need to be extensively manipulated in order to print acceptably. Like a photograph shot with a Polaroid camera, the immediate satisfaction gained by drawing with the freehand tool results in the sacrifice of accuracy and elegance in your image. For this reason, we recommend that you use the tool primarily for sketching images and that you prepare yourself to spend the time required to properly reshape them (as described in Chapter 7, *Reshaping Existing Paths*).

Bézier paths

Every path in Aldus FreeHand is a *Bézier* (pronounced bā´·zē·ā) *path*; that is, it relies on a handful of mathematical curve definitions, pioneered by Pierre Bézier, that have developed into an integral part of the Post-Script printer language. The Bézier curve model allows for zero, one, or two levers to be associated with each point in a line or shape. These levers are called *Bézier control handles*. Each handle may be moved in relation to a point, bending and tugging at a curved segment like a piece of elastic taffy.

The geometric path tools and the freehand tool gloss over the nuts and bolts of path building. However, if you really want to understand how to draw in Aldus FreeHand, you must master the creation of lines and shapes on a point-by-point basis. The remainder of this chapter is devoted to a thorough examination of points, segments, and Bézier control handles, all centered around a discussion of FreeHand's four *point tools*—the corner tool, curve tool, connector tool, and pen tool.

As we discussed in Chapter 4, FreeHand defines lines and shapes as the combination of two or more points. Each point determines how a segment in the path enters it and how another exits it. Each of the four point tools works by defining a single point.

The corner tool

Select the *corner tool*, the sixth tool on the left side of the toolbox, and click at some location on the screen to create a *corner point* that shows up as a tiny hollow square, indicating that it is *selected*.

The point you just created is *open-ended*, meaning that it does not have both a segment coming into it and a segment going out from it. In fact, this new corner point—we'll call it point A—is associated with no segment whatsoever. It is a lone point, open-ended in two directions.

In FreeHand, a point that is both open-ended and selected, like point A, is waiting for additional points and segments to be added to it. For example, if you again click with the corner tool at a new location on the screen, as demonstrated in Figure 5.16, a straight segment will be drawn from the original corner point A to the new corner point B. Notice that point A now appears black rather than hollow. This shows that point A is the member of a selected path, but is itself *deselected*. Our new corner point B is selected and open-ended. A point always becomes selected, thereby deselecting all other points, immediately after it is created.

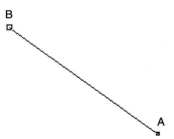

Figure 5.16: Create a straight line by clicking at each of two separate locations with the corner tool.

Points A and B now make up a path. The fact that point B is both open-ended and selected signifies that the path is *active*, meaning that it is ready to receive a point. A segment will be drawn between the selected point and the next point you create. If the path is selected, but no point is both open-ended and selected (no endpoint appears hollow), the path is said to be *passive*. When all paths are passive, any point created with a point tool becomes the first point in a new path.

If you click a third time with the corner tool, you create a new point, point C. As shown in Figure 5.17, point A remains open-ended, since it is associated with only one segment, by which it is attached to point B. Likewise, a segment goes from point B to point C. Because a point may be associated with no more than two segments, point B is no longer open-ended. Such a point is called an *interior point*. Point C was just created, so it and only it is selected. And because this last point is also open-ended, the path remains active.

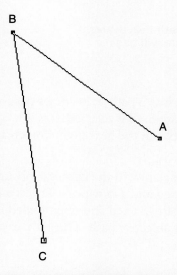

Figure 5.17: Point B is now an interior point, incapable of receiving additional segments.

We will now *close* our path, changing it from a line into a shape. All open-ended points will be eliminated. This is done quite easily. Merely click with the corner tool on point A, the first point in the path. Since point A is open-ended, it willingly accepts the segment drawn between it and point C, as shown in Figure 5.18 on the following page.

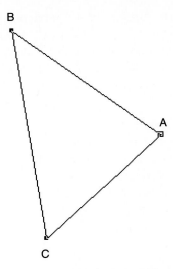

B

A

C

Figure 5.18: Closing a path deactivates it.
The next point you create will begin a
new path.

The moment you close a path, it becomes passive. For example, although point A in Figure 5.18 is selected, it is not open-ended. No segment will be drawn between the next point you create and any point in the selected shape.

Suppose you click again with the corner tool cursor. The triangle shape becomes deselected and a new point D is created, as shown in Figure 5.19. Point D is both selected and open-ended in two directions, making it a member of an active path. The path-creation process has begun anew.

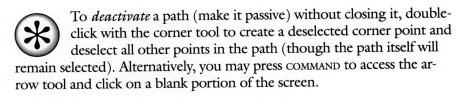

To *deactivate* a path (make it passive) without closing it, double-click with the corner tool to create a deselected corner point and deselect all other points in the path (though the path itself will remain selected). Alternatively, you may press COMMAND to access the arrow tool and click on a blank portion of the screen.

Pressing the 9 key—either in the standard key set or on the keypad—will select the corner tool at any time, except when a dialog box is displayed.

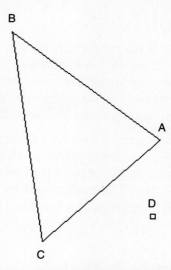

Figure 5.19: Creating a point D that is independent of the previous path deselects that path.

Drawing perpendicular segments

To constrain a point so it is created at an angle that is a multiple of 45° from the selected, open-ended point, press SHIFT as you click with the corner tool. This technique allows you to create horizontal, vertical, and diagonal segments. In Figure 5.20, for example, the location at which we actually click with the corner tool is shown by the position of the + cursor. However, since the SHIFT key is pressed, the new point is constrained to a 0° angle from its neighbor, resulting in a horizontal segment.

+

Figure 5.20: Shift-click with the pen tool to create a horizontal, vertical, or diagonal segment.

The effect of pressing the SHIFT key can be altered by rotating the constraint axes using the CONSTRAIN... command from the ELEMENT menu, as described in *Geometric paths at an angle*, earlier in this chapter.

The curve tool

The next point tool we will discuss is the *curve tool,* fifth tool on the right side of the toolbox. When you click with this tool, you create a *curve point,* which ensures a smooth arc between one curved segment and the next. A curve point sports two crosslike *Bézier control handles.* These handles act as levers, bending segments relative to the curve point itself.

The first example in Figure 5.21 shows a curve point bordered on either side by corner points. All three points are shown as they appear when selected. Notice that the curve point is a hollow circle and the corner points are hollow squares. The small crosses are the Bézier control handles belonging to all three points. Each control handle pulls at a segment, causing it to curve outward.

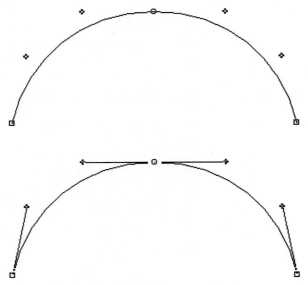

Figure 5.21: Points and Bézier control handles shown as they appear with levers hidden (top) and displayed (bottom).

Notice that *levers* connect the control handles to their points in the second example. This is a result of selecting the "Display curve levers" option in the PREFERENCES dialog box. Levers demonstrate the relationship between points and Bézier control handles. For example, in Figure 5.21, you can see that the curve point has two control handles, which are initially positioned symmetrically about the point. It is this symmetrical quality that makes two segments always form an even, smooth arc through a curve point.

Each of the corner points in Figure 5.21 also has a Bézier control handle. While this is not the standard configuration for a corner point— none of our previous corners points, for example, have had control handles—a curve point tends to dominate the form of a segment over a corner point. A point created with the curve tool always attaches a Bézier control handle to each of its neighboring points. We will see more about how this works in later sections.

Curve points act no differently than corner points when it comes to building paths. Clicking with the curve tool creates a curved segment between the current curve point and the previously selected, open-ended point in the active path. If no path is active, the curve point becomes the first point in a new path. Clicking on the first point in an active path closes the path. Double-clicking with the curve tool deselects all points in the current path, making it passive.

 Pressing the 8 key—either in the standard key set or on the keypad—will select the curve tool at any time, except when a dialog box is displayed.

The versatile pen tool

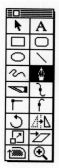

If you're familiar with previous versions of FreeHand, you've no doubt noticed that the combination tool has disappeared, having been replaced by the *pen tool*, fourth tool on the right side of the toolbox. To what do we owe this change? Probably because the combination tool was so ugly. In any case, the pen tool operates almost identically to its predecessor, so experienced users should have little problem adapting.

The pen tool is capable of creating both corner and curve points. It also enables the user to precisely determine the placement and quantity of Bézier control handles. The pen tool offers less automatic software control, and leaves more control in the hands of the user.

If you click with the pen tool, as you would with the corner or curve tool, you create a corner point with no Bézier control handle. But if you drag with the pen tool, you create a curve point: The point at which you begin dragging with the pen tool determines the location of the curve point; the point at which you release becomes a Bézier control handle that affects the next segment you create. A second handle appears symmetrically about the curve point to the first. This handle determines the curvature of the most recent segment, as demonstrated in Figure 5.22.

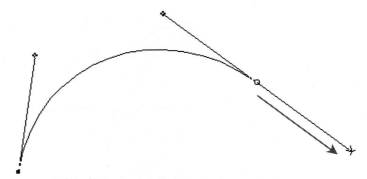

Figure 5.22: Drag with the pen tool to create a curve point flanked by two Bézier control handles.

When dragging with the pen tool, you might think of a curve point as if it were the center of a small seesaw, with the Bézier control handles acting as opposite ends. If you push down on one handle, the opposite handle goes up, and vice versa. Figure 5.23 shows four examples of dragging different distances from the same curve point with the pen tool. Notice that the placement of both Bézier control handles is determined by the release location, since the second handle is symmetrical about the curve point to the first. It is this seesaw quality that forces two segments to always form a continuous, seamless arc through a curve point.

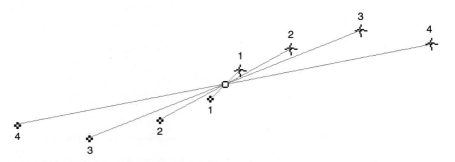

Figure 5.23: When dragging with the pen tool, the release location determines the placement of both Bézier control handles.

Creating a cusp

As mentioned previously, a curve point must always have two Bézier control handles, each positioned in an imaginary straight line with the point itself. A corner point, however, is much more versatile: It may have zero, one, or two handles. We have seen that clicking with the pen tool creates a corner point with no control handle and that dragging with the pen tool creates a curve point. You may also create a corner point that has one or two Bézier control handles—sometimes called a *cusp*—by pressing the OPTION key as you drag with the pen tool. If you press OPTION after you begin to drag, but before you release the mouse button, you create a corner point with two independent Bézier control handles.

Suppose you are dragging with the pen tool, creating a curve point. As shown in the first example of Figure 5.24, the handle beneath your cursor will control the next segment that you create; the symmetrical handle controls the preceding segment. After correctly positioning the symmetrical handle, press OPTION. This changes the round curve point to a square corner point, as shown in the second example in Figure 5.24. While pressing OPTION, you may move the handle belonging to the next segment independently of the handle for the preceding segment. This latter handle is motionless throughout the remainder of your OPTION-drag.

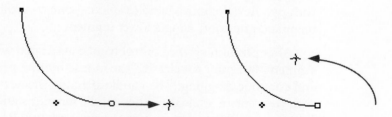

Figure 5.24: Pressing option while dragging with the pen tool changes the curve point (left) to a corner point with two independent Bézier control handles (right).

The following are three examples of how this technique can be applied:

- **Option 1**: *Move one curve point handle independently of the other.*

The first two examples begin with the semicircle shown in progress in Figure 5.25 on the following page. You may create this path by dragging three times with the pen tool: Begin by dragging downward from the right point; then drag leftward from the bottom point; and finally drag upward from the left point. Figure 5.25 catches us in the process of performing the final drag.

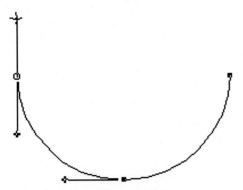

Figure 5.25: Creating a curve point in a semicircular path with the pen tool.

Suppose you wish to close the path with a rounded top, like the one shown in Figure 5.28. All segments in this path are curved, and yet the upper segment meets with the lower segments to form two cusps. This means that you must change the two top curve points to corner points with two Bézier control handles apiece—one controlling the upper segment and one controlling a lower segment.

After positioning the control handle associated with the preceding segment, but prior to releasing the mouse button, press the OPTION key and continue dragging. The handle affecting the next segment moves with your cursor while the other handle remains stationary, as shown in Figure 5.26. The result is a corner point with two Bézier control handles, each fully independent of the other.

You may close the shape in a similar manner. First, drag with the pen tool from the first curve point in the path. While dragging, concentrate on placing the symmetrical Bézier control handle, which is associated with the new curved segment. In this case, to make the path symmetrical, you should drag down and to the right, as shown in Figure 5.27. After the symmetrical handle is properly placed, but again prior to releasing the mouse button, press OPTION and continue dragging to restore the handle beneath your cursor to its original location, as shown in Figure 5.28. Using the OPTION key, you have simultaneously closed the shape and converted the first point in the path to a corner point.

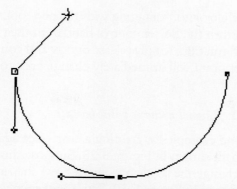

Figure 5.26: Press the option key and drag from the selected curve point to convert the point to a cusp.

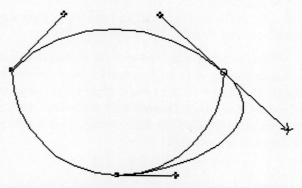

Figure 5.27: Close the shape by dragging down and to the right from the first point in the path.

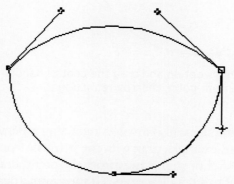

Figure 5.28: Press option and drag the control handle beneath your cursor back to its original location.

If, while OPTION-dragging with the pen tool, you decide you want to return the Bézier control handles to their original symmetrical configuration, simply release OPTION and continue dragging. The current corner point will immediately change back to a curve point.

● **Option 2**: *Retract a curve point handle.*

This second example for creating a cusp once again begins with the semicircular path shown in Figure 5.25. Suppose this time, however, that you want to change the semicircle into a bowl-shaped path with a flat top, like the one shown in Figure 5.30. This shape involves three segments, two of which meet to form a single large arc, and a third which is straight, flattening off the shape. Since curve points and Bézier control handles may be associated only with curved segments, corner points must exist on both sides of the top segment and the top segment may be associated with no control handle.

While dragging with pen tool (as shown in Figure 5.25), press OPTION to change the curve point to a corner point. Now drag the control handle beneath the cursor back to the current point, as shown in Figure 5.29, and release the mouse button and OPTION key. Notice that one of the Bézier control handles has disappeared. This technique is known as *retracting* a control handle.

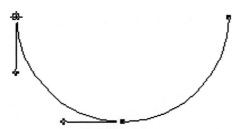

Figure 5.29: Press option and drag the control handle back to the current point, thereby retracting it.

Closing the shape also involves retracting a Bézier control handle. As in the previous example, drag with the pen tool from the first curve point in the path. After dragging away from the point, drag back toward it until at least one of handles disappears. (If the symmetrical handle does not disappear completely, don't worry. You may always retract it further during the reshaping process, as described in Chapter 7, *Reshaping Existing*

Paths.) After retracting the handles, but prior to releasing the mouse button, press OPTION and continue dragging to restore the handle beneath your cursor to its original location, as shown in Figure 5.30. The new segment is flat, bordered on both sides by corner points with one Bézier control handle apiece.

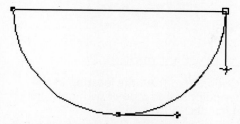

Figure 5.30: Once again, press option and drag the control handle beneath your cursor back to its original location.

● **Option 3**: *Press option before beginning to drag.*

This third example demonstrates how you can create a corner point with only one Bézier control handle by pressing OPTION before dragging with the pen tool. We will start with the straight-segment path shown in Figure 5.31. Suppose that you want to create a curved top for this path, as shown in Figure 5.34 on page 153. The following paragraphs describe how.

Figure 5.31: An active straight-segment path with a selected, open-ended corner point.

The left point in the path in Figure 5.31 is selected and open-ended, making the path active. Press OPTION and drag from a point horizontally aligned with the first point in the path, as shown in Figure 5.32. Because the OPTION key is pressed, the pen tool automatically creates a corner point with only one Bézier control handle. The new segment is straight, since the control handle is positioned to affect the next segment you create. After dragging the control handle to the location shown in Figure 5.32, release both your mouse button and the OPTION key.

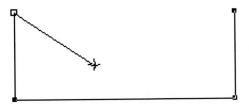

Figure 5.32: Option-drag from the location of the selected corner point to add a point with only one Bézier control handle.

To close the path, drag with the pen tool from the first point (top right point) in the path. Dragging at this point automatically converts it from a corner point to a curve point. This may seem like a mistake, since we want the final point to be a corner point, but this is the only way to correctly position the control handle associated with the new curved segment. To make the path symmetrical, drag up and to the right, as shown in Figure 5.33. After the symmetrical handle is properly placed, but prior to releasing the mouse button, press OPTION and continue dragging to convert the current point back to a corner point. Retract the handle beneath your cursor by OPTION-dragging back to the corner point, as shown in Figure 5.34. The shape is now complete.

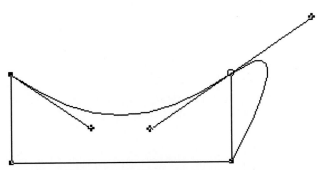

Figure 5.33: Close the shape by dragging on the first corner point in the path.

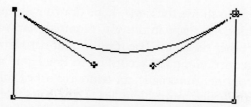

Figure 5.34: Press option and retract the control handle back to its corner point.

Why the pen tool is so great

You will probably find that the pen tool is the tool of choice for creating complex paths, rather than trading back and forth between the corner and curve tools. The reason is control. Take as an example the fish shape shown in Figure 5.35. This fish is the product of five corner points and five curve points, all created with the pen tool. By clicking, dragging, and OPTION-dragging, we have manually determined the placement of each point and every Bézier control handle in the shape.

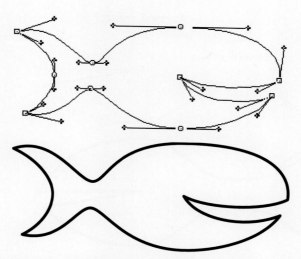

Figure 5.35: Shown as it appears on screen (top) and when printed (bottom), this fish demonstrates how the pen tool allows you to determine the exact location of every point and Bézier control handle.

Figure 5.36 shows the same shape drawn with the corner and curve tools. Creating the shape in this way required that we switch from one tool to the other six times. The result of our hard work is a rather malformed specimen, designed according to FreeHand's built-in *automatic curvature* routine. Automatic curvature is a set of rules that guides the placement of Bézier control handles. These rules include the following:

- Each point that neighbors a curve point gets one Bézier control handle on the curve-point side. The segment between the curve point and its neighbor is formed according to the definition of a circle and according to the locations of other neighboring points.

- If a corner point neighbors another corner point, the segment between the two points gets no Bézier control handle whatsoever.

The first rule results in the distortion of the tail, exaggerating the curvature of the tail segments so they appear like arcs in a circle. The second rule straightens out the mouth, since the mouth is defined using corner points only.

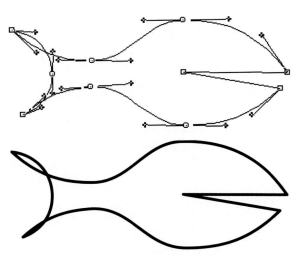

Figure 5.36: When creating a path using the corner and curve tools, FreeHand automatically determines the quantity and location of Bézier control handles, as demonstrated by this more haphazard creature.

We are not suggesting that by using the corner and curve tools, you limit yourself to producing ugly results. However, the results may not exactly suit your needs. Figure 5.36 displays a fish, but Figure 5.35 shows the fish we want. The pen tool offers the greatest control.

 You may have noticed that by dragging with the corner tool or the curve tool, you may move the current point around on the screen. This can prove extremely useful, allowing you to view a point at several locations before proceeding to the next point in a path. You may likewise move points as they are created with the pen tool by pressing the COMMAND key as you drag.

KE Pressing the 6 key—either in the standard key set or on the keypad—will select the pen tool at any time, except when a dialog box is displayed.

The connector tool

The pen tool can create every kind of point except the *connector point*, which is used to ensure a smooth transition between straight and curved segments. The connector point may be created using the *connector tool* only, which is the sixth tool on the right side of the toolbox.

Some people will live their entire lives without once using a connector point. However, connector points can be useful in very specific situations, as demonstrated by the following example. Figure 5.37 shows a path composed of six corner points and two curve points. The four selected corner points join straight segments to curved segments.

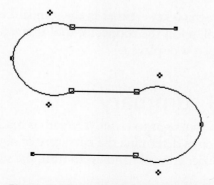

Figure 5.37: Four selected corner points join straight segments to curved segments.

FreeHand's automatic curvature routine causes the curved edges of the path to bulge outward, resulting in definite corners. Perhaps you desire a different effect. Suppose you want the progression from straight segment to curved segment to occur smoothly, without any interfering corner. A gentle transition is guaranteed if you substitute each of the selected corner points with connector points, as shown in Figure 5.38. Connector points, which display as hollow triangles when selected, are designed to provide seamless links between straight segments and curved segments. To accomplish this, the Bézier control handle belonging to each connector point is locked into alignment with the straight segment that precedes it, as demonstrated in the figure.

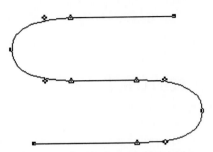

Figure 5.38: Four selected corner points join straight segments to curved segments.

 Use connector points to create any straight object that ends in a rounded tip, such as a finger or other cylindrical object. Connector points may also be useful for creating rounded corners.

 Pressing the 0 key—either in the standard key set or on the keypad—will select the connector tool at any time, except when a dialog box is displayed.

Point tool summary

Regardless of the tool used to create it, a path is made up of points and segments. The points determine the curvature of segments based on the positioning of Bézier control handles. In turn, the segments define the form of the path.

Although you may adjust the placement of points and Bézier control handles by reshaping a path created with any drawing tool (as described in Chapter 7, *Reshaping Existing Paths*), the point tools—corner tool, curve tool, pen tool, and connector tool—allow you to exactly position points during the creation process. And since any illustration may be constructed as the combination of a series of lines and shapes, there is absolutely no illustration that cannot be created using the point tools alone.

The following items summarize the ways in which the point tools can be used to build paths in Aldus FreeHand:

- To build a path, create one point after another until the path is the desired length and shape. As long as the path is *active* (an endpoint is selected), a segment will be created between each point.

- To close a path and, in the process, make the path *passive*, click on the first point in the active path. Click again to begin a new path.

- To make an open path passive, double-click with the current point tool, thus deselecting the final point in the path. Click again to begin a new path.

- To activate an open path (you may not activate a closed path), select one of its endpoints with the arrow tool.

The next items explain the specific kinds of points and segments that may be created with the most useful point tool, the pen tool:

- Click to create a *corner point*.

- Click at two separate locations to create a straight segment.

- Click at one location and SHIFT-click at another to create a perpendicular segment (at any angle that is a multiple of 45°).

- Drag to create a *curve point* with two *Bézier control handles*.

- Drag at two separate locations to create a curved segment.

- Drag, press SHIFT, begin a new drag, and then release SHIFT while still dragging to create a curved segment whose points align with respect to the constraint axes. Pressing SHIFT constrains the point; releasing SHIFT before you complete the drag allows you to move the Bézier control handles freely. An example of such a curve is shown in Figure 5.39 on the next page.

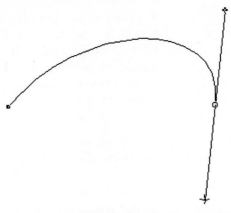

Figure 5.39: Press shift before dragging but then
release to create a curve along the constraint axes.
Notice how the points align horizontally.

● Press SHIFT after beginning a drag to constrain the Bézier control
handles without affecting the placement of the curve point. An example of this is shown in Figure 5.40.

Figure 5.40: Begin the drag before pressing shift to align
the Bézier control handles to the constraint axes without
constraining the curve point.

● Press SHIFT and drag at two separate locations to create a perfect
dome, as shown in Figure 5.41.

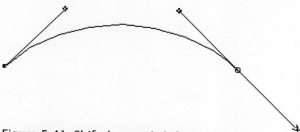

Figure 5.41: Shift-drag and shift-drag
again to constrain both points and Bézier
control handles to create a symmetrical dome.

- Press OPTION while dragging to create a corner point with two independent Bézier control handles. Be sure to properly position the handle belonging to the preceding segment before pressing OPTION.

- To create a corner point with only one Bézier control handle associated with the preceding segment, press OPTION while dragging, then retract the control handle beneath your cursor while still pressing OPTION.

- Press OPTION before dragging to create a corner point with only one Bézier control handle associated with the next segment.

- Release OPTION while dragging to change the current point back to a curve point.

- Press COMMAND while dragging to move the current point in the drawing area.

Tracing
Bitmapped
Images

Not everyone can be a Rembrandt. Some of us are lucky to draw a straight line, much less triumph over the gamut of complex strategies inherent in the operation of the pen tool. Others can draw quite adequately with pencil and paper, but have problems making the transition to the computer-graphics environment.

If you fall into any of these categories, you may breathe a sigh of relief. FreeHand allows you to trace scanned images and artwork created in painting programs. It also automates the conversion process by providing a trace tool. Even skilled computer artists are well advised to sketch their ideas on paper or in a painting program before executing them in Aldus FreeHand. The following section explains why.

Why trace a bitmap?

It is not easy to draw from scratch in Aldus FreeHand. Even if you draw exclusively with the freehand tool, you will frequently have to edit your lines and shapes, point by point (as we will discuss in Chapter 7, *Reshaping Existing Paths*). Also, to build an image in FreeHand is to do just that: *build*. Heaps of mathematically defined lines and shapes must be combined and layered much like girders at a construction site.

With this in mind, you'll probably have the most luck with Aldus FreeHand if you're part artist and part engineer. But for those of us who aren't engineers and can't even *imagine* how engineers think, a painting application like MacPaint or Studio/1 provides a more artist-friendly environment.

Painting programs provide simple tools such as pencils and erasers. And since little interpretation is required by your software, these tools work just like their real-life counterparts. Your screen displays the results of your mouse movements instantaneously. This allows you to draw, see what you've drawn, and make alterations, all in the time it takes the appropriate neurons to fire in your brain.

But despite the many advantages of painting software, its single failing—the graininess of its output—is glaringly obvious, so much so that people who have never used a computer can immediately recognize a bitmapped image as computer-produced artwork. Object-oriented drawings, on the other hand, are smooth.

This jaggedness is particularly noticeable in the case of black-and-white artwork. For example, the bitmapped fish in Figure 6.01 was fairly easy to create. It is well executed, but its jagged edges are far too obvious for it to be considered professional-quality artwork. By introducing a few shades of gray to the image, we can soften much of its jaggedness, as demonstrated by Figure 6.02. However, it now appears fuzzy and out of focus. This makes gray-scale scanning more suited to photography than to line art.

Figure 6.01: A typically jagged black-and-white image created in MacPaint.

Figure 6.02: Gray pixels soften the edges, but make the image appear out of focus.

Only in a drawing application such as Aldus FreeHand can you create pristine line art. The fish in Figure 6.03, for example, required more time and effort to produce, but the result is a smooth, highly focused, professional-quality image.

Figure 6.03: By tracing the bitmapped fish image, we are able to arrive at this smooth, exemplary drawing.

By tracing a bitmapped image in a drawing program, you can have the best of both worlds. You can sketch your idea traditionally onto a piece of paper and then scan it into your computer, or you can sketch directly in a painting program. Either way, your sketch will be bitmapped. You may then import the sketch as a *tracing template* into Aldus Free-Hand using the PLACE... command, as discussed in the following section. Finally, use FreeHand's drawing tools to convert the image to a collection of free-form lines and shapes.

Importing
tracing templates

FreeHand is capable of importing any bitmapped image saved in one of the following standardized graphic formats:

- MacPaint
- PICT (QuickDraw picture)
- TIFF (Tag Image File Format)
- EPS (Encapsulated PostScript)

MacPaint-format documents may originate not only from MacPaint itself but also from other popular painting programs, like DeskPaint, SuperPaint, PixelPaint, and Studio/1, as well as from scanning applications like ThunderWare. The MacPaint format is one of the most widely supported graphics formats for the Macintosh computer. Unfortunately, it is also the most limited. MacPaint files are exclusively *monochrome* (black and white—no colors or gray values), no larger than 8 inches by 10 inches, vertically oriented, and always bitmapped at a resolution of 72 dots per inch. (See Chapter 1, *Drawing on the Macintosh.*)

The *PICT format*, on the other hand, provides much more flexibility. The PICT format is most commonly associated with moderately powerful drawing applications such as MacDraw, Canvas, and MacDraft. But, in fact, PICT goes much farther. It is the original file-swapping format developed by Apple for the purpose of transferring both bitmapped and object-oriented pictures from one graphics application to another. PICT can accommodate any size graphic, resolutions exceeding 300 dots per inch, and over 16 million colors. For this reason, many scanning and image-editing applications, such as ImageStudio, PixelPaint, Studio/32, and PhotoShop, support this format. In addition to converting object-oriented PICT files into FreeHand drawings using the OPEN... command (asdescribed in the section *Opening files inside FreeHand 3.0* in Chapter 3) FreeHand allows you to import and trace both bitmapped and object-oriented PICT files.

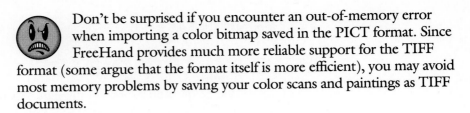Don't be surprised if you encounter an out-of-memory error when importing a color bitmap saved in the PICT format. Since FreeHand provides much more reliable support for the TIFF format (some argue that the format itself is more efficient), you may avoid most memory problems by saving your color scans and paintings as TIFF documents.

Like MacPaint, the *TIFF format* is an exclusively a bitmapped format. But, like PICT, it is otherwise unrestricted, accommodating graphics of any size, resolutions exceeding 300 dots per inch, and over 16 million colors. TIFF was developed by Aldus in an attempt to standardize images created by various scanners. Most painting and image-editing programs support the TIFF format.

The *EPS format* combines a pure PostScript-language description of a graphic with a PICT-format screen representation. The EPS format was designed by Altsys (the developers of FreeHand) in cooperation with Aldus and Adobe for the swapping of high-resolution images from one Post-Script-compatible application to another. It is not, however, an efficient format for saving bitmaps. A color EPS bitmap, for example, is typically twice to three times as large as the same bitmap saved in the TIFF format.

Due to the poor performances of the PICT and EPS formats, we recommend that you save gray-scale or color bitmaps in the TIFF format only prior to importing the image into FreeHand.

Kinds of tracing templates

The best way to think of a tracing template is in terms of its purpose, which may fall into one of three broad categories:

- **Scans** are electronic images of photographs, prints, or drawings. Black-and-white scans are commonly saved as MacPaint documents. Oversized or color scans may use the PICT format. Scans, especially when taken from photographs, offer exceptionally accurate tracing backgrounds. They are useful for detail work, such as schematic drawings, medical illustrations, and other situations where accuracy is paramount. They are also useful for people who wish to draw, but do not consider themselves very skilled in drawing. Scans can be the perfect bridge between an amateur effort and a professional product.

- **Sketches** are deeply embedded in the artistic tradition. If you were creating an oil painting, for example, you might make several sketches before deciding how the finished piece should look. After arriving at a satisfactory design, you would pencil it onto the canvas. Only after finalizing the sketch would you begin laying down the oils. Like oil paint, FreeHand is ill-suited to sketching. Sketches are best created in a painting application like MacPaint, DeskPaint, or SuperPaint. Painting programs provide an environment conducive to spontaneity, allowing you to scribble, erase, and create much like the pencil you use in sketching—quickly and freely. Once the final sketch has been completed, you may use it as a template in Free-Hand, where the high-resolution, final artwork is created.

- **Drafts** are CAD (*computer-aided design*), schematic, or structured drawings created in MacDraw, MacDraft, Claris CAD, and similar applications. Perhaps the original drawing program did not provide the array of free-form illustration tools and capabilities available in FreeHand 3.0, or you wish to add details that may be coupled with the graphic in a page-layout software like PageMaker or Quark-XPress. Draft templates are typically transported via the PICT format.

Placing a template file

To import a template—regardless of format—into an open FreeHand illustration, follow these steps:

1. Choose the PLACE... command from the FILE menu. The PLACE DOCUMENT dialog box will display, as shown in Figure 6.04 on the next page.

2. Select a template file from the scrolling list and press RETURN. Free-Hand will read the file from disk and display the *graphic placement cursor* that corresponds to the graphic format for the selected file. Each of these cursors is displayed in Figure 6.05.

3. Position the graphic placement cursor at the prospective location of the upper left corner of the template, then click. The selected template image will display in the illustration window, deselecting all previously selected objects, as demonstrated in Figure 6.06.

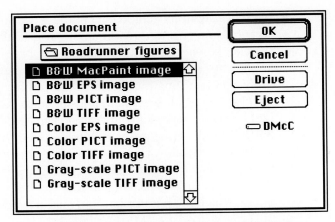

Figure 6.04: The Place document dialog box allows you to import a tracing template saved in one of four graphic formats.

Figure 6.05: The graphic placement icons for (from left to right) a MacPaint template, a PICT template, a TIFF template, and an EPS template.

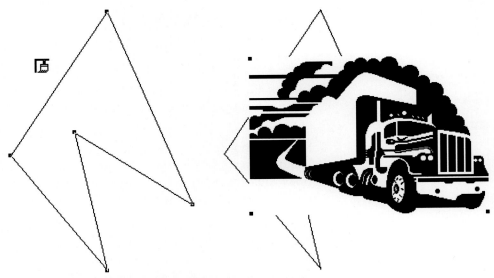

Figure 6.06: The graphic placement icon (left) represents the position of the upper left corner of an imported template (right).

For best results, send the template image to a background layer. This may be accomplished by clicking on the "Background" option name in the LAYERS palette while the template is selected. (If the LAYERS palette is not displayed, first choose the "Layers" option from the WINDOWS pop-up in the VIEW menu or press ⌘-6.) The template will then appear grayed, as shown in Figure 6.07, which will make it easier to trace. Also, imported artwork on a background layer is displayed in both the preview and keyline modes, versus imported artwork on a foreground layer, which displays only in the preview mode. Finally, background artwork does not print, so you can isolate it from the actual illustration.

Figure 6.07: A tracing template appears grayed when placed on a background layer, thus distinguishing the template from the lines and shapes that make up your illustration.

Pasting a template file

You may also import a tracing template via the Macintosh Clipboard using the CUT, COPY, and PASTE commands common to the EDIT menus of all Macintosh applications. The following procedure explains how:

1. While inside a painting program, such MacPaint or Studio/32, select the portion of the picture that you wish to use as a template and choose COPY from the EDIT menu (⌘-C).

2. Switch to the FreeHand application.

    a. If you are using the standard Macintosh Finder, choose Quit from the paint program File menu (⌘-Q). If the copied image is sufficiently large, an alert box will display requesting that you convert the contents of the Clipboard, much like the one shown in Figure 6.08. Press RETURN or click the Yes button to approve the conversion. Then launch FreeHand, as described in the section *Starting FreeHand* in Chapter 3, and open an existing FreeHand illustration or create a new one.

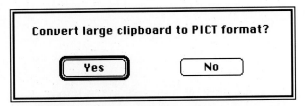

Figure 6.08: This alert box confirms the conversion of a Clipboard image to a format readable by other Macintosh applications.

    b. If you are working under MultiFinder and FreeHand is currently running, click the application icon in the far right corner of the menu bar until the FreeHand toolbox comes to front, or choose the Aldus FreeHand 3.0 icon (⟳) from the list of running applications in the Apple menu.

3. Choose Paste from the FreeHand Edit menu (⌘-V). The selected template image will display in the center of the illustration window.

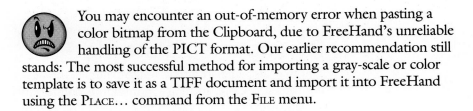

You may encounter an out-of-memory error when pasting a color bitmap from the Clipboard, due to FreeHand's unreliable handling of the PICT format. Our earlier recommendation still stands: The most successful method for importing a gray-scale or color template is to save it as a TIFF document and import it into FreeHand using the Place... command from the File menu.

Automated tracing

Any of the freehand drawing tools we have described so far—including the freehand tool and any of the four point tools—may be used to trace a bitmapped image. Simply follow the outline of the bitmap, using the tools as directed in the previous chapter. However, if this seems too complicated, or you just want to speed things up, FreeHand provides an additional drawing tool that automates the tracing process. This tool is the subject of the remainder of this chapter.

The trace tool

The *trace tool*, the last tool on the left side of the toolbox, is used to trace the borders of a template image. You operate the trace tool by dragging to create a rectangular marquee around the portion of the template that you desire to trace. FreeHand does the rest. The tool is easy to operate—certainly easier than tracing a template image by hand—but the results are predictably less precise and require more adjustments than paths created with the pen tool or even the freehand tool.

Figure 6.09: A hornet image created in MacPaint.

Suppose that you have created the hornet shown in Figure 6.09 in MacPaint. This image will act as your template. After you import the hornet bitmap, using either the PLACE... or PASTE command, and send it to the background layer (as explained earlier in this chapter), the template will appear grayed in the drawing area of the current window. The image is now ready to be converted with the trace tool. Drag with the trace tool as if you were drawing a rectangle around the template image. A marquee will track the movements of your cursor, as shown in Figure 6.10. After the marquee entirely surrounds the template, release the mouse button. Several seconds later, FreeHand produces several selected closed paths that trace the various outlines of the template, as shown in Figure 6.11.

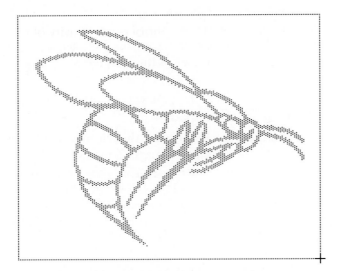

Figure 6.10: Drag with the trace tool to marquee the portion of the template that you wish to trace.

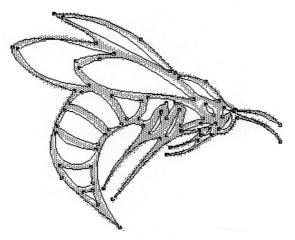

Figure 6.11: A few moments later, FreeHand produces several closed paths that trace the outline of the marqueed image.

Note that the trace tool always produces closed paths. Even if you marquee the template image of a line, FreeHand will trace entirely around the line to create a long and very thin shape.

Trace curve fit

FreeHand allows you to control the sensitivity of the trace tool using the "Tight" option in the TRACE dialog box. Selecting this option results in a tight *curve fit*, which in turn causes FreeHand to trace every single pixel of a bitmapped template. If you deselect the option, the software ignores jags in the outline of a template image and smooths out excessively imprecise forms.

To access the "Tight" option, double-click the trace tool icon in the toolbox. The TRACE dialog box, shown in Figure 6.12, will display. Select the "Tight" option to increase the sensitivity of the trace tool; deselect the option to smooth out your traced paths.

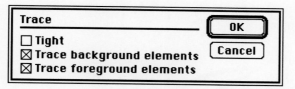

Figure 6.12: Double-click the trace tool icon in the toolbox to access the Trace dialog box.

Figure 6.13 on the following page shows how FreeHand interprets the hornet image depending on the selection of the "Tight" option. The path on left was created with "Tight" selected. The path on right is the result of deselecting "Tight" before tracing. The two circled areas in each hornet highlight major differences between the two images. If you compare these images to those back in Figure 5.08, you will see that the "Tight" option affects the performance of the trace tool and freehand tool very similarly. However, unlike freehand tool curve fit, you should adjust the curve fit of the trace tool to compensate for inaccuracies in the image you are tracing, rather than inaccuracies in your personal drawing ability.

Figure 6.13: The paths created by the trace tool when the "Tight" check box is selected (left) and deselected (right). Circled areas highlight major differences.

All paths created by the trace tool are filled and stroked with the default attributes. Therefore, to complete a traced image, you will need to apply the desired fill and stroke the each path, as explained in Chapters 9 and 10 of this book. Figure 6.14 shows the hornet image after being converted to object-oriented paths, then filled and stroked to match the template.

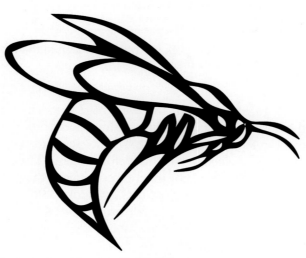

Figure 6.14: The finished hornet, traced from a template, as it appears when printed from FreeHand 3.0.

Tracing layer control

The two last options in the Trace dialog allow you to determine which elements in a trace tool marquee are evaluated by FreeHand. Select "Trace background elements" to trace any marqueed images on a background layer. Select "Trace foreground elements" to trace any marqueed images on the foreground layer. For example, suppose that there are two bitmapped images in the current illustration, one directly in front of another. If one image is positioned on a background layer and the other is on some foreground layer, you may use the options in the Trace dialog box to trace one image without tracing the other. For more information about layering, see the section *Layering objects* in Chapter 12.

Note that FreeHand traces *all* marqueed images on the specified layers, regardless of whether they were imported or created directly in FreeHand.

Tracing comparisons

The trace tool's greatest strengths are that it traces images automatically and that it is the only drawing tool capable of creating more than one path at a time. However, do not mistake it for a precise drawing tool. More often than not, you will have to spend a good deal of time reshaping your traced paths, as described in the next chapter.

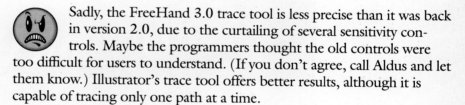 Sadly, the FreeHand 3.0 trace tool is less precise than it was back in version 2.0, due to the curtailing of several sensitivity controls. Maybe the programmers thought the old controls were too difficult for users to understand. (If you don't agree, call Aldus and let them know.) Illustrator's trace tool offers better results, although it is capable of tracing only one path at a time.

If you're a tracing fanatic, the best product for automatically converting bitmaps into object-oriented drawings is Streamline from Adobe Systems, (415) 961-4400. Priced at $195, Streamline 2.0 can convert multiple paintings at a time and at a much higher level of quality than either FreeHand or Illustrator trace tools can hope to match.

For those interested in how well the FreeHand trace tool works in comparison to Streamline, we provide the following figures. Figure 6.15 shows an image created in MacPaint. Figure 6.16 shows how the image is interpreted by both FreeHand and Streamline. The "Tight" option was selected to produce the FreeHand image. However, because of Streamline's more exacting controls, you will notice, even under a brief scrutiny, that the Streamline conversion is more accurate and more elegant. Notice, for example, the line defining the back of the eagle's head, evident in the Streamline illustration but missing entirely from the FreeHand graphic. Also notice the differences between the treatments of the area around the eye and underneath the beak.

Figure 6.15: A monochrome painting composed largely of loose, shading pixels.

But, in all fairness, when you consider that we're comparing a single tool, in the case of FreeHand, to an stand-alone utility, the trace tool performs quite admirably. In fact, if FreeHand provided a few more controls and automatically filled its paths (as does Streamline), we would find it very difficult to justify the purchase of Streamline to any but the most affluent user.

Figure 6.16: Traced versions of the eagle bitmap created using the FreeHand trace tool (top) and the Adobe Streamline utility (bottom).

Tracing color images

Although FreeHand allows you to import color images saved in the PICT, TIFF, or EPS format, the trace tool will not necessarily interpret color images accurately. The trace tool treats *all* images as if they were monochrome, seeing only two color levels. All colors lighter than medium gray are seen as white; all colors darker than medium gray are seen as black. Figures 6.17 and 6.18 demonstrate how the trace tool sees a typical gray-scale scan.

Figure 6.17: A color template is displayed accurately in the FreeHand illustration window (top), but the trace tool can only identify its black and white components (bottom).

Figure 6.18: The still life image as converted by the trace tool.

In other words, regardless of whether you trace the color image or the monochrome image shown in Figure 6.17, you will get the result shown in Figure 6.18 because the trace tool sees them the same way. The color image will take longer to trace, however, since the trace tool has to spend more time computing the boundaries between the light and dark portions of the image.

To trace a color scan, first marquee the image with the trace tool. After FreeHand's automated tracing concludes, trace any ignored details manually using the freehand and point tools, as described in Chapter 5.

Okay, okay, so that's not the most insightful tip in the world. Actually, there is a better tip, but it's harder to describe and, at least in some respects, messier to execute. But, it's still one heck of a tip. So here goes:

1. Prior to importing the color image into FreeHand, convert the image from color to gray scale in your painting or image-editing software. Most of the detail will be retained, but FreeHand will be better able to interpret the image. Save the gray-scale image as a TIFF document.

2. Import the template and send it to the background layer.

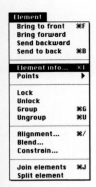

3. While the bitmap is still selected, choose the ELEMENT INFO... command from the ELEMENT menu (⌘-I) or OPTION-double-click the bitmap with the arrow tool. The IMAGE dialog box will display, as shown in Figure 6.19. (If the COLOR IMAGE dialog box appears, you did not correctly convert the bitmap to a gray-scale image. You will have to return to your painting or image-editing software and try again. If your favorite paint program does not allow you to save or convert an image to a gray-scale format, use a different application that can, such as Studio/32 or Adobe Photoshop.)

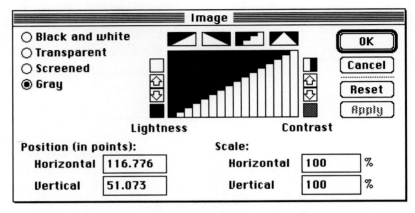

Figure 6.19: The Image dialog box allows you to edit an imported gray-scale TIFF image.

The IMAGE dialog box (described in depth in Chapter 13, *Importing and Exporting Graphics*) allows you to edit each of 16 gray values in an imported bitmap using one of the 16 vertical bars that form a stair-step pattern in the center of the dialog box. Each bar may be dragged up and down. Dragging up lightens the corresponding gray value; dragging down darkens the value. Since the trace tool can only discern one color at a time (as in black against a white background), you can use the IMAGE dialog box to isolate each of the 16 gray values, one by one.

4. To begin, select the "Black and white" radio button in the upper left corner of the dialog box. Notice that the vertical bars shift to form a new pattern—half move all the way down (disappearing from view) and the other half move all the way up. This is

FreeHand's way of telling you that all the dark grays have become black and all the light grays have become white. Then press RETURN to close the dialog box and return to the illustration window. The image, which previously appeared as shown in the first example of Figure 6.17, has now been *polarized*, so that it looks like the second example in that same figure.

5. Marquee the image with the trace tool. FreeHand automatically traces the bitmap, just as it would have if you hadn't altered it using the IMAGE dialog box (except faster, since you have clearly identified blacks and whites for the trace tool).

6. You have now isolated all values lighter than medium gray from those that are darker than medium gray. Now, you must isolate the very darkest values from the others. Press OPTION and double-click the template to again display the IMAGE dialog box. To isolate the dark gray values, change all other gray values to white. Try clicking near the top of the box containing the vertical bars, inside the black area. One of the vertical bars will jump to the top of the box, as demonstrated by the first example in Figure 6.20. That gray value is now converted to white. Drag along the top of the box to change all gray values except the very darkest shade (represented by the leftmost bar) to white, as shown in the second example of Figure 6.20. If you accidentally display the leftmost bar, click at the base of the bar to hide it.

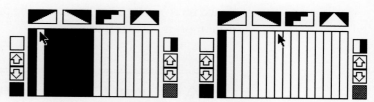

Figure 6.20: To isolate the darkest gray value, click above one of the bars (left) and drag across the top of the box (right), displaying all but the leftmost vertical bar.

7. Press RETURN to implement your changes to the selected image. Only the darkest portions of the template image will remain visible, as shown in Figure 6.21 on the following page.

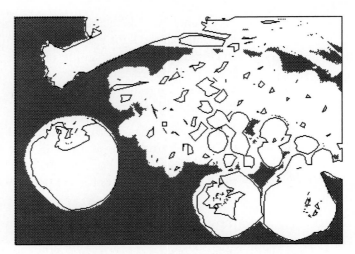

Figure 6.21: The template after changing all but the darkest gray value to white. The lines, created in step 5 with the trace tool, represent the previous boundaries of the image.

8. Again marquee the image with the trace tool. The alert box shown in Figure 6.22 will display, informing you that you are trying to trace images of different resolutions. In other words, you are trying to trace both bitmapped and object-oriented images. The bitmapped image is the template. The object-oriented images are the paths you created when you used the trace tool back in step 5. Since there's no reason to retrace the paths, click the CANCEL button or press COMMAND-PERIOD.

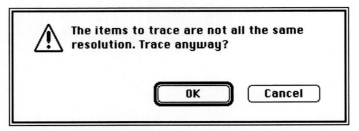

Figure 6.22: This alert box displays when you try to trace both bitmapped and object-oriented images.

9. Double-click the trace tool to display the TRACE dialog box. Assuming the tracing template is on a background layer and the object-oriented paths are on a foreground layer, you can isolate the template image by deselecting the "Trace foreground elements" option. Only "Trace background elements" remains selected, so only the template image will be traced.

10. Press RETURN to close the TRACE dialog box. Again marquee the image with the trace tool. The lightened version of the template will be traced, creating a new collection of paths.

11. Repeat step 6 for other gray values. For example, to trace all but the very lightest value, drag along the bottom of the bars in the IMAGE dialog box to hide all except the rightmost bar, as shown in Figure 6.23. Depending on how accurate you want your converted image to be (and how much time you want to spend on this project), you won't necessarily want to isolate every one of the 16 gray values. However, you probably will want to isolate the medium-dark and medium-light gray values, as shown in Figure 6.24. Marquee the image with the trace tool between each alteration with the IMAGE dialog box.

Figure 6.23: Drag along the bottom of the bars to blacken all but the lightest gray value.

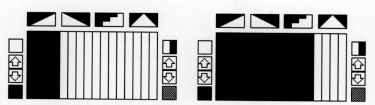

Figure 6.24: Isolating the medium-dark gray values (left) and medium-light values (right).

12. After you finish tracing the template, you will have to spend several additional minutes filling, stroking, and layering the paths, as described in Chapters 9, 10, and 12, respectively. The completed illustration will look something like the one shown in Figure 6.25.

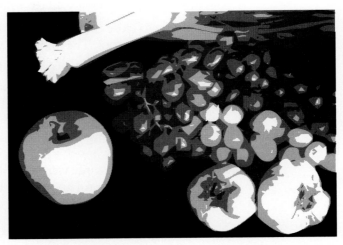

Figure 6.25: The still life created by isolating and tracing each of five gray values.

⁑ To simplify the process of filling and stroking traced paths, change the default settings in the COLOR palette before each application of the trace tool. In this way, you may determine the fill and stroke of traced paths *before* you create them. This will help distinguish one round of traced paths from the next. (For a complete discussion of the COLOR palette, see Chapter 11, *Assigning Colors and Styles*.)

There's no denying that this technique is complicated and time consuming, but until FreeHand automates the process of tracing gray values, this is the most efficient means available. And, if you compare Figure 6.25 to Figure 6.18 (back on page 179), you'll see that your additional effort is well rewarded.

Reshaping Existing Paths

After you create a graphic object in FreeHand, the object is by no means permanent. Any path may be changed. And, assuming you do most of your drawing with the freehand and trace tools, your paths are going to need adjustment. As a matter of fact, almost every path you create will need to be altered in some way. Adjusting a path in FreeHand is like painting over the same area on a canvas; it is a fine-tuning process.

This chapter examines how to *reshape* both geometric and free-form paths. To reshape a path is to alter the placement or identity of a point or segment within a single path. The adjustment of whole paths is discussed in Chapter 12, *Transforming and Duplicating Objects*.

Selecting elements

Before you may reshape a path, you must *select* one of more of its *elements*—a handle, a point, or just about any other small or large portion of an illustration. Selecting an element in FreeHand is not unlike selecting an element in some other object-oriented program on the Macintosh. Merely position your arrow tool cursor over part of an image and click. Points or corner handles display to indicate that the next action you perform will affect the selected element.

Selecting a path

Like most manipulations covered in this chapter, selecting is performed with the *arrow tool* (also called the *selection tool* or the *pointer tool*), the first tool in the toolbox. Clicking on a point or segment with any arrow tool selects the path containing that point or segment.

Different kinds of paths have different ways of showing that they are selected. For example, if you click on a geometric path, such as a rectangle or ellipse, four small black *corner handles* surround the shape, as demonstrated in Figure 7.01, signifying that these are *grouped objects* that may be subject to special manipulations, as described in the section *Reshaping geometric paths*, later in this chapter.

When you click on a free-form path, all points in the path are displayed as small black squares, as shown in Figure 7.02. This indicates that the path is selected, but the individual points in the path are deselected. Any manipulation you perform will affect all elements in the path equally. To select a specific point in a path, first select the path, then click directly on the desired point. A selected point appears as a small hollow square, as shown in Figure 7.03 on page 188. All Bézier control handles associated with the selected point and the two neighboring segments also display. Other deselected points in the path appear as small black squares.

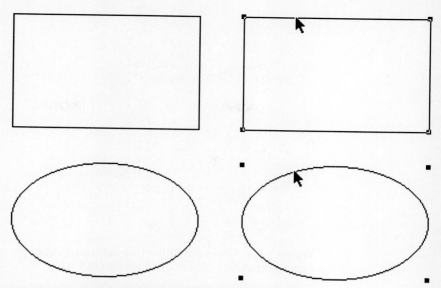

Figure 7.01: A rectangle and ellipse, each shown as it appears when deselected (left) and after selecting it with the arrow tool (right).

Figure 7.02: Normally invisible (left), the points in a free-form path may be displayed by selecting the path with the arrow tool (right).

To select multiple points in a selected path, click on the first point you want to select, then press SHIFT and click on each additional point.

Figure 7.03: After selecting a free-form path, you can
select a specific point in the path by clicking on it.

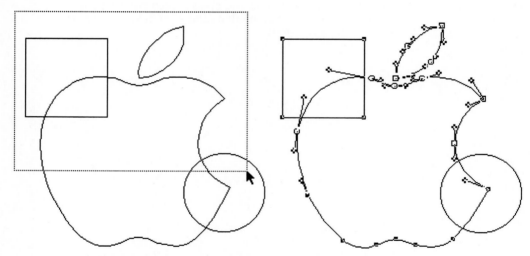

Figure 7.04: All points surrounded by a marquee (left)
become selected (right). A geometric path or other group
must be entirely surrounded to be selected.

Another way to select multiple elements is too *marquee* them. Drag
at an empty portion of your screen to create a rectangular marquee with a
dotted outline, as shown in the first example of Figure 7.04. One corner

of the marquee is positioned at the location at which you begin to drag; the opposite corner follows the movements of your cursor as you drag. All points within the marquee that belong to free-form paths will become selected when you release your mouse button. To select a grouped object, such as a geometric path, the entire group must be surrounded by the marquee. Notice in the second example of Figure 7.04 that the square is selected, but the circle is not. The square was entirely marqueed; the circle was only partially marqueed.

KE Marqueeing is possibly the most convenient means for selecting multiple elements. However, marqueeing selects not only paths, but also their points. If you want to manipulate whole paths and speed up the screen display, press the TILDE key (~) to deselect specific points while leaving all selected paths selected.

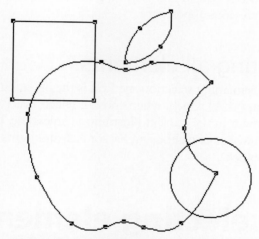

Figure 7.05: The paths from the second example in the previous figure as they appear after pressing the tilde key. The paths remain selected, but the all points are deselected.

Marqueeing may be combined with SHIFT-clicking to select multiple paths and elements. You may also marquee while pressing SHIFT, thereby adding the marqueed elements to an existing set of selected elements.

These and other ways to select elements with the arrow tool are summarized in the following list:

- Click on an element to select that element and deselect the previous selection.

- Drag on an empty portion of the drawing area to create a marquee. All points and groups inside the marquee become selected, and the previous selection becomes deselected.

- Press SHIFT and click or marquee deselected elements to add them to the current selection. (If you SHIFT-click or SHIFT-marquee an element that is already selected, it will become deselected, as described in the following section, *Deselecting elements*.)

 To temporarily access the arrow tool at any time, press and hold the COMMAND key. Releasing COMMAND returns the cursor to its previous appearance.

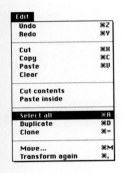

Selecting all elements

The only remaining selection method is the SELECT ALL command in the EDIT menu (⌘-A) which, when chosen, selects every point, group, and other element in the current illustration (unless the TEXT dialog box is displayed, in which case choosing SELECT ALL highlights all text in the current text block).

Deselecting elements

Sometimes you will want to *deselect* elements to prevent them from being affected by a command or mouse operation. To deselect all elements, simply click with the arrow tool on an empty portion of the drawing area.

 If an empty portion of the drawing area is not available—that is, the entire window is filled with images—press the TAB key to deselect all elements in the current illustration.

All currently selected elements will also deselect when you perform any one of the following items:

- Select an element that was not previously selected by clicking on it with the arrow tool.

- Click or drag with one of the geometric path tools.

- Click or drag with a free-form drawing tool (line, freehand, corner, curve, connector, or pen) on an empty portion of the drawing area.

- Marquee an image with the trace tool.

- Click or drag with the type tool.

- Choose the PLACE... command from the FILE menu.

- Choose PASTE (⌘-V), DUPLICATE (⌘-D), or CLONE (⌘-=, COMMAND-EQUAL) from the EDIT menu.

Deselecting individual elements

You don't have to deselect every element in an illustration. You may also deselect specific elements without affecting other selected elements.

To deselect a single selected element, such as a point, SHIFT-click on it with the arrow tool. To deselect an entire path, SHIFT-click on any segment in the path with the arrow tool.

Also, any selected elements that are surrounded by a marquee when pressing the SHIFT key will be deselected. You may not, however, deselect entire free-form paths by SHIFT-marqueeing.

Reshaping geometric paths

Try this little experiment: Draw a rectangle with the rectangle tool. The shape and size doesn't matter. Now select the arrow tool and try to select a specific point in the shape.

Can't do it, huh? When you click a point, is does not become hollow, as it would in a free-form path. If you SHIFT-click a point, the entire rectangle becomes deselected. That's because all geometric shapes—rectangles, rectangles with rounded corners, and ellipses—are created as *grouped objects*, also called simply *groups*. All elements in a group are fused into a single object, locking points into relative alignment so the path cannot be reshaped.

Using handles

Grouped geometric paths are not necessarily immutable. The easiest way to alter a geometric shape is to *scale* it—change its size—by dragging at one of its four corner handles. As shown in Figure 7.06, the shape's original size and form is displayed during the drag for reference. The center point for the shape's current size displays as an ×, allowing you to more precisely align the shape with other objects in the drawing area.

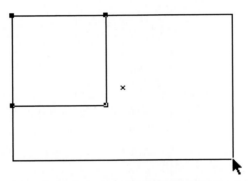

Figure 7.06: Scale a geometric path by dragging one of its corner handles with the arrow tool.

If you OPTION-drag a corner handle, you will scale the path with respect to its center point, as demonstrated in Figure 7.07. Press SHIFT while dragging to constrain a rectangle to a square or an ellipse to a circle. Press both SHIFT and OPTION while dragging to scale the square or circle with respect to its center point.

 After beginning to SHIFT-drag a corner handle, but before releasing the mouse button, press CONTROL to scale a geometric path exclusively horizontally or vertically. Press CONTROL while SHIFT-OPTION-dragging to scale the path about its center point.

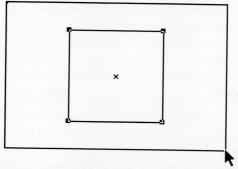

Figure 7.07: Scale a geometric path about its center point by option-dragging a corner handle with the arrow tool.

 To scale a rectangle or ellipse *proportionally*—that is, to maintain a constant ratio between height and width—SHIFT-drag with the scale tool as described in the section *Scaling objects* in Chapter 12.

Rectangle info

One of the most basic ways to manipulate any element in FreeHand is to choose ELEMENT INFO… from the ELEMENT menu (⌘-I). This brings up a dialog box customized for the kind of element that you have selected.

 You may also initiate the ELEMENT INFO… command by OPTION-double-clicking any segment or handle in a geometric path with the arrow tool.

If you select a rectangle and choose ELEMENT INFO…, the RECTANGLE dialog box will display, as shown in Figure 7.08. This dialog box contains options specifically applicable to rectangles and squares.

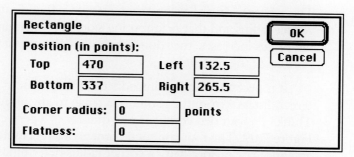

Figure 7.08: Press option and double-click a rectangle to display the Rectangle dialog box.

The four "Position" option boxes display the location of the four sides of the shape in relation to the *ruler origin*; that is, the location at which the horizontal and vertical coordinates are 0, as discussed in the section *Using the rulers* in Chapter 12. By default, the ruler origin is positioned at the lower left corner of the page size.

Notice that the "Position" header in Figure 7.08 is followed by the message "(in points)." This refers to the unit of measure for the current illustration, which is determined using the "Unit of measure" option in the DOCUMENT SETUP dialog box (discussed in Chapter 3, in the section *Setting up the illustration*). Instead of points, the unit of measure may be picas, inches, decimal inches, or millimeters, depending on your personal preference.

✳ When entering values for the "Position" options, you may override the current unit of measure by adding the following abbreviations: *i* for inch, *m* for millimeter, and *p* for pica, with any value following *p* indicating points. (Forgive us for repeating the tip from page 65, but it's so good, we felt obliged to say it twice.)

You may modify the "Position" options to alter the height or width of the selected rectangle. To determine the height, subtract the "Bottom" value from the "Top" value; to figure the width, subtract the "Left" value from the "Right." You may also make precise movements to the selected rectangle by adding or subtracting equal amounts to both the "Top" and "Bottom" values and the "Left" and "Right" values, respectively.

Corner radius

The next option in the RECTANGLE dialog box, "Corner radius," allows you to alter the extent to which the corners of a rectangle are rounded. The *corner radius* of a standard rectangle is 0, indicating that there is no corner radius and that neighboring sides meet perpendicularly. As the corner radius increases, the rounded corner consumes a larger and larger portion of the rectangle.

It is necessary here to introduce a little geometry. The *radius* is the direct distance from the center of a circle to any point on its outline. Think of a rounded corner as one quarter of a perfect circle, as shown in Figure 7.09. The four rounded corners of a rectangle therefore make up an entire circle. Specifying a corner radius determines the radius of this circle. Since the size of the circle will increase as the radius increases, a rounded corner with a large radius consumes more of a rectangle than a rounded corner with a small radius. Notice how the rounded corner displayed in Figure 7.10 occupies a larger space than the corner in Figure 7.09. This is because the value for its corner radius is larger. The radius arrows from Figure 7.09 are superimposed on those of Figure 7.10 to demonstrate this difference.

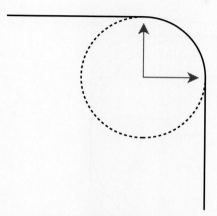

Figure 7.09: The corner of a rounded rectangle is actually a quarter circle. Arrows represent its radius.

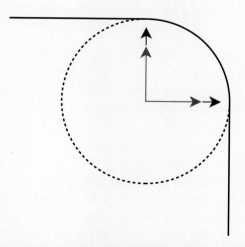

Figure 7.10: An enlarged corner radius with the smaller corner radius superimposed.

A radius of a circle is half the circle's total width, which is called the *diameter*. If the diameter of a rounded corner is at least equal to the longest side of a rectangle—that is, if the radius is at least *half* the longest side of a rectangle—then the rounded corner will consume the entire rectangle. Figure 7.11, for example, shows a series of inset squares, each with a larger corner radius than that of its predecessor. Eventually, the radius of a round corner becomes so large that the corner takes over the square, resulting in a circle.

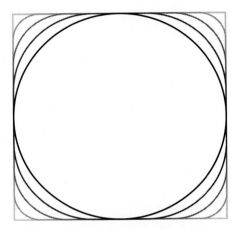

Figure 7.11: The largest of rounded corners will completely consume a rectangle and will result in a circle.

To change the corner radius of a selected rectangle, enter a new value into the "Corner radius" option of the RECTANGLE dialog box. Like the "Position" options, the "Corner radius" value is subject to the current unit of measure. The default radius for a rounded corner is 14 points.

Flatness

The final option in the RECTANGLE dialog box, "Flatness," has less to do with reshaping a path and more to do with printing it, specifically to a PostScript output device, such as a LaserWriter or Linotronic. PostScript printers imitate curves as a collection of hundreds or even thousands of tiny, straight lines. The "Flatness" option determines the greatest distance, in device pixels, that any of these lines many stray. Enter any number between 0 and 100 for this option. Higher values allow fewer straight lines, and therefore result in more jagged curves. Leave this option as 0 unless you experience problems printing the current illustration. See the *Splitting long paths* section of Chapter 14 for complete information.

Oval info

If you select an ellipse with the arrow tool and choose ELEMENT INFO... from the ELEMENT menu (⌘-I, ⬱-➘➘), the ELLIPSE dialog box will display, as shown in Figure 7.12. Like the RECTANGLE dialog box, the ELLIPSE dialog box provides four "Position" options for relocating the sides of the selected ellipse with respect to the ruler origin and a "Flatness" option for modifying the printed appearance of the shape. See the previous sections for details about these options.

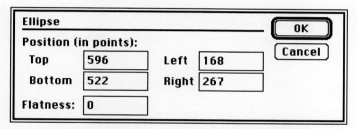

Figure 7.12: Press option and double-click an ellipse to display the Ellipse dialog box.

 FreeHand cannot communicate information for more than one element at a time. Therefore, the ELEMENT INFO... command is dimmed if more than one element is selected.

Ungrouping geometric shapes

As described in the preceding pages, FreeHand provides a number of ways to modify geometric paths. But none of these methods allows you to move one point in a path independently of its neighbors. The only way to truly reshape a geometric path is to ungroup it by selecting it and choosing the UNGROUP command from the ELEMENT menu (⌘-U). Ungrouping frees the points in a geometric path so they can be manipulated independently, just like points in a free-form path. Figure 7.13 on the next page shows the effect of ungrouping each of three geometric shapes.

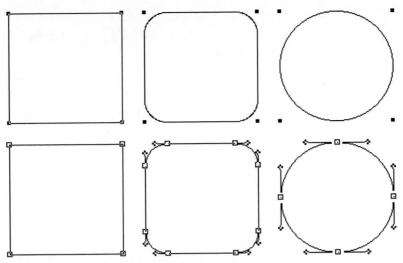

Figure 7.13: Three geometric paths before (top) and after (bottom) choosing the Ungroup command. All points in the ungrouped paths have been selected to display Bézier control handles.

When you ungroup a path, its corner handles and center point disappear, and you gain access to points, segments, and Bézier control handles. Notice that in Figure 7.13 all selected points are hollow squares, indicating that they are corner points. This provides greater flexibility in reshaping the paths, as we will see in later sections.

A few words of warning: Once a geometric path is ungrouped, you can never again access the RECTANGLE or ELLIPSE dialog box for that path (not even if you regroup the path by choosing the GROUP command), unless you choose UNDO UNGROUP from the EDIT menu (⌘-Z) immediately after ungrouping the path. In the case of an ellipse, ungrouping is not much of an issue, since the ELLIPSE dialog box does not provide any unique options. But you should pause before ungrouping a rectangle. The RECTANGLE dialog box is the only place you may access the "Corner radius" option. FreeHand provides no means for numerically adjusting the corner radius of an ungrouped rectangle. You must either reshape the rectangle, as described throughout the remainder of this chapter, or recreate it.

Also, you may not scale an ungrouped path by dragging at its corner; you must instead use the scale tool as described in Chapter 12, in the section *Scale tool*.

Moving elements

The most common method for reshaping a path is to move some element in the path. FreeHand allows you to move selected points independently of deselected points in a path. You may also reshape a segment by moving the Bézier control handles associated with the segment, thus altering the curvature of a path. The next few pages explain all aspects of moving and dragging elements in Aldus FreeHand.

Moving points

To move one or more points in a path, select the points you want to move and drag one of the selected points. All selected points will move the same distance and direction. When you move a point while a neighboring point remains stationary, the segment between the two points shrinks or stretches in length to accommodate the change in distance, as displayed in Figure 7.14. If a point has any Bézier control handles, the handles move with the point. Thus, a curved segment must not only shrink or stretch, but also bend, to accommodate the movement of a point. Segments located between two deselected points or two selected points remain unchanged during a move, as demonstrated in Figure 7.15 on the following page.

Figure 7.14: Dragging the selected point on left stretches the segments between the point and its deselected, stationary neighbors, as shown on right.

Figure 7.15: Dragging at any selected point in a shape (left) moves all selected points an identical distance and direction (right). Notice that any segment bordered on both sides by selected points is not reshaped.

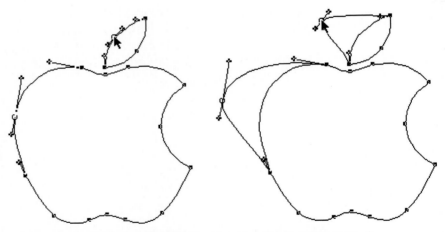

Figure 7.16: You may even move multiple points when selected points reside in different paths.

When moving an element, FreeHand displays both its previous and current locations. As demonstrated in Figures 7.14 through 7.16, this useful feature allows you to gauge the full effect of a move as it progresses.

Constrained movements

To constrain the movement of selected points to an angle that is a multiple of 45°, press the SHIFT key after beginning your drag and hold the key down until after you release the mouse button. (If you press and hold SHIFT before beginning your drag, you will deselect the selected point on which you click.) Horizontal, vertical, and diagonal movements are all multiples of 45°.

The effects of pressing the SHIFT key may be altered by rotating the *constraint axes*. This is accomplished using the CONSTRAIN dialog box (see Figure 7.17), which is displayed by choosing the CONSTRAIN... command from the ELEMENT menu.

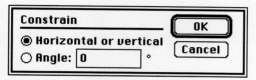

Figure 7.17: The Constrain dialog box permits you to rotate the horizontal and vertical constraint axes.

The constraint axes, displayed in Figure 7.18 on the following page, specifies the eight directions in which an element may be moved. By default, these directions include the following:

- Right (0°)
- Diagonally up and to the right (45°)
- Straight up (90°)
- Diagonally up and to the left (135°)
- Left (180°)
- Diagonally down and to the left (225° or –135°)
- Straight down (270° or –90°)
- Diagonally down and to the right (315° or –45°).

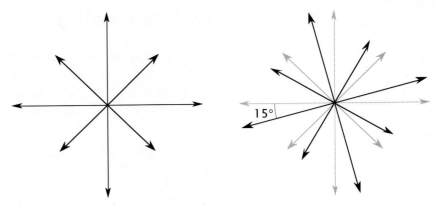

Figure 7.18: The default constraint axes (left) and the axes as they appear when rotated 15° (right).

Each direction differs from its neighbor by an angle of 45°. By entering a number between –360 and 360 for the "Angle" option in the CONSTRAIN dialog box, you may rotate the contraint axes. The second example in Figure 7.18 displays the effect of rotating the axes 15°. If you were to SHIFT-drag an element under these conditions, your movements will be constrained to a direction of 15°, 60°, 105°, 150°, 195° (–165°), 240° (–120°), 285° (–75°), or 330° (–30°). Horizontal and vertical SHIFT-dragging will not be possible until you return the "Angle" value to 0 (or select the "Horizontal or vertical" radio button).

Exercise caution when altering the "Constrain angle" option, since it also affects the creation of geometric paths, as explained in the section *Geometric paths at an angle* in Chapter 5.

Snapping

While dragging an element, you may find that it has a tendency to move sharply toward another element. Called *snapping*, this effect is one of FreeHand's ways of ensuring that elements belonging together are positioned flush against each other to form a perfect fit. When you drag an element within 1 to 5 pixels of any point on your drawing area (as determined using the "Snap-to distance" option in the MORE PREFERENCES dialog box), your cursor will snap to the point, so that both point and cursor occupy an identical horizontal and vertical location.

There may be times when you'll want to snap a point in one path to a point in another, as shown in Figure 7.19. However, if you drag at a point in a selected free-form path, only that point will move. To move the entire path, either 1) select all points in the path prior to dragging at a point or 2) CONTROL-drag at a point in a selected path.

Figure 7.19: Your cursor is attracted to stationary points when the Snap to point command is active.

Your cursor will snap to stationary points as well as to the previous locations of points that are currently being moved. Snapping also occurs in proximity to text block handles and to points in geometric paths (even if the points are invisible because the paths have not been ungrouped).

FreeHand's snapping feature may be turned on and off by choosing the SNAP TO POINT command from the VIEW menu (⌘-', COMMAND-QUOTE). A check mark precedes the command when the feature is active.

The interval at which a dragged object will snap toward a stationary point may be altered by entering a new value into the "Snap-to distance" option in the MORE PREFERENCES dialog box (introduced in the *Setting preferences* section of Chapter 3). Any value between 1 and 5 is permitted, as measured in screen pixels. The default value is 3.

Using arrow keys

Another way to move a selected element is to press one of the four arrow keys (↑, ←, ↓, →). Each arrow key moves a selection in the direction of the arrow. The → key, for example, moves the selection to the right.

The distance by which a single keystroke moves a selected element is determined by specifying a "Cursor key distance" value in the MORE PREFERENCES dialog box, as introduced in the *Setting preferences* section of Chapter 3. The value that you enter is measured in points, picas, inches, or millimeters, depending on the current unit of measure specified in the DOCUMENT SETUP dialog box.

Arrow keys can be used to move points and whole paths. Arrow keys may not be used to move a specific Bézier control handle (as described in the *Dragging Bézier control handles* section later in this chapter).

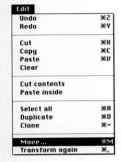

Using the Move elements dialog box

You may also specify the movement of a selected element numerically, via the MOVE ELEMENTS dialog box, which is shown in Figure 7.20 and is accessed by choosing the MOVE... command from the EDIT menu (⌘-M). To use the MOVE ELEMENTS dialog, enter values for each of the "Offset" options. These values represent distances which are measured in points, picas, inches, or millimeters, depending on the currently selected "Unit of measure" option in the DOCUMENT SETUP dialog box.

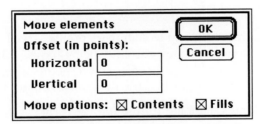

Figure 7.20: The Move elements dialog box allows you to specify a horizontal and vertical distance by which to move one or more selected elements.

Use the "Horizontal" and "Vertical" options as follows:

- Enter a positive "Horizontal" value to move the selection to the right.
- Enter a negative "Horizontal" value to move the selection to the left.
- Enter a positive "Vertical" value to move the selection upward.
- Enter a negative "Vertical" value to move the selection downward.
- Enter 0 in the "Horizontal" option to specify a purely vertical move.
- Enter 0 in the "Vertical" option to specify a purely horizontal move.

If a path in the current selection serves as a clipping path, select the "Contents" option to move the masking elements along with the selection. Select "Fills" to move tile patterns with an object. (Clipping paths and tile patterns, as well as the "Contents" and "Fills" options, are discussed in Chapter 9, *Filling Type and Graphic Objects*.)

⊛ The MOVE dialog box also acts as a recorder: After moving an element by hand, you may choose the MOVE... command to display the numerical increments of this previous move. This allows you to exactly repeat the most recent move in the current session, regardless of how long ago the move was made.

Dragging Bézier control handles

The only element that we have neglected to move so far is the Bézier control handle. We save it until last because it is the most difficult element to manipulate. So far, we have only introduced and briefly discussed the qualities of Bézier control handles, the elements that control the arc of a segment as it exits or enters a point. Regardless of the identity of its point, a Bézier control handle may be moved in much the same way that a point may be moved. To display a Bézier control handle, select the point to which the handle belongs. Then drag the handle you wish to move. Bézier control handles may only be moved with the mouse; they cannot be moved using an arrow key or the MOVE ELEMENTS dialog box.

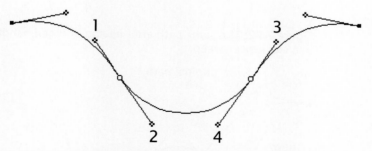

Figure 7.21: A path composed of four curve points, two of which are selected to display their Bézier control handles.

Figures 7.21 through 7.25 feature four curve points. Each point in each figure is located in the exact same position as its counterpart in the other figures. From one figure to the next, only the numbered Bézier control handles have been moved. However, these simple adjustments have a dramatic impact on the appearance of each path. The affected handles have been numbered to show the exact manner in which a handle is relocated from figure to figure. For the record, handle number 1 controls the left segment, handles 2 and 4 control the middle segment, and handle 3 controls the right segment.

When one Bézier control handle for a curve point is moved, the other handle for that point moves in the opposite direction. Hence, the two handles of a curve point form a constant lever. Compare Figure 7.22 below with Figure 7.21 on the preceding page. In Figure 7.22, handles 3 and 4 have been moved only slightly. Handles 1 and 2, however, have been moved dramatically. Handle 1 was dragged in a clockwise sweep, sending handle 2 upward. Figure 7.23 shows the path as it appears during the drag. A gray line representing the motion of the drag has been inserted to clarify the figure.

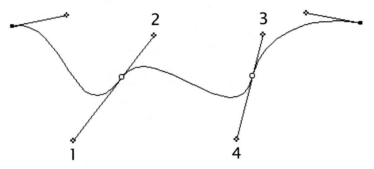

Figure 7.22: The same path after having dragged handle 1 in a clockwise sweep.

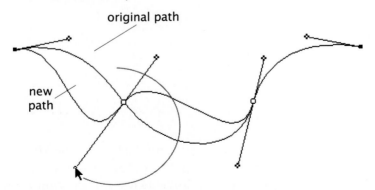

Figure 7.23: The act of dragging handle 1, shown in progress.

In Figure 7.22, handle 2 forces the center segment to ascend as it exits the left curve point. But because of handle 4, the segment also ascends as it enters the right curve point. So somewhere between the two points, the segment has to change direction. Handles 2 and 4 pull at the beginning and at the end of the segment, respectively. The farther the handles are moved from the center segment and from each other, the more desperately the segment stretches to keep up, as shown in Figure 7.24. Here, both handles 2 and 4 have been moved far away from each other. The result is a segment that bulges out in three directions—left, right, and downward.

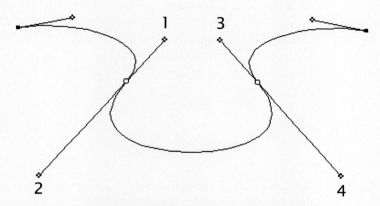

Figure 7.24: Dragging handles 2 and 4 far away from each other forces the center segment to bulge outward.

The final example, shown in Figure 7.25 on the next page, shows that there is basically no limitation to how far you may drag a Bézier control handle from its point, nor to how severely you may stretch a curved segment. The segment will always stretch to keep up, turning around only when necessary to meet the demands of the opposite point and its Bézier control handle.

However, dragging Bézier control handles is not so much a question of what can you do as when you should do it. One of the most common problems users have when learning to use Aldus FreeHand is trying to determine the placement of Bézier control handles. Several rules have been developed over the years, but the best are the *all-or-nothing rule* and the *30% rule*. The all-or-nothing rule states that every segment in your path should be associated with either two Bézier control handles or none at all.

In other words, no segment should rely on only one control handle to determine its curvature. In the 30% rule, the distance from any Bézier control handle to its point should be approximately 30% the length of the segment.

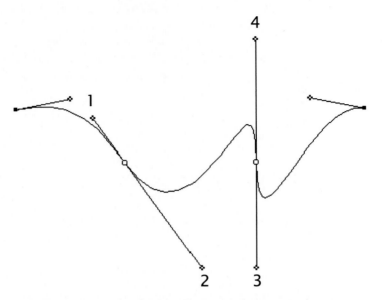

Figure 7.25: There is no limit to the extent that you may drag a handle or stretch a segment.

The top path in Figure 7.26 violates the all-or-nothing rule. Its two curved segments are controlled by only one handle apiece, resulting in weak, shallow arcs. Such curves are to be avoided at all costs. The second example obeys the all-or-nothing rule. As the rule states, its straight segment is associated with no handle and both curved segments have two handles apiece. The result is a full-figured, properly pumped-up dome, a credit to any illustration.

The first path in Figure 7.27 violates the 30% rule. The handles for the central point are much too long, about 60% the length of their segments, and the two outer handles are too short, about 15% the length of their segments. The result is an ugly, misshapen mess. In the second example, the two handles belonging to the left segment each take up about 30% of the length of the segment. The right segment is shorter, so its handles are shorter as well. The curvature of this path is smooth and consistent, giving the path a naturalistic appearance.

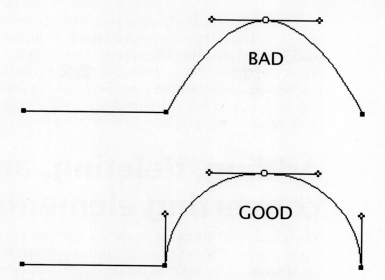

Figure 7.26: The all-or-nothing rule states that every curved segment should be controlled by two handles, one for each of its points.

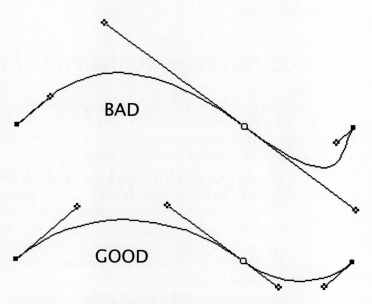

Figure 7.27: The 30% rule states that every Bézier control handle should extend about 30% the length of its segment.

Moving points and adjusting control handles are fundamental ways to change the shape of a path. But sometimes, no matter how much time you spend adjusting the placement of its points or the curvature of its segments, a path fails to meet the requirements of your illustration. In such a case, you may want to expand the path by adding points, or simplify the path by deleting points.

Adding, deleting, and converting elements

The quantity and identity of points and segments in a path is forever subject to change. Whether closed or open, a path may be reshaped by adding, deleting, and converting points. In turn, adding or deleting a point forces the addition or deletion of a segment. The conversion of a point, from corner to curve or from curve to corner, frequently converts a segment, from curved to straight or from straight to curved. The following pages describe how all these reshaping techniques may be applied to any existing path.

Adding points to the end of a path

As discussed in Chapter 5, *Drawing Paths from Scratch*, a point associated with less than two segments is open-ended. Such a point is always located at one end or the other of a line. For this reason, an open-ended point is called an *endpoint*. An open path always has two endpoints. A closed path contains no endpoint, since each point in a shape is connected to another.

An active endpoint is waiting for a segment to be drawn from it. To *activate* an endpoint in a passive path so that a new segment may be drawn from it, select it with the arrow tool. Then, you may click or drag anywhere else on your screen with any of the four point tools—corner, curve, connector, or pen—to create a segment between the selected endpoint and the newly created point. Following this, your original endpoint will be bound by segments on both sides, no longer an endpoint. It must relinquish this title to the newest point in the line.

You can also use this technique to close an existing path. Just select one endpoint, then click on the remaining endpoint with any point tool. A segment is drawn between the two endpoints, closing the path to form a shape and eliminating both endpoints by converting them to interior points. This brings up an interesting question: What happens if you close a path by clicking an endpoint with a tool other than the one used to create it? For example, if you click a corner point with the curve tool, does the point remain a corner point, convert to a curve point, or change to some other kind of point? The answer: It remains a corner point. A closing point retains its original identity if you click on it with the corner, curve, or connector tool. Only the pen tool may be used to convert an endpoint as you close a path, as described below:

- Click on a closing point to make it a corner point.

- Drag on a closing point to change it to a curve point.

- Drag on a closing point and press OPTION before completing the drag to change the point to a corner point with two independent Bézier control handles.

- Press OPTION and drag on a closing point to change it to a corner point with only one Bézier control handle.

You may also lengthen an open path by drawing from one of its endpoints with the freehand tool. To close a path, drag from one endpoint to the other. To close a path with a straight segment, OPTION-drag from one endpoint to the other with the freehand tool.

Adding points within a path

We have demonstrated how you may add points to the end of an existing line. But sometimes you may wish to add points in the middle of a path. In FreeHand, this procedure has been made extremely convenient and may be accomplished using any of the four point tools.

First, select the path to which you wish to add a point. Then click with the corner, curve, or connector tool on some segment in the path. A new corner, curve, or connector point will appear at this location, according to the tool used. The segment to which the point was added is broken into two segments.

You may also use the pen tool to insert points in a path. Click on an existing segment to insert a corner point; drag on a segment to insert a curve point. Dragging with the pen tool allows you to determine the precise placement of Bézier control handles.

Suppose that you want to change an ordinary, ungrouped circle composed of four curve points into a crescent. This may be accomplished by adding points within the path. The following steps describe one way to perform this task:

1. Select the path. Press 8 to select the curve tool, then click at a similar location on each of the right-hand segments. Both inserted points appear as selected in Figure 7.28.

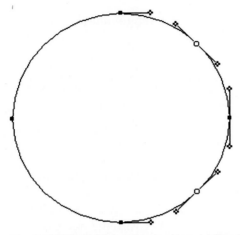

Figure 7.28: Add a point in the middle of each of the right-hand segments of an ungrouped circle.

2. Press and hold the COMMAND key to access the arrow tool. Drag at the rightmost point, moving it toward the center of the shape, as shown in Figure 7.29.

3. Release COMMAND to redisplay the curve tool cursor. Click in the middle of each of the two segments between the crescent tips and the dragged point. The new points are displayed as selected in Figure 7.30.

4. Finally, move the most recently created points outward from the center of the shape, as shown in the first example in Figure 7.31 on page 214. The Bézier control handles of the point at the center of the mouth will require some adjustment as well.

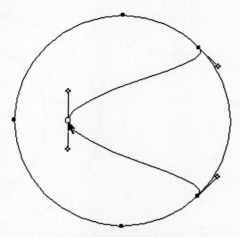

Figure 7.29: Drag the rightmost point toward the center of the shape.

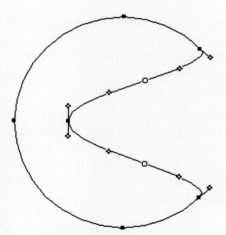

Figure 7.30: Add a point to the middle of each of the segments forming the mouth of the shape.

The completed image is displayed on the right side of Figure 7.31 on the next page.

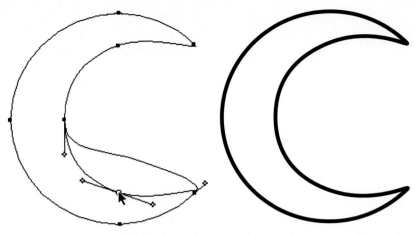

Figure 7.31: Drag the most recent points into position. The completed image is shown on right as it appears when printed from FreeHand.

You may click with a point tool on a segment in any selected ungrouped path. You may also insert points into a grouped or composite path, provided that the points in the path have been displayed by OPTION-clicking on the path with the arrow tool (as described in the section *Selecting elements within groups* in Chapter 12).

Also, although it is possible, we do not recommend clicking with a point tool directly on a point in a selected path. A new point will be created and it will be a member of the selected path, but it will be located directly in front of the previous point. It is unlikely you will want two points in the same path to be positioned in such close proximity, and you may have to zoom in to separate them.

Adding Bézier control handles

If you want to bend an existing straight segment, or if a curved segment doesn't curve sufficiently, you may want to add a Bézier control handle to a neighboring point. FreeHand allows you to add control handles to either a corner point or a connector point long after the point has been created. You may not add a Bézier control handle to an existing curve point or to any other point that already has two control handles.

To add a control handle, select the desired point and OPTION-drag from the point with the arrow tool. The segment affected by the new control handle depends on the following criteria:

- If no control handle yet exists for the point, the new control handle will affect the more recent of the two neighboring segments.

- If one control handle already exists for the point, the new control handle will affect the opposite segment.

- If two control handles already exist for the current point, OPTION-dragging simply moves the point to a new position.

It is not always possible to predict which of two neighboring segments will be affected when adding a Bézier control handle, since there is no way to determine the direction of an existing path (unless you happen to remember how you drew it). We can only suggest that you adopt a trial-and-error attitude when OPTION-dragging a point.

If the first control handle does not affect the desired segment, OPTION-drag the point again to produce another control handle. This second handle will necessarily be the one you want, since no more than two control handles may exist for a point. Finally, delete the unwanted handle by dragging it back to the point until it snaps in place. (This technique is described in *Retracting Bézier control handles*, later in this chapter.)

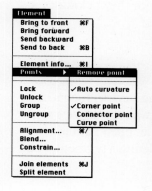

Deleting points from a path

The simplest way to delete a point is to select the point and press either BACKSPACE or DELETE. You may also choose the "Remove point" option from the pop-up menu that displays when you choose the POINTS command from the ELEMENT menu. The selected point will disappear, as will the two segments associated with the point. To prevent a gap in outline of the path, FreeHand connects the two points that neighbored the deleted point with a new segment, as shown in the second example of Figure 7.32 on the next page.

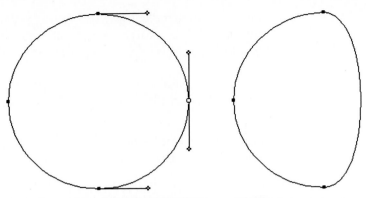

Figure 7.32: Selecting an interior point (left) and pressing the delete key deletes the point but retains a segment (right).

The first example in Figure 7.32 shows the familiar ungrouped circle path with the right point selected. The second example shows the path after pressing the DELETE key. The two segments surrounding the deleted point are fused into a single segment, the curvature of which is determined by the remaining points in the path. The result is a path that remains closed and selected, although all points are deselected.

If you delete an endpoint from an open path, you delete the single segment associated with the point. No new segment is drawn in its place. Also, the new endpoint in the path becomes selected, allowing you to extend the path using the freehand tool or the point tools, or to shorten the path by deleting additional endpoints.

Multiple points may also be deleted, whether or not they belong to the same path.

Deleting a segment

FreeHand maintains the integrity of a path by drawing new segments in place of deleted ones. However, sometimes you may want to delete a segment entirely, either to open a closed path or to split an open path in two. Although FreeHand provides no direct means for deleting a segment, you may do so by following these steps:

1. Select the path that you want to open or split.

2. Press 7 to select the knife tool.

3. Click on the segment that you want to delete, as shown in the first example of Figure 7.33. You have now split the segment and inserted two endpoints into the path.

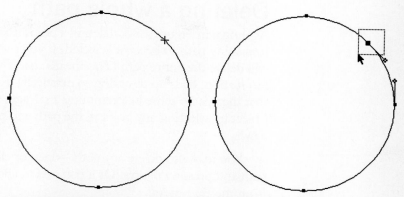

Figure 7.33: Click on a segment with the knife tool (left) to split the segment and insert two endpoints (right).

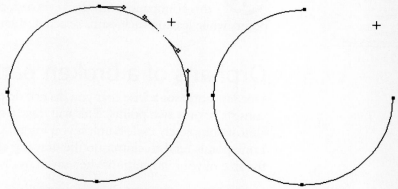

Figure 7.34: After selecting the two coincident points (left), press the delete key to open the path.

4. To ensure that both new endpoints are selected, press COMMAND to access the arrow tool and marquee the points, as shown in the second example of Figure 7.33. Because the selected points overlap, they disappear, as shown in the first example of Figure 7.34.

5. Press DELETE or choose the "Remove point" option. Both points will disappear, as shown in the second example, leaving a break in the outline of the path.

For a complete discussion of the knife tool, see the section *Splitting an element*, later in this chapter.

Deleting a whole path

As shown in Figure 7.32, deleting a point from a closed path causes the remaining path to become selected. If you press DELETE a second time, you will delete the entire path. This means that if a closed path, in the course of its creation, ends up deviating so drastically from your original intention that there is no sense in attempting a salvage, you may delete the entire object by selecting any point in the path and pressing DELETE twice in a row.

You may also delete any path—open or closed—by selecting the entire path and pressing DELETE. Or if you prefer, choose the CLEAR command from the EDIT menu.

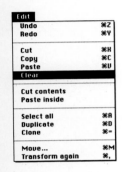

 The CLEAR command deletes entire selected paths, whether or not one or more points in the path are also selected. To perform this command from the keyboard, press TILDE (~) to deselect all points while leaving their paths selected, then press DELETE.

Orphans of a broken path

One last note: we advise that you do not delete a point from a line that consists of only two points. This will leave a single-point path, which is almost completely useless unless you intend to build on it immediately. Lone points tend to clutter up the drawing area and needlessly increase the size of your illustration when saved to disk.

Retracting Bézier control handles

To put away, or *retract*, a Bézier control handle, drag the control handle back to its point and release. If the SNAP TO POINT command is active (⌘-', COMMAND-QUOTE), the control handle will snap to its point as you retract it.

The first example in Figure 7.35 shows the arrow tool cursor positioned over the control handle belonging to the selected point in the lower left corner. In the second example, the control handle has been dragged back to its point. Notice that the lower segment is now straight, since it is no longer associated with any control handle.

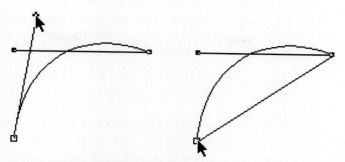

Figure 7.35: To retract a Bézier control handle for either a corner or connector point, drag the handle back to its point.

Generally, you will only want to put away Bézier control handles belonging to corner points or connector points. It is possible to put away handles belonging to curve points, but why do it? The seesaw lever of a curve point functions properly only if it includes two control handles.

Converting points

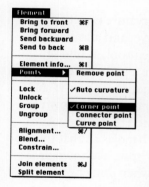

FreeHand allows you to change the identity of an interior point; that is, to convert any point within an existing path to a curve, corner, or connector point. All point conversions are performed using the "Corner point," "Connector point," and "Curve point" options, all of which are displayed by choosing the POINTS command from the ELEMENT menu.

If a single point is selected, a check mark will display in front of the corresponding option. For example, if a corner point is selected, a check mark will precede the "Corner point" option. If more than one point is selected, no check mark will display, even if all points share a common identity. If no point is selected, the POINTS command will be dimmed.

When you convert a point using one of the POINTS options, FreeHand automatically determines the quantity and position of any associated Bézier control handle, based on its definition of *automatic curvature*, as described in the following section.

Automatic curvature

When you create a point with any point tool except the pen tool, Free-Hand automatically determines the location of any Bézier control handle for the point. Called the *automatic curvature* of a point, this determination is based on both the identity and the location of the point with respect to the identities and locations of its immediate neighbors.

The number of Bézier control handles assigned to any point is determined according to two simple rules:

- A point created with either the corner or connector tool is given one control handle for each neighboring curve point. No control handle is assigned neighboring corner and connector points.

- A point created with the curve tool is always assigned two symmetrical control handles, regardless of the identity or location of preceding and succeeding points.

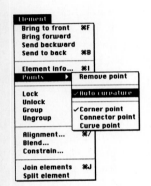

Anytime you move, add, or retract a Bézier control handle, the affected point deviates from FreeHand's perception of automatic curvature. To restore the control handles to their predetermined locations, choose the "Auto curvature" option from the Points pop-up in the Element menu.

Perhaps the best way to understand automatic curvature is to think of a line that is made up of three points—a corner, a curve, and another corner. Suppose that you draw this entire line with the pen tool, dragging the Bézier control handles of the curve point to create a path like the one shown in the first example of Figure 7.36. Now imagine that there is an center spot, equidistant from all three points. This center spot is shown in the figure as a small ×. If you select the curve point and choose the "Auto curvature" option, FreeHand will moves the control handles so that the path curves symmetrically about the imaginary center spot, as shown in the second example of Figure 7.36. In other words, when you choose "Auto curvature," FreeHand moves the control handles of selected curve points and their neighbors to mimic the perfect arc of a circle.

Once implemented, the rules of automatic curvature guide the manipulation of a point. The first example in Figure 7.37 shows the path from Figure 7.36 with all Bézier control handles displayed. Automatic curvature is in effect for all three points. If we move the curve point to the left, as shown in the second example, FreeHand will simultaneously reposition all control handles. In this way, we move a point and reshape its segments in a single operation.

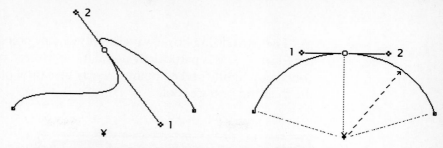

Figure 7.36: A curve point created with the pen tool (left) and subjected to automatic curvature (right).

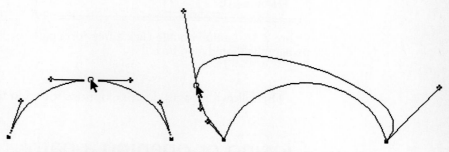

Figure 7.37: Dragging a point when automatic curvature is active simultaneously moves the point and reshapes its segments.

You may turn off automatic curvature for a selected point in one of two ways:

- Move at least one control handle for that point.

- Choose "Auto curvature" from the POINTS pop-up menu to deactivate the option (hide the check mark).

Free-form path info

If you want to make several changes at once, FreeHand provides a one-stop path manipulation dialog box. Choose ELEMENT INFO... from the ELEMENT menu (⌘-I) or OPTION-double-click a selected path to display the PATH dialog box shown in Figure 7.38 on the next page. This dialog applies to any free-form path—whether created with the line tool, freehand tool, one of the point tools, or the trace tool—as well as any ungrouped geometric path.

The Path dialog box always lists how many points reside in the selected path. This is particularly useful if the selected path is complicated, containing tightly packed points, as may be typical of a path created with the freehand or trace tool.

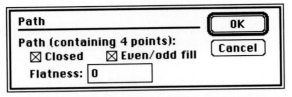

Figure 7.38: Option-double-click a free-form path to display the Path dialog box.

The following pages describe options found in the PATH dialog box.

Closing or opening a path

As you may remember from Chapter 4, *The Graphic Creation Process*, to *close* a path is to draw a segment from the last point in the path to the first so that no point remains open-ended; the resulting path is a shape. In turn, to *open* a path is to disconnect these points by eliminating the final segment; the resulting path is a line.

Selecting the "Closed" check box inserts a segment between the two endpoints of the selected path. The identities of the endpoints dictate the form of the new segment. Deselecting the "Closed" option opens the selected path by eliminating the segment between the first and last points, as determined by the order in which the points were created.

Even/odd fill

The "Even/odd fill" option controls the manner in which overlapping portions of a selected closed path are filled. This option is dimmed when the "Closed" option is deselected. For complete information, see the *Filling theory* section at the end of Chapter 9.

Flatness

The "Flatness" option controls the manner in which the selected path is printed to a PostScript output device, such as a LaserWriter or Linotronic. PostScript printers imitate curves as a collection of hundreds or even thousands of tiny, straight lines. The "Flatness" option determines the greatest distance, in device pixels, that any of these lines many stray. Enter any number between 0 and 100 for this option. Higher values allow fewer straight lines, and therefore result in more jagged curves. Leave this option set to 0 unless you experience problems printing the current illustration. For complete information, see *Splitting long paths* in Chapter 15.

Selected point options

If a single point in a path is selected when you choose the ELEMENT INFO… command (⌘-I, ⌥-♦♦), the PATH/POINT dialog box will display, as shown in Figure 7.39. This dialog box contains the aforementioned options, as well as a number of other options that affect the identity of the selected point and the locations of the point and its Bézier control handles.

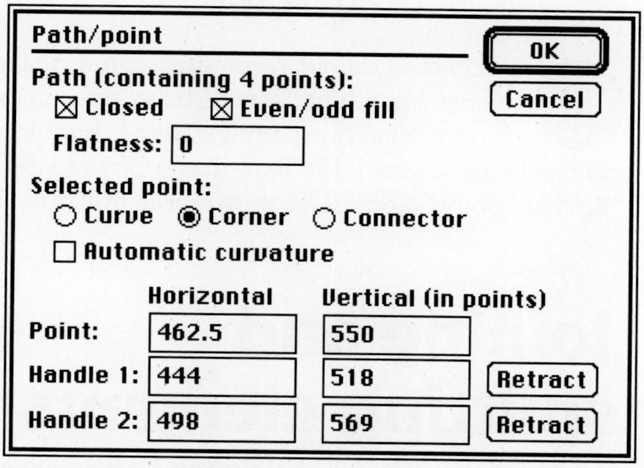

```
┌─────────────────────────────────────────────────┐
│ Path/point                        ┌─────────────┐│
│                                   │     OK      ││
│ Path (containing 4 points):       └─────────────┘│
│   ⊠ Closed      ⊠ Even/odd fill   ┌─────────────┐│
│                                   │   Cancel    ││
│   Flatness: │0          │         └─────────────┘│
│                                                  │
│ Selected point:                                  │
│   ○ Curve   ● Corner   ○ Connector               │
│   □ Automatic curvature                          │
│                                                  │
│           Horizontal    Vertical (in points)     │
│ Point:   │462.5    │   │550    │                  │
│                                                  │
│ Handle 1:│444      │   │518    │   [ Retract ]    │
│                                                  │
│ Handle 2:│498      │   │569    │   [ Retract ]    │
└─────────────────────────────────────────────────┘
```

Figure 7.39: Option-double-click a selected point in a free-form path to display the Path/point dialog box.

The "Selected point" options in the PATH/POINT dialog box include the following:

- **Curve, Corner, Connector**. Select any one of these radio buttons to convert the identity of the current point.

- **Automatic curvature**. Select this check box to subject the current point to the rules of automatic curvature, as described in the *Automatic curvature* section, earlier in this chapter.

- **Point**. Use the "Horizontal" and "Vertical" option boxes to reposition the current point with respect to the ruler origin. These values represent distances which are measured in points, picas, inches, or millimeters, depending on the currently selected "Unit of measure" option in the DOCUMENT SETUP dialog box.

- **Handle 1, Handle 2**. Use these options to determine the location of the Bézier control handles associated with the current point with respect to the ruler origin. Click the RETRACT button to drag the corresponding control handle back to the current point, as described in the *Retracting Bézier control handles* section earlier in this chapter. If the "Handle" values match the "Point" values, the handle has been retracted.

FreeHand cannot communicate information for more than one element at a time. The ELEMENT INFO... command is dimmed if more than one path is selected. If multiple points within the same path are selected, the PATH dialog box will display without the "Selected point" options, as shown back in Figure 7.38.

Joining and splitting elements

Many of the reshaping techniques we have described so far are available, in some form or another, in just about every drawing software for the Macintosh. MacDraw, for example, although providing no Bézier curve capacity, allows you to move elements, add and delete points, and convert straight segments to curved segments. Yet MacDraw is commonly considered too remedial for tackling a complex illustration. This section discusses two areas in which FreeHand stands heads above the common drawing crowd: the joining and splitting of points and segments. These features make it possible to break up portions of a path like pieces in a tailor-made puzzle, then assemble them in any way you see fit.

Joining endpoints in different paths

The JOIN ELEMENTS command in the ELEMENT menu (⌘-J) serves to combine various kinds of elements in FreeHand. First and foremost, this command may be used to join endpoints from two different open paths to form a single free-form line. If two endpoints from separate paths are *coincident*—that is, one point is positioned exactly on top of the other in the drawing area—the JOIN ELEMENTS command will fuse the two into a single interior point.

Joining open paths is a three-step process:

1. Drag one endpoint onto another with the arrow tool so the two points are coincident. The points will snap together if the SNAP TO POINT command is active (⌘-', COMMAND-QUOTE).

2. Marquee both points to select them. No other point should be selected.

3. Choose the JOIN ELEMENTS command from the ELEMENT menu (⌘-J).

We will demonstrate this process with an example. Figure 7.40 on the following page shows two selected endpoints, each belonging to a different open path. After dragging one endpoint directly in front of the other, we marquee the two points to select them, as shown in Figure 7.41, also on the next page. (Marqueeing is the only possible means of selection, since one point is located inaccessibly in back of the other.)

Having selected the points, we choose the JOIN ELEMENTS command. If the endpoints are correctly positioned one directly in front of the other, the two endpoints will join to form a single, selected interior point.

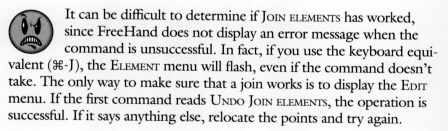

It can be difficult to determine if JOIN ELEMENTS has worked, since FreeHand does not display an error message when the command is unsuccessful. In fact, if you use the keyboard equivalent (⌘-J), the ELEMENT menu will flash, even if the command doesn't take. The only way to make sure that a join works is to display the EDIT menu. If the first command reads UNDO JOIN ELEMENTS, the operation is successful. If it says anything else, relocate the points and try again.

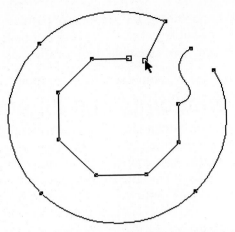

Figure 7.40: Two open paths with one selected endpoint apiece.

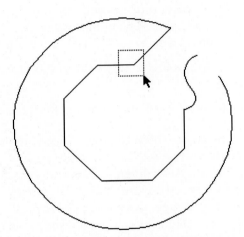

Figure 7.41: Marqueeing the two coincident endpoints prior to choosing the Join elements command.

Because the JOIN ELEMENTS command may also be used to join type to a path and to combine multiple objects into a composite path (as described in Chapters 8 and 9), the command is dimmed only when less than two paths are selected.

Auto joining

The JOIN ELEMENTS command is not needed when joining two endpoints in a single path. This is because endpoints in an open path will *auto join* when made coincident. Simply select one endpoint and drag it in front of the other endpoint in the same path, as shown in Figure 7.42. The two points automatically bond to form a selected interior point (see Figure 7.43). If you choose ELEMENT INFO..., the PATH dialog box will confirm that the path is closed.

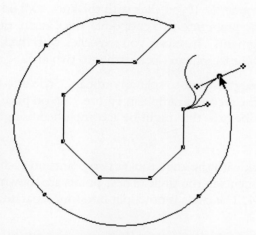

Figure 7.42: Dragging one endpoint in front of the other endpoint in the same path.

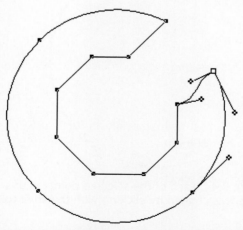

Figure 7.43: The endpoints auto join, closing the path.

Regardless of their original identities, endpoints auto join to form a single corner point. The original Bézier control handles will be retained.

Splitting an element

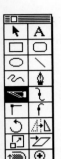

The *knife tool*, fifth tool on the left side of the toolbox, is used to split a point or segment. By choosing the knife tool and clicking at some location on a selected segment, you insert two endpoints into the segment, each associated with one segment apiece. This means the segment is split into two segments. If you click with the knife tool on an interior point, you split the point into two endpoints; once again, each is associated with a single segment. Therefore, you may click with the knife tool to open a closed path or to split an open path into two lines.

Suppose you want to split an ordinary circle into the three shapes shown in the second example in Figure 7.46 on page 230. The following steps describe how this might be accomplished using the knife and pen tools:

1. Click with the knife tool at two points on each of the right-hand segments in the circle. These points are shown as selected in Figure 7.44. The circle is now split into four separate lines.

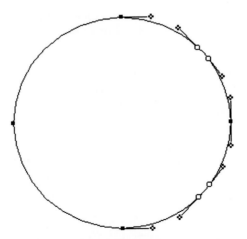

Figure 7.44: Each of the selected points in this circle was created by clicking with the knife tool.

2. Press TAB to deselect all elements. Select the arrow tool and click on the topmost of the single-segment lines created with the knife tool. Then SHIFT-click on the lower single-segment line to add it to the selection.

3. Drag both lines away from the remaining paths of the circle, as shown in Figure 7.45. Neither line is a part of the prospective final image, so press the BACKSPACE or DELETE key to delete them both. You are now left with two open paths.

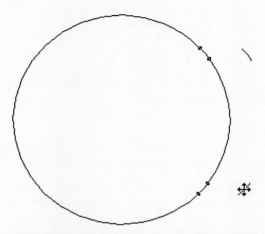

Figure 7.45: Drag the two single-segment lines away from the rest of the circle and delete them.

4. Select the right-hand path, then select the top point in the path. Press the OPTION key and drag down and to the left from the selected point. This adds a Bézier control handle to the corner point, making it a cusp.

5. Press 6 to select the pen tool. Drag at a location that mirrors the center curve point of the right-hand path.

6. Drag at the bottom point in the right-hand path, closing the path. In the middle of the drag, press OPTION to convert the curve point to another cusp. Finish the drag up and to the right, forming a leaf-shaped path.

7. Close the second, larger path in a similar manner, adding two segments that are parallel to those that closed the right-hand shape. The result is the first example in Figure 7.46 on the next page.

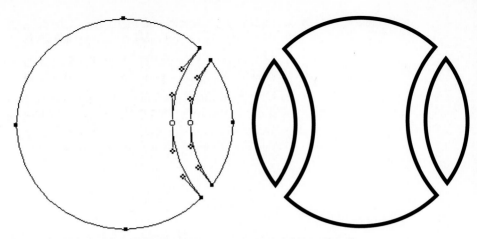

Figure 7.46: Draw segments closing the two remaining paths. Repeating the exercise on the left side of the shape results in the image shown on right.

The second example in Figure 7.46 shows the completed image after repeating steps 1 through 7 on the left side of the circle.

You may click with the knife tool on a point or segment in any selected ungrouped path. You may also split elements in a grouped or composite path, provided that the points have been displayed by OPTION-clicking on the path with the arrow tool (as described in the *Selecting elements within groups* section of Chapter 12). However, FreeHand does not allow you to click with this tool at some empty location in the drawing area.

Pressing the 7 key—either in the standard key set or on the keypad—will select the knife tool at any time, except when a dialog box is displayed.

Splitting multiple points

You may also split an interior point into two endpoints by selecting the point and choosing the SPLIT ELEMENT command from the ELEMENT menu. The only advantage this command has over the knife tool is that it may be used to split multiple points simultaneously. Otherwise, the knife tool is more convenient to use. This command will be dimmed if no point is selected.

Reneging the past

Because we all make mistakes, especially when drawing and tracing complicated paths, FreeHand provides you with the ability to nullify the results of previous operations. In fact, FreeHand is provides you with a greater capacity to mull over past actions than any other drawing program currently available on any platform. So when drawing anxiety sets in, remember this simple credo: *Undo, redo, revert.* That's Latin for "Relax, it's just a computer."

Undo

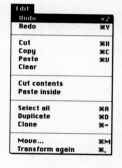

If you are familiar with other Macintosh programs or Microsoft Windows applications on the IBM PC, such as PageMaker or CorelDraw, you are no doubt familiar with the Undo command in the Edit menu (⌘-Z). This command allows you to negate the last action performed. For example, suppose that you have added a point to a path and then decide that you do not like how it looks. Choose the Undo command and the new point will disappear. You will in fact be returned to the moment before you added the point. You may even undo such minor alterations as changing an option in a dialog box, a level of precision unmatched by most other applications. And you may *always* undo the last action, even if you have since clicked on screen or performed some minor action that the command does not recognize. FreeHand is truly amazing in this respect.

Get this: FreeHand goes so far as to allow you to undo an operation performed prior to the most recent Save operation (although you may not undo the Save command itself). You can delete an element, save the illustration, then choose Undo to make the element reappear. Absolutely phenomenal, dude.

The Undo command, however, does have it limits. You may not undo an operation performed in a previous FreeHand session.

FreeHand lists the name of the operation that may be undone under the Edit menu following the word Undo, so that you fully realize the consequences of choosing the command. Examples include Undo FreeHand and Undo Move elements.

Multiple undos

In a typical application, after you undo an operation, the UNDO command changes to a REDO command, providing a brief opportunity to reperform an operation, just in case you decide you didn't want to undo it after all. In FreeHand, the UNDO command remains available, so that you may undo the second-to-last operation, and the one before that, and so on. In fact, you may undo up to 99 consecutive operations. This power-user feature takes a great deal of the worry out of using FreeHand. Even major blunders may be whisked away.

You adjust the number of possible consecutive undos by entering any value from 1 to 99 for the "Number of undo's" option in the MORE PREFERENCES dialog box (introduced in the *Setting preferences* section of Chapter 3). The default value is 8. To make this value take affect, you must quit FreeHand and relaunch the application, allowing FreeHand the opportunity to create an adequately sized undo buffer in your computer's RAM.

 Conventional wisdom suggests your machine must have at least 4 megabytes of RAM to support no more than 10 consecutive undos. If FreeHand cannot build a buffer large enough when launching, you may be presented with an out of memory error and returned to the Finder. In this worst-case scenario, you may reset the MORE PREFERENCES and related dialog boxes to their original settings by dragging the FreeHandPrefs file—found in the System folder or in the FreeHand application folder—into the Trash icon at the Finder level. Then choose the EMPTY TRASH command from the SPECIAL menu and relaunch FreeHand.

After you undo the maximum number of operations, the UNDO command will appear dimmed in the EDIT menu. Pressing COMMAND-Z will produce no effect until a new operation is performed.

Redo

Just as you may undo as many as 99 consecutive actions, you may redo up to 99 consecutive undos using the REDO command in the EDIT menu (⌘-Y). You may utilize the REDO command only if an UNDO command was the most recent action performed. The command will otherwise be dimmed. Also, if you undo a series of actions, perform a new series of actions, and then undo the new series of actions to the point where you had stopped undoing previously, you are not allowed to go back and redo the first series of undos. Instead, you may simply continue to undo from where you had left off.

FreeHand lists the name of the operation that may be redone under the EDIT menu following the word REDO, so that you fully realize the consequences of choosing the command. Examples include REDO FREEHAND or REDO MOVE ELEMENTS.

Revert

Suppose you revise your illustration by performing a series of actions. After making these changes, you decide that the illustration looked better before you started. You might use the UNDO command to reverse all your changes one operation at a time. However, not only does this take a lot of time, but there's no guarantee you have enough undos at your disposal.

A better solution is to use the REVERT command in the FILE menu to return your illustration to its exact state immediately following the last save operation. This is useful when you have made major changes in your illustration that you now regret, such as deleting important elements or editing text content.

To revert to the version of the current illustration saved to disk, choose the REVERT command from the FILE menu. The REVERT TO LAST VERSION SAVED? alert box will display, requesting that you confirm that you wish to dispose of all changes made since the last SAVE command.

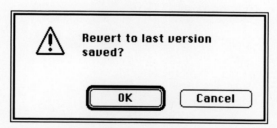

Figure 7.47: The Revert to last version saved? alert box.

Once you have reverted to the last version saved to disk, you cannot return to the current version of the illustration. If this is what you want, click the OK button or press RETURN; if not, click CANCEL or press COMMAND-PERIOD. If you click OK, your document will be restored to the version saved by the last SAVE command.

If you have not saved your illustration since opening it, or if you are working on a new illustration that has never been saved to disk, the REVERT command will be dimmed.

Creating and Editing Type

Once upon a time, FreeHand provided more text-handling capabilities than any other drawing program for the Macintosh. That was before Adobe Illustrator 3.0 changed the rules, sporting type features comparable with those in dedicated page-layout programs like PageMaker and QuarkXPress. Sadly, type in FreeHand 3.0 has changed almost imperceptibly. By recent text standards, FreeHand has fallen from state-of-the-art grace to mere acceptability.

Creating text blocks

Type in FreeHand is created and manipulated as a specific kind of element known as a *text block*. As we shall see, text blocks are both similar and dissimilar to graphic objects in FreeHand. Their similarity is based on the fact that most of FreeHand's general commands, including those covered in later chapters, may be applied to text blocks as easily as they are to graphic objects. Text blocks differ from graphic objects in that a special set of tools, commands, and options is used for the creation and alteration of type, which is the sole content of a text block.

Using the type tool

The only purpose for the *type tool* is to create a new text block in the drawing area. Unlike similar tools in other Macintosh programs, the Free-Hand type tool may not be used to edit an existing text block. As we will see in later sections of this chapter, the editing of text—like the editing of graphic objects—is a function served primarily by the arrow tool.

The type tool may be used to create a text block in one of two ways:

- Click anywhere on the page to indicate the placement of the bottom left corner of the text block.

- Drag to draw a horizontal dotted line representing the *column width* (the width of the text block), as shown in Figure 8.01. Text entered into the TEXT dialog box will wrap to fit inside this column.

Figure 8.01: When dragging with the type tool, FreeHand tracks the cursor movement with a horizontal dotted line.

After clicking or dragging with the type tool, the TEXT dialog box will display, as shown in Figure 8.02.

Pressing the A key will select the type tool at any time, except when a dialog box is displayed. Pressing SHIFT-A will also select the type tool.

Entering text

At first glance, the TEXT dialog box is little more than an empty window. It offers a title bar, a few buttons, and a large *text entry area* surrounded by scroll bars. Enter the desired text from your keyboard as you would in a word processor. Each letter will appear in the text entry area. A blinking *insertion marker* will move rightward with the addition of each letter, indicating the location at which the next letter you enter will appear, as shown in Figure 8.02. If a word threatens to extend beyond the edge of the text entry area, it will automatically wrap to begin a new line of type.

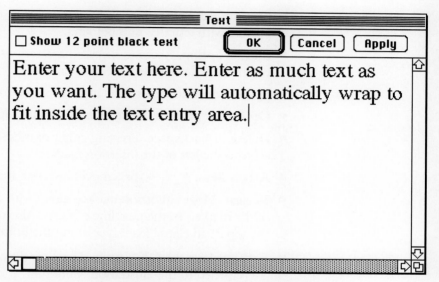

Figure 8.02: Click or drag with the type tool to display the Text dialog box, where all text is entered.

The text entry area will accept as much as 32 kilobytes of text (32,000 characters), which is equivalent to about 5,000 words, much more than you can cram onto a single page. The vertical scroll bar provides an easy method of browsing through text that extends above or below the boundaries of the window.

 As in previous versions of FreeHand, the horizontal scroll bar in the TEXT dialog box serves no function. Since text always wraps to fit within the horizontal confines of the text entry area, scrolling to the right displays only emptiness.

To display more or less text in the text entry area, drag the size box in the lower right corner of the TEXT dialog box.

When entering text from the keyboard, you may use keys to perform the same functions as in any word-processing software. Most keys insert the character that appears on the key. Keys that perform other functions include the following:

- **Caps lock**. Accesses uppercase letters when pressed with letter keys.
- **Shift**. Accesses uppercase letters when pressed with letter keys and special characters printed at the top of number keys.
- **Option**. Accesses special characters—such as £, ¢, ∞, §, ¶—when pressed with letter or number keys.
- **Shift + option**. Accesses special characters—such as fi, fl, ‡, °—when pressed with letter or number keys.
- **Spacebar** or **tab**. Inserts a standard space into a text block.
- **Option + spacebar**. Inserts a non-breaking space into a text block.
- **Delete** or **backspace**. Pressing either of these keys deletes the character to the left of the insertion marker.
- **Arrow keys**. ←, ↑, →, or ↓ moves insertion marker inside text block.
- **Return**. Moves insertion marker, along with any text to the right of the marker, to the next line of type. (Also separates type along the top of an ellipse from type along the bottom of an ellipse.)
- **Enter**. Selects the OK button. The TEXT dialog box closes and you are returned to the illustration window.

Click the APPLY button to display the current text in the drawing area without leaving the TEXT dialog box. If you cannot see the drawing area because the dialog box is in the way, drag its title bar to move the box partially off screen. This allows you to enter additional text and change the formatting (as explained later in this chapter) if the current text is not satisfactory.

Both the OK and CANCEL buttons function as they do in any other dialog box. You may even cancel your changes after clicking OK or pressing the ENTER key by choosing the UNDO ELEMENT INFO… command from the EDIT menu (⌘-Z).

After accepting the text entered into the TEXT dialog box—either by clicking OK or pressing the ENTER key—the text block will appear selected in the drawing area, as shown in Figure 8.03. A rectangle represents the boundary of the text block. It features four *corner handles* and four *side handles*, much like the handles that surround a selected rectangle or ellipse. If you created the text block by dragging with the type tool, the width of the text block matches the length of your drag. If you clicked with the type tool, the column width is around six to seven inches (the default width of the text entry area in the TEXT dialog box).

Enter your text here. Enter as much text as you want. The type will automatically wrap to fit inside the text entry area.

Enter your text here. Enter as much text as you want. The type will automatically wrap to fit inside the text entry area.

Figure 8.03: A text block shown as it appears when selected (top) and when printed (bottom).

Creating text on a path

The second kind of text block you may create in FreeHand 3.0 is *text on a path*, in which the baseline of a line of type is fixed to the outline of an existing path, as shown in Figure 8.04 on the following page.

Creating type on a path is a four-step process:

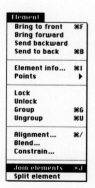

1. Create a path using one of the geometric or free-form path tools.

2. Create a standard text block using the type tool, as described in the previous section. Do not insert any carriage return (by pressing the RETURN key) unless you intend to create type on an ellipse. Type on an ellipse may contain one carriage return to separate type along the top of the ellipse from type along the bottom of the ellipse.

3. Select both the path and the text block with the arrow tool.

4. Choose the JOIN ELEMENTS command from the ELEMENT menu (⌘-J). The type will bind to the path, as demonstrated in Figures 8.05 and 8.06 on the following page.

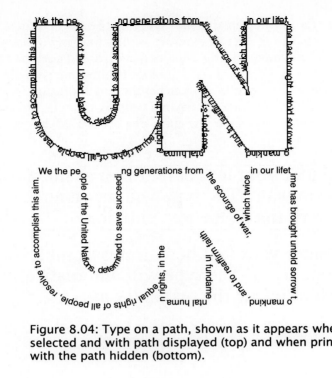

Figure 8.04: Type on a path, shown as it appears when selected and with path displayed (top) and when printed with the path hidden (bottom).

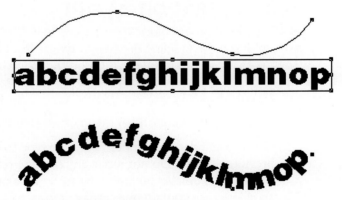

Figure 8.05: After selecting a standard text block and a path (top), choose the Join elements command to bind the baseline of the text to the path (bottom).

Figure 8.06: When joining text to an ellipse (left), a carriage return may be used to separate type along the top of the ellipse from type along the bottom (right).

Although any text block can be joined to a path—even 32,000 characters' worth—text on a path is ill-suited for long documents. Ultimately, the length of your path determines the length of your text. When a word extends beyond the last point in an open path, or beyond the first point in a closed path, the remaining type disappears from view.

Paths composed exclusively of curve points—no corners—serve best for creating path text. When type has to flow around a corner, it may interrupt a word, as verified by several instances in Figure 8.04. FreeHand does not keep whole words together in path text. Also, type may overlap inside sharp corners. We avoided this in the figure by inserting spaces to spread apart overlapping letters, but the results still appear rather odd and, frequently, illegible.

Adjusting text blocks

Like other objects in Aldus FreeHand, standard text blocks and text on a path may be adjusted in a variety of ways. For example, the column width of a text block may be adjusted to allow more or fewer words to fit on each line. You may also alter the way in which type fits on a path, as well as whether or not the path itself is displayed. These and related topics are explained in the following pages.

Changing the column width

When creating a text block, you do not have to accept the default column width provided by FreeHand or the original column width specified by dragging with the type tool. You may at any time change the column width of an existing text block simply by selecting the object and dragging at one of its four corner handles.

Suppose, for example, that a text block is too narrow to hold one of the words on a single line. Even though the word is not hyphenated, FreeHand is forced to break it onto two lines, as demonstrated by the word *determined* in Figure 8.07. This problem generally occurs only if the path is very narrow or the type is very big. To remedy the problem, you may: 1) reduce the size of the type (as described in the *Formatting text* section later in this chapter), 2) manually hyphenate the word by inserting a hyphen followed by a space, as in *deter- mined*, or 3) increase the width of the text block, as shown in Figure 8.08.

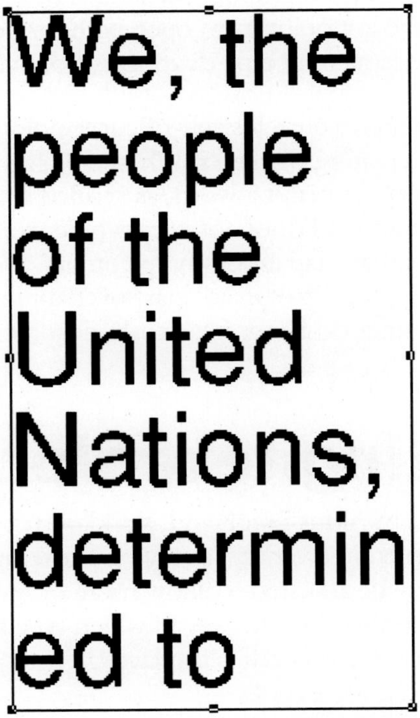

> # We, the people of the United Nations, determin ed to

Figure 8.07: If a word is too long to fit on a single line, FreeHand arbitrarily breaks it onto two lines.

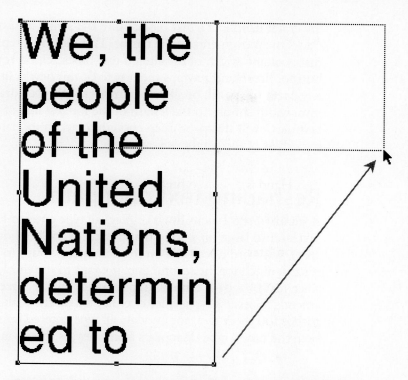

Figure 8.08: After dragging the lower right corner handle of the text block (top), the text rewraps to fit the new column width (bottom).

Changing the column width of a path allows you to fit long words on a single line, include more or less text on each line, or simply change the appearance of a text block. Figure 8.08 shows the result of dragging the lower left handle of a text block using the arrow tool. A dotted rectangle tracks the movements of the cursor. This rectangle represents the approximate column width of the altered text block. Upon releasing the mouse button, FreeHand rewraps the text to fit this new column width. The altered text block will be slightly narrower than your drag, since the column width shrinks to the length of the longest line of type. However, the text block will always be deep enough to accommodate all lines of type, regardless of the height of your drag.

Reshaping text on a path

A standard text block always displays all type entered into it (provided the text isn't so large or so long that it exceeds the boundaries of the drawing area). If a word doesn't fit on the first line, it wraps to the second line. If it's too much for the second line, it wraps to the third, and so on. But since text on a path cannot wrap to a second line, FreeHand cannot make amends for excess type. A letter either fits on the path or it doesn't. If the path is too short to accommodate all type entered into the TEXT dialog box, the excess type disappears from view, as shown in Figure 8.09.

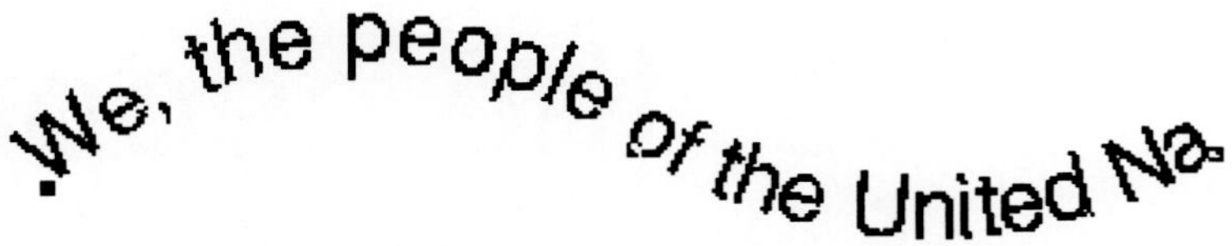

Figure 8.09: A string of type may break in the middle of a word if its path is not long enough to accommodate it.

You have three choices for fixing the appearance of type along an inadequate path: 1) reduce the size of the type (as described in the *Formatting text* section later in this chapter), 2) edit the text until it fits on the path, or 3) lengthen the path until all text is visible.

To lengthen a path with type fixed to it, you may drag points and Bézier control handles with the arrow tool in any manner you desire. After each drag, the text will refit to the new shape of the path.

Suppose that you want to lengthen the path shown in Figure 8.09 so that the last word fits completely on the path. The following steps demonstrate a few reshaping methods:

1. Using the arrow tool, drag the right endpoint, as shown in Figure 8.10. The type will immediately adjust to follow the altered path, as shown in Figure 8.11.

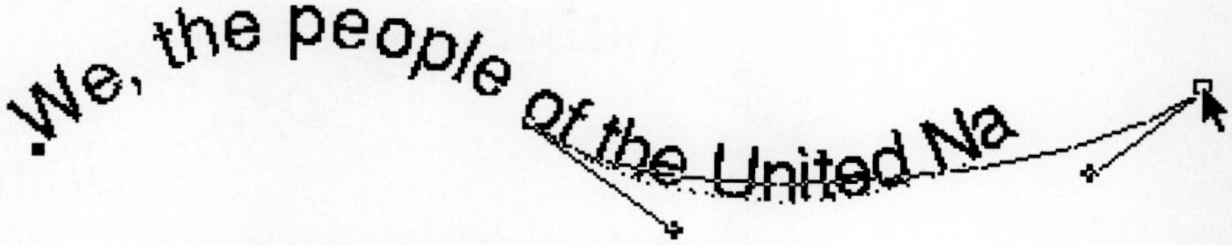

Figure 8.10: Use the arrow tool to drag the endpoint of an open path independently of its type.

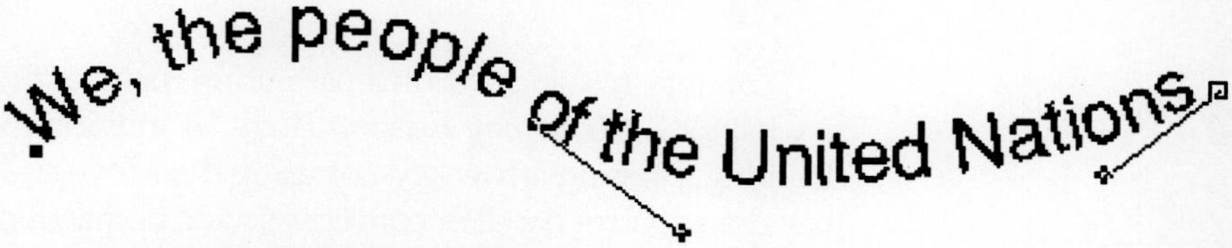

Figure 8.11: The type refits to the path immediately following the drag.

2. Notice that the path now curves neither as fluidly nor as symmetrically as it did in Figure 8.09. Dragging an endpoint initially results in a less pleasing path. To compensate, drag down on the rightmost Bézier control handle to adjust the segment, as shown in Figure 8.12.

Figure 8.12: You may also move the Bézier control handles of type on a path.

3. You may even change the identity of a point in the path. The middle point in the path is currently a curve point. If you select the point and choose the "Corner point" option from the POINTS pop-up in the ELEMENT menu, the point will convert to a corner point. You may then drag its Bézier control handles independently, as shown in Figure 8.13.

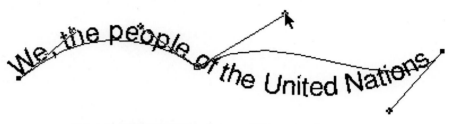

Figure 8.13: After converting the middle point from a curve point to a corner point, you may drag the control handles independently of each other.

You may reshape text on a path using many of the techniques discussed in Chapter 7, *Reshaping Existing Paths*. In addition to moving points by dragging, pressing arrow keys, or using the MOVE ELEMENTS dialog box, you may drag control handles; convert selected points using the options in the POINTS pop-up menu; delete selected points by pressing DELETE or BACKSPACE or using the "Remove point" option; and join the two endpoints of the same path by dragging one endpoint in front of the other to create a closed path.

Some reshaping techniques, however, are not applicable to a path, while text is joined to it. These include the following:

- You may not extend an open text path using any of the free-form drawing tools, nor may you insert a point into the path using a point tool.

- You may not join an open text path to a separate open path using the JOIN ELEMENTS command.

- You may not split a point in a path with text fixed to it using the knife tool or the SPLIT ELEMENT command. (SPLIT ELEMENT separates the text block from the path, as described in the next section.)

To perform any of these techniques, you must first split the text from the path as explained in the next section.

Splitting text from a path

The fact that you can't add points to text on a path can be a real imposition. But don't think you're stuck. Just as you can join text to a path, you can split it apart. To return text and path to two separate objects, select the path and choose the SPLIT ELEMENT command from the ELEMENT menu. You may then edit the path using any of the reshaping techniques described in Chapter 7, including those mentioned in the bulleted list on the previous page. After you have added points and performed other desired manipulations, rejoin the text to the path using the JOIN ELEMENTS command from the ELEMENT menu (⌘-J).

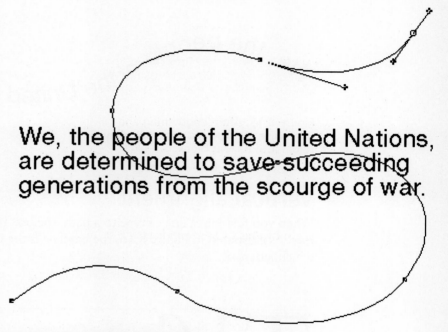

Figure 8.14: You may add points
to a text path only after separating text
and path using the Split element command.

Although the text block shown in Figure 8.14 contains three lines of type, all lines will fit onto the lengthened path (see Figure 8.15 on the next page). This is because the text contains no carriage return. Every line break is the natural result of the column width of the text block, and therefore does not translate to text on a path.

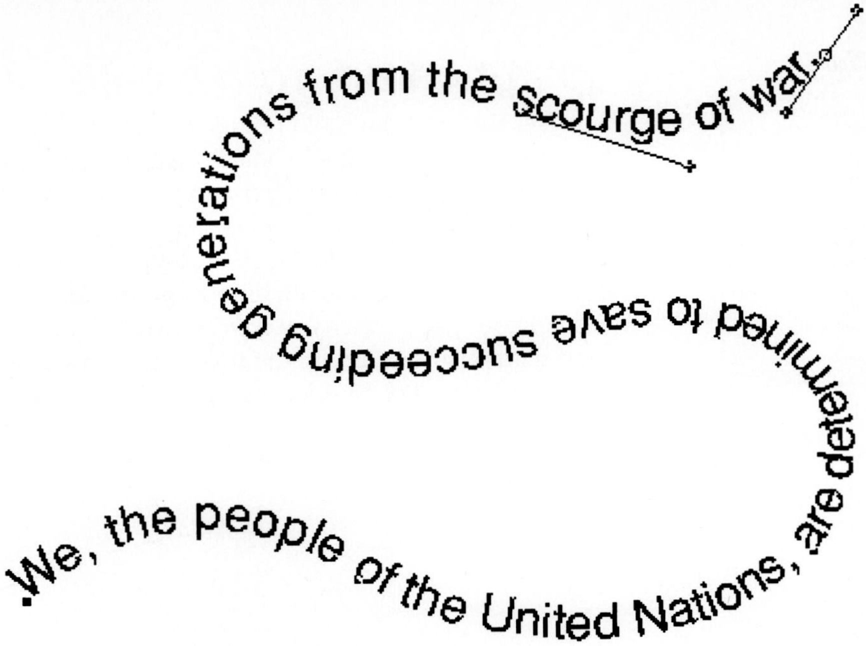

Figure 8.15: After lengthening and
otherwise reshaping a path, you may
rejoin it to its text block.

Vertical alignment

When you first join a line of type to a path, the text is joined by its *base-line*. As illustrated in Figure 8.16, the baseline is the imaginary line on which letters sit.

Tdƒnpg

— Ascent —
— Baseline
— Descent —

Type size

Figure 8.16: Text in originally joined to a path by its
baseline, but it may also be joined at the ascent or
descent.

Figure 8.17: When you join the text to a path, the baseline, ascent, and descent of each letter curves to follow the exact form of the path.

Only a few lowercase letters—*f, g, j, p, q,* and *y*—descend below the baseline. These are called *descenders*. Other lowercase letters are slightly taller than capital letters. These, including—*b, d, f, h, k,* and *l*—are called *ascenders*. Shown in Figure 8.16, the *descent* marks the lower boundary for a line of type; the *ascent* marks the upper boundary.

In FreeHand, a line of type may follow a path along its baseline, its ascent, or its descent. This feature is known as the *vertical alignment* of text on a path. For example, suppose that you want to create two lines of type that follow the same path, one above and one below. This is a job for vertical alignment:

1. Create two text blocks and one free-form path, similar to those shown in Figure 8.18.

2. Select the path and choose the CLONE command from the EDIT menu (⌘-=, COMMAND-EQUAL). This creates a duplicate of the path directly in front of the original.

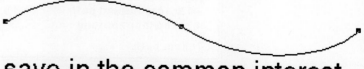

Figure 8.18: Create a free-form path and clone it, providing identical paths for both text blocks.

3. Using the arrow tool, SHIFT-click the first text block to add it to the current selection.

4. Choose the JOIN ELEMENTS command from the ELEMENT menu (⌘-J). The first text block joins to the path.

5. Choose the SEND TO BACK command from the ELEMENT menu (⌘-B). The selection is placed behind all other objects in the illustration.

6. Press TAB to deselect all elements. Click the remaining path and SHIFT-click the second text block to select both objects.

7. Choose JOIN ELEMENTS again. The second text block joins its path, overlapping the first text on path. This makes for the extremely illegible effect shown in Figure 8.19.

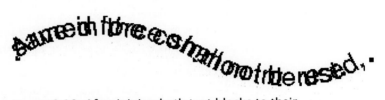

Figure 8.19: After joining both text blocks to their paths, the two lines of type overlap.

8. Choose ELEMENT INFO... from the ELEMENT menu (⌘-I, ⬦-★★). The TEXT ALONG A PATH dialog box will appear, as shown in Figure 8.20. This dialog box allows you to control the vertical alignment of a selected text path.

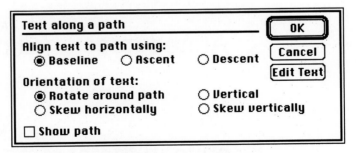

Figure 8.20: Option-double-click path text to display the Text along a path dialog box.

9. The path that is currently selected contains the second line of type. This type should be positioned below the first line of type. With this in mind, select the "Ascent" radio button to force the upper boundary of the type to follow the path. Then press the RETURN key. Figure 8.21 shows the result.

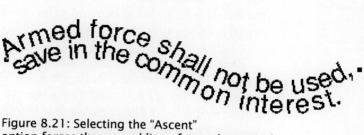

Figure 8.21: Selecting the "Ascent"
option forces the second line of type downward.

10. Choose SEND TO BACK to send the selected text object behind the first line of type.

11. Press TAB to deselect all objects. Click on the baseline of the top line of type to select it, then choose the ELEMENT INFO... command.

12. Again, the TEXT ALONG A PATH dialog box displays. To position the selected line of type above its path, select the "Descent" radio button and press RETURN. The finished result is shown in Figure 8.22.

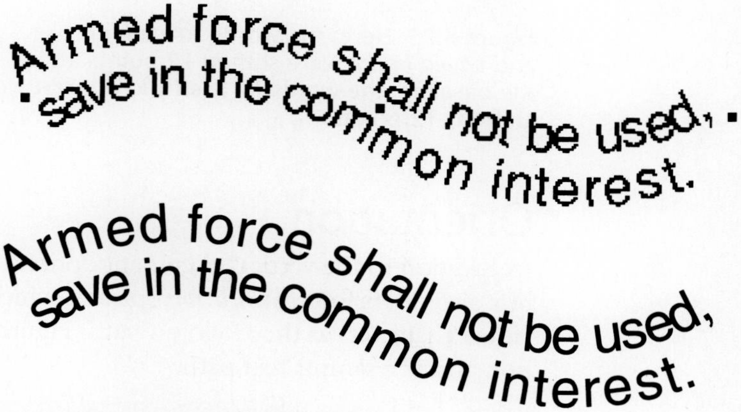

Figure 8.22: Selecting the "Descent"
option forces the first line of type upward, as it
appears on screen (top) and when printed (bottom).

The options in the TEXT ALONG A PATH dialog box allow you to move type vertically with respect to a path in three gross increments. But you may also fine-tune vertical alignment using *baseline shift*, which raises or lowers selected text in relation to its own baseline. To use this feature, select a text path and choose the BASELINE SHIFT... command from the TYPE menu. Enter a value into the option in the BASELINE SHIFT dialog box and press RETURN. Positive values raise type, negative values lower type.

You may also raise or lower individual words or letters in a selected text path, as demonstrated in Figure 8.23. This is accomplished by displaying the TEXT ALONG A PATH dialog box (⌘-I), clicking the EDIT TEXT button to display the TEXT dialog box in which you may edit and format type, then highlighting the desired type and applying the BASELINE SHIFT... command. This process is explained in depth in the *Raising and lowering type* section later in this chapter.

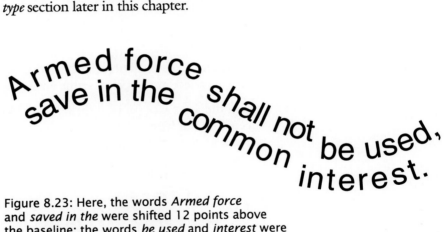

Figure 8.23: Here, the words *Armed force* and *saved in the* were shifted 12 points above the baseline; the words *be used* and *interest* were shifted −12 points.

Orientation

In addition to the vertical alignment options, the TEXT ALONG A PATH dialog box also offers four *orientation* options, which control the angle of individual characters as they follow a path. Figure 8.24 shows how each option affects a sample text path.

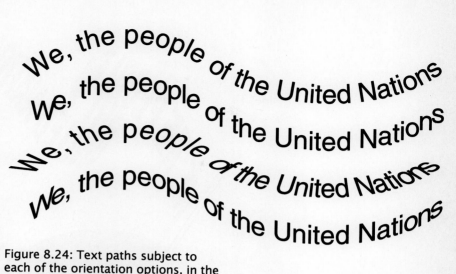

Figure 8.24: Text paths subject to each of the orientation options, in the order described below.

These options work as follows:

- **Rotate around path**. Each letter is tangent to its position on the path, so that letters tilt back and forth as the path twists and turns. This option—the default—is the most useful.

- **Vertical**. Though the baseline curves with the path, each letter is positioned straight up and down, as it would appear if it were in a standard text block. Letters frequently overlap when this option is selected.

- **Skew horizontally**. Letters slant with the inclination of the path. Though the name of this option implies that the type slants only horizontally, letters may slant both horizontally and vertically, like slats in a fan.

- **Skew vertically**. Letters slant vertically only with the inclination of the path. Characters remain upright, rather than leaning from side to side, without overlapping. Generally, this setting is preferable to the "Vertical" option, and is useful for creating exciting three-dimensional effects like those shown in Figure 8.25 on the following page.

Figure 8.25: Vertically oriented type can be useful for
creating 3-D effects, like type around a globe. Both of
these text paths were grouped and rotated.

Normally, when you manipulate text on a path using one of
the transformation tools—scale, reflect, rotate, or skew (each
described in the corresponding section of Chapter 12)—you
transform the path without transforming the type. For example, if you
reduce the path to half its original size, the type will remain at its original
size. If you rotate a text path with vertically oriented type, the type will
remain vertical rather than tilting to the new angle. To tilt the text, as
demonstrated in Figure 8.25, read on.

To transform the type along with its path, you must prepare your text path as described in the following steps:

1. Select the text path and choose the GROUP command from the ELE-MENT menu (⌘-G). This groups text and path into a single object.

2. Choose the ELEMENT INFO... command (⌘-I, ⬱-🡑🡑) to display the GROUP dialog box, shown in Figure 8.26.

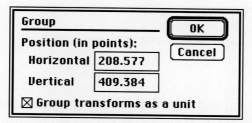

Figure 8.26: Prepare a text path for a transformation by grouping the object and selecting the above option.

3. Select the "Group transforms as a unit" check box, as shown in the figure. This option ensures that all elements in the group will be transformed identically, including the text.

4. Press RETURN to close the GROUP dialog box, then perform the desired transformation.

Type on an ellipse

Because users have expressed more interest in joining text to circles and ovals than to any other kinds of shapes, FreeHand 3.0 provides some special options for type on an ellipse.

As mentioned earlier in this chapter, a carriage return may be used to separate type along the top of an ellipse from type along the bottom of the ellipse. FreeHand also allows you to manipulate these two portions of text separately. After you join type to an ellipse, choose the ELEMENT INFO... command from the ELEMENT menu (⌘-I, ⬱-🡑🡑) to display the TYPE ON AN ELLIPSE dialog box, shown in Figure 8.27 on the next page. Here, you may access vertical alignment options for both the upper and lower lines of type. (This dialog box will display only if the text is joined to a ellipse drawn with the oval tool that has *not* been ungrouped.)

```
┌─────────────────────────────────────────────────────┐
│ Text on an ellipse                        ┌────────┐  │
│ ─────────────────                         │   OK   │  │
│ Align text to top of ellipse using:       └────────┘  │
│   ○ Baseline    ○ Ascent    ● Descent   ┌──────────┐ │
│                                         │  Cancel  │ │
│ Align text to bottom of ellipse using:  └──────────┘ │
│   ○ Baseline    ● Ascent    ○ Descent   ┌──────────┐ │
│                                         │ Edit Text│ │
│ Orientation of text:                    └──────────┘ │
│   ● Rotate around path   ○ Vertical    ○ Skew       │
│                                                      │
│   ☐ Show path      ☒ Centered                       │
└─────────────────────────────────────────────────────┘
```

Figure 8.27: Option-double-click text on an ellipse to
display the specialized Text on an ellipse dialog box.

By default, type before the carriage return (top text) is aligned by its
descent and type after the carriage return (bottom text) by its ascent. This
ensures that both lines of type match up with each other. As demonstrated in Figure 8.28, the descent of text above an ellipse coincides with
the ascent of the text below the ellipse, and vice versa. Therefore, revers-
ing the options will achieve a similar effect (although letters will be
cramped together, since the text will be on the inside rather than on
the outside of the ellipse, as shown in Figure 8.29).

Figure 8.28: The descent for type above an ellipse
is the ascent for type below the ellipse.

Figure 8.29: Type on an ellipse lines up even if you select "Ascent" for the top line of type and "Descent" for the bottom. The text is spaced more tightly, but you can loosen the spacing using formatting commands, as described later in this chapter.

The TEXT ON AN ELLIPSE dialog box offers only three orientation options. In addition to the "Rotate around path" option, used to create the examples in Figure 8.28 and 8.29, FreeHand offers "Vertical" and "Skew" options, both of which are demonstrated in Figure 8.30. "Skew" performs the same function as the "Skew vertically" option in the standard TEXT ALONG A PATH dialog box.

Figure 8.30: Type on an ellipse oriented vertically (left) and skewed relative to the path (right).

If the text is sufficiently long, skewed type will wrap around to the other side of the ellipse, as demonstrated in Figure 8.31. The *a*'s occupy the top portion of the ellipse, the *B*'s occupy the bottom.

Figure 8.31: Skewed type appears to wrap around an ellipse in a three-dimensional manner.

Selecting text on a path

When you join type to a path, the path disappears. Unfortunately, it is visible in neither the preview nor keyline mode. Ironically, to select text on a path, you must click on its invisible path. Generally, this is not much of a problem, since the path usually coincides with the baseline of the type, and you can recognize the baseline quite easily. Type on an ellipse is a special case, however, since it is usually aligned by its ascent or its descent. Finding the path can be quite difficult.

There are two ways to remedy this problem: 1) learn how to find the ellipse and 2) display the ellipse so it can be easily seen. The former is less work, if you can master it. Rather than clicking at the base of the line of type (which no doubt has become a habit to users familiar with previous versions of FreeHand), click just above the lower line of type on an ellipse, as demonstrated in Figure 8.32. In this way, you will be clicking on the ascent of the lower text, which is aligned with the ellipse.

Figure 8.32: Click above the lower line of type to select text on an ellipse (left). If you click below the upper line (right), you will miss the path.

If this technique proves unsatisfactory, here's a surefire tip. Select the path and choose ELEMENT INFO… (⌘-I, ⌥-↖↖) to bring up the TEXT ON AN ELLIPSE dialog box. Select the "Show path" check box to display the path, and press RETURN. Then, assuming you don't want the path to appear when printed, choose the REMOVE LINE command from the ATTRIBUTES menu. Now you can view the path in the keyline mode and hide it in the preview mode.

You may also use the "Show path" option in the TEXT ALONG A PATH dialog box to display text on a free-form path. This option is examined in further detail in Chapters 9 and 10 as it relates to filling and stroking a path independently of the type joined to it.

Horizontal alignment and direction

The final option in the TEXT ON AN ELLIPSE dialog box is the "Centered" check box. This determines how text is *horizontally aligned* on the path; that is, the location of the type back and forth along the length of the path. When "Centered" is selected, the type before the carriage return is centered along the top half of the circle, type after the carriage return is centered along the bottom half. If you deselect "Centered," the type before the carriage return will slide counterclockwise, so it begins at the leftmost point in the ellipse, considered the first point in the path. The type after the carriage return will disappear. In other words, deselect "Centered" to align the text as it would appear on a free-form path, or on an ungrouped ellipse.

Which brings up an interesting question: Just how is type joined to a free-form path? The best way to demonstrate the answer is by way of an example. Suppose that you want to join the text block and path shown in the first example of Figure 8.33 to create the finished artwork shown in the second example of the figure.

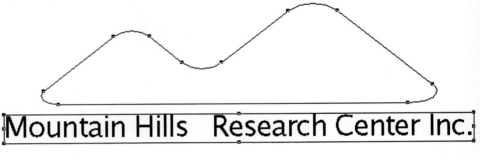

Figure 8.33: When joining a text block to a free-form path (top) the type begins at the first point in the path and follows the direction of the path (bottom).

Type begins at the first point in the path. Also, it follows the direction of a path. For example, in the case of an ellipse, the direction of a path is clockwise, so text on an ellipse reads in a clockwise direction. The direction of a free-form path is determined by the order in which you added points with the point tools, or the direction in which you drew the path with the freehand or line tool.

You say you can't remember the direction in which you drew a path, or which point is the first point? Welcome to the club. Few people can remember how a path was created three seconds after drawing it, and you can't discern this information by looking at the path or using the ELEMENT INFO... command. Therefore, when joining a text block to a free-form path, you should expect at least one of two problems to occur. First, the text may begin at the wrong point in the path, as shown in Figure 8.34. (This problem will most likely occur when you join text to a closed path, since an endpoint is the obvious first point in an open path.) Second, the text may flow in the wrong direction, causing it to appear on the inside rather than the outside of the path, as shown in Figure 8.35.

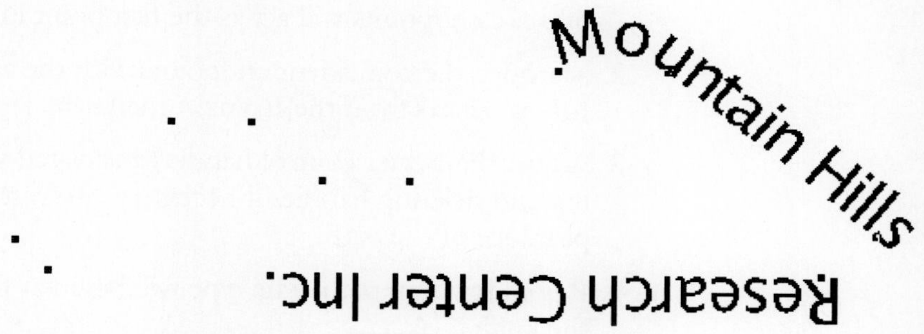

Figure 8.34: Type may begin at an undesirable point in a path.

Figure 8.35: Also, type may flow in an undesirable direction.

Every expert we've ever talked to claims that a problem like Figure 8.35 can't be solved without redrawing the path. (Note that flipping is *not* an alternative, since the path is asymmetrical.) We know different, and, shortly, so will you.

● **Problem 1**: *Changing the first point in a path.*

The first thing you should do if either of these problems occurs is to choose the Undo Join elements command from the Edit menu (⌘-Z) to separate type and path. Then deselect the text block by shift-clicking it with the arrow tool.

A moment ago, we mentioned that one of the endpoints in an open path is guaranteed to be the first point in the path. Therefore, the easiest way to determine the first point in a closed path is to open it.

1. Select the knife tool and click on the location in the path (either on a point or a segment) at which you want the type to begin. Two endpoints will be inserted, one directly in front of the other. One of these endpoints will act as the first point in the path.

2. Marquee the coincident endpoints with the arrow tool and choose Join elements from the Element menu (⌘-J), reclosing the path.

3. Adjust the Bézier control handles associated with the point—adding and deleting handles if necessary—to restore the original appearance of the path.

4. Rejoin text and path. The type will begin at the point clicked with the knife tool.

If the text is flowing on the inside rather than the outside of the path, the above steps solve only half your problem. To change the direction of a path, read on.

● **Problem 2**: *Changing the direction of a path.*

The simplest way to change the direction of a path is to flip it:

1. Select the reflect tool and option-click near the center of the selected shape. The Reflect dialog box will display.

2. Select "Vertical" from the "Axis" radio buttons and press return to close the dialog box.

3. Rejoin text and path. The type will now flow in the opposite direction.

The reflect tool and Reflect dialog box are discussed in full detail in the *Flipping objects* section of Chapter 12.

Unfortunately, because this technique involves creating a mirror image of your path, it may be used only to change the direction of a symmetrical path. If your path is asymmetrical and you don't want to alter its basic appearance, you must replace one of the segments in the path with a new segment that flows in the opposite direction:

1. First you need to remove a segment from the path, so select the knife tool.

2. If the path is open, click on one of the points that neighbors the endpoints (the second point in from either side of the path). If the path is closed, click on two points, both of which border a single straight segment. (A straight segment is most easily replicated.)

3. Press TAB to deselect all elements. Then select the separated segment and delete it.

4. Draw a new segment matching the deleted one, except in the opposite direction. (If the deleted segment was straight, use the line tool for convenience.) This segment must be drawn independently of the path.

5. While the new segment is still selected, choose SEND TO BACK from the ELEMENT menu (⌘-B). The direction of the rear path takes precedent in FreeHand.

6. Select both points in the segment and drag it by one of its points until it snaps onto one of the endpoints in the path.

7. Marquee the coincident endpoints with the arrow tool and choose JOIN ELEMENTS from the ELEMENT menu (⌘-J) to join segment and path.

8. If the path was closed, auto-join the remaining endpoints in the path by dragging one in front of the other.

9. Adjust the Bézier control handles associated with the joined points—adding and deleting handles if necessary—to restore the original appearance of the path.

10. Rejoin text and path. The type will now flow in the opposite direction.

This may seem like a lot of work, but it will go quickly after you try it out a few times. Even after your first try, you'll probably find it preferable to redrawing the path from scratch, which is your only other alternative.

Formatting text

Text editing features can be broken into two categories: those that are applied to characters of type and those that are applied to an entire text block. To properly apply formatting commands, it is important to understand the distinction and to know which features fall into which category.

- **Character-level formatting** includes almost everything—typeface, size, leading, type style, effects, spacing, kerning, horizontal scaling, and baseline shift. To change the formatting of one or more characters, you first select the specific characters in the TEXT dialog box and then apply the desired options. Only the selected characters will be modified.

- **Block-level formatting** includes everything mentioned above plus alignment. To change the formatting of an entire text block, select the block with the arrow tool. Alignment is the odd feature out: it always affects entire text blocks, even if you select a single character in the TEXT dialog box.

You may also set character-level or block-level formatting for a new text block before typing it. After clicking with the type tool to display the TEXT dialog box, specify the desired formatting options and then begin typing.

Selecting and editing text

Text is formatted in FreeHand using the arrow tool. You may select the entire text block or text on a path by clicking on it. Any formatting changes will therefore affect all characters. By selecting multiple text blocks with the arrow tool, you may format multiple text objects.

To select individual characters, you must first display the TEXT dialog box. This may be accomplished in one of two ways:

- To edit characters in a text block, select the text block and choose the ELEMENT INFO... command from the ELEMENT menu (⌘-I) or simply double-click the text block (you don't have to press OPTION).

- To edit characters in text on a path, select the text path, choose ELEMENT INFO... (⌘-I, ⬉-↖↖) to display the TYPE ALONG A PATH or TYPE ON AN ELLIPSE dialog box, then click the EDIT TEXT button.

Once the TEXT dialog box appears, your cursor will change to an I-beam (I), allowing you to select and edit text. You may format text only within a single text block. However, you may select individual characters, words, and paragraphs of type with the I-beam, something that may not be accomplished using the arrow tool.

The following items explain how the I-beam cursor may be used to select type in the TEXT dialog box:

- Drag over the characters that you want to select. Drag to the left or to the right to select characters on the same line of type and drag upward or downward to select characters on multiple lines, as shown in Figure 8.36. The selected text will become *highlighted*, white against a black background on a monochrome monitor, black against a colored background on a color monitor.

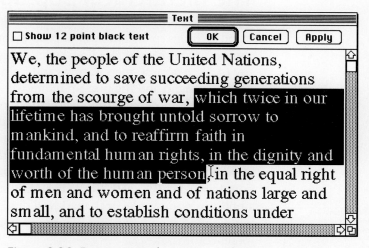

Figure 8.36: Drag across characters in the Text dialog box to select letters and words.

- Double-click on a word to select that word. Hold down the mouse button on the second click and drag to select additional words.
- Click to set the insertion marker at one end of the text you want to select, then SHIFT-click at the opposite end of the desired selection. All text between the first click and the SHIFT-click will become highlighted.

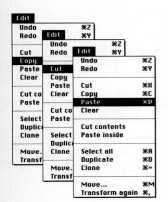

- Click anywhere in a text block and choose SELECT ALL from the EDIT menu (⌘-A) to select all text in the current text block.

Highlighted text may be formatted, as discussed in the following pages, or replaced by entering new text from the keyboard. You may also delete selected text by pressing the DELETE or BACKSPACE key. You may copy selected text to the Macintosh Clipboard by choosing the COPY command from the EDIT menu (⌘-C). Or you may delete the selected text and at the same time send a copy to the Clipboard by choosing CUT from the EDIT menu (⌘-X). Finally, you may replace the selected text with some type that you copied earlier to the Clipboard by choosing PASTE from the EDIT menu (⌘-V). Pasted text always adopts the formatting of the text block into which it is pasted.

The hierarchical pop-up menus

All commands used to format type are included in the TYPE menu. The menu includes six hierarchical pop-up menus that allow you to quickly choose a typeface, size, leading, style, special effect, and alignment. To use any of these pop-up menus, press and hold the mouse button on the desired command and the pop-up menu will display to the right or left of the TYPE menu (depending on available screen space), listing available options. Drag your cursor horizontally onto the pop-up menu and then drag vertically to choose the desired option. If the pop-up menu is not completely displayed, arrows will indicate that more options are available by scrolling the menu up or down. The currently selected option will be noted with a check mark. If the currently selected text is not formatted to a uniform option, no check mark will display. An option is chosen by highlighting it and releasing the mouse button, just as with any other menu command.

Choosing a font

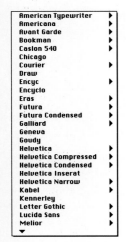

The FONT command brings up a pop-up menu listing all *fonts* (typefaces) currently loaded into your System file or *attached* to it using a font utility like MasterJuggler or Suitcase. If you are also using Adobe Type Manager, or a similar font organization utility, the FONT pop-up menu will offer access to additional pop-up menus for accessing type styles, as shown at left.

If your artwork contains any font that is not currently loaded into or attached to your System file, the name of the missing font will appear dimmed in the pop-up menu. If you add the missing font to your System file and then relaunch FreeHand, the font name will no longer be dimmed and the typeface will display properly.

Choosing a type size

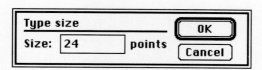

The SIZE command allows you to control the *type size* of the currently selected text. Type size is measured in points from the top of an ascender (such as an *f* or *l*) to the bottom of a descender (such as a *g* or *p*). The SIZE pop-up menu provides access to several common sizes and to the "Other…" option. To select a size that is not displayed in the SIZE pop-up menu, choose "Other…" to display the TYPE SIZE dialog box shown in Figure 8.37. Any value between 0.1 and 3000 in 0.01-point increments can be entered in the "Size" option box.

```
Type size                    ┌──────────┐
                             │    OK    │
Size: │24          │ points  └──────────┘
                             ┌──────────┐
                             │  Cancel  │
                             └──────────┘
```

Figure 8.37: The Type size dialog box allows you to specify a custom type size value.

KE You may adjust the type size of a selected text block dynamically by pressing SHIFT and OPTION and dragging at a corner handle. Drag away from the text block to increase the type size; drag inward to reduce the type size. To determine the effect the drag has made on the type size, choose "Other…" from the SIZE pop-up menu. The new type size will be displayed in the "Size" option.

Choosing a leading

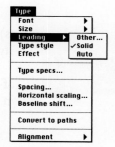

The LEADING command allows you to control the *leading* of the selected text; that is, the distance between a selected line of type and the line above it, as measured in points from one baseline to the other. The LEADING pop-up menu provides access to three options: "Other…," "Solid," and "Auto." The default "Solid" option matches the leading to the type size. Choose the "Auto" option to make the leading 120 percent of the current type size (rounded to the nearest 1/100-point). To specify a custom leading, choose the "Other..." option, which displays the LEADING dialog box shown in Figure 8.38. Any value between 0 and 3000 in 0.01-point increments can be entered in the "Leading" option box.

Leading
Leading: 24 points
OK
Cancel

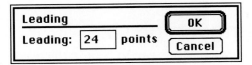

Figure 8.38: The Leading dialog box allows you to specify a custom leading value.

Use 0 leading to create overlapping text effects. Figure 8.39 shows a text block with differently colored lines of type subjected to solid leading. Figure 8.40 shows the same text block with a leading value of 0. Notice that the characters in the lower lines appear in front of those above them.

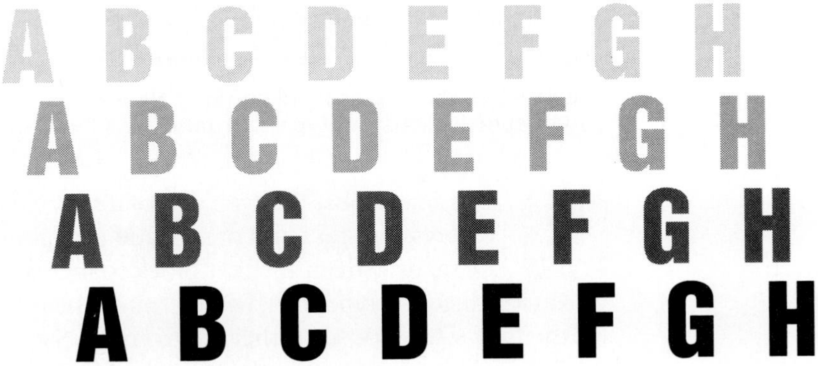

A B C D E F G H
A B C D E F G H
A B C D E F G H
A B C D E F G H

Figure 8.39: A text block with solid leading and differently colored lines of type. Characters are separated with spaces.

A B C D E F G H

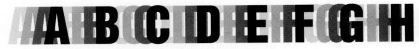

Figure 8.40: The same text block with 0 leading.

Any time that one line of text contains characters with two different leading specifications, the larger leading will prevail. When making a large initial capital letter, for example, you might have a 24-point character on the same line as 12-point characters. If both the 24-point character and the 12-point character use "Auto" leading, then the entire line will be set at 28.8-point leading (120% the 24-point type size).

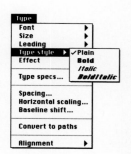 You may adjust the leading of a selected text block dynamically by dragging at the top or bottom handle of the text block. Drag up from the top handle or down from the bottom handle to increase the leading; drag in toward the text block to reduce the leading. To determine the effect the drag has made on the leading, choose "Other…" from the LEADING pop-up menu. The new leading will be displayed in the "Leading" option.

Because leading controls the distance between lines of type, it has no effect on text on a path.

Choosing a type style

The TYPE STYLE command offers a pop-up menu listing the *type styles* (plain, italic, bold) available for the current font. FreeHand relies strictly on *stylized fonts*, which provide separate font information for each type style in a *family*. The Times family, for example, includes PostScript-language definitions for the fonts Times-Roman (plain), Times-Bold, Times-Italic, and Times-BoldItalic. This configuration is somewhat of a standard. However, some families contain more or fewer styles. The family Zapf Dingbats, for example, offers only one PostScript font. If you attempt to choose a style from the TYPE STYLE pop-up menu, you will find all options except "Plain" dimmed. This is because FreeHand knows that the printer font for the current typeface offers no bold or italic style.

To guarantee the best use and accuracy in all your Macintosh typography, we recommend that you always load or attach complete PostScript font families, including a separate screen font for each style the family offers. For the Times family, for example, you should load the screen fonts Times, B Times Bold, I Times Italic, and BI Times BoldItalic. However, even if you load the plain screen font only, FreeHand will determine which styles are available and will display stylized fonts on screen, although their appearance will be approximate in accuracy.

FreeHand also clearly separates the use of true stylized fonts from mathematical effects, such as outline and shadow, by placing effects in a separate pop-up menu, as discussed in the next section. Figure 8.41 demonstrates the difference between true type styles and FreeHand's special type effects as applied to the typeface Times Roman.

Plain style
Bold style
Italic style
Bold-italic style

Heavy effect
Oblique effect
Outline effect
Shadow effect

Figure 8.41: PostScript type styles (first four) for the Times family compared with FreeHand's mathematical effects (bottom four) applied to Times plain.

Special type effects

The EFFECT command brings up a pop-up menu of options for special type effects, as well as access to standard fill and stroke functions. Each option is described here in alphabetical order, as it appears in the pop-up menu:

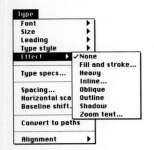

- **None**. Selected by default, this option applies no special effect to the selected text.

- **Fill and stroke**.... Choose this option to display the FILL AND STROKE dialog box shown in Figure 8.42, which allows you to define the color of the interior of each selected character of type as well as the thickness and color of its outline. To define the interior, called the *fill*, select the "Fill" check box, then select an existing color or define a new one using the "Color" pop-up option. To assign an outline, called a *stroke*, check the "Stroke" option, enter a *line weight* (thickness) value into the "Width" option box, and choose a color from the lower "Color" pop-up option. If desired, enter a value into the "Miter limit" option. This value represents the smallest angle at which a stroke is allowed to form a sharp corner. If either "Fill" or "Stroke" is not checked, the fill or stroke of the selected type will be transparent. For a complete description of filling and stroking type, both in a standard text block and in text on a path, see Chapters 9 and 10, respectively. A thorough discussion of the "Miter limit" option is also included in Chapter 10.

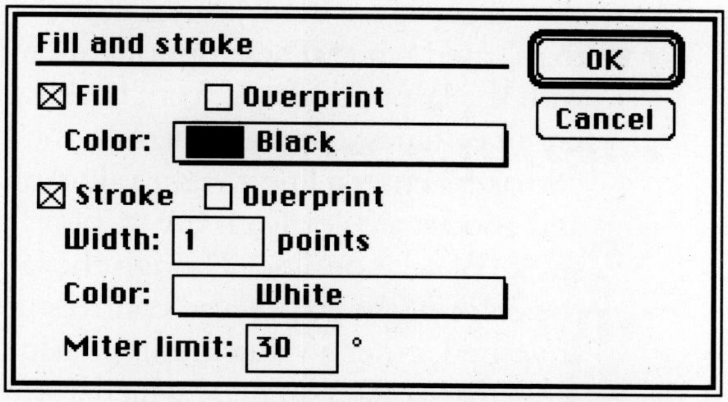

Figure 8.42: The Fill and stroke dialog box allows you to determine the colors of the interior and outline of the selected type.

"Overprint" check boxes appear next to both the "Fill" and "Stroke" options. These options apply strictly to color illustrations that are printed as color separations. When selected, overlapping colors in different separations are allowed to blend with each other. Colors may not *overprint* within a single separation or print. See the section *Overprinting colors* in Chapter 11 for a complete description of the "Overprint" option. Printing is the subject of Chapter 14.

fill   stroke   fill and stroke

Figure 8.43: An example of type that has been
filled, stroked, and both filled and stroked.

- **Heavy**. Choose this option to make the selected text appear bolder by adding a thin outline to each character (the thickness of the outline depends on the current type size) and widening the letter spacing.

- **Inline**.... Choose this option to display the INLINE dialog box shown in Figure 8.44, which allows you to assign multiple outlines to selected type. (These options are most easily explained if we start with the last option and work backward.) To determine the number of outlines, enter a value into the "Iterations" option. Under "Stroke," enter a line weight value into the "Width" option box and choose a color from the "Color" pop-up option to define the stroke of each outline. Though the label does not make this clear, the color of the stroke also controls the color of the fill of the type. If desired, enter a value into the "Miter limit" option, which represents the smallest angle at which a stroke is allowed to form a sharp corner (see the *Basic strokes* section in Chapter 10). Under background, enter a line weight and select a "Color" option to determine the thickness and color of the areas between each stroke, as demonstrated by the gray area in Figure 8.45.

- **Oblique**. This option slants the selected text approximately 10° to the right to give text an italicized appearance.

- **Outline**. This option combines a transparent interior with a thin outline (about ½ point thick) around each selected character.

- **Shadow**. Choose this option to create an offset, medium-gray shadow behind each selected character. The shadow is always gray, regardless of the color of the type.

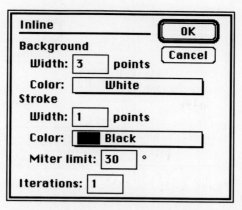

Figure 8.44: The Inline dialog box allows you to apply multiple outlines to the selected type.

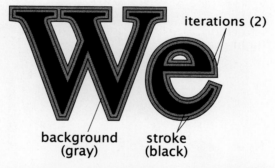

iterations (2)

background
(gray)

stroke
(black)

Figure 8.45: A word subjected to the inline effect.

• **Zoom text....** Choose this option to display the ZOOM TEXT dialog box shown in Figure 8.46 on the following page. This option allows you to create a series of repetitions of the text selection, stacked one upon another, sized and offset to create the appearance of type zooming off the page. An example of a word subjected to the "Zoom text..." option is shown in Figure 8.47.

The "Zoom to" option determines the type size of the rearmost repetition, measured as a percentage of the original type size. Enter values into the "Zoom offset" options to specify the distance from the original selection to the rearmost repetition. The "Horizontal" option is measured from the center of the selected text. Positive is right, negative is left. The "Vertical" option is measured from the baseline. Positive is up, negative is down.

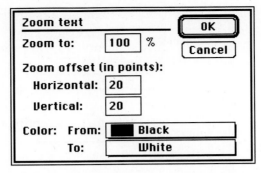

Figure 8.46: The Zoom text dialog box allows you
to create type that appears to leap off the page.

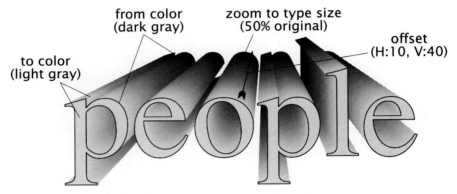

Figure 8.47: A word subjected to the zoom effect.
The central arrow shows the direction of the offset.

Choose a color from the "From" pop-up option to define the
color of the rearmost repetition, as well as the outline of the original selection. Choose a color from the "To" pop-up menu to
determine the fill color of the original selection. Each of the repetitions between the original selection and rearmost repetition is automatically assigned a size, position, and color to create a smooth
gradation.

 Only one EFFECT option may be applied at a time. For example,
you may not choose both "Heavy" and "Oblique" for the same
selected type. Each option cancels any previously selected effect.

However, you may combine special effects with type styles, such as "Bold" and "Heavy," since these options appear in different pop-up menus. FreeHand will allow multiple effects within a single text block, provided that each effect is applied to separate characters.

Unlike other formatting options, effects do not display accurately in the TEXT dialog box. Special effects may be displayed in the drawing area by selecting the "Display text effects" option in the PREFERENCES dialog box (introduced in the *Setting preferences* section of Chapter 3).

Spacing letters and words

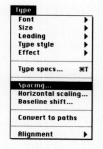

As in previous versions of Aldus FreeHand, you may control the amount of space that is placed between selected characters and words. These features are called *letter spacing* and *word spacing*. To access these spacing options, choose the SPACING... command from the TYPE menu. The SPACING dialog box shown in Figure 8.48 will display.

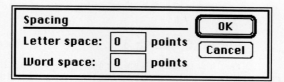

Figure 8.48: The Spacing dialog box controls the amount of space between selected letters and words.

All values in the SPACING dialog box are measured in points, regardless of the current unit of measure. For example, a "Letter space" value of 2 inserts two points between each pair of selected characters. A "Word space" value of 6 inserts 6 points (½ pica) between each pair of selected words, in addition to the normal space character. Negative values squeeze letters and words closer together.

Figure 8.49 on the next page shows a paragraph with various letter spacing and word spacing specifications. The letter spacing changes from one column of paragraphs to the next. The word spacing changes between rows.

Letter: -1, Word: -3

Wethepeopleof the United Nations, determined to save
succeeding generations from the scourge of war which
twice in our lifetime has brought untold sorrow to
mankind and to reaffirm faith in fundamental human
rights in the dignity and worth of the human person in the
equal right of men and women and of nations large and
small and to establish conditions under which justice
and respect for the obligations arising from treaties and
other sources of international law can be maintained,
and to employ international machinery for the

Letter: 0, Word: -3

We, the people of the United Nations,
determined to save succeeding
generations from the scourge of war,
which twice in our lifetime has brought
untold sorrow to mankind, and to reaffirm
faith in fundamental human rights, in the
dignity and worth of the human person, in
the equal right of men and women and of
nations large and small, and to establish
conditions under which justice and

Letter: 1, Word: -3

We, the people of the United
Nations, determined to save
succeeding generations from
the scourge of war, which twice
in our lifetime has brought
untold sorrow to mankind, and to
reaffirm faith in fundamental
human rights, in the dignity and
worth of the human person, in
the equal right of men and

Letter: -1, Word: 0

We, the people of the United Nations,
determined to save succeeding generations
from the scourge of war, which twice in our
lifetime has brought untold sorrow to mankind,
and to reaffirm faith in fundamental human rights,
in the dignity and worth of the human person, in
the equal right of men and women and of
nations large and small, and to establish
conditions under which justice and respect for
the obligations arising from treaties and other

Letter: 0, Word: 0

We, the people of the United
Nations, determined to save
succeeding generations from the
scourge of war, which twice in our
lifetime has brought untold sorrow to
mankind, and to reaffirm faith in
fundamental human rights, in the
dignity and worth of the human
person, in the equal right of men and
women and of nations large and

Letter: 1, Word: 0

We, the people of the United
Nations, determined to save
succeeding generations from
the scourge of war, which
twice in our lifetime has
brought untold sorrow to
mankind, and to reaffirm faith
in fundamental human rights,
in the dignity and worth of
the human person, in the

Letter: -1, Word: 3

We, the people of the United Nations,
determined to save succeeding generations
from the scourge of war, which twice in
our lifetime has brought untold sorrow to
mankind, and to reaffirm faith in
fundamental human rights, in the dignity
and worth of the human person, in the
equal right of men and women and of
nations large and small, and to establish
conditions under which justice and respect

Letter: 0, Word: 3

We, the people of the United
Nations, determined to save
succeeding generations from the
scourge of war, which twice in
our lifetime has brought untold
sorrow to mankind, and to
reaffirm faith in fundamental
human rights, in the dignity and
worth of the human person, in
the equal right of men and

Letter: 1, Word: 3

We, the people of the
United Nations, determined
to save succeeding
generations from the
scourge of war, which
twice in our lifetime has
brought untold sorrow to
mankind, and to reaffirm
faith in fundamental human
rights, in the dignity and

Figure 8.49: Labeled paragraphs demonstrating the effects
of different letter spacing and word spacing values.

 You may adjust the letter spacing of a selected text block dynamically by dragging at a side handle. Press OPTION and drag a side handle to alter the word spacing. In both cases, drag away from the text block to increase the spacing; drag inward to reduce spacing. To determine the exact effect a drag has made on the spacing of a text block, choose SPACING… from the TYPE menu. The new spacing values will be displayed in the "Letter space" and "Word space" options.

Kerning

FreeHand offers another method for controlling the amount of space between characters of type. Called *kerning*, this technique can be applied only inside the TEXT dialog box.

First, a little background: To determine the positioning of each character in a text block relative to the characters immediately before and after it, FreeHand relies on information included with the screen font. This information specifies the width of a character as well as the amount of space that should be placed before and after the character, known as the left and right *side bearing*, as shown in Figure 8.50. In most cases, the space between any two characters is determined by the right bearing of the first character plus the left bearing of the second.

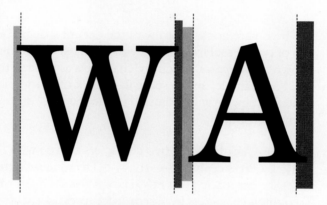

Figure 8.50: Each character has a width (demonstrated by the dotted lines) as well as right and left side bearings (shown as the light and dark gray areas). Together, these elements constitute the horizontal space occupied by a letter.

To increase readability, font designers can specify that certain pairs of letters, called *kerning pairs*, should be positioned more closely together than the standard character spacing would allow. Whenever two characters of a kerning pair appear next to each other, they are spaced according to the special information provided with the font, as demonstrated by Figure 8.51.

Figure 8.51: Certain pairs of letters are defined as kerning pairs. The screen font includes special spacing information for each pair, regardless of the letters' normal widths and side bearings.

If you are not satisfied with the default spacing between two characters of type, FreeHand allows you to adjust the kerning using increments known as *em spaces*, which are characters as wide as the current type size is tall. For example, an em space in a block of 12-point type is 12 points wide. Kerning may be adjusted inside the TEXT dialog box using the following technique.

 Click between two characters of type with the I-beam cursor. Press COMMAND-← (or ⌘-⌫) to squeeze letters together by ¹⁄₁₀₀ em space; press COMMAND-→ (or ⌘-⇧-⌫) to spread them apart. To tighten characters by ¹⁄₁₀ em space, press COMMAND-SHIFT-←; to insert ¹⁄₁₀ em space, press COMMAND-SHIFT-→.

You may notice that the information bar (just beneath the menu bar) displays the message "kerning: 0 ems" anytime the TEXT dialog box is displayed. Not only will this message change to reflect the default kerning between the current pair of letters, as shown in Figure 8.52, it will also update as you kern characters from the keyboard. For a complete explanation of the information bar, see the *Controlling movements* section of Chapter 12.

---

    kerning:-0.02 ems

Figure: 8.52: The information bar monitors the amount of kerning between the current pair of characters.

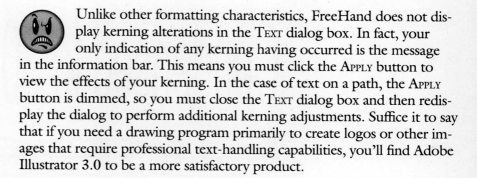

Unlike other formatting characteristics, FreeHand does not display kerning alterations in the TEXT dialog box. In fact, your only indication of any kerning having occurred is the message in the information bar. This means you must click the APPLY button to view the effects of your kerning. In the case of text on a path, the APPLY button is dimmed, so you must close the TEXT dialog box and then redisplay the dialog to perform additional kerning adjustments. Suffice it to say that if you need a drawing program primarily to create logos or other images that require professional text-handling capabilities, you'll find Adobe Illustrator 3.0 to be a more satisfactory product.

Kerning becomes a necessity when formatting text on a path. In FreeHand, letters curve apart from each other as they pass over convex curves, while they tend to overlap when passing through concave curves. If you tighten the kerning in convex areas and loosen the kerning in concave areas, your letter spacing will appear more consistent. (Again, Illustrator is the better type handler, automatically kerning text on a path to account for convex and concave curves.)

Horizontal scale

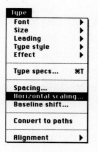

Choose the HORIZONTAL SCALING… command to display the HORIZONTAL SCALING dialog box, shown in Figure 8.53. In FreeHand, the *horizontal scale* of the selected type is its current width, measured as a percentage of its normal width. In this way, you may expand or condense type to any extent from 0.1% to 10,000% ($\frac{1}{1000}$ to 100 times its normal width). The "Scale factor" option is used primarily to achieve special graphic effects with type. Take care not to modify any type so severely that its legibility is compromised, as shown in Figure 8.54 on the following page.

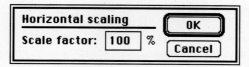

Figure 8.53: The Horizontal scaling dialog box allows you to stretch or squeeze selected type.

Condensed to 30%

Expanded 400%

Figure 8.54: Decreasing the horizontal scaling of a text block may result in fat horizontal character strokes and skinny vertical strokes. Increasing the option may result in fat vertical strokes and skinny horizontal strokes. Both effects decrease the legibility of the text.

 You may adjust the horizontal scaling of a selected text block dynamically by OPTION-dragging horizontally at a corner handle. Drag away from the text block to increase the horizontal scale; drag inward to reduce the scale. To determine the effect the drag has made on the text block, choose HORIZONTAL SCALING… from the TYPE menu. The new scale will be displayed in the "Scale factor" option.

You may reset the selected type to its normal width by changing the "Scale factor" option to 100%.

Baseline shift

Choose the BASELINE SHIFT… command to display the BASELINE SHIFT dialog box, shown in Figure 8.55, which allows you to alter the distance between the selected type and its baseline. You may use this option to create superscripts or subscripts, or to adjust the vertical alignment of text on a path. Enter any value between –10,000 and 10,000 points into the "Offset" option box. A negative value lowers selected type; a positive value raises it.

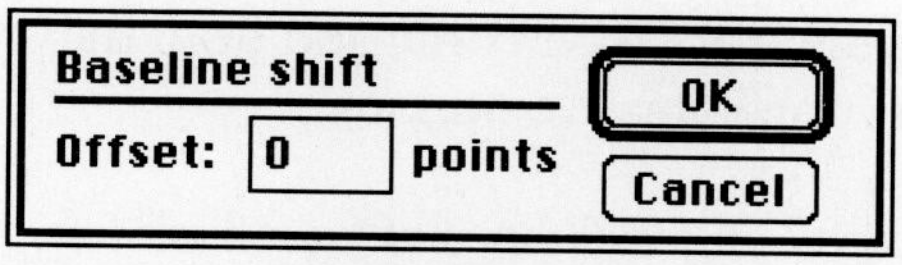

Figure 8.55: The Baseline shift dialog box allows you to raise or lower selected type with respect to its baseline.

To create a perfect fraction in Aldus FreeHand, enter the fraction using the real fraction symbol (⇧-⌥-1) rather than the standard slash. Select the numerator, make it about half its current type size, and enter a baseline shift value equal to about one-third the original type size. Then select the denominator and match its type size to that of the numerator, but do not adjust the baseline shift. The result will be a fraction such as the one shown in Figure 8.56.

35/38

Figure 8.56: You can make any fraction by varying type size and baseline shift. The fraction above was first set in 100-point type. The numerator (35) was then changed to 50-point and shifted 33 points up. The denominator (38) was also changed to 50-point type.

Changing the alignment

The lines of type in a text block may be aligned along their left edges (*flush left*), their right edges (*flush right*), or both (*fully justified*). Lines of type may also be centered with respect to each other. Finally, text may be arranged in vertical columns, so that it reads from top to bottom, then from left to right..

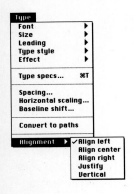

Choosing the ALIGNMENT command from the TYPE menu displays a pop-up menu containing five options:

- "Align left" aligns all lines of type flush left.

- "Align center" centers all lines of type.

- "Align right" aligns all lines of type flush right.

- "Justify" aligns all lines of a paragraph to meet the length of the longest line of type in the text block. The last line of type will also be justified, as shown in Figure 8.57, if the unjustified length of the line is 85% or more of the column width.

- "Vertical" aligns all lines of type into vertical columns, reading from top to bottom, as shown in Figure 8.57.

We, the people of the
United Nations, determined
to save succeeding
generations from the
scourge of war, which twice
in our lifetime has brought
untold sorrow to mankind,

We, the people of the
United Nations, determined
to save succeeding
generations from the
scourge of war, which twice
in our lifetime has brought
untold sorrow to mankind,

We, the people of the
United Nations, determined
to save succeeding
generations from the
scourge of war, which twice
in our lifetime has brought
untold sorrow to mankind,

We, the people of the
United Nations, determined
to save succeeding
generations from the
scourge of war, which twice
in our lifetime has brought
untold sorrow to mankind,

```
W U t g s i u
e n o e c n n
, i   n o   t
  t s e u o o
t e a r r u l
h d v a g r d
e   e t e
  N   i   l
p a s o o i s
e t u n f f o
o i c s e   r
p o c   n e r
l n e w t o o
e s f a i w
  ,   r r m   t
o   d o , e
f i m   t o
  d n   w h
  e g t h a m
  t   h i s a
h e   i c   n
e r   h b   k
  m   r i
i   t o n
n   w o u d
e   i u g ,
d c g h
  h t
  e t
```

Figure 8.57: Clockwise, from top left, text blocks flush left, centered, vertical, fully justified, and flush right.

Each ALIGNMENT option will affect all lines of type in a selected text block, even if only some portion of the text is highlighted.

The Type specifications dialog box

Choosing the TYPE SPECS... command in the TYPE menu (⌘-T) brings up the TYPE SPECIFICATIONS dialog box shown in Figure 8.58. This dialog box provides access to every formatting function discussed so far. This dialog box is most useful when you want to access several formatting options at a central location.

Figure 8.58: The Type Style dialog box provides access to every formatting option at a central location.

The following pages describe each option available in this dialog box:

- **Font.** Click and hold down your mouse button on this option to display a pop-up menu listing all typefaces and styles loaded and attached to the current System file. The "Font" option box will appear empty if the current selection contains more than one typeface.

- **Style.** Click and hold down your mouse button on this option to display a pop-up menu listing four possible type styles applicable to the current font. If the current font does not offer one or more styles, the unavailable styles will be dimmed. The "Style" option box will appear empty if the current selection contains more than one style.

- **Size.** Enter any value from 0.1 to 3000 in 0.01-point increments, or choose an option from the pop-up menu to determine the type size of the currently selected text. The value is measured in points. The "Size" option will appear empty if the current selection is set to more than one type size.

- **Leading**. Enter any value from 0 to 3000 in 0.01-point increments to determine the leading for the currently selected text. The value is measured in points. You may also choose the "Solid" option from the pop-up menu to make the leading match the type size, or choose the "Auto" option to make the leading 120% of the current type size. The "Leading" option will appear empty if the current selection uses more than one leading value.

- **Color**. Click and hold down your mouse button on this option to display a pop-up menu listing all existing colors, as well as options for creating new colors. The selected color will be applied to the fill of the selected type. The "Color" option box will appear empty if the current selection is filled with more than one color.

- **Effect**. Click and hold your mouse button down on this option to display a pop-up menu of eight mutually exclusive special effects. The specific options are discussed in the *Special type effects* section earlier in this chapter. The "Effects" option box will appear empty if the current selection contains more than one style.

- **Letter space**. The value in this option box determines the distance between selected letters of type. A negative value squeezes letters together; a positive value spreads them apart.

- **Word space**. The value in this option box is added or subtracted from a standard space character to determine the distance between selected words of type. A negative value squeezes words together; a positive value spreads them apart.

- **Horizontal scaling**. The value in this option determines the horizontal scale of the selected type. Enter any value from 0.01 to 10,000. A value greater than 100% expands selected type; a value less than 100% condenses selected type.

- **Baseline shift**. The value in this option box determines the distance between the selected type and its baseline. You may use this option to create superscripts or subscripts or to adjust text on a path. Enter any value from −10,000 to 10,000 points. A positive value raises selected type; a negative value lowers selected type.

- **Alignment**. The four "Alignment" icons allow you to change the alignment of the lines of type in a partially selected text block. Select the first icon () to align the text block flush left; select the second icon () to center the text block; select the third icon () to align the text block flush right; select the forth icon () to justify the text block; and select the last icon () to align the text block into vertical columns.

Both the OK and CANCEL buttons function as they do in any other dialog box. You may undo your changes after clicking OK by choosing the UNDO TYPE SPECS command from the EDIT menu (⌘-Z).

Converting type to paths

The final type surprise in FreeHand 3.0 is the best and the easiest to use. By choosing the CONVERT TO PATHS command from the TYPE menu, you can convert any selected text block into a collection of editable paths. To successfully implement the CONVERT TO PATHS command, the following conditions must be met:

- The type that you wish to convert must be selected with the arrow tool (it cannot be highlighted inside the TEXT dialog box).

- The selected type may be set in a Type 1 (Adobe) or Type 3 (Fontographer) font. These types include all fonts designed for PostScript printers.

- The printer font for the current typeface must be available in either the System folder or the folder that contains the FreeHand application. If the font is attached using MasterJuggler or Suitcase, the printer font may be located in the folder that contains the corresponding screen font.

The left example in Figure 8.59 on the next page shows a three-character text block selected using the arrow tool. The second example shows the characters after choosing CONVERT TO PATHS. The characters are now a single *composite path*, which, like a grouped object, is surrounded by four corner handles.

Figure 8.59: Select the text block with the arrow tool (top) and choose the Convert to paths command to produce a composite path surrounded by corner handles (bottom).

In a composite path, some paths may create holes in the paths behind them. For example, notice that the ampersand has been converted into three paths. The fact that these paths have been combined into a composite path makes the two interior paths transparent, essentially cutting holes in the larger, outer path behind them. In this way, you can see through the character to images behind it, as discussed in Chapter 9, *Filling Type and Graphic Objects*. However, to reshape a letter, you must use a special selection technique. Press OPTION and click one of the paths in the composite path with the arrow tool. The four corner handles will disappear, and all points and segments in the selected path will display. You may now manipulate these points just as if they belonged to a standard path. To select multiple paths in a composite path, SHIFT-OPTION-click each additional path. Figure 8.60 shows the result of OPTION-clicking and SHIFT-OPTION-clicking each of the paths that make up the converted letters.

To perform complex manipulations, such as joining part of one path to another, it may be necessary to separate the composite path into one or more standard paths by choosing the SPLIT ELEMENT command from the ELEMENT menu.

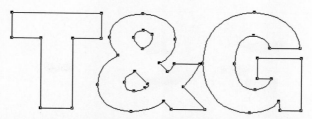

Figure 8.60: Option-click a character in a composite path to display its points and segments.

After choosing the CONVERT TO PATHS and SPLIT ELEMENT commands, converted type may be reshaped, transformed, duplicated, and otherwise manipulated in any manner, as demonstrated by the fantastic image in Figure 8.61. It may not be art, but at least it's possible.

Figure 8.61: And to think, once this was Helvetica.

Filling Type and Graphic Objects

In the keyline display mode, every path has a transparent interior surrounded by a thin, solid black outline. All type is black. But when you preview or print an illustration, all this changes. The interior of type or a graphic object may be black or red or may fade from blue to yellow with green between. Outlines may be as thick or thin as you like, dashed or solid, orange or purple, and you may now select from a collection of arrowheads. One of Aldus FreeHand's greatest strengths is the complete freedom its allows you to determine the appearance of a path or text object.

The qualities that may be ascribed to type and graphic objects are called *fills* and *strokes*. Fill determines the appearance of the interior of an object, and is the subject of this chapter. Stroke is applied to the outline of an object. Detailed coverage of this attribute is included in Chapter 10, *Stroking Type and Graphic Objects.*

How fill affects an object

In FreeHand, any path or text block may be filled. When a closed path is filled, its entire interior is affected. Figure 9.01 shows a closed path as it appears in the keyline mode and the same path as it appears when printed. The shape acts like a kind of malleable water balloon—the fill seeps into every nook and cranny of the shape.

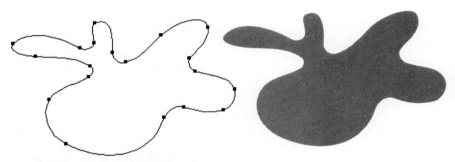

Figure 9.01: In the keyline mode, the fill of a closed path is invisible (left). But when you preview or print the path, its fill seeps into every nook and cranny of the shape (right).

Although you may assign a fill to an open path, the fill will neither preview nor print. The open path in the first example in Figure 9.02 has been filled with gray. However, the fill does not display until we close the path, as demonstrated by the second example in the figure.

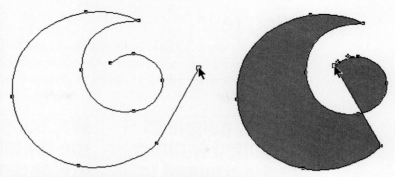

Figure 9.02: An open path (left) may be assigned a fill, but it will neither preview nor print until the path has been closed (right).

It's unfortunate that FreeHand can't display or print the fill of an open path, because indefinite boundaries can be created by filling a shape that is not bordered on all sides by a stroke. Notice, in Figure 9.03, that on the side of the plane facing the viewer, the wings appear as open paths. Imaginary segments define the boundaries of the white fills of the wings. If either path were closed, a stroke along the closing segment would appear at the junction of the wing and the plane. How do you create such a graphic in FreeHand? While closed, we assigned a white fill and *no* stroke to each path. Then we cloned both paths, deleted the closing segment from each, removed the fills, and applied black strokes.

Figure 9.03: To create the wings on the facing side of the plane, you must create two paths for each wing, one closed and filled, the other open and stroked.

Filling text

Text objects—which include both text blocks and text on a path—may also be filled. If you select a text object with the arrow tool and apply a fill, the fill will affect all type in the text object, as demonstrated in Figure 9.04.

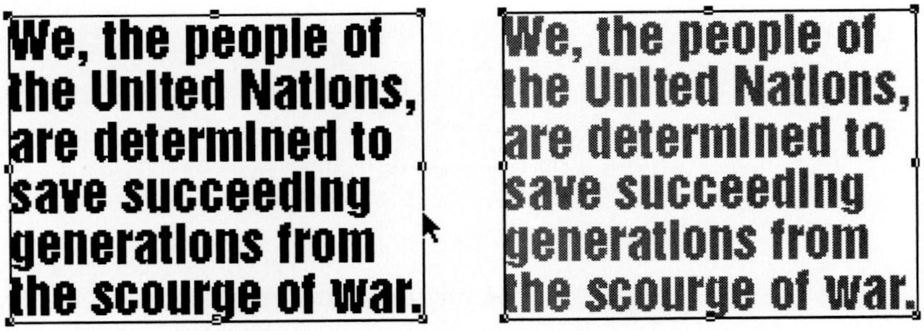

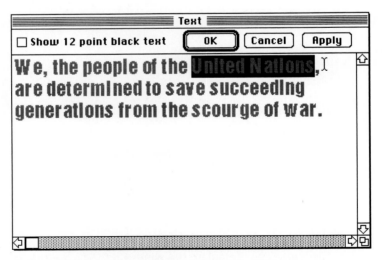

Figure 9.04: If you fill a text block selected with the arrow tool (left), all characters in the block will be filled (right).

You may also fill single words and other collections of specific characters inside the TEXT dialog box. Like any character-level formatting option, such as font or type size, fill affects only highlighted characters, as demonstrated in Figures 9.05 and 9.06. In this way, FreeHand 3.0 allows you to apply several different fills to a single text object.

Figure 9.05: By highlighting text using the I-beam cursor inside the Text dialog box...

Figure 9.06: ...you may fill specific characters of type without affecting other characters in the block.

Due to FreeHand's self-imposed restrictions, you may not apply special fill effects, such as gradations and tile patterns, to type. If you want to create an effect like the one shown in Figure 9.07, you must first convert the text to composite paths using the CONVERT TO PATHS command from the TYPE menu, as described in the last section of Chapter 8. The type may then be filled and stroked like any other graphic object.

Figure 9.07: After converting a text block to composite paths, you may assign complicated fill effects, such as gradations, tile patterns, and masking, the last of which is shown here.

Assigning the fill

To fill or stroke any graphic object (not text), you must select the object and choose FILL AND LINE... from the ATTRIBUTES menu (⌘-E). The FILL AND LINE dialog box will display, as shown in Figure 9.08. Almost every characteristic of a fill or a stroke can be manipulated within this dialog box.

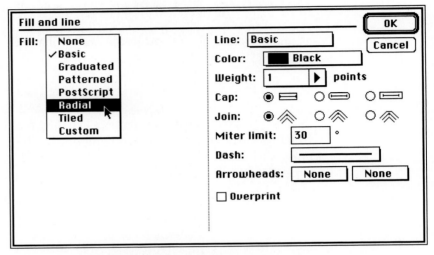

Figure 9.08: The Fill and line dialog box provides access to most of FreeHand's fill and stroke features.

All options in the FILL AND LINE dialog box fall into one of two categories: those that affect fill and those that affect stroke. All options on the left side of the dialog box apply to the fill of a selected object. All options on the right side apply to the stroke. See Chapter 10, *Stroking Type and Graphic Objects*, for complete information on the stroking options.

Using the "Fill" pop-up option

After displaying the FILL AND LINE dialog box, click and hold on the "Fill" option to display a pop-up menu listing various kinds of fills, as demonstrated in Figure 9.08. Only one "Fill" option may be selected at a time. Many options display other options that request additional specifications in determining the colors in a fill. Each variety of fill and its related options are discussed in the following sections.

No fill

The "None" option makes the interior of the selected path transparent. This same function may also be performed by choosing the REMOVE FILL command from the ATTRIBUTES menu. The "None" option is useful for filling paths when you want only the stroke to be visible. You may also assign both a transparent stroke and a transparent fill to a path. An entirely transparent path may be viewed in the keyline mode but will neither preview nor print. Such a path may be used for alignment purposes or to surround an image that you intend to export as an EPS file, as described in the *Exporting an illustration* section of Chapter 13.

Fill: | None |

Figure 9.09: No additional option is associated with the "None" option.

Basic fills

Choosing the "Basic" option fills the selected path with a uniform color. The "Color" pop-up option will appear below the "Fill" option, as shown in Figure 9.10. Click and hold on this option to display every color defined in the current illustration, as well as several commands used to create new colors and access colors from the Pantone color library. See Chapter 11, *Assigning Colors and Styles*, for complete information about creating and accessing colors in FreeHand.

Fill: | Basic |

Color: | ▓ Black |

☐ **Overprint**

Figure 9.10: The "Basic" options include the "Color" pop-up menu and the "Overprint" check box.

An "Overprint" check box appears below the "Color" option when the "Basic" option is selected. This option applies strictly to color illustrations that are to be printed as color separations. When selected, overlapping colors in different separations are allowed to blend with each other. Colors may *not* overprint within a single separation. See Chapter 11 for a complete description of the "Overprint" option. Printing is the subject of Chapter 14.

Gradient fills

Choose the "Graduated" option to create a *gradient fill*, which fades from one color to another. For example, if the left side of a path is filled with black and the right side is filled with blue, the two colors will fade together throughout the middle of the path.

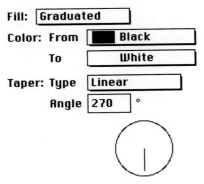

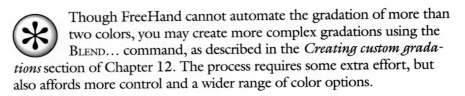

Figure 9.11: The "Graduated" options include the "Color" pop-up menus and the "Taper" controls.

When using the "Graduated" option, the differently colored portions of a gradient fill must be positioned directly opposite of each other. For example, if the gradation begins at the top of a shape, it must end at the bottom. Colors may not fade in and out, and no more than two colors may be included in a single gradation.

Though FreeHand cannot automate the gradation of more than two colors, you may create more complex gradations using the BLEND... command, as described in the *Creating custom gradations* section of Chapter 12. The process requires some extra effort, but also affords more control and a wider range of color options.

When "Graduated" is selected, two "Color" pop-up options appear beneath the "Fill" option. They are labeled "From" and "To"; that is, the first and last colors in the gradation, respectively. Click and hold on this option to display every color defined in the current illustration, as well as several commands used to create new colors and access colors from the Pantone color library that accompanies the FreeHand application. Note that gray values, process colors, and tints of the same spot color may be used in a single gradation, but different spot colors may not, nor may you blend from a spot color to a gray value or process color. (See Chapter 11, *Assigning Colors and Styles*, for complete information about creating and accessing gray values, process colors, spot colors, and tints in FreeHand.)

After the "Color" options come the "Taper" controls, which allow you to determine the manner in which the first and last colors fade together. It is not enough to know that a fill begins at one color and fades into another. FreeHand needs to know *how* these colors mesh. Where exactly is the first color in reference to the selected shape? Does the gradation favor one color, or are both colors given equal treatment?

The "Type" pop-up option allows you to choose either a *linear gradation* or a *logarithmic gradation*. In a linear gradation, every increment between the first and last colors is given equal treatment. In a logarithmic gradation, each progressive gradation is slightly larger than its predecessor. In other words, the gradation will contain more of the last color than the first. The fill fades drastically at the beginning, then more moderately as the gradation progresses.

Figure 9.12: An image filled with a linear gradation (top) and another filled with a logarithmic gradation (bottom).

The first image in Figure 9.12 contains a linear gradation. The first color is black; the last color is white. The fill fades from black at the top to white at the bottom in a consistent manner. The second image in Figure

9.12 contains a logarithmic gradation. Again, the first color is black and the last color is white. As a result, black receives the least emphasis and white receives the most.

The "Angle" option gives you control over the direction of the gradation. This may be set either by entering a value between –360° and 360° into the option box or by using the wheel below the "Angle" option. To use the wheel, drag its hand around the circle. The option box value and wheel hand act congruously. If you enter 90 in the option box, the hand will move around to the 12 o'clock position. Likewise, if you move the hand to the 12 o'clock position, the option box value will change to match. The default taper angle is 270° (–90°), or straight downward.

The top path in Figure 9.13 shows the results of setting the "Angle" value to 45° (between 1 and 2 o'clock) with a first color of black and an last color of white. The lower path contains identical first and last colors, but the "Angle" value has been changed to 225° (–135°), forcing the gradation to progress in the opposite direction.

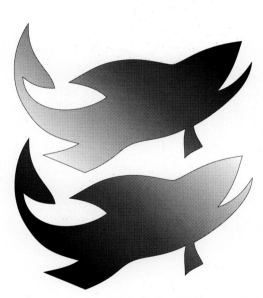

Figure 9.13: Images filled with a 45°angle gradation
(top) and a 225°angle gradation (bottom).

 Pressing the SHIFT key while dragging the hand of the "Angle" wheel will constrain the direction of the current gradation in 5° increments.

Keep in mind that the color and angle of a gradation work together. The following exercise examines how the "Color" and "Angle" options may be used to change the amount of emphasis applied to colors in a logarithmic fill:

1. Select a closed path and choose the FILL AND LINE... command from the ATTRIBUTES menu (⌘-E).

2. Choose "Graduated" from the "Fill" pop-up option. Then choose "Black" as the first color and "White" as the last.

3. Under "Taper," choose "Logarithmic" from the "Type" pop-up option. Leave the "Angle" option at 270° (straight down).

4. Press RETURN to close the FILL AND LINE dialog box. The result is a fill that fades from black to white, quickly at the top and slowly at the bottom, as seen in the first example of Figure 9.14. Suppose, however, that you want to create a slightly different fill that fades slowly at top and quickly at the bottom, as displayed in the second example of the figure. Which options do you have to adjust to achieve this fill?

Figure 9.14: Images filled with logarithmic gradations, each of which uses different first and last colors and flows in the opposite direction of the other.

5. The logarithmic tapering cannot be changed. That is to say, it always fades quickly at first and slowly at the end. Therefore, you must turn everything upside down. Assuming the path is still selected, choose FILL AND LINE... to again display the FILL AND LINE dialog box.

6. Change the "Angle" value to 90° (straight up).

7. Reverse the first and last colors, so that the gradation begins with white ("From") at the bottom of the path and fades upward into black ("To").

8. Press RETURN. Your path now contains a gradation that appears to flow in the same direction as before. However, white—being the last color—now receives more emphasis than black.

Bitmapped patterns

Choose the "Patterned" option to fill the selected path with a bitmapped pattern, similar to those offered by MacPaint, MacDraw, and other low-end applications. In fact, the primary purpose for the inclusion of bitmapped patterns is to make FreeHand compatible with graphics created in MacDraw.

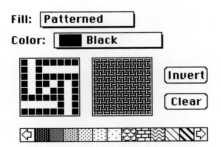

Figure 9.15: The "Patterned" options include the "Color" pop-up menu and a series of controls for editing bitmapped patterns.

Among the options that appear when you choose "Patterned" from the "Fill" pop-up option is a scrolling collection of 64 patterns included with FreeHand 3.0. Display additional patterns by clicking on the left and right scroll arrows. Select a pattern by clicking on it. Above the scrolling patterns are two boxes. The left box contains an enlarged version of the pattern, allowing you to edit the pattern by clicking pixels on and off. The right box shows the pattern as it appears at actual size. (Clicking in this box produces no result.) Two buttons are also provided to enhance your editing abilities. The INVERT button changes all black pixels in a pattern to white, and all white pixels to black. This is useful for creating a negative image of the current pattern. You may also erase all pixels in a pattern by clicking CLEAR.

The white pixels in a bitmap pattern are always white and opaque. The black pixels may be colored using the "Color" pop-up option.

FreeHand 3.0 doesn't allow you to color bitmapped patterns any better than its predecessors. Although you can apply any color that you desire, a color that requires a screen value will not print correctly. This excludes all tints (including gray values) and almost every process color. Also, regardless of whether you enlarge or reduce a path, its bitmapped pattern will always print at 72 dots per inch, the same resolution as MacPaint. They don't even enlarge on-screen when you magnify the view size. Our unhappy recommendation: Don't use bitmapped patterns. They are provided strictly to aid in the conversion of PICT graphics originally created in MacDraw or a similar program and opened in FreeHand.

PostScript-language fills

Choose the "PostScript" option from the "Fill" pop-up menu to fill the selected path with a PostScript-language routine. Type up to 255 characters (including spaces) into the "PostScript code" text entry area, shown in Figure 9.16 on the following page. The text must be "stable" PostScript code (no *nulldevice*, no *initgraphics*, that kind of thing). Do *not* use return characters. An entry error will very likely prevent the entire illustration from printing, so check your code carefully.

You may color your PostScript fill by choosing a color from the "Color" pop-up option. If your PostScript code contains any color information of its own, your "Color" option selection will be ignored during the printing process.

A PostScript routine is displayed in the drawing area as a series of *PS*s, colored according to your selection in the "Color" pop-up option, regardless of whether your PostScript code contains color information. However, the fill will print according to the PostScript definition.

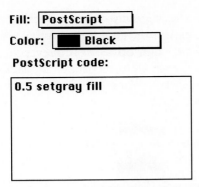

Figure 9.16: The "PostScript" options include the "Color" pop-up menu and the "PostScript code" text entry area.

If this all sounds like Greek to you, don't worry. Most of us can get by without ever using the "PostScript" option. Still, it's a great feature for the frustrated programmer. It can also be useful for calling up custom fills created by third-party developers, as examined in Appendix B, *FreeHand and the PostScript Language*.

Radial gradient fills

In addition to linear and logarithmic gradations, FreeHand offers access to another variety of gradient fill called a *radial gradation*. In such a fill, the first color emanates from the center of the selected path, the last color appears at the perimeter of the path. In between, the colors fade into one another in concentric circles, creating a sunburst effect.

To create a radial gradation, choose the "Radial" option from the "Fill" pop-up menu. Two "Color" options will appear. The "From" selection determines the central color in the gradation; the "To" selection determines the color around the perimeter of the path.

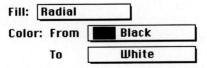

Figure 9.17: The "Radial" options include two "Color" pop-up menus.

Figure 9.18 shows two images enhanced with radial gradations. For the top fish, the "From" color was white and the "To" color was black. For the bottom fish, the color options were reversed.

Figure 9.18: A radial gradation from white to black (top) and another from black to white (bottom).

Edit	
Undo	⌘Z
Redo	⌘Y
Cut	⌘H
Copy	⌘C
Paste	⌘U
Clear	
Cut contents	
Paste inside	
Select all	⌘A
Duplicate	⌘D
Clone	⌘=
Move...	⌘M
Transform again	⌘,

You've probably heard this oft-repeated tip before, but it's a good one to know, so here goes: FreeHand automatically positions the first color in a radial gradation at the exact center of the selected path. To change the location at which a radial graduation begins, draw a larger shape that completely covers your path and fill it with a radial gradation. Then reposition the center of the shape relative to your path. When you are satisfied, cut the shape (using the CUT command from the EDIT menu, ⌘-X), select your original path, and choose the PASTE INSIDE command. This process is demonstrated in Figure 9.19 on the following page. This masks the radial gradation so the highlight—assuming the "From" color is lighter than the "To" color—begins at the location defined by the larger shape. For complete information on masking, see the *Clipping paths* section later in this chapter.

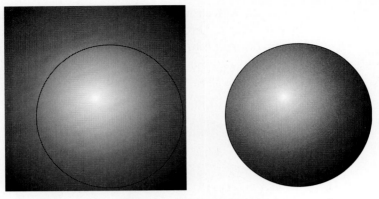

Figure 9.19: Mask a large radial gradation (left) to control
the location of its highlight inside a path (right).

Tile patterns

The "Tiled" option in the "Fill" pop-up menu allows you to define a
tile pattern, which is an object-oriented pattern or design composed of
stroked and filled objects. Like the surface of a kitchen linoleum, a
single, rectangular *tile* is repeated over and over throughout a selected
path. This is the first of two techniques that allows you to achieve the appearance of one object being set within another. The other technique,
masking, is described in the *Clipping paths* section later in this chapter.

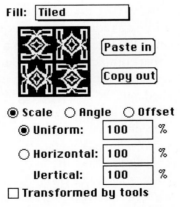

Figure 9.20: The "Tiled" options allow you to define
and fill a selection with a repeating tile pattern.

Creating and applying a tile pattern is a more complicated process than any of the filling options we have examined so far. To simplify our discussion, we will analyze the process in three major parts: Creating a tile pattern and assigning the pattern to a selection, transforming the pattern independently of the selection, and transforming the pattern along with the path that it fills.

- **Part 1**: *Creating and assigning a tile pattern.*

In FreeHand, all tile patterns are rectangular. This fact is very important for understanding and creating patterns in FreeHand. The appearance of a pattern can be far from rectangular, but when you create a tile, it must exist completely within a rectangular boundary. It is sometimes advisable to first create a rectangle to represent the perimeter of the pattern tile and then create your pattern objects within this perimeter. Other times it may be better to create the objects first, then draw your rectangle around the objects.

Fill and stroke all pattern objects (including the rectangle) and position the rectangle in relation to the pattern objects. If necessary, select the rectangle and choose the SEND TO BACK command from the EDIT menu (⌘-B) to ensure that it doesn't obscure any pattern objects. Note: No pattern objects should exceed the perimeter of the rectangular boundary (although they may be flush with the edge).

After completing the objects, you may define them as a tile pattern and applied to the fill of a path as described below:

1. Select the rectangle and all objects that you want to include in the tile, and choose the CUT command from the EDIT menu (⌘-X) to transfer the objects to the Clipboard.

2. Select the path or paths to which you want to apply the pattern.

3. Choose the FILL AND LINE... command from the ATTRIBUTES menu to display the FILL AND LINE dialog box. (If you want to save the pattern as an attributes style for use in filling future objects, access the FILL AND LINE dialog box via the STYLES... command, as described in Chapter 11, *Assigning Colors and Styles.*)

4. Choose the "Tiled" option from the "Fill" pop-up menu. The options shown in Figure 9.20 will display.

5. Click the PASTE IN button to paste the contents of the Clipboard into the FILL AND LINE dialog box. A preview of your tile will appear to the left of the button.

6. Click the OK button or press RETURN to confirm the creation of your new tile pattern and apply it to the current selection.

The following exercise demonstrates how to create a pattern that looks like the cover of a manhole, with alternating horizontal and vertical ridges appearing to stand up from a metal plate, as shown in Figure 9.21. You'll find that a mechanical tile pattern such as this is well-suited to a computer-graphics environment.

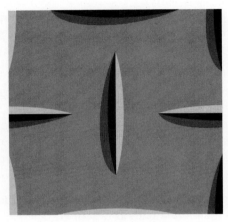

Figure 9.21: A tile that mimics metal ridges like those on a manhole cover.

The exercise is slightly longer than previous ones in this book, since creating a tile pattern involves several steps. However, the procedure is not particularly difficult:

1. Create the first ridge as a combination of three paths, as shown in Figure 9.22. Each path is filled with a different shade of gray to impart a sense of depth and shadow, as shown in the second example in the figure.

2. Select the three paths and choose the GROUP command from the ELEMENT menu (⌘-G).

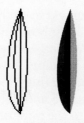

Figure 9.22: A single ridge made up of three paths (left)
and the ridge as it appears when printed (right).

3. Choose the CLONE command from the EDIT menu (⌘-=, COMMAND-EQUAL) to create a duplicate of the group directly in front of the original.

4. Drag the duplicated group while pressing SHIFT to move it about one inch to the left.

5. Choose the DUPLICATE command from the EDIT menu (⌘-D), to create a second duplicate of the group. You now have three ridges, spaced equidistantly.

6. Next, select the middle group. Using the reflect tool, OPTION-click near the center of the selected group. After the REFLECT dialog box displays, select the "Angled" radio button, enter 45 in the corresponding option box, and press RETURN. The object will flip and rotate, as shown in Figure 9.23. (For complete information about the reflect tool and the REFLECT dialog box, see the *Flipping objects* section of Chapter 12.)

Figure 9.23: Clone two additional ridges and flip the
middle one about a 45° axis.

7. The first row of ridges is now complete. Select the three ridges and choose CLONE from the EDIT menu to duplicate all three objects.

8. Choose the Move… command from the EDIT menu (⌘-M) to display the MOVE ELEMENTS dialog box. Enter 72 for the "Horizontal" option and –72 for the "Vertical" option, then press RETURN. (This assumes you are working in points. If you are using picas, enter 6 and –6, respectively; if you are using inches, enter 1 and –1; if you are using millimeters, enter 25 and –25.) The duplicated ridges, which appear below and to the right of the originals, act as the beginning of a second row.

9. Select the two rightmost ridges in the second row and choose CLONE. Position your arrow cursor at the top point in the selected vertical ridge and drag the duplicates to the left while pressing SHIFT. Release your mouse button when this point snaps to the similar point in the stationary vertical ridge in the same row, as shown in Figure 9.24. By snapping, you ensure that the space between all ridges is constant.

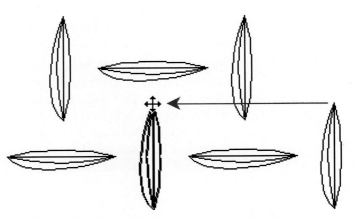

Figure 9.24: Duplicate the two rightmost ridges in the second row and drag them to the left until they snap to the stationary vertical ridge in the same row.

10. You now have two coincident vertical ridges in the middle of the second row, one in front of the other. Select the front one and press DELETE or BACKSPACE to get rid of it. The right vertical ridge is also extraneous, so delete it as well.

11. To create a third row of ridges, select the three grouped objects in the top row and choose CLONE. Then choose the MOVE... command to again display the MOVE ELEMENTS dialog box. Enter 0 for the "Horizontal" option and –144 (–12 picas, –2 inches, or –50 millimeters) for the "Vertical" option, then press RETURN. Figure 9.25 shows the three rows of ridges.

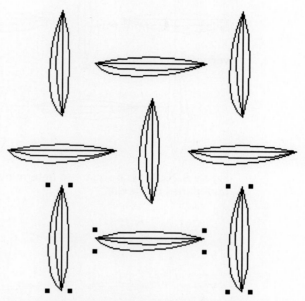

Figure 9.25: Clone the top row of ridges and move the clones down 144 points, or two inches.

12. Draw a square surrounding the portions of the ridge objects that you want to repeat in the pattern, as shown in Figure 9.26 on the next page. This square determines the boundaries of the tile.

✳ When you draw your rectangle around the tile objects, try to visualize of how it will look when the pattern is repeated. Objects that touch the left edge of the rectangle will be flush with the objects that touch the right edge of an adjoining tile. Likewise, objects that touch the top of the rectangle will meet with the objects that touch the bottom of another tile. Figure 9.27 on the next page shows six copies of the manhole-cover tile arranged in a pattern. Each object flows continuously through one tile and into another.

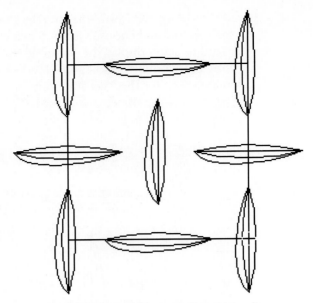

Figure 9.26: Draw a square to determine the boundaries of the tile.

Figure 9.27: When drawing the boundary rectangle, visualize how the tiles will fit together.

13. While the square is selected, choose the SEND TO BACK command from the EDIT menu (⌘-B). Then fill the square with a medium shade of gray to act as a background for the ridges.

14. The pattern objects may not exceed the boundaries of the square. Therefore, you must clip the excess ridges away before defining the pattern. The easiest way to accomplish this is to mask the ridges with the square. Select all nine ridge groups and choose the CUT command from the EDIT menu (⌘-X). Next, select the square and choose the PASTE INSIDE command from the EDIT menu. All portions of the ridge objects that previously exceeded the boundary of the square are now clipped away, as shown in Figure 9.21 back on page 306. (Masking is explained in detail in the *Clipping paths* section later in this chapter.)

15. While the square is still selected, choose CUT again, sending the square and its contents to the Clipboard.

16. Choose the STYLES… command from the ATTRIBUTES menu to display the STYLES dialog box, shown in Figure 9.28. This dialog box allows you to name a pattern for future use (as discussed in Chapter 11, *Assigning Colors and Styles*).

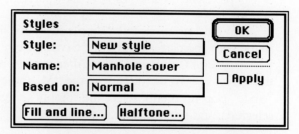

Figure 9.28: The Styles dialog box allows you to name a fill or stroke for future use.

17. Click on the FILL AND LINE… button to display the FILL AND LINE dialog box. Choose the "Tiled" option from the "Fill" pop-up menu to display the tile pattern options.

18. Click the PASTE IN button. A preview of the tile will appear to the left of the button. If the preview does not match the one shown in Figure 9.29 on the next page, press COMMAND-PERIOD twice to cancel out of both the FILL AND LINE and the STYLES dialog boxes, paste the pattern elements back into the drawing area. Then manipulate the elements as necessary and repeat steps 16 and 17. If your preview matches the figure, press RETURN to confirm the pattern and close the FILL AND LINE dialog box.

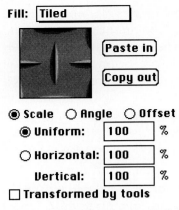

Fill: ⬚ Tiled

[Paste in]

[Copy out]

◉ Scale   ◯ Angle   ◯ Offset
  ◉ **Uniform:** `100` %
  ◯ **Horizontal:** `100` %
    Vertical: `100` %
☐ **Transformed by tools**

Figure 9.29: The Pattern dialog box previews the selected pattern tile.

19. You are returned to the STYLES dialog box. Enter the name *Manhole cover* into the "Name" option box and press RETURN to complete the creation of your new pattern.

You have now created a simple tile pattern. You may now fill any shape with the pattern using the STYLES palette, as described in Chapter 11, *Assigning Colors and Styles*. Alternatively, select a closed path, choose the STYLES... command, choose the "Manhole cover" option from the "Style" pop-up menu, select the "Apply" check box (if it is not already selected), and press RETURN.

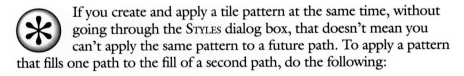

If you create and apply a tile pattern at the same time, without going through the STYLES dialog box, that doesn't mean you can't apply the same pattern to a future path. To apply a pattern that fills one path to the fill of a second path, do the following:

1. Select the path filled with the tile pattern and choose the FILL AND LINE... command from the ATTRIBUTES menu (⌘-E).

2. Inside the FILL AND LINE dialog box, click the COPY OUT button to the right of the tile preview. A copy of the tile is transferred to the Clipboard. Press RETURN to close the dialog box.

3. Select the second path and choose FILL AND LINE... again. Choose "Tiled" from the "Fill" pop-up menu and click the PASTE IN button. The copied tile appears in the preview box. Press RETURN to accept the pattern fill and close the dialog box.

The Copy out button may also be used to copy a tile so it may be pasted into the drawing area and manipulated. The Copy out button does not remove the tile pattern from the current fill, but simply makes a copy of it.

● **Part 2**: *Transforming a tile pattern independently of a path.*

After applying a tile pattern, you may scale, rotate, or move the pattern inside the object it fills. Directly beneath the pattern preview in the FILL AND LINE dialog box are three radio button options, shown in Figure 9.29. These options include the following:

● **Scale**. The options in this box allow you to enlarge or reduce a pattern inside an object. If you want to scale the pattern proportionally, select the "Uniform" radio button and enter a percentage in the corresponding option box. Values less than 100% will reduce the pattern; values greater than 100% will enlarge it. If you want to scale the horizontal and vertical dimensions of the pattern differently, select the radio button that precedes "Horizontal" and enter values in the "Horizontal" and "Vertical" option boxes.

● **Angle**. Select this radio button to display the option box and wheel shown in Figure 9.30. Enter a value in the option box or drag the wheel hand around the circle to rotate the pattern by a specific number of degrees. A positive value indicates a counterclockwise rotation; a negative value produces a clockwise rotation.

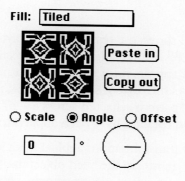

Figure 9.30: Select "Angle" to rotate a tile pattern inside a path.

Pressing the SHIFT key while dragging the hand of the "Angle" wheel will constrain the angle of the rotation in 5° increments.

- **Offset**. Select this radio button to display the two option boxes shown in Figure 9.31, which allow you to reposition a pattern within an object. Enter the horizontal and vertical components of a move into the "H" and "V" option boxes. These value are measured in points, picas, inches, or millimeters, depending on the setting of the "Unit of measure" option in the DOCUMENT SETUP dialog box.

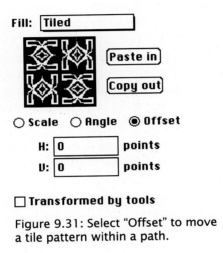

Figure 9.31: Select "Offset" to move a tile pattern within a path.

Figure 9.32 shows the results of transforming the manhole cover pattern within the fill of a rectangle. The first example in the figure shows the pattern as it appears prior to any transformation. The second example on the left shows the pattern scaled to 200%; the first example on the right shows the pattern reflected across a −45° axis. In the final example, both scaling and rotating have been applied to the pattern.

Notice that transformations applied from inside the FILL AND LINE dialog box do not transform the filled object itself, only the tiles within the object. Also, a pattern is transformed only within the current selection. Transforming a pattern within one object does not transform that pattern within other objects filled or stroked with the same pattern.

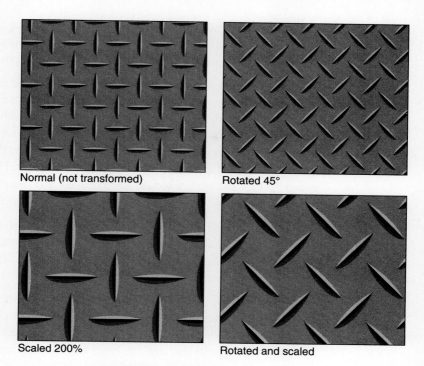

Normal (not transformed) Rotated 45°

Scaled 200% Rotated and scaled

Figure 9.32: The manhole cover pattern
subjected to various transformations.

Incidentally, when you fill an object with a pattern, the relative location of each tile is based on its distance from lower left corner of the page size. This location acts as the origin point for all tile patterns, even if an object filled with a pattern appears far from this origin. All manipulations performed in the FILL AND LINE dialog are performed with respect to the this location. For example, when you rotate a pattern 45°, you rotate it 45° around the lower left corner of the page.

● **Part 3**: *Transforming a tile pattern along with a path.*

Finally, you may transform a tile pattern along with a filled object. The MOVE ELEMENTS dialog box (discussed in the *Using the Move elements dialog box* section in Chapter 7) as well as the SCALE, REFLECT, ROTATE, and SKEW dialog boxes (see Chapter 12, *Transforming and Duplicating Objects*) all contain check boxes that toggle the transformation of patterns within a transformed object. Rather than conforming strictly to the lower left corner of the page, a tile pattern may conform momentarily to the location and orientation of the object filled with that pattern.

If all of this seems a little confusing, consider the following example: Suppose that you select a rectangle filled with the manhole cover pattern and choose the MOVE... command from the EDIT menu (⌘-M). In the MOVE ELEMENTS dialog box, you specify a vertical move of 24 points and select "Fills" from the "Move options" check boxes. Both the selected rectangle and its fill pattern move upward two picas. (Had you not selected "Fills," the object would have moved and the tiles would have remained stationary.)

When you first launch the FreeHand application, patterns are by default transformed along with filled objects. This means that the "Fills" check boxes in the MOVE ELEMENTS, SCALE, REFLECT, ROTATE, and SKEW dialog boxes will be selected.

Each "Fill" option in each dialog box operates independently, so if you change the setting for one check box, the other check boxes will be unaffected. However, the default setting for that dialog box will be changed throughout the current FreeHand session or until changed again.

These options do *not* affect manual transformations. Transforming a path with the scale, reflect, rotate, or skew tool affects both path and tile pattern equally, regardless of the default setting of the "Fill" check box. Moving a path with the arrow tool or using the arrow keys moves the path only, without affecting the tile pattern.

To see if a pattern has been transformed inside an object, select the object and choose the FILL AND LINE... command from the ATTRIBUTES menu (⌘-E). The "Scale," "Angle," and "Offset" options will display information concerning only those transformations that have been performed from inside the FILL AND LINE dialog box. If a pattern has been transformed in the course of transforming the filled object, the "Transformed by tools" check box will be selected. If you deselect this check box, you reverse the effects of all pattern transformations applied in the course of transforming the selected object, although the object itself will remain transformed. Transformations applied using the FILL AND LINE dialog box options will also remain intact.

The "Transformed by tools" option is dimmed if the current pattern has not been affected by transforming the selected object.

● *Tile pattern wrap-up.*

A couple of final notes: Tile patterns may *not* be applied to type, as shown in Figure 9.33, unless you first convert the text block using the CONVERT TO PATHS command in the TYPE menu. Generally, large sans serif type is best suited to this purpose.

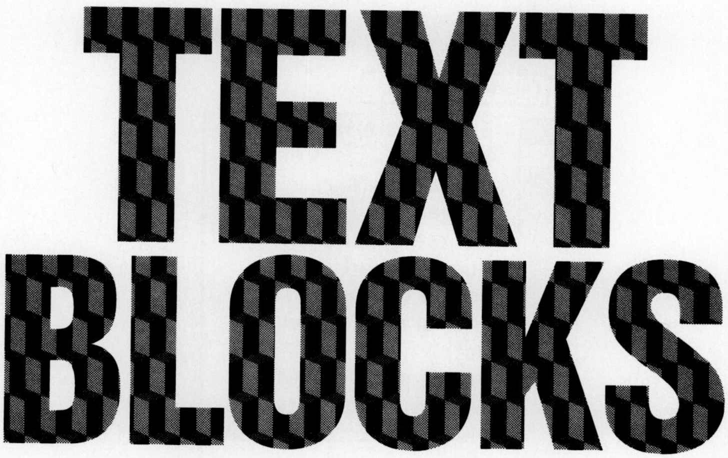

Figure 9.33: A tile pattern can only be applied to text converted to a path.

Patterns may be beautiful to look at, but they take a lot of effort to create and they eat up disk space and printer memory like you wouldn't believe. For a more efficient filling technique that doesn't restrict you to using repeating images, create a mask as described in the *Clipping path* section later in this chapter. Or use FreeHand's collection of custom Post-Script fills. They're easy to use, they print quickly, and they're introduced on the following page.

Custom PostScript fills

Choose the "Custom" option from the "Fill" pop-up menu to fill the selected path with a predefined PostScript routine included with the FreeHand 3.0. After choosing "Custom," you may choose any one of the 19 options included in the "Effect" pop-up menu, as shown in Figure 9.34. If you choose any but the "Black & white noise" option, a dialog box will display. It will contain a "Color" pop-up menu, as well as other options depending on the variety of custom fill you have chosen.

Custom fill routines are displayed in the drawing area as a series of *C*s, colored according to your selection in the "Color" pop-up option.

Fill: Custom

Effect:
- ✓ Black & white noise
- Bricks
- Burlap texture
- Circles
- Coarse gravel texture
- Coquille texture
- Denim texture
- Fine gravel texture
- Hatch
- Heavy mezzo texture
- Light mezzo texture
- Medium mezzo texture
- Noise
- Random grass
- Random leaves
- Sand texture
- Squares
- Tiger teeth
- Top noise

Figure 9.34: The "Custom" options include an "Effect" pop-up menu, which contains 19 PostScript fill options.

Figure 9.35 shows the result of accepting the default values presented by FreeHand for each custom fill. Appendix B, *FreeHand and the PostScript Language*, describes how to specify the various options for each custom fill. We also examine PostScript-language fills created by third-party developers for use with FreeHand.

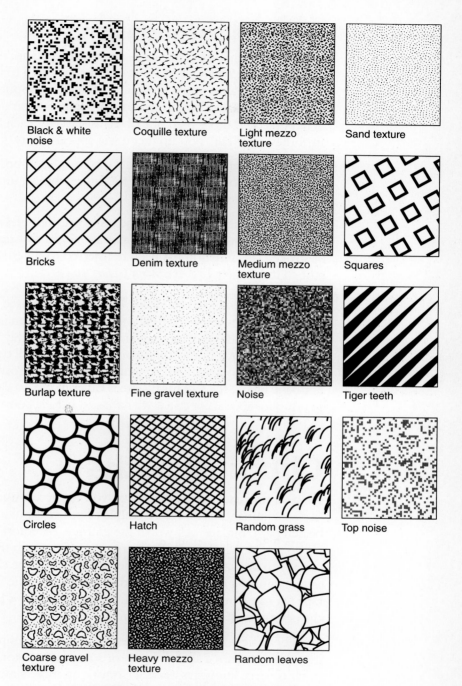

Black & white
noise

Coquille texture

Light mezzo
texture

Sand texture

Bricks

Denim texture

Medium mezzo
texture

Squares

Burlap texture

Fine gravel texture

Noise

Tiger teeth

Circles

Hatch

Random grass

Top noise

Coarse gravel
texture

Heavy mezzo
texture

Random leaves

Figure 9.35: FreeHand's 19 custom fill patterns as each
appears if you accept its default settings.

Fill and line conclusion

If you're familiar with previous versions of FreeHand, note that the FILL AND LINE dialog box replaces most options that used to be contained in over ten commands in the FILL and LINE menus. About time, eh? Not only that, the dialog box always contains information pertinent to the selected object. If more than one object is selected, each having different fill attributes, the "Fill" pop-up menu will appear empty.

Attributes entered into the FILL AND LINE dialog box become the default fill and stroke characteristics for future objects, until new default characteristics are set.

Finally, unlike similar dialog boxes in previous versions of FreeHand, the FILL AND LINE dialog box does not allow you to assign a name to a fill or stroke. This function has been transferred to the STYLES palette, as described in Chapter 11, *Assigning Colors and Styles*.

The FILL AND LINE dialog box may not be used to fill text. Instead, you must use the "Fill and stroke…" option in the EFFECTS pop-up under the TYPE menu. As described in the *Special type effects* section of Chapter 8, this command allows you to fill type only with a single color—no gradation, no pattern, no custom PostScript fill, no fun. For basic filling, the COLORS palette is easier to use, as described in Chapter 11. And for special effects, as we have said before, convert to paths.

Clipping paths

We have discussed all the fills effects you can access using the FILL AND LINE… command. However, a couple of other techniques are a bit off the beaten path, but are well worth the journey. Foremost among these is the *clipping path*, which is the PostScript term for a path that is created specifically to be filled with other objects. It may also be called a *masking object*, or simply a *mask*, after the airbrushing technique in which masking tape (or some other masking tool, such as a frisket) is laid down to define the perimeter of a spray-painted image.

The basic concept behind the clipping path is simple: Rather than filling an object with a shade of gray or some other color, you fill it with other objects, known as *masked elements* or, more simply, *contents*. Almost any graphic object created in FreeHand may be used as a clipping path.

The only exception is a group (although a single path in a group may be a clipping path, as discussed later in this section). Any number of lines, shapes, and other objects—grouped or ungrouped—may fill a clipping path. Even another clipping path may be masked.

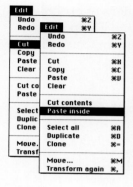

Creating a clipping path

FreeHand has allowed for the straightforward creation of clipping paths since version 1.0. The process remains unchanged. After filling and stroking all objects, assemble the mask and contents in their desired relative locations. Select all prospective contents and choose CUT from the EDIT menu (⌘-X) to transfer the selection to the Clipboard. Next, select the prospective mask and choose the PASTE INSIDE command from the EDIT menu. The contents of the Clipboard are pasted into the interior of the mask. All portions of the contents that exceed the boundary of the masking object are hidden.

Figure 9.36: The following exercise demonstrates how to color the bomb-pop (left) with the stripes (right).

Figure 9.36 shows a popsicle next to some stripes. The following exercise demonstrates how to set the stripes inside the body of the popsicle to create a . . . a whatchamacallit, a *bomb-pop*; you know, one of those

---

three-color frozen treats kids like to rub all over their faces. The problem is this: how to set the stripes inside the bomb-pop body without affecting the drip or the stick.

1. In order to create the clipping path, you must first move the prospective contents—the stripes—into position relative to the bomb-pop. Figure 9.37 shows the proper relative locations of masked elements and mask, as viewed in the keyline mode. This positioning will determine the exact manner in which the contents will fill the clipping path.

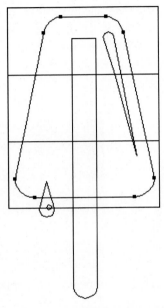

Figure 9.37: Mask and contents assembled, as viewed in the keyline mode.

2. Select the three stripes and choose the Cut command (⌘-X). They will be removed from the illustration and placed in the Clipboard.

3. Select the bomb-pop body (shown as selected in Figure 9.37) and choose Paste inside from the Edit menu. That's all there is to it. Figure 9.38 shows the resulting image as it appears when previewed or printed.

Figure 9.38: The finished image as
it appears when printed.

Provided that the stick was behind the bomb-pop body and the drip
and reflection elements were in front of it, you will get the result shown
in Figure 9.38, regardless of the layering of the stripes. When pasted into
an object using the PASTE INSIDE command, the contents assume the layering of the masking object.

The contents of a clipping path display only when the illustration is
previewed or printed. Contents are not displayed in the keyline mode.

Adjusting masked elements

If you decide you do not care for the appearance of a clipping path, you
may make adjustments in one of the following three ways:

- To alter one or more masked elements inside an existing clipping
  path, select the clipping path and choose the CUT CONTENTS command from the EDIT menu. All elements inside the path will be deleted from the mask and placed directly in front of the mask. (They
  will *not* be transferred to the Clipboard.) After making the required

alterations to the masked elements, select them, choose CUT, select the clipping path, and choose PASTE INSIDE, returning the masked elements to the interior of the selected object.

● To add elements to an existing clipping path, position the elements relative to the path, select the elements, choose CUT, select the clipping path, and choose PASTE INSIDE. Both new and original masked elements will appear inside the clipping path, with the new elements being in front of the original elements.

● To subtract elements from an existing clipping path, select the clipping path and choose CUT CONTENTS, deleting the contents from the mask and placing them directly in front of the mask. After deleting the offending masked elements, select all remaining elements, choose CUT, select the mask, and choose PASTE INSIDE, returning the desired contents to the interior of the clipping path.

Pasting elements inside a group

The PASTE INSIDE command can be applied to geometric paths, free-form paths, and composite paths (such as converted type). It may not be applied to a selected group, because FreeHand cannot paste elements into more than one path at a time. However, you may make a single path inside a group a clipping path. To select the single path, press OPTION and click on it with the arrow tool. Then choose PASTE INSIDE to fill the selected path with the current contents of the Clipboard.

Creating multiple masks

You may not choose PASTE INSIDE while more than one path is selected. However, you may apply a single set of masked elements to multiple paths, one at a time.

For example, Figure 9.39 displays a logo made up of four similar clipping paths. Each path is shaped differently and filled differently. However, each path is filled with what appear to be part of one large pattern of objects. To accomplish this, we created a set of masked elements that was as large as all four clipping paths combined. After sending the masked elements to the Clipboard using the CUT command, we selected the left masking object and chose PASTE INSIDE. We then selected the next clipping path over, chose PASTE INSIDE again, and so on, until the masked element had been pasted into all four clipping paths. The final logo creates a puzzle-piece effect, in which the contents of each clipping path seem to flow into the contents of its neighbor.

Figure 9.39: The graphic portion of this logo comprises four clipping paths filled with continuous masked elements.

Making holes

Another way to display objects within objects is to create one or more holes in the middle of a path using the JOIN ELEMENTS command under the ELEMENT menu (⌘-J). For example, consider the cartoon man in Figure 9.40 on the following page. The first example in the figure displays his full face. But suppose you need to add a ski mask to the image. (Who knows? Maybe he's cold. Maybe he robs banks professionally.) A real-life ski mask has holes cut into it for the eyes. Therefore your cartoon ski mask must also have holes for the eyes, as shown in the second example in the figure. The holes in the cartoon ski mask, however, are actually paths that have been combined with the ski mask path using the JOIN ELEMENTS command.

Figure 9.40: A cartoon face (left) and the same face with the addition of a composite path (right). Composite paths may contain holes through which underlying images are visible.

Eye holes and mask together are known as a *composite path*, because in a few key respects, FreeHand treats the object as a single path. All objects included in the composite path must be filled and stroked identically using options available in the FILL AND LINE dialog box. And, like a group, selecting any part of a composite path with the arrow tool selects all objects in the composite path. But also, like a group, you may OPTION-click with the arrow tool to manipulate objects independently within a composite path.

Creating a composite path

Like a clipping path, a composite path is easily created in FreeHand. First assemble the objects that you want to combine in their desired relative positions. One path will act as the background path and one or more other paths will act as the holes. For best results, all holes should overlap some portion of the larger background path. Select the background path and choose the SEND TO BACK command from the EDIT menu (⌘-B). Then

select all paths—background path and all holes—and choose the JOIN ELE-
MENTS command from the ELEMENT menu (⌘-J). Background and holes
are now combined.

To change the fill or stroke of all objects in a composite path, select
any object using the arrow tool and choose FILL AND LINE... from the AT-
TRIBUTES menu (⌘-E). Any change you make inside the FILL AND LINE dialog box will affect every object in the composite path.

Figure 9.41: This doughnut would look more like a
doughnut if you could see through its center.

Figure 9.41 shows a doughnut on a checkered napkin. Unfortunately,
it does not look much like a doughnut because the doughnut hole has
not yet been removed. You can save this doughnut from a heartbreaking
existence on the Island of Misfit Pastry by completing the following exercise. You will also create a shadow beneath the doughnut that is itself a
composite path:

1. The doughnut is made up of two circles, both drawn with the oval
   tool. As discussed in the *Reshaping geometric objects* section of
   Chapter 7, the oval tool always draws grouped shapes. However,
   one of the JOIN ELEMENTS command's little rules is that it does not
   allow you to combine objects from different groups. So select both
   circles and choose UNGROUP from the ELEMENT menu (⌘-U).

2. A doughnut consists of a background shape and a single hole. To ensure that the larger circle acts as the background, select the shape and choose SEND TO BACK (⌘-B). This step is not essential, since the smaller shape will automatically act as a hole in the larger shape, but it may help you to better see the results of the next operations.

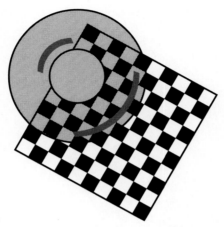

Figure 9.42: Send the large circle to the back of the illustration.

3. The large circle now appears in back of the napkin, as shown in Figure 9.42. That's a little too far back, but the problem will take care of itself. Select both circles and choose the JOIN ELEMENTS command (⌘-J). The doughnut now has a hole, as shown in Figure 9.43. Notice that the large circle is in front of the napkin. The JOIN ELEMENTS command always moves all selected objects to directly in back of the frontmost object in the selection.

4. To create the shadow, clone the doughnut by choosing the CLONE command from the EDIT menu (⌘-=, COMMAND-EQUAL). Drag the clone with the arrow tool about a half inch down and to the right.

5. Send the clone to the back of the illustration (⌘-B).

6. Choose FILL AND LINE… from the ATTRIBUTES menu (⌘-E). Choose "Basic" from the "Fill" pop-up option (if it isn't already chosen). Choose "60% gray" from the "Color" pop-up option below the "Fill" option. Next, choose "None" from the "Line" pop-up option on the right side of the dialog box. Then press RETURN. The finished illustration appears as shown in Figure 9.44.

Figure 9.43: Joining the circles makes a hole and brings the large circle in front of the napkin.

Figure 9.44: The finished doughnut with shadow.

In case you're wondering, the shadow appears to shade the napkin because the napkin is filled with a partially transparent tile pattern. The pattern contains only black squares. The appearance of white squares is created by an absence of black squares. Therefore, you can see through the "white" squares to the shadow at the back of the illustration. (Recall that all objects on a single separation are opaque. So if the shadow were in front of the napkin, it would obscure portions of the black squares.)

Composite masking

In FreeHand 3.0, a composite path may double as a clipping path, allowing you to create a path that is filled with objects and has holes punched out of it. After creating a composite path, position the masked elements in front of the composite path, cut all masked elements to the Clipboard, select the composite path, and choose the PASTE INSIDE command.

Figure 9.45: The next exercise demonstrates how to fill the doughnut with these stripes of icing.

In Figure 9.45, we have added several stripes of icing in front of the doughnut. The following two-step exercise describes how to use the doughnut as a clipping path for the icing:

1. Select the icing stripes and the two curved reflection lines with the arrow tool. Choose CUT from the EDIT menu (⌘-X), transferring the paths to the Clipboard.

2. Select the doughnut and choose PASTE INSIDE from the EDIT menu. The stripes will be pasted into the large circle. The small circle continues to form a hole in the path, inside of which the stripes do not appear. The completed image is shown in Figure 9.46.

Figure 9.46: The finished doughnut with icing.

Composite paths and text

Type may *not* be associated with a composite path. However, you may convert a text block to a series of paths using the CONVERT TO PATHS command from the TYPE menu, and then combine these paths with other graphic objects using the JOIN ELEMENTS command (⌘-J). You should note that type is automatically converted to composite paths. The entire text block is converted into a composite path, which in turn contains a separate composite path for each character. This allows you to apply a single fill over the entire length of a line of converted type, as shown in Figure 9.47.

Figure 9.47: Because it is converted to a large composite path, a single fill may be applied to an entire line of type (top). If you split the converted text block, each character contains its own unique fill (bottom).

It is sometimes a good idea to break the paths apart using the SPLIT ELEMENT command before combining them with other paths. If you do split converted type, each character may be filled individually, as shown in the second example in Figure 9.47 on the preceding page.

Breaking composite paths

To break apart a composite path, select the object and choose the SPLIT ELEMENT command from the ELEMENT menu. All paths will be restored to opaque fills. This command is especially handy if you want to dramatically reshape type that has been converted using the CONVERT TO PATHS command, as described in the *Converting type to paths* section in Chapter 8.

Filling theory

If you OPTION-double-click or choose the ELEMENT INFO… command (⌘-I) for a selected composite path, you will display the COMPOSITE PATH dialog box, shown in Figure 9.48. In addition to the standard "Flatness" option box (introduced in the *Free-form path info* section of Chapter 7), this dialog box contains a sole check box labeled "Even/odd fill." Like the identical option in the standard PATH and PATH/POINT dialog boxes, this option determines the method by which FreeHand fills paths with overlapping segments. The question is: When is part of a path considered to be outside the path and when is it considered inside? To determine the answer, FreeHand uses one of two PostScript routines. If "Even/odd fill" is selected, as by default, FreeHand relies on the *even/odd rule*. If the option is deselected, FreeHand uses the *non-zero winding number rule* . To save paper, we'll call the latter the *Ø-rule*.

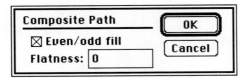

Figure 9.48: Option-double-click a composite path to display the Composite Path dialog box, which allows you to determine the manner in which a composite path is filled.

To demonstrate both rules, we'll use the complex path shown in Figure 9.49. We have designed this path so that every segment overlaps at least two other segments in the path. In Figure 9.50 on the next page, we have enhanced the shape with directional arrows. These arrows demonstrate the direction in which each segment in the shape progresses from point to point. If you start at any point in the path and trace along the path in the direction indicated by the arrows, you will eventually arrive back at the point at which you started, having traced every segment exactly one time. Therefore, the arrows represent the consistent progression of the path through its points.

Figure 9.49: Every segment in this path overlaps at least two and as many as five other segments.

The manner in which we have drawn the path divides it into 19 *subsections*, that is, portions of the path separated from other portions by part of a segment. If a subsection is bordered entirely by other subsections, then we say it is *encompassed*. Any subsection that is *not* encompassed is obviously inside the path and will be filled just like a path whose segments do not overlap. In Figure 9.50, the four encompassed subsections are identified by flagpoles, labeled 1 through 4. These are the subsections that are subjected to either the Ø-rule or the even/odd rule.

Figure 9.50: A filled version of the same path notated with arrows and flags, and filled according to the Ø-rule.

The Ø-rule

Figure 9.50 is filled according to the Ø-rule; the "Even/odd fill" check box has been deselected. Each flagpole in the figure begins inside an encompassed subsection and extends to a location outside of the path. Each pole crosses two or more segments. Each segment, according to its arrows in the figure, progresses at least partially in a rightward or leftward direction. To illustrate the winding number rule, we will use the metaphor of raising flags up the flagpoles. Before we begin raising the flag, we have a "flag variable" of zero. As we raise the flag, it will cross a number of segments. For each rightward-progressing segment that it crosses, we add 1 to our flag variable. For each leftward-progressing segment crossed, we subtract 1 from our flag variable. Once the flag is raised beyond all crossing segments, we compute the total.

This final flag variable will lead us to one of two conclusions:

- If it is zero, then the encompassed subsection from which the flag-pole emanates is *outside* the shape, and will *not* be filled.

- If it is not equal to zero, the encompassed subsection is *inside* the shape and will be filled.

Flag 1 in Figure 9.50 crosses both a rightward- and leftward-progressing segment. The flag variable is $0 + 1 - 1 = 0$, so its subsection is outside the shape by the Ø-rule. The same is true for flags 3 and 4. However, flag 2 crosses two rightward-progressing segments. Its flag variable is $0 + 1 + 1 = 2$. Therefore, its subsection is inside the shape.

The conclusion: Of all the encompassed subsections, only the center one is filled, as shown in Figure 9.50.

Perhaps an easier way to think of the Ø-rule is this:

- If all directional arrows surrounding an encompassed subsection do *not* progress in a consistently clockwise or counterclockwise formation, the subsection is considered by FreeHand to be *outside* the shape.

- If all directional arrows *do* progress in a consistently clockwise or counterclockwise formation, the subsection is considered by Free-Hand to be *inside* the shape.

The arrows surrounding the subsection containing flag 2 establish a consistently clockwise order; thus the subsection is filled. The subsections containing flags 1, 3, and 4, however, each have one or more dissenting arrows that flow against the majority direction. These dissenting arrows are grayed in Figure 9.50.

Even/odd rule

Figure 9.51 on the following page shows the same path filled according to the even/odd rule; that is, when the "Even/odd fill" check box is selected. According to this much more straightforward rule, every subsection that is *not* encompassed is filled; every subsection that *is* encompassed is considered to be outside the path and is therefore transparent, forming a hole through which other objects may be viewed.

Figure 9.51: Another version of the path filled according to the even/odd rule.

Keep in mind that both rules affect only free-form and composite paths with overlapping segments. Paths with no overlapping segments are always filled according to your directions, as described in previous sections of this chapter. If you do have to create a path with overlapping segments and these rules seem too complex, just preview the path with the "Even/odd fill" check box selected, then preview the path with the check box deselected, and see which one you like better.

Stroking Type and Graphic Objects

Like the fill attribute, the *stroke* attribute is applied to both type and graphic objects to determine the appearance of your printed artwork. Fill is applied to the interior of an object while stroke is applied to its outline. Strokes share many similarities with fills: they may be colored with gray values, bitmapped patterns, and even with custom PostScript effects. Or they may be transparent, so that only the fill can be seen. If you apply a transparent fill as well, you may create an invisible object, which can be used for alignment purposes. However, a stroke may not be subjected to gradations, tile patterns, masking, or hole making—features that can be applied only to the interior of a shape. By the same token, stroke provides options that are irrelevant to fill: line weight, dash patterns, caps, joins, and so on, all of which are explained in this chapter.

How stroke affects objects

Stroke may be applied to any object in Aldus FreeHand. Applying a stroke to a path is a straightforward process. If you want to see a path's outline, apply a stroke. Otherwise, do not.

Figure 10.01 shows an identical stroke applied to an open path and to a closed path. In both cases, we have displayed the path in white to show how the stroke is always centered on its path. This is important to keep in mind when trying to determine the amount of space a stroke will occupy when you print your artwork. You may also exploit this feature to create useful effects, as described in the section *Mixing stroke attributes* later in this chapter.

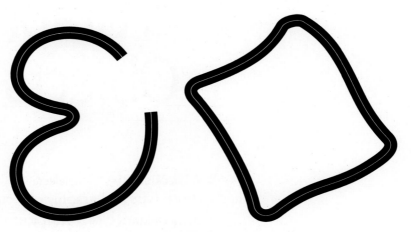

Figure 10.01: An open path (left) and a closed path (right), each stroked with a heavy line. The actual paths are displayed in white.

Stroking text

Text objects may also be stroked. If you select a text block or text on a path with the arrow tool, the stroke will affect all type in the text object, as shown in Figure 10.02.

Figure 10.02: If you stroke a text block selected with the arrow tool, all characters in the text object will become stroked.

In the case of text on a path, the path may be stroked separately from the type. First, select the "Show path" check box in the TEXT ALONG A PATH dialog box (displayed by OPTION-double-clicking the text path). Then use the FILL AND LINE... command under the ATTRIBUTES menu (⌘-E) to stroke the path and use the "Fill and stroke..." option in the EFFECT pop-up under the TYPE menu to stroke the type.

Figure 10.03: Text may be stroked separately from its path once the "Show path" check box has been selected.

You may also stroke single words and other collections of specific characters without affecting the path by selecting the text with the type tool. Like any character-level formatting option, such as font or type size, stroke affects only highlighted characters, as demonstrated in Figure 10.04 on the next page. In this way, FreeHand 3.0 allows you to apply several different strokes to a single text object.

Figure 10.04: By highlighting text using the I-beam cursor inside the Text dialog box, you may stroke specific characters of type.

Just as FreeHand doesn't allow you to apply certain kinds of fills to text objects, several stroking attributes—including line joins, dash patterns, and arrowheads—cannot be applied to type. If you want to create an effect like the one shown in Figure 10.05, you must first convert the text to composite paths using the CONVERT TO PATHS command from the TYPE menu, as described in the section *Converting type to paths* in Chapter 8. The characters may then be filled and stroked, since they are now graphic objects.

Figure 10.05: After converting a text block to paths, you may assign any stroking attribute, including round line joins, dash patterns, and arrowheads, all of which are shown above.

Assigning the stroke

To stroke a graphic object (not text), you must select the object and choose the FILL AND LINE... command from the ATTRIBUTES menu (⌘-E). The FILL AND LINE dialog box will display, as shown in Figure 10.06. Every characteristic of a stroke can be determined or manipulated from this dialog box.

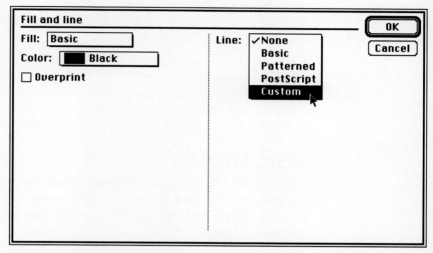

Figure 10.06: The Fill and line dialog box provides access to all of FreeHand's stroking options.

All options on the right-hand side of the FILL AND LINE dialog box apply to the stroke of a selected object. These options are described in the following pages. See Chapter 9, *Filling Type and Graphic Objects*, for complete information on the left-side ("Fill") options.

Using the "Line" pop-up option

After displaying the FILL AND LINE dialog box, click and hold on the "Line" option to display a pop-up menu listing various kinds of strokes, as demonstrated in Figure 10.06. Only one "Line" option may be selected at a time. Many "Line" options display other options that request additional specifications in determining the color in a stroke. Each variety of stroke and its related options are discussed in the following sections.

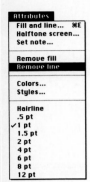

No stroke

The "None" option makes the outline of the selected path transparent. This same function may also be performed by choosing the REMOVE LINE command from the ATTRIBUTES menu. The "None" option is useful for stroking a path when you want only the fill to be visible. You may also assign both a transparent stroke and a transparent fill to a path. An entirely transparent path may be viewed in the keyline mode but will neither preview nor print. Such a path may be used for alignment purposes or to surround an image that you intend to export as an EPS file, as described in the *Exporting an illustration* section of Chapter 13.

Line: | None |

Figure 10.07: No additional option is associated with the "None" option.

Basic strokes

Choosing the "Basic" option strokes a selected path with a uniform color and thickness. You may also determine how the ends and corners of the stroked path will look, specify dash patterns, and assign arrowheads using the "Basic" options.

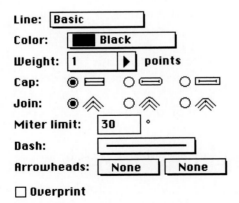

Figure 10.08: The "Basic" options control the color, thickness, cap, join, dash pattern, and arrowheads associated with the selected stroke.

Each of the "Basic" stroking options controls the stroke of a path in a unique, and sometimes complicated, manner. For this reason, we divide our discussion into eight parts, each of which corresponds to a specific option: 1) "Color," 2) "Weight," 3) "Cap," 4) "Join," 5) "Miter limit," 6) "Dash," 7) "Arrowheads," and 8) "Overprint."

● **Part 1**: *Specifying a line color.*

The first option below the "Line" option is the "Color" pop-up menu. Click and hold on this option to display every color defined in the current illustration, as well as several commands used to create new colors and access colors from the Pantone color library. Chapter 11, *Assigning Colors and Styles*, contains complete information about creating and accessing colors in FreeHand.

● **Part 2**: *Specifying a line weight.*

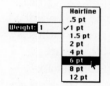

The next option is the "Weight" option box, which controls the thickness, or *line weight*, of a stroke. Line weight in FreeHand is specified in points, picas, inches, or millimeters, depending on the selected "Unit of measure" option in the DOCUMENT SETUP dialog box (as discussed in the section *Creating a new illustration* in Chapter 3). Click and hold on the right-pointing arrowhead icon (▶) to display a menu of common line weights. These are the same line weights that appear at the end of the ATTRIBUTES menu. The current line weight, if any, will be preceded by a check mark. FreeHand also allows you to enter any value from 0 to 288 points (the latter being equal to 4 inches).

Generally, we advise against specifying a line weight value smaller than 0.15. FreeHand defines a *hairline*—the thinnest line weight traditionally available—as ¼ point. Thus, 0.15-point is just over half the weight of a hairline. As an example, suppose you specify a 0-point line weight. This instructs FreeHand to print the thinnest line available from the current output device. The thinnest line printable by 300-dpi laser printer is 0.24-point thick (⅟₃₀₀ inch), approximately equal to a hairline. But higher-resolution printers, such as Linotronic and Compugraphic imagesetters, easily print lines as thin as 0.03 point, or eight times thinner than a hairline. Because any line thinner than 0.15-point is almost invisible to the naked eye, such a line will probably drop out when reproduced commercially.

- **Part 3**: *Specifying a line cap.*

The next set of options that affect stroke is the three "Cap" options. Here, you may select a *line cap*, which determines the appearance of a stroke at an endpoint. Therefore, line caps are generally useful only when stroking an open path. The only exception to this is when line caps are used in combination with dash patterns, as described in the *Dash patterns and line caps* section, later in this chapter.

The "Cap" options function as follows:

- **Butt cap** (⊟). The first radio button is the *butt cap* option, the default setting and by far the most commonly used line cap. Notice the black line that runs through the center of each of the "Cap" icons. This line denotes the position of the path relative to the stroke. When the butt cap option is selected, the stroke ends immediately at an endpoint and is perpendicular to the final course of the path, as its icon suggests.

- **Round cap** (⊝). The second radio button is a *round cap* option. Giving a stroke a round cap is like attaching a circle to the end of a path. The endpoint acts as the center of this circle, and its radius is half the line weight, as demonstrated by Figure 10.09. For example, suppose you have a 4-point line weight with round caps that follows a horizontal path. A 2-point portion of the stroke is on top of the path and the other 2-point portion is underneath. Since the path is itself invisible, the two halves of the stroke meet with no break between them. Upon reaching the end of the path, the top half of the stroke wraps around the endpoint in a circular manner to meet with the bottom half of the stroke; hence the end of the path is a semicircle with a 2-point radius.

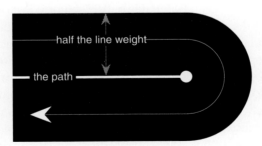

half the line weight

the path

Figure 10.09: When the round cap option is selected, the stroke wraps around each endpoint in a path to form a semicircle.

When combined with round joins (described in the next section), round caps may be used to give an open path an informal appearance. Figure 10.10 shows several letters drawn entirely using open paths. The first example is stroked with square caps (described below), the second is stroked with round caps. Which do you think looks more friendly?

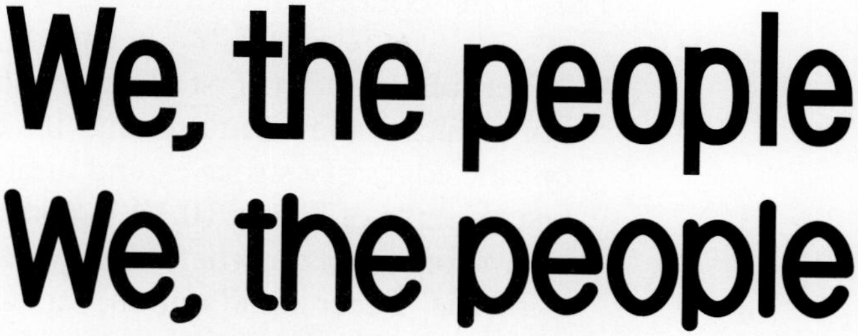

We, the people
We, the people

Figure 10.10: Two lines of converted type composed of open paths, one stroked with square caps (top) and one with round caps (bottom).

- **Square cap** (☐). The third radio button is the *square cap* option. Here, a square is attached to the end of a line; the endpoint is the center of the square. It is similar to the rounded cap in the sense that the size of this square is dependent on the line weight. The width and height of the square are equal to the weight of the stroke, so that the square projects from the endpoint a distance equal to one half the weight of the stroke. If the path in Figure 10.11 has a 4-point line weight, for example, the upper corner of the stroke would be located 2 points above and 2 points to the right of the endpoint.

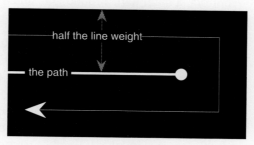

half the line weight

the path

Figure 10.11: When the square cap option is selected, the stroke wraps around the endpoints in a path to form perpendicular corners.

- **Part 4**: *Specifying a line join.*

Below the "Cap" radio buttons are the three "Join" radio buttons. Here, you may select a *line join*, which determines the appearance of a stroke at places in a path where two segments meet at a corner formed by a corner point or connector point. Line joins have no affect on the appearance of stroked curve points.

The "Join" options function as follows:

- **Miter join** (⩓). The first "Join" radio button is the *miter join* option, which is the default setting. If a corner has a miter join, the outside edges of a stroke extend until they meet, as shown in the first example of Figure 10.12. A corner with a true miter join will always form a crisp corner. Miter joins can, however, be cut short using the "Miter limit" option, explained in the next section.

Figure 10.12: Three corners and three joins: from top to bottom, a miter join, a round join, and a bevel join.

- **Round join** (⩓). The second radio button is the *round join* option, which is identical in principal to the round cap. Half the line weight wraps around the corner point to form a semicircle. In fact, rounded joins and rounded caps are so alike that they are used together almost exclusively. We recommend that you do not use round joins in combination with butt caps. This goes doubly if any dash pattern is involved, because round joins actually form complete circles around corner points. See the *Dash patterns and line joins* section later in this chapter for more information.

- **Bevel join** (⋀). The third and last radio button is the *bevel join* option. The bevel join is very similar to a butt cap. Instead of allowing the outer edges of a stroke to meet, as in the case of a miter join, the stroke is sheared off at the corner point. The result appears to be two very closely situated corners. Unlike a butt cap, however, a bevel join is not sheared perpendicularly to any one segment. Since two segments meet at a corner point, a compromise is struck. As you may notice in the last example of Figure 10.12, the angle at which the sheared edge of the bevel join meets with one segment is identical to the angle at which it meets with the other.

- **Part 5**: *Bevelling excessive miter joins.*

  Below the "Join" radio buttons is the "Miter limit" option box, which allows you to bevel excessively long miter joins. Measured in degrees, the *miter limit* is the smallest angle at which two segments may meet and still be allowed to form a miter join. If two segments meet at an angle smaller than the value entered into the "Miter limit" option box, the join is converted into a bevel join at that corner point only.

Figure 10.13: Three versions of a path stroked with miter joins but with different miter limits: from top to bottom, the "Miter limit" value is 10°, 20°, and 30°.

The top path in Figure 10.13 includes two pairs of segments that meet to form sharp corners. The stroke of this path includes miter joins. The top and right-hand corners are so sharp that the joins must extend an extreme distance before the two outer edges of the stroke can finally meet. Occasionally, you will discover that excessively long tips at the corners of a path may protrude into other paths or simply appear unattractive. Unfortunately, FreeHand does not allow you to give one corner a different line join than any other corner in a single path. But it does allow you to do the next best thing.

The top corner forms an angle of approximately 24°; the right-hand corner is half that, or about 12°. The miter limit of the top path has been set to 10°. Since both corners are larger than 10°, neither miter join is bevelled.

In the middle path of Figure 10.13, the miter limit has been increased to 20°. Since the right corner is less than 20°, FreeHand automatically converts this miter join to a bevel join. However, the stroke at the top corner of this path remains a miter join, since it is slightly less acute.

To create the bottom path in the figure, the miter limit has been changed to 30°, the default value. Because both top and right-hand corners are sharper than 30°, both miter joins are sliced off to form bevel joins.

The "Miter limit" value may be any angle from 2° to 180°, the default value being 30°. A miter limit of 180° specifies that every corner in a path should be beveled, and is therefore identical to selecting the bevel join option from the "Join" radio buttons. The "Miter limit" option is useful only with miter joins. If either the round join or bevel join radio button is selected, the "Miter limit" option will produce no effect.

Choosing between a huge corner tip and no tip at all is a harsh compromise. If you wish to preserve the attractive quality of a miter join without allowing it to take over too large a portion of your drawing, you may prefer to adjust your path to increase the angle between a pair of segments, thus decreasing the length of the tip formed by the stroke. A miter limit should be used only as a last resort.

Part 6: *Choosing a dash pattern.*

The "Dash" option allows you to select from a pop-up menu of ten *dash patterns*, which are variations in the manner in which a stroke follows its path. Most often, this results in repetitive interruptions in a stroke. For example, a standard coupon border in an advertisement is a dash pattern.

The first dash pattern offered in the "Dash" pop-up menu is the solid stroke, the default setting and by far the most common dash pattern. A solid stroke simply means that a stroke remains constant throughout the length of its path.

All the remaining patterns are dashed strokes. These are most popularly used to indicate cut-out lines. They may surround mail-in coupons, paper dolls, or any number of other items that are specifically created to be clipped from a page. Dash patterns may also indicate a ghostly or translucent image.

KE Press OPTION while choosing any but the first option from the "Dash" pop-up menu to display the LINE PATTERN dialog box shown in Figure 10.14. This dialog box displays the length of each dash and gap in the current dash pattern. Change the values to create a new dash pattern based on the existing one.

```
┌──────────────────────────────────────────┐
│  Line pattern                  ┌────────┐ │
│                                │   OK   │ │
│  Segment lengths (in points):  └────────┘ │
│  On │12    │    Off │2    │    ┌────────┐ │
│                                │ Cancel │ │
│  On │2     │    Off │2    │    └────────┘ │
│                                            │
│  On │2     │    Off │2    │                │
│                                            │
│  On │0     │    Off │0    │                │
└──────────────────────────────────────────┘
```

Figure 10.14: Press option when choosing a pattern to display the Line pattern dialog box, which allows you to create your own custom dash pattern.

Each option box in the LINE PATTERN dialog box represents the interval—measured in points, picas, inches, or millimeters, depending on the selected "Unit of measure" option in the DOCUMENT SETUP dialog box—during which a dash will be "On" or "Off" in the course of stroking a path. "On" values determine the length of the dashes; "Off" values determine the length of the gaps between the dashes. Dash pattern values may range from 1 to 200 points (2¾ inches).

Suppose that you want to create a dashed line composed of a series of 8-point dashes followed by 4-point gaps. After displaying the LINE PATTERN dialog box, enter 8 in the first "On" option box and 4 in the first "Off" option box. Leave the remaining six option boxes blank. If a series of consecutive "On" and "Off" options are blank, they are simply ignored. Therefore, once FreeHand has completed created the first 8-point dash and following 4-point gap, it repeats the sequence over and over throughout the length of the selected path.

This same pattern may be indicated in many different ways. For example, instead of leaving the last six options blank, you might fill them with 8/4/8/4/8/4. Many other variations will produce the same effect.

All sorts of line patterns can be created, since every "On" and "Off" indicator may contain a different value. You may create a pattern that repeats one, two, three, or four dash/gap combinations. Also, you need not specify an "Off" value for every "On" value. A solid stroke, for example, is all dashes and no gaps. Its dash pattern may contain any positive number for its first option value while the remaining options may be left blank. However, the first "On" option must contain a value. Also, once a value of 0 has been entered for any option, all following "On" and "Off" options will be ignored.

You may create an unlimited number of custom dash patterns in FreeHand 3.0. After editing the values in the "On" and "Off" option boxes, click the OK button or press RETURN to create a new dash pattern, which is added to the end of the "Dash" pop-up menu.

All custom dash patterns are saved with an illustration. They will be transferred from one illustration to the next if you cut a line stroked with the pattern and paste it into another document. To create a library of patterns that will be available in all new illustrations, create a new Aldus FreeHand Defaults file as described in the *Changing defaults* section of Chapter 3.

●	**Part 7**: *Choosing an arrowhead.*

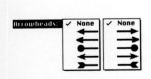

We have no idea why it's taken so long, but with version 3.0, FreeHand finally offers automatic arrowheads. Two "Arrowheads" pop-up menus allow you to determine the arrowheads or tails assigned to the first and last endpoints of a selected path, making them applicable to open paths only.

In addition to "None," FreeHand provides five arrowhead and tail options. Each arrowhead varies in size depending on the current line weight. Figure 10.15 shows all arrowheads as they appear in various common line weights.

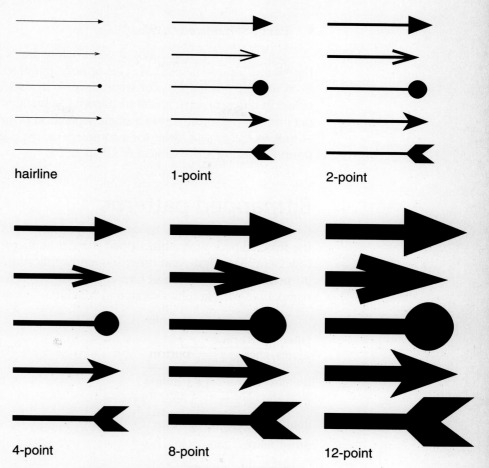

hairline   1-point   2-point

4-point   8-point   12-point

Figure 10.15: The five "Arrowhead" options subjected
to each of six different line weights.

FreeHand does not allow you to edit arrowhead options or design your own, as you can in MacDraw and Canvas, nor may
you vary the size of an arrowhead except by adjusting the associated line weight. You may, however, create and apply any number of
custom arrowheads. For complete information, see the *Designing custom
arrowheads* section later in this chapter.

Arrowheads are not affected by line caps or line joins. However, the
second arrowhead option (➡) may be bevelled using the "Miter limit"
option. A miter limit greater than 40° will bevel the arrowhead; a miter
limit less than 30° will allow it to taper to a sharp point.

- **Part 8**: *Overprinting inks.*

An "Overprint" check box appears below the "Color" option when the "Basic" option is selected. This option applies strictly to color illustrations that are printed as color separations. When selected, overlapping colors in different separations are allowed to blend with each other. Colors may *not* overprint within a single separation or print. See Chapter 11, *Assigning Colors and Styles*, for a complete description of the "Overprint" option. Printing is the subject of Chapter 14.

Bitmapped patterns

Choose the "Patterned" option from the "Line" pop-up menu to stroke the selected path with a bitmapped pattern, similar to those offered by MacPaint, MacDraw, and other low-end applications. In fact, the primary purpose for the inclusion of bitmapped patterns is to make FreeHand compatible with graphics created in MacDraw.

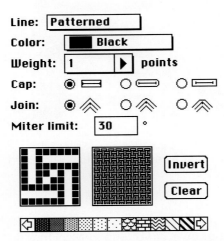

Figure 10.16: The "Patterned" options control the color, thickness, cap, join, and bitmap pattern associated with the current stroke.

Among the options that appear when you choose "Patterned" is a scrolling collection of 64 patterns included with FreeHand 3.0. Display additional patterns by clicking on the left and right scroll arrows. Select a pattern by clicking on it. Above the scrolling patterns are two boxes. In the left box, you may edit an enlarged version of the pattern by clicking pixels on and off. The right box shows the pattern as it appears at actual size. (Clicking in this box produces no result.) Two buttons are also provided to enhance your editing abilities. The INVERT button changes all black pixels in a pattern to white, and all white pixels to black. This is useful for creating a negative image of the current pattern. You may also erase all pixels in a pattern by clicking CLEAR.

The white pixels in a bitmap pattern are always white and opaque. The black pixels may be colored using the "Color" pop-up option.

 Although you can apply any color that you desire to a bitmapped pattern, only solid colors will print correctly. The color will *not* print correctly if it is defined as a gray value or tint or if it includes a percentage of less than 100% of any process-color ink.

Other options—including "Weight," "Cap," "Join," and "Miter limit"—function as described in the previous section.

PostScript-language strokes

Choose the "PostScript" option from the "Line" pop-up menu to stroke the selected path with a PostScript routine. Type up to 255 characters (including spaces) into the "PostScript code" text-entry area, shown in Figure 10.17. Do *not* use return characters. Any entry error will very likely prevent your entire illustration from printing, so enter your code carefully.

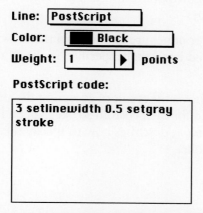

Figure 10.17: The "PostScript" options include the "Color" and "Weight" pop-up menus and the "PostScript code" text entry area.

You may color your PostScript stroke by choosing a color from the "Color" pop-up option. The value in the "Weight" option box will determine the thickness of the stroke. If your PostScript code contains any color information of its own, your "Color" option selection will be ignored during the printing process. Likewise, if the code contains line weight information, the "Weight" value will be ignored.

PostScript strokes are displayed as solid lines in the color and line weight specified in the "Color" and "Weight" options, regardless of whether your PostScript code contains color or weight information.

If this all sounds like Greek to you, don't worry. Most of us can get by without ever using the "PostScript" option. Still, it's a great feature for the frustrated programmer. It can also be useful for calling up custom strokes created by third-party developers, as examined in Appendix B, *FreeHand and the PostScript Language*.

Custom PostScript strokes

Choose the "Custom" option from the "Line" pop-up menu to stroke the selected path with a predefined PostScript routine included with the FreeHand 3.0. Each routine strokes a line with a series of repeated images, such as hearts, stars, or triangles. After choosing "Custom," choose one of the 23 strokes included in the "Effect" pop-up menu, as shown in Figure 10.18. Following this, a dialog box will display, requesting that you specify the color and length of each image in the stroke, the height of each image (which corresponds to the line weight), and the amount of space between images.

Custom stroke routines are displayed in the drawing area as solid lines, in the color and line weight specified in the "Color" and "Pattern width" options.

Figure 10.19 shows the result of accepting the default values presented by FreeHand for each custom stroke. Appendix B, *FreeHand and the PostScript Language*, describes how to specify the various options for each "Custom" stroke.

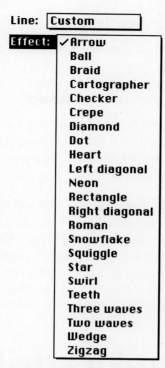

Line: | Custom |

Effect: | ✓Arrow
Ball
Braid
Cartographer
Checker
Crepe
Diamond
Dot
Heart
Left diagonal
Neon
Rectangle
Right diagonal
Roman
Snowflake
Squiggle
Star
Swirl
Teeth
Three waves
Two waves
Wedge
Zigzag

Figure 10.18: The "Custom" options include an "Effect" pop-up menu, containing 23 PostScript stroke routines.

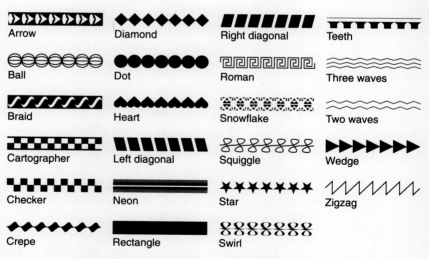

Arrow   Diamond   Right diagonal   Teeth

Ball   Dot   Roman   Three waves

Braid   Heart   Snowflake   Two waves

Cartographer   Left diagonal   Squiggle   Wedge

Checker   Neon   Star   Zigzag

Crepe   Rectangle   Swirl

Figure 10.19: FreeHand's 23 "Custom" stroke patterns as they appear if you accept the default settings.

"Line" pop-up conclusion

Some final notes: If more than one object is selected, each having different stroke attributes, the "Line" pop-up menu will appear empty. Attributes entered into the FILL AND LINE dialog box become the default stroke characteristics for future objects, until new default characteristics are set.

Unlike similar dialog boxes in previous versions of FreeHand, you cannot assign a name to a stroke from the FILL AND LINE dialog box. This function has been transferred to the STYLES palette, as described in Chapter 11, *Assigning Colors and Styles*.

To stroke text, you must use the "Fill and stroke..." option in the EFFECTS pop-up under the TYPE menu. As described in the *Special type effects* section of Chapter 8, this option allows you to stroke type only with a color and line weight—no line caps, no line joins, no dash patterns, no arrowheads, no custom PostScript strokes. For basic stroking, the COLORS palette is easier to use, as described in Chapter 11. And for special effects, as we have said before, convert to paths.

Mixing stroke attributes

Stroking effects may be created by mixing dash patterns with caps, joins, and line weights. More complicated effects may be achieved by layering duplicates of an object, one copy in front of another, each with a slightly different stroke. Provided that the line weight of each stroke is thinner than the line weight of the stroke behind it, portions of each stroke will show through to create unusual effects.

Layering strokes

The simplest stroking effect may be achieved by layering duplicate paths stroked with increasingly thinner line weights. The following exercise demonstrates how to use this technique to change a word of text that has been converted to a composite path and then stroked with a single outline, as shown in Figure 10.20, into a block of *inline* text, as shown in Figure 10.22 on page 358:

1. Start with something large, like a line of 120-point type converted using the CONVERT TO PATHS command under the TYPE menu. This will act as the first object in the stroking effect.

2. For best results, you should apply the thickest line weight to the backmost object in a series of layered strokes. In this case, select the converted type, choose FILL AND LINE… from the ATTRIBUTES menu (⌘-E), choose "Basic" from the "Line" pop-up menu, and enter 6 in the "Weight" option box.

3. While the FILL AND LINE dialog box remains displayed, select "None" from the "Fill" pop-up menu. The result is a line of type similar to the one shown in Figure 10.20.

Figure 10.20: A block of 120-point type converted and stroked with a 6-point line weight. The fill is transparent.

4. Duplicate the selected type by choosing the CLONE command from the EDIT menu (⌘-=, COMMAND-EQUAL).

5. Display the FILL AND LINE dialog box again (⌘-E). Select "White" from the "Color" pop-up menu under the "Line" option and enter 4 into the "Weight" option. Then press RETURN. The result is the type shown in Figure 10.21.

Figure 10.21: Clone the converted type and apply a thinner, white stroke.

6. Choose CLONE again. Display the FILL AND LINE dialog box and change the stroke to a black, 2-point line weight. The finished image is shown in Figure 10.22.

Figure 10.22: Clone the type again and apply an even thinner, black stroke. Ta-da, inline type, better than the stuff FreeHand creates automatically via the "Inline..." option.

Note that this effect is similar to, but more versatile than, the effect produced using the "Inline..." option in the EFFECT pop-up under the TYPE menu. For example, using our technique, inline strokes may be different in color and weight. But don't take our word for it. Compare the figure above to the automated inline type displayed in Figure 8.45 back on page 273.

Other stroking effects can be accomplished by layering duplicated objects with progressively thinner line weights. By lightening the color of a line each time you reduce the line weight, you can create neon type. In Figure 10.25, for example, the backmost text block is stroked with a 100% black, 6-point line weight. The text block front of that is stroked with a 90% black, 5.5-point line weight, and so on, until the frontmost text block, which is stroked with a white, 0-point line weight. All paths were given round joins to emulate the curves associated with neon tubes.

The next section goes one step further by adding dash patterns and line caps to the scenario.

Figure 10.23: Neon type is made up of duplicated text blocks, each of which is stroked with a thinner, more lightly colored stroke than the object behind it.

Dash patterns and line caps

Forget layering duplicate objects for a moment. Even if you are stroking only a single object, you can achieve interesting effects by combining dash patterns with line caps. This is because FreeHand treats the beginning and ending of each dash in a pattern as the beginning and ending of a stroke. Therefore, both ends of a dash are affected by the selected line cap. This allows you to create round dashes as well as rectangular ones.

Suppose that you have created a black stroke with round caps and a 12-point line weight. You add to this by pressing OPTION and choosing an option from the "Dash" pop-up menu in the FILL AND LINE dialog box. When the LINE PATTERN dialog box appears, enter 1 for the "On" value (the smallest permitted by FreeHand) and 16 for "Off." The resulting line is shown in Figure 10.24.

Figure 10.24: A dash pattern with a 1-point dash, a 16-point gap, a 12-point line weight, and round caps.

The diagram in Figure 10.25 on the next page shows how each dash is constructed. By specifying the length of each dash to be 1, you instruct FreeHand to allow only one point between the center of the round cap at the beginning of the dash and the center of the round cap at the end of the dash. This implies that a series of black ovals exist, the centers of which are 1-point dashes (the endpoints of the dash are shown as small white circles in Figure 10.25). The cap of each oval has a 6-point radius and the complete oval has a 13-point diameter. Because 13 points of each 17-point dash/gap sequence is consumed by a round cap oval, a distance of only four points appears between each oval. In conclusion, a dash pattern that is essentially rarely on, but nearly always off in 16-point intervals appears to be on for 13 points and off for only four points when a stroked with a 12-point line weight and rounded caps.

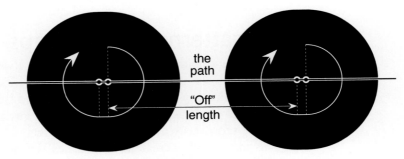

Figure 10.25: Round caps wrap around the ends of each dash in a dash pattern. Small dashes result in near-perfect circles.

Each non-zero "On" value in the LINE PATTERN dialog must be 1 if you want to create a stroke with near-round dashes. Also, each "Off" option must contain a gap value (if any) that is larger than the line weight to prevent the dashes from touching each other.

Layering dash patterns and line caps

Even more interesting results may be achieved by layering dash patterns in front of other dash patterns. Using a technique similar to layering solid strokes, you make the line weight of each path thinner than the line weight of the path behind it. Also, although you may vary the line caps, you will generally want to keep the dash pattern constant throughout all layered paths; that is, the length of each dash and length of each gap—what we call the *periodicity* of the pattern—should not vary.

The following example begins with the line shown back in Figure 10.24. The periodicity of this line is 17 points—a 1-point dash plus a

16-point gap. In the exercise, you will layer two additional paths in front of this line to create a pattern of inline circles.

1. Clone the line (⌘-=, COMMAND-EQUAL).

2. Using the FILL AND LINE dialog box (⌘-E), change the color of the stroke to white and decrease the line weight to 10 points. The result is displayed in Figure 10.26. The frontmost white ovals all but cover up the larger black ovals of the original line. Since the periodicity of the dash pattern remains constant, the ovals of the white line fit exactly within the ovals of the black line to produce a series of outlined dots.

Figure 10.26: The pattern from Figure 10.24 after adding a 10-point white stroke in front of it.

3. To create the line shown in Figure 10.27, create another clone of the path, then change the color of the stroke to black and decrease the line weight to 6 points. The effect is a series of black dots surrounded by white outlines, which are themselves surrounded by black outlines.

Figure 10.27: Layering a 6-point, black line in front of the other paths makes an inline effect.

If you know line weights, you may notice that the outlines around the ovals in Figure 10.26 are one point thick. This may seem incongruous with the fact that the first line is stroked with a 12-point line weight and the second line is stroked with a 10-point line weight. After all, the difference between the strokes is two points, not one. But because it is the radius of a rounded cap that wraps around the end of a dash, you must subtract the radius of the smaller round cap from that of the larger round cap to determine the amount of the original stroke that remains exposed. Since the radius of a round cap oval is equal to half its line weight, the outline of each dot appears to be 6 minus 5, or one point thick.

Whenever one path exactly covers another path, regardless of dash patterns or line caps, always subtract half the weight of the front stroke from half the weight of the back stroke to determine the amount of the back path that will remain visible.

Dash patterns and line joins

Dash patterns can also produce unusual effects when combined with line joins. The stroke of the path in Figure 10.28, for example, is made of a 32-point line weight with round joins and a lively dash pattern. The path itself is displayed in the figure as a thin, white line. Each corner point in the path is numbered. Notice that corners 1 and 2 coincide with gaps in the dash pattern, so they appear to be cut off, or beveled—not what you might expect from a line with round joins. By contrast, corners 3 and 4 meet with dashes in the pattern. Due to constraints of the PostScript language, FreeHand is forced to represent the round joins at these corners as black circles, interrupting the flow of the pattern. This problem is less noticeable for paths with smaller line weights, although a high-resolution printer will uncover these mistakes, even with narrow lines.

Figure 10.28: When combined with a lively pattern, round joins form circles at corners that coincide with dashes (3 and 4) and bevel at corners that coincide with gaps (1 and 2).

To avoid the problem shown in Figure 10.28, you may either select beveled or miter joins, or move the corner points of a path so they coincide with gaps rather than with dashes.

Designing custom arrowheads

As discussed in the *Basic strokes* section earlier in this chapter, FreeHand now offers five varieties of arrowheads, but it neither allows you to edit them nor to create your own. However, with only a little effort, you can create a library of custom arrowheads and apply these manually to end-points when required. The process requires some extra work, but it also produces versatile and unusual results.

The easiest way to create an awesome library of arrowheads is to convert characters from the Zapf Dingbats font. This is an unusual type-face made up of arrows, stars, boxes, pointing hands, and other symbols, which is built into most PostScript printers, including the Apple Laser-Writer. Assuming the printer font is available inside the System folder (or inside the folder that contains the FreeHand 3.0 application), you may convert all arrow characters in the Zapf Dingbats font by following these simple steps:

1. Click on an empty portion of the drawing area with the type tool. The TEXT dialog box will display.

2. Choose "Zapf Dingbats" from the FONT pop-up under the TYPE menu. Any text entered from the keyboard will now appear inside the text entry area in the Zapf Dingbats typeface.

3. Display the TYPE SIZE dialog box by choosing the "Other..." option from the SIZE pop-up under the TYPE menu. Enter 60 for the "Size" option and press RETURN. Your text will now appear in 60-point characters.

4. Create a text block containing all the arrowheads that you want to include in your library. Table 10.01 on the following page displays the arrows available in Zapf Dingbats and the keystrokes required to access them.

Table 10.01: Arrow characters available in the Zapf Dingbats font

ZAPF DINGBATS CHARACTER	KEYSTROKE
→	⌥-] (OPTION-RIGHT BRACKET)
→	⇧-⌥-] (SHIFT-OPTION-RIGHT BRACKET)
→	⇧-⌥-~ (SHIFT-OPTION-TILDE)
→	⇧-⌥-2
→	⇧-⌥-3
→	⇧-⌥-4
→	⇧-⌥-5
➤	⇧-⌥-0
➤	⇧-⌥-W
➤	⇧-⌥-E
▶	⇧-⌥-Y
➡	⇧-⌥-U
⇨	⇧-⌥-I
⇨	⇧-⌥-S
⇦	⇧-⌥-D
⇨	⇧-⌥-F
⇨	⇧-⌥-G
⇨	⇧-⌥-H
⇨	⇧-⌥-J
⇨	⇧-⌥-L
⟳	⇧-⌥-; (SHIFT-OPTION-SEMICOLON)
➤➤➤→	⇧-⌥-Z
➤→	⇧-⌥-B
➤➤→	⇧-⌥-, (SHIFT-OPTION-COMMA)
→	⌥-H
●→	⌥-K

5. Press ENTER to close the TEXT dialog box. The text block will appear selected in the drawing area.

6. Choose the CONVERT TO PATHS command from the TYPE menu. The arrows will be converted to standard paths.

7. Choose the S<small>PLIT</small> <small>ELEMENT</small> command from the E<small>LEMENT</small> menu to split the large composite path that includes all arrowheads into individual composite paths that include one arrow apiece.

8. Save the illustration as *Arrows* or whatever name you prefer, in the folder containing the FreeHand application.

To use an arrowhead, you must apply it manually to the end of your line. First open the Arrows document and copy an arrowhead (⌘-C). Then return to the document containing your line and paste the arrowhead (⌘-V). If you are creating either a horizontal or vertical straight line, you need only rotate the arrowhead by some 90° angle. This may be accomplished by selecting the entire arrowhead path and O<small>PTION</small>-clicking with the rotate tool, as described in the *Rotating objects* section of Chapter 12. Since all Dingbats arrowheads point to the right, enter 90 to create an upward-pointing arrow, 180 to point it to the left, or 270 to point it downward. Then press R<small>ETURN</small>.

If your arrowhead character does not contain its own line, such as the one shown in Figure 10.29, draw a horizontal or vertical line by S<small>HIFT</small>-dragging with the line tool. Then, using the arrow tool, drag the arrowhead by the point in the center of its base so that it snaps to the endpoint in the line, as shown in Figure 10.29.

Figure 10.29: Drag the arrowhead by the center of its base to snap it to the endpoint of a line (top). In this way, line and arrowhead will appear continuous when printed (bottom).

If the arrowhead has its own line, select the rear portion of the line, farthest from the arrowhead, by O<small>PTION</small>-clicking with the arrow tool to display the points in the composite path, then clicking and S<small>HIFT</small>-clicking to select individual points, as shown in the first example of Figure 10.30 on the next page. Then drag while pressing S<small>HIFT</small> to move it vertically or horizontally away from the arrow, as shown in the second example, until the stretched segment becomes the desired length.

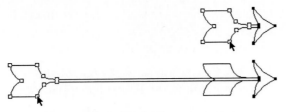

Figure 10.30: To extend an arrow, select its tail (top)
and drag away from the arrowhead (bottom).

If you want to use an arrow that has its own line, but you want
to attach it to an existing stroked path, as shown in Figure
10.29, convert the arrow into an arrowhead. Select the
rear points in the line—except the center rear point—by OPTION-clicking
and SHIFT-clicking with the arrow tool, and press DELETE to get rid of
them. Then select the center rear point and drag it to a position inside the
arrowhead, as demonstrated in Figure 10.31.

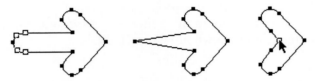

Figure 10.31: Select the rear points, except the center rear point (left),
and delete them. Next, drag the remaining rear point—which will be
connected to the arrowhead by two straight segments (middle)—into
position inside the arrowhead (right).

What if you want to add an arrowhead to a free-form line? This is a
more difficult operation, requiring more exacting use of the rotation tool.
First, drag the arrowhead so that its center point snaps to one of the endpoints in the free-form path. Then drag with the rotate tool to rotate the
selected arrowhead until it appears to match the angle of the line, as demonstrated in Figure 10.32.

Figure 10.32: Rotate an arrowhead to match it to the angle of a free-form path (top). If rotated properly, line and arrowhead will appear continuous when printed (bottom).

Assigning Colors and Styles

There was a time when the Macintosh computer was seen as a strictly monochrome machine. To this day, most users own Pluses, SEs, and Classics, computers with built-in monitors that display only black and white pixels. Even so, a growing number of users are branching into color machines, color monitors, and color output. If you are such a user, you will find that the degree of color control offered by Aldus FreeHand 3.0 continues to be some of the best available in any software, including support for four-color process colors, spot colors, tints, and the entire 747-color Pantone Matching System library. If you don't use a color display device, you can still access FreeHand's color capabilities; you'll just have to become a little more adept at predicting the results.

After coloring your fills and strokes, you can bundle specific attribute settings using *attribute styles*. New to FreeHand 3.0, styles allows you to name attribute settings so that they can be easily applied to graphic objects and transferred between illustrations.

Displaying colors

FreeHand's color abilities are available to anyone who can run the software; they are not limited by the monitor on which you are working or by the printer on which you proof your work. When using a monochrome monitor, specified colors appear in corresponding shades of gray. When using a color monitor, FreeHand will take full advantage of it, displaying up to 16 million colors at one time, depending on the capacity of your monitor and video card.

Preparing your color monitor

If you are going to work with a color monitor, you will want your screen to display colors that match commercially printed results as closely as possible. Since the color display varies widely from one brand of monitor to another, and even between monitors from the same manufacturer, FreeHand 3.0 includes the ability to reset the color definitions used by your monitor display.

When using FreeHand in color, you will generally want to set your Monitors *Control Panel device* to display as many colors as possible—16 colors if you are using a 4-bit video card, 256 colors if you are using an 8-bit video card, and "Millions" if you are using a 24-bit video card or better. A Control Panel device, also known by the acronym *cdev* (pronounced see-dev), is accessed by choosing CONTROL PANEL from the APPLE (🍎) menu and selecting the appropriate icon from the scrolling list, as shown in Figure 11.01. However, during the creation of a color document, you may wish to reduce the number of colors displayed or even turn off the color entirely for a while in order to speed up the preview of your illustration. These changes will not affect the color definitions used for your illustration, and the color settings can be safely changed as often as desired. You may even use a color-switching utility that allows you to toggle between display modes. Our favorite is Switch-A-Roo, a free Fkey from Bill Steinberg available over CompuServe (where Bill's account number is 76703,1027) and other national bulletin board systems.

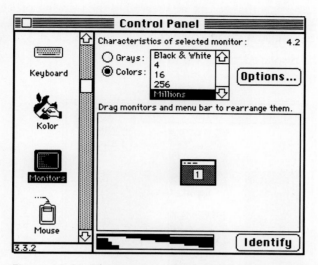

Figure 11.01: The Monitors Control Panel device allows you to set the number of colors that can be displayed simultaneously on your monitor.

Any adjustment to the Monitors cdev affects the colors used by all Macintosh software. You may also customize your screen display strictly for FreeHand from within the application. This color adjustment process serves to alter certain key screen colors to match printed samples as closely as possible. For best results, you will need to obtain a sample color bar from the commercial printer who will be reproducing your illustrations. This sample should include a separate color square for each of the four process colors—cyan, magenta, yellow, and black—plus combinations of each pair—cyan plus magenta, cyan plus yellow, magenta plus yellow— and all three process colors—cyan plus magenta plus yellow. If you cannot obtain these samples from your printer, or you don't work with a single commercial print house on a consistent basis, you may use the *Color Monitor Adjustment Card*, generally located inside the pouch at the front of the FreeHand user manual.

To begin the color adjustment, choose the PREFERENCES... command from the FILE menu. After the PREFERENCES dialog box appears, click the COLORS... button to bring up the DISPLAY COLOR SETUP dialog box (see Figure 11.02), which shows the current appearance of each primary process color and primary process color combination. The goal is to adjust each color so that it is as close as possible to the appropriate printed color sample. Be aware, however, that monitors do not create colors in the same way that colors are created in the printing process, so perfect matches will be unlikely. To adjust the on-screen representation of a color, click the color you wish to adjust. The APPLE COLOR WHEEL dialog box will be displayed, as shown in Figure 11.03.

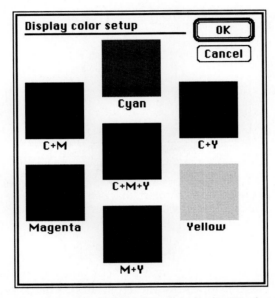

Figure 11.02: Click a color box in the Display color setup dialog box to adjust the color to better match a printed sample.

The APPLE COLOR WHEEL dialog box provides specific control over the display of the selected primary process color. To alter a color, you may use one of two color models: *RGB* (red, green, blue) or *HSB* (hue, saturation, brightness). Each model is explained in one of the following sections.

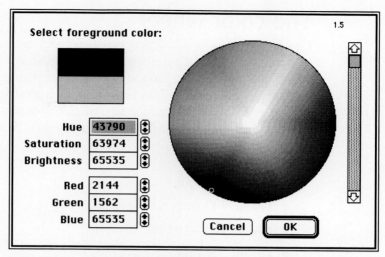

Select foreground color:

Hue	43790
Saturation	63974
Brightness	65535
Red	2144
Green	1562
Blue	65535

1.5

Cancel   OK

Figure 11.03: The Apple Color Wheel dialog box allows you to define on-screen colors according to one of two color models.

Coloring with light

When using the RGB color model, colors are defined by mixing two or more *primary hues*. The amount of each hue mixed is called its *intensity*, as measured from 0 (no hue) to 65,535 (full intensity). The RGB model is also called the *additive primary model*, because a color becomes lighter as you add higher intensities of primary hues. All monitors and other projection devices—including televisions that use light to display colors—rely on the additive model.

The additive primary model consists of three hues—red, green, and blue—from which all colors in the visible spectrum may be derived. These primary hues can be mixed as follows:

- Equal intensities of red and green make yellow. Subtract some red to produce chartreuse; subtract some green to produce orange.

- Equal intensities of green and blue make cyan. Subtract some green to produce turquoise; subtract some blue to produce jade.

- Equal intensities of blue and red make purple. Subtract some blue to produce magenta; subtract some red to produce violet.

- Equal intensities of red, green, and blue make gray or white.

- No light results in black (or darkness).

The color wheel

The APPLE COLOR WHEEL dialog box also provides a second model for adjusting the amount of light in a color. This HSB color model, as it is called, makes use of the properties of hue, saturation, and brightness. The *hue* of a color is measured on a color wheel representing the entire visible spectrum. The wheel is divided into 65,535 sections. Some of the most popular hues are found at the following numeric locations:

- Red—0.
- Orange—5500.
- Yellow—11,000.
- Chartreuse—16,500.
- Green—22,000.
- Jade—27,500.
- Cyan—33,000.
- Blue—44,000.
- Violet—49,000.
- Purple—54,500.
- Magenta—60,000.

Saturation represents the purity of a color. A saturation of 0 is always gray; a saturation of 65,535 is required to produce the most vivid versions of each of the colors listed above. You can think of the saturation value as the difference between a black-and-white television and a color television. When the saturation value is low, all information about a color is expressed except the hue itself. Most natural colors require moderate saturation values. Highly saturated colors appear vivid.

Brightness is the lightness or darkness of a color. A brightness of 0 is always black; a brightness of 65,535 is used to achieve each of the colors listed above. For example, if the hue is red, a brightness value of 65,535 will produce bright red; 49,000 produces medium red; 32,500 produces dark red; and 16,000 makes a red so dark that it appears almost black.

Changing screen colors

To change a color using the RGB color model, enter values from 0 to 65,535 in the "Red," "Green," and "Blue" option boxes. Alternatively, you may click the up or down arrow next to each option box to raise or lower the corresponding value. Press TAB to advance from one option box to the next.

To change a color using the HSB model, alter the values in the "Hue," "Saturation," and "Brightness" option boxes. Or you may reposition the *color-adjustment dot* inside the *color wheel* on the right-hand side of the dialog box. The color wheel works in association with the nearby scroll bar. The color wheel and scroll bar may be adjusted as follows:

- To change the hue, move the color-adjustment dot around the perimeter of the wheel.

- To alter the saturation, move the color-adjustment dot between the perimeter and center of the wheel. Colors along the perimeter have a saturation value of 65,535; the center color has a saturation value of 0.

- To change the brightness, move the scroll box within the scroll bar. The top of the scroll bar equates to a brightness value of 65,535; the bottom equates to 0.

After you press the TAB key or complete an adjustment to the color wheel or scroll bar, the new color will display in the *new color box* above the option boxes. Directly below the new color box is the *original color box*, which shows the color as it appeared prior to the new changes, so that you may continuously compare the current color to the original setting.

Click the OK button or press RETURN when you are satisfied with your color adjustment, or click the CANCEL button to close the dialog and revert to the previous color settings. When all the colors presented in the DISPLAY COLOR SETUP dialog have been adjusted satisfactorily, click the close box in the upper left corner of the dialog, then click the OK button or press RETURN after subsequently returning to the PREFERENCES dialog.

 It is generally a good idea to let your monitor warm up at least 20 minutes before adjusting its color. Also, be sure the colors in the DISPLAY COLOR SETUP dialog are properly adjusted before creating or editing colors using the COLORS palette or COLORS... command.

Coloring illustrations

FreeHand's color capabilities have changed little since FreeHand 1.0, but its organization has changed dramatically. Previous versions of FreeHand offered a COLOR menu that allowed you to create, edit, and apply colors. In version 3.0, FreeHand introduces the COLORS palette, an independent palette that appears in front of the foremost window and is displayed by choosing "Colors" from the WINDOWS pop-up under the VIEW menu (⌘-9). As shown in Figure 11.04, all existing colors in the current illustration are displayed as options in a scrolling list inside the COLORS palette. These options may be defined and manipulated using another set of options, made available by clicking and holding on the right-pointing arrowhead icon. The ▶ pop-up menu will display, as shown in the figure.

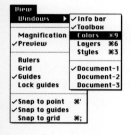

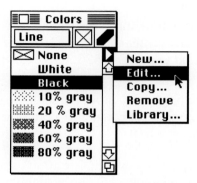

Figure 11.04: Choosing an option from the Colors palette pop-up menu.

The following section describes how to apply colors to a selected text block or graphic object using the COLORS palette. Following that, we discuss how to create new colors, edit existing colors, and access predefined color libraries.

Assigning colors

Below the COLORS palette title bar is a pop-up menu that offers three options—"Fill," "Line," and "Both"—each of which is used, respectively, to view or alter the fill, the stroke, or both the fill and the stroke of a selection.

KE Clicking the fill icon (⊠ or ■) immediately to the right of the pop-up menu chooses the "Fill" option. Clicking the stroke option (✐ or ⊠) along the right side of the palette chooses "Line." To choose "Both," click one icon, then SHIFT-click the other.

When you select a text or graphic object in the illustration window, or when you highlight type in the TEXT dialog box, the color name for the corresponding fill or stroke (depending on the chosen option) becomes highlighted in the scrolling list. Also, both the fill and stroke icons beneath the title bar adopt the colors of the fill and the stroke of the selection (⊠ if "None").

To change the color of one or more selected objects, choose the desired option—"Fill," "Line," or "Both"—then click on a color name in the scrolling list. Click "None" to delete a selected fill and/or stroke.

The COLORS palette is the one place from which you can change the fill and/or stroke of both type and graphics. However, the result of changing an option in the COLORS palette varies, depending on the fill and stroke currently assigned to the selection and whether the selection is a text block or a graphic object. If text, changing the "Fill" color generally changes the fill of the selected type, but changing the "Line" color produces no effect (always "None"). The only exceptions occur when the text has been filled or stroked using an option from the EFFECT pop-up under the TYPE menu. Then the results of choosing a color name become less predictable, as listed below. (Unless otherwise noted, changing the "Line" color produces no effect.)

- **Filled and stroked type**. "Fill" color affects the fill of the selected type; "Line" color affects the stroke.

- **Heavy type**. "Fill" color affects the fill of the selected type.

- **Inline type**. "Fill" color affects both the fill and strokes associated with the selected type (defined by the "Stroke" color in the INLINE dialog box).

- **Oblique type**. "Fill" color affects the fill of the selected type.

- **Outline type**. "Fill" color affects the outline (stroke) of the selected type.

- **Shadow type**. "Fill" color affects the fill of the foremost characters (the shadow is always gray).

- **Zoom text**. "Fill" color affects the stroke of the foremost version of the selected type and the fill of the rearmost version (defined by the "From" color in the ZOOM TEXT dialog box).

If that doesn't seem perfectly logical to you, join the club. We don't understand the reasoning behind a lot of the FreeHand interface. Fortunately, the effects of changing the fills and strokes of graphic objects are more predictable, but they are still dependent on current fill and stroke attributes. "Fill" colors function as follows:

- **No fill**. Selecting a "Fill" color adds a basic fill to the selected object.

- **Basic fill**. "Fill" color affects the fill of the selected object.

- **Graduated fill**. "Fill" color affects the beginning color in the selected gradation (defined by the "From" color in the FILL AND LINE dialog box).

- **Patterned fill**. "Fill" color affects the color of the pixels in the bit-mapped pattern.

- **PostScript fill**. "Fill" color affects the color of the current Post-Script pattern (unless the code contains its own color information, in which case the "Fill" color produces no effect).

- **Radial fill**. "Fill" color affects the beginning color in the selected gradation (defined by the "From" color in the FILL AND LINE dialog box).

- **Tiled fill**. Selecting a "Fill" color deletes the tile pattern from the selected object and adds a basic fill.

- **Custom fill**. "Fill" color affects the color of the current predefined PostScript pattern (unless "Black & white noise" is chosen from the "Effect" pop-up menu in the FILL AND LINE dialog box, in which case the "Fill" color produces no effect).

Similarly, "Line" colors work like this:

- **No stroke**. Selecting a "Line" color adds a basic stroke with a 1-point line weight to the selected object.

- **Basic stroke**. "Line" color affects the stroke of the selected object.

- **Patterned stroke**. "Line" color affects the color of the pixels in the bitmapped pattern.

- **PostScript stroke**. "Line" color affects the color of the current PostScript pattern (unless the code contains its own color information, in which case the "Line" color produces no effect).

- **Custom stroke**. "Line" color affects the color of the current pre-defined PostScript pattern.

If all selected objects do not share a common fill and/or stroke color (depending on the chosen option), no color option will be highlighted.

You may also apply a color to the fill and stroke of one or more selected objects by choosing options from the "Color" pop-up menus inside the FILL AND LINE dialog box. To color a selected text block or one or more highlighted characters in the TEXT dialog box, use the "Color" pop-up menus in the FILL AND STROKE, INLINE, and ZOOM TEXT dialog boxes.

Overprinting colors

Any time you apply a basic fill or stroke, whether to type or to a graphic object, the current dialog box offers an "Overprint" option check box. This option controls whether the color that fills or strokes the selected object will be printed on top of another color that is directly behind it in the current illustration. When this option is selected, an object is allowed to *overprint* the object behind it, provided the color assigned to the object behind it is printed to a different *separation* (as defined in Chapter 14, *Printing Your Illustrations*). For example, if your drawing consists of two colors—orange and blue—then orange may overprint blue, blue may overprint orange, and either may overprint or be overprinted by black, because orange, blue, and black will print to their own separations during the printing process. However, a 30% tint of blue may not overprint a 70% tint of blue, because all blue objects will print to the same separation.

If the "Overprint" option is deselected, as by default, portions of an object covered by another object will be *knocked out* (won't print) when the two objects are printed to different separations.

For example, suppose that the faces in Figure 11.05 on the following page are filled and stroked in tints of orange, and that the hats are colored in tints of blue. In the first example in the figure, the portion of the orange object under the hat has been knocked out. In the second example, the objects overprint, allowing the colors to blend, giving the hat a transparent appearance.

Figure 11.05: An orange face with a blue hat as it appears when the "Overprint" option is deselected (left) and selected (right).

Defining new colors

Only named colors may be assigned to type and graphic objects in Free-Hand 3.0. There are three ways to define or introduce colors to the list of named colors in the COLORS palette:

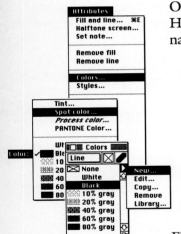

- Choose the COLORS... command from the ATTRIBUTES menu.

- Choose one of the four color-creation options from the "Color" pop-up menu in the FILL AND LINE, FILL AND STROKE, INLINE, or ZOOM TEXT dialog box. These are the "Tint...," "Spot color...," "Process color...," and "Pantone color..." options.

- Choose the "New...," "Copy...," or "Library..." option from the ▶ pop-up menu in the COLORS palette.

Most of these actions will display the COLORS dialog box, shown in Figure 11.06. The only exception—choosing the "Library..." option from the ▶ pop-up menu—displays the SELECT LIBRARY COLOR(S) dialog box, discussed later in this chapter.

The following sections describe the kinds of colors you may create in Aldus FreeHand.

Creating process colors

After the COLORS dialog box displays, choose the "Process" option (in italicized type) from the "Type" pop-up menu. This allows you to create a *process color*, a color that is defined and printed by mixing various concentrations of four primary process hues—cyan, magenta, yellow, and black. Each hue is represented by a scroll bar followed by an option box, as shown in Figure 11.06.

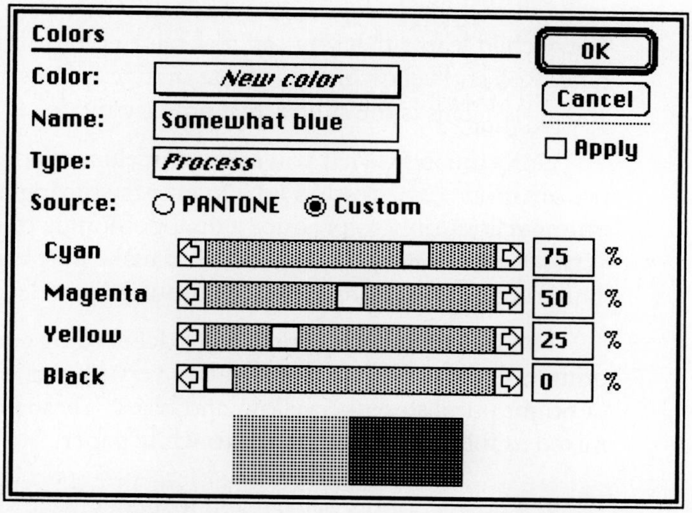

Figure 11.06: The Colors dialog box allows you to define process colors, spot colors, and tints. You may also access Pantone-brand ink simulations.

Although process colors resemble other on-screen colors in that they are defined by mixing two or more primary hues, *pigment*-based colors on paper behave differently than light-based colors on your monitor. Rather than projecting light, pigments reflect light. Therefore, process colors use an entirely different color model, known as the *subtractive primary model* because a resulting color becomes darker as you add higher concentrations of primary hues.

Coloring with pigments

In nature, most colors are created using the subtractive color model, which works like this: Sunlight contains every visible color found on earth. When sunlight is projected on an object, the object absorbs (subtracts) some of the light and reflects the rest. This reflected light is the color that you see. For example, a fire engine is red because it absorbs all other colors from the white-light spectrum.

Pigments on a sheet of paper work the same way. A purple crayon absorbs all nonpurple colors; green ink absorbs all colors that aren't green. Every child learns that you can make any color using red, yellow, and blue. Red and yellow mix to create orange, yellow and blue make green, and so on. This is the subtractive primary model.

Unfortunately, what you learned in elementary school is a rude approximation of the truth. Did you ever try mixing a vivid red with a bright yellow, only to produce a disappointingly drab orange? And the very idea that deep blue and vivid red make purple is almost laughable. The true result is more of a washed-out gray.

The true subtractive primary model used by commercial artists and printers consists of four hues: cyan (a very pale greenish blue), magenta (a bright purplish pink), yellow, and black. These primary hues can be mixed as follows, when applied to white paper:

- Equal amounts of cyan and magenta make violet. Additional cyan produces blue; additional magenta produces purple.

- Equal amounts of magenta and yellow make red. Additional magenta produces carmine; additional yellow produces orange.

- Equal amounts of yellow and cyan make green. Additional yellow produces chartreuse; additional cyan produces turquoise.

- Equal amounts of cyan, magenta, and yellow make brown.

- Black pigmentation added to any other pigment darkens the color.

- No pigmentation results in white (assuming that white is the color of the paper).

To create a process color in the COLORS dialog box, enter percentage values from 0% (no concentration) to 100% (full concentration) in the "Cyan," "Magenta," "Yellow," and "Black" option boxes. Or you may use the corresponding scroll bars. Drag a scroll box to the left to lower the concentration of a color; drag it to the right to increase the color concentration.

Two *color-display boxes* appear at the bottom of the COLORS dialog box. The right color box shows the color as it originally appeared before displaying the COLORS dialog. When creating a new color, this color box is generally black. The left color box shows the color as it now appears, according to your most recent specifications. Keep in mind that the on-screen version of the color will not exactly match the final printed version, since screen and paper rely on different color models. To accurately gauge the printed appearance of a process color, examine the 20% mixtures included on the *Process Color Card*, generally located inside the pouch at the front of the FreeHand user manual.

If you intend to pursue commercial art professionally, you may want to purchase a comprehensive 5%-increment process color guide from a local printer or art supplies dealer. Among those available commercially is a $300 guide from Pantone, (201) 935-5501. But we recommend that you first check with your printer to see if they provide a guide of their own, assuming the guide is printed in-house from the same ink, paper, and presses used to print artwork for clients.

When you are satisfied with your specifications, enter a color name into the "Name" option, up to 32 characters in length. (Note that Free-Hand does *not* allow you to replace an existing color by creating a new color with the same name.) Then press RETURN or click the OK button. If you want to apply the new color to a selected object, select the "Apply" check box before pressing RETURN. Your new process color will display in the COLORS palette and in all "Color" pop-up menus in italicized type to set it apart from spot colors and tints.

Creating spot colors

FreeHand also allows you to create a *spot color*; that is, a color that is printed using a single ink. For example, suppose that you want to create a simple illustration that contains only two colors, red and dark gray. Rather than printing each of these colors as a mixture of cyan, magenta, yellow, and black inks, you may select red and dark gray inks that exactly meet your requirements. Because your printer has to print only two colors instead of four, you save money. And because there's no mixing in the final printing stage, the colors will print exactly the way you expect.

To create a spot color, choose the "Spot" option from the "Type" pop-up menu in the COLORS dialog box, as shown in Figure 11.07. Even though your spot color will print as a single ink, you must mix primary hues to display the color on-screen. Three scroll bars followed by option boxes are provided for this purpose. Prior to mixing, you may pick from one of three color models: "RGB" (red, green, blue), "HLS" (hue, lightness, saturation, identical in theory to the HSB color model described on page 374), and "CMY" (cyan, magenta, yellow).

- Figure 11.07 shows the scroll bars that display when the "RGB" radio button is selected. Enter percentage values from 0% (no intensity) to 100% (full intensity) in the "Red," "Green," and "Blue" option boxes. To use the scroll bars, drag a scroll box to the left to lower the intensity; drag it to the right to increase the intensity. Higher intensities produce lighter colors.

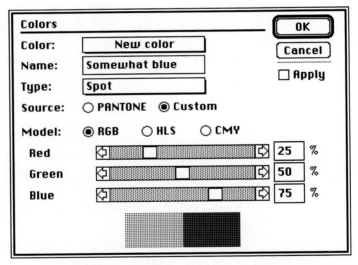

Figure 11.07: Defining a spot color using the RGB color model.

- Figure 11.08 shows the scroll bars that display when the "HLS" radio button is selected. Enter a degree value in the "Hue" option box. The hue is measured on a wheel, but unlike the one in the APPLE COLOR WHEEL dialog box, FreeHand's wheel is divided into 360°.

Values correspond to hues as follows:

Red—0°.	Green—120°.	Blue—240°.
Orange—30°.	Jade—150°.	Violet—270°.
Yellow—60°.	Cyan—180°.	Purple—300°.
Chartreuse—90°.	Sky blue—210°.	Magenta—330°.

Enter a percentage value from 0% (black) to 100% (white) in the "Lightness" option box. Likewise, enter a value from 0% (gray) to 100% (vivid color) in the "Saturation" option box. A "Lightness" value of 50% and a "Saturation" of 100% were used to produce the colors listed above. You may also use the scroll bars. We recommend that you experiment with this color model if you intend to use it on a regular basis.

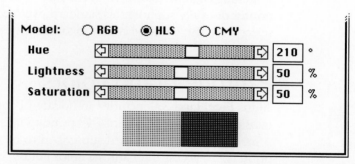

Figure 11.08: Defining a spot color using the HLS color model.

● Figure 11.09 on the following page shows the scroll bars that display when the "CMY" radio button is selected. Enter percentage values from 0% (no concentration) to 100% (full concentration) in the "Cyan," "Magenta," and "Yellow" option boxes. Unlike the options presented for defining a process color, the CMY model does not offer a "Black" option, since the color black is necessary only for creating printed reproductions. All colors may be represented on screen without black. To use the scroll bars, drag a scroll box to the left to lower the concentration; drag it to the right to increase the concentration. Higher intensities produce darker colors.

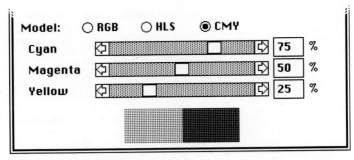

Figure 11.09: Defining a spot color using the CMY color model.

You should always define spot colors that match ink colors available from your printer. In other words, you can't create a color on-screen, and later expect your printer to fabricate an ink in that same color. Various spot color standards exist. One of the most popular is the Pantone Matching System, described in the next section. In fact, unless your printer does *not* support this standard, we recommend that you always select from the Pantone colors to satisfy your spot color requirements.

Pantone-brand colors

Aldus FreeHand 3.0 includes an updated Pantone Colors file, which contains the complete library of 747 printing inks that make up the *Pantone Matching System*, a standard subscribed to by most major commercial printers. To access the Pantone color library, select "Pantone" from the "Source" radio buttons in the COLORS dialog box. A scrolling list of colors and a "Pantone ___ CV" option box will display, as shown in Figure 11.10, along with an exhaustive copyright statement. (No doubt we're all dying to steal their color definitions or something. It's not enough to display *PANTONE* in capital letters at every possible opportunity like we're all supposed to stand up and salute. But alas, we digress...)

A Pantone color may be defined either as a spot color or a process color by choosing the desired option from the "Type" pop-up menu. In most cases, you will want to print a Pantone color as a spot color, since it corresponds to a specific mixture of inks. However, if you need to match a Pantone color in a document that otherwise contains process colors—as when reproducing a logo in a full-color illustration—FreeHand can simulate the Pantone color using process colors. The simulations are performed according to Pantone specifications.

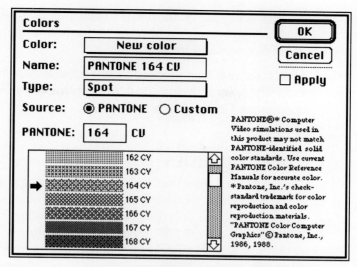

Figure 11.10: Click the "Pantone" radio button to display a scrolling list of 747 Pantone-brand colors.

To select a Pantone color, click on a color in the scrolling list or, if you're looking for a specific color, enter the number for the color in the "Pantone ___ CV" option box.

Process color versus custom color

Although it is not difficult to define a fill or stroke as either a process color or a custom color, it can be difficult to determine which technique is more appropriate for the current object. Generally, the rule of thumb is this: Process colors should be applied in an illustration that contains many colors and will therefore be separated as a four-color process image. You should also use process colors under any of the following situations:

- The current illustration contains one or more blends or gradations that span different colors (not just different tints of the same color).

- The current illustration contains one or more imported images that require process-color separation, such as a color scan stored in the TIFF format.

Spot colors are better suited to illustrations in which only two or three specific inks are required or to documents that incorporate logos or other color-sensitive images.

A color may be converted from a process color to a spot color, or vice versa, simply by choosing the desired option from the "Type" pop-up menu in the COLORS dialog box.

Creating tints

Choose "Tint " from the "Type" pop-up menu, as shown in Figure 11.11, to create a *tint* based on any existing color. A tint is a lightened variation of a color, specified as a percentage value from 0% (white) to 100% (the solid color). When used in spot color printing, tints provide an inexpensive way to create shades of a single ink to achieve the effect of using multiple colors. Tints are also used to create gray values in monochrome artwork.

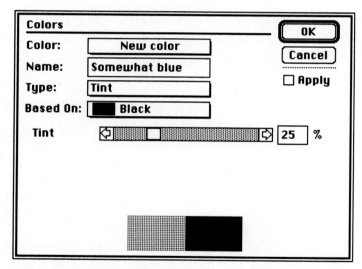

Figure 11.11: Choose "Tint" from the "Type" pop-up menu to create a lighter version of an existing color.

New color defaults

As we discussed earlier, there are many ways to display the COLORS dialog box to create a new color. However, you should be aware that the manner in which you access the COLORS dialog will have an effect on the default settings it contains:

- **Choose** 1) COLORS… from the ATTRIBUTES menu, 2) "Spot color…" from a "Color" pop-up menu, or 3) "New…" from the ▶ pop-up menu when a spot color, "Black," or "White" is currently selected in the COLORS palette. *Default*: Black spot color using RGB color model.

- **Choose** 1) "Process color…" from a "Color" pop-up menu or 2) "New…" from the ▶ pop-up menu when a process color is currently selected in the COLORS palette. *Default*: White process color using CMYK color model.

- **Choose** 1) "Pantone color…" from a "Color" pop-up menu or 2) "New…" from the ▶ pop-up menu when a Pantone color is currently selected in the COLORS palette (whether defined as a spot or process color). *Default*: Pantone yellow (first option in scrolling list) defined as a spot color.

- **Choose** 1) "Tint…" from a "Color" pop-up menu or 2) "New…" from the ▶ pop-up menu when a tint is currently selected in the COLORS palette. *Default*: 100% black tint.

- **Choose** "Copy…" from the ▶ pop-up menu when any color name is selected in the COLORS palette. *Default*: Settings exactly matching the selected color.

These are the default settings only. You may, of course, choose different options and alter values as you see fit.

Note that although choosing the "Copy…" option from the COLORS palette ▶ pop-up menu displays all settings relevant to the current color, the "Name" option in the COLORS dialog box will be blank, allowing you to create a duplicate or similar color under a different name.

You may also copy an existing color by double-clicking the color name in the COLORS palette, then choosing the "New color" option from the "Color" pop-up menu in the COLORS dialog box. As when choosing "Copy…," all settings relevant to the selected color will display and the "Name" option will be empty.

Using color libraries

Because the process of defining a color is time consuming, and because you may want to use the same colors in many documents, FreeHand allows you to organize colors into *color libraries,* or *clibs* (pronounced see-libs), which may be loaded into any illustration. As an example, FreeHand includes a color library named CrayonLibrary.clib, which contains 64 colors that correspond to the colors found in a large pack of Crayola-brand crayons. (Although Crayola has recently updated many of its colors, FreeHand has not, making FreeHand's collection something of a Crayola Classic pack.)

Using existing clibs

To load colors from an existing clib, choose the "Library…" option from the ▶ pop-up menu in the COLORS palette. A standard Macintosh OPEN DOCUMENT dialog box will appear, requesting that you locate and select the name of the color library you wish to open. These CrayonLibrary.clib files will be in the same folder as the FreeHand application.

After selecting a library name and pressing RETURN, the SELECT LIBRARY COLOR(S) dialog box will display, as shown in Figure 11.12. The names of colors contained in the open color library will display in a scrolling list.

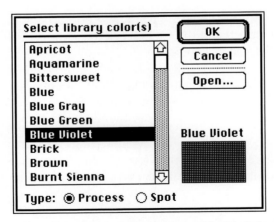

Figure 11.12: The Select library color(s) dialog box allows you to select one or more colors for use in the current illustration.

When you select a color name from the scrolling color list, the color will display on the right side of the dialog box. You may select multiple colors by SHIFT-clicking or SHIFT-dragging over color names. Select "Process" or "Spot" from the "Type" radio buttons to determine whether the selected color is imported as a process color or a spot color. ("Process" is generally the wisest choice, since clib colors do not correspond to any commercial printing standard.)

After selecting the color(s) and specifying the type, click the OK button or press RETURN to add the selected color(s) to the current illustration. These colors will appear in the COLORS palette as well as in "Color" pop-up menus inside various dialog boxes.

Once a color library has been opened, choosing "Library…" from the ▶ pop-up menu in the COLORS palette will bring up the SELECT LIBRARY COLOR(S) dialog box directly. Colors that are not contained in the current illustration will display in the scrolling list. You may then select one or more of these colors and add them to the current illustration.

To open a different color library and select from its colors, click the OPEN… BUTTON in the SELECT LIBRARY COLOR(S) dialog box and the OPEN DOCUMENT dialog will again display. Select the name of the new clib file you wish to open and press RETURN. Colors from this library will now appear in the SELECT LIBRARY COLOR(S) dialog box. You may add colors from several clibs to a single illustration.

Creating new clibs

A FreeHand color library is nothing more than an *ASCII* (text-only) file that contains straightforward color definitions in a format recognized by FreeHand. Therefore, defining a new clib for use in FreeHand, or modifying an existing clib, is a very simple procedure. All you need is a standard word processor, such as MacWrite, Microsoft Word, or WriteNow.

To begin, launch your favorite word processing application and open an existing clib or create a new text file. A FreeHand clib file must contain the library name on the first line of text and the word "BeginColorDefs" on the second line. Comments may also be included, provided they begin with a percent symbol (%). Each subsequent line of text contains the name of a color you wish to include in the library, followed by the percentages of each appropriate primary process hue that makes up the color.

The format for defining a color is as follows:

name=(*NewColor*) cmyk=(*.00, .00, .00, .00*) rgb=(*.00, .00, .00*)

in which *NewColor* is any color name up to 32 characters long, consisting of no special characters and beginning with an alphabetic character, and in which *.00* can be substituted with any number between .0 (0%) and 1.0 (100%) in 0.01 increments. It is not necessary to define colors in both the CMYK and RGB color models. However, if you do not include a CMYK definition, you will not be permitted to import the color into an illustration as process color.

The last two lines of text in a clib file must read "EndColorDefs" and "EndColorLibrary" to instruct Freehand it has reached the end of the file. To illustrate this format, the contents of the CrayonLibrary.clib file are listed below:

```
ColorLibrary 1.0
% These are from the 64 crayon box - sharpener NOT included
LibraryType Crayon Colors
BeginColorDefs

name=(Apricot) cmyk=(.0, .15, .3, .0) rgb=(1.0, .85, .7)
name=(Aquamarine) cmyk=(1.0, .1, .1, .0) rgb=(.0, .9, .9)
name=(Bittersweet) cmyk=(.15, .7, 1.0, .0) rgb=(.85, .3, .0)
name=(Blue) cmyk=(.71, .70, .21, .0) rgb=(.29, .30, .79)
name=(Blue Gray) cmyk=(.5, .38, .28, .0) rgb=(.5, .62, .72)
name=(Blue Green) cmyk=(1.0, .31, .37, .0) rgb=(.0, .69, .63)
name=(Blue Violet) cmyk=(.91, 1.0, .67, .0) rgb=(.09, .0, .33)
name=(Brick) cmyk=(.32, 1.0, 1.0, .0) rgb=(.68, .0, .0)
name=(Brown) cmyk=(.5, .85, 1.0, .0) rgb=(.5, .15, .0)
name=(Swamp Fire) cmyk=(.13, .72, 1.0, .0) rgb=(.87, .28, .0)
name=(Burnt Sienna) cmyk=(.41, .75, 1.0, .0) rgb=(.59, .25, .0)
name=(Gray Blue) cmyk=(.65, .44, .38, .0) rgb=(.35, .56, .62)
name=(Carnation) cmyk=(.0, .25, .25, .0) rgb=(1.0, .75, .75)
name=(Copper) rgb=(.7, .2, .04) %No cmyk equivalent
name=(Cornflower) cmyk=(.36, .43, .0, .0) rgb=(.64, .57, 1.0)
name=(Forest Green) cmyk=(1.0, .63, 1.0, .0) rgb=(.0, .37, .0)
name=(Gold) rgb=(1.0, .8, .0) %No cmyk equivalent
name=(Goldenrod) cmyk=(.0, .25, .8, .0) rgb=(1.0, .75, .2)
name=(Gray) cmyk=(.4, .4, .4, .0) rgb=(.6, .6, .6)
name=(Green) cmyk=(1.0, .18, 1.0, .0) rgb=(.0, .82, .0)
name=(Green Blue) cmyk=(1.0, .4, .37, .0) rgb=(.0, .6, .63)
```

name=(Green Yellow) cmyk=(.2, .0, 1.0, .0) rgb=(.8, .0, 1.0)
name=(Chinese Red) cmyk=(.5, .95, 1.0, .0) rgb=(.5, .05, .0)
name=(Lavendar) cmyk=(.0, .3, .0, .0) rgb=(1.0, .7, 1.0)
name=(Lemon) cmyk=(.0, .0, .7, .0) rgb=(1.0, 1.0, .3)
name=(Magenta) cmyk=(.0, 1.0, .0, .0) rgb=(1.0, .0, 1.0)
name=(Mahogony) cmyk=(.29, .75, 1.0, .0) rgb=(.71, .25, .0)
name=(Maize) cmyk=(.0, .25, .9, .0) rgb=(1.0, .75, .1)
name=(Maroon) cmyk = (.22,1.0, .74, .0) rgb=(.78, .0, .26)
name=(Melon) cmyk=(.0, .65, .78, .0) rgb=(1.0, .35, .22) %
name=(Midnight) cmyk=(1.0, .92, .6, .0) rgb=(.0, .8, .40)
name=(Mulberry) cmyk=(.16, 1.0, .53, .0) rgb=(.84, .0, .47)
name=(Navy) cmyk=(1.0, 1.0, .42, .0) rgb=(.0, .0, .58)
name=(Olive) cmyk=(.16, .16, .73, .0) rgb=(.84, .84, .27)
name=(Orange) cmyk=(.0, .4, 1.0, .0) rgb=(1.0, .6, .0)
name=(Orange Red) cmyk=(.0, .9, 1.0, .0) rgb=(1.0, .1, .0)
name=(Orange Yellow) cmyk=(.0, .25, 1.0, .0) rgb=(1.0, .75, .0)
name=(Orchid) cmyk=(.0, .5, .0, .0) rgb=(1.0, .5, 1.0)
name=(Peach) cmyk=(.0, .2, .35, .0) rgb=(1.0, .8, .65)
name=(Periwinkle) cmyk=(.3, .3, .15, .0) rgb=(.7, .7, .85)
name=(Pine Green) cmyk=(.93, .59, .76, .0) rgb=(.07, .41, .24)
name=(Plum) cmyk=(.72, 1.0, .6, .0) rgb=(.28, .0, .4)
name=(Purple) cmyk=(.76, 1.0, .67, .0) rgb=(.24, .0, .33)
name=(Raw Sienna) cmyk=(.31, .73, 1.0, .0) rgb=(.69, .27, .0)
name=(Raw Umber) cmyk=(.67, .92, 1.0, .0) rgb=(.33, .08, .0)
name=(Red) cmyk=(.12, 1.0, 1.0, .0) rgb=(.88, .0, .0)
name=(Red Orange) cmyk=(.0, .75, 1.0, .0) rgb=(1.0, .25, .0)
name=(Red Violet) cmyk=(.13, 1.0, .27, .0) rgb=(.87, .0, .73)
name=(Salmon) cmyk=(.0, .5, .6, .0) rgb=(1.0, .6, .5)
name=(Seafoam) cmyk=(1.0, .0, .6, .0) rgb=(.0, 1.0, .4)
name=(Sepia) cmyk=(.54, .85, .98, .0) rgb=(.46, .15, .2)
name=(Sky) cmyk=(.28, .08, .0, .0) rgb=(.72, .92, 1.0)
name=(Silver) rgb=(.65, .65, .65) %No cmyk equivalent
name=(Spring Green) cmyk=(1.0, .0, 1.0, .0) rgb=(.0, 1.0, .0)
name=(Tan) cmyk=(.27, .61, 1.0, .0) rgb=(.73, .39, .0)
name=(Rose) cmyk=(.0, .5, .3, .0) rgb=(1.0, .5, .7)
name=(Turquoise) cmyk=(1.0, .2, .2, .0) rgb=(.0, .8, .8)
name=(Violet Blue) cmyk=(.8, 1.0, .67, .0) rgb=(.2, .0, .33)
name=(Violet Red) cmyk=(.1, 1.0, .0, .0) rgb=(.9, .0, 1.0)
name=(Yellow) cmyk=(.0, .0, 1.0, .0) rgb=(1.0, 1.0, .0)
name=(Yellow Green) cmyk=(.3, .0, 1.0, .0) rgb=(.7, .0, 1.0)
name=(Yellow Orange) cmyk=(.0, .35, 1.0, .0) rgb=(1.0, .65, .0)

EndColorDefs
EndColorLibrary

If you are interested in obtaining more color libraries, public domain clibs may be available from your local Macintosh user's group or through a Macintosh bulletin board system (such as the Aldus forum on Compu-Serve or the Aldus folder on MacNet).

Editing existing colors

Regardless of how a color is defined—whether as a process color, spot color, Pantone color, tint, or clib color—any color displayed in the COLORS palette (except black or white) may be altered or deleted. You may change its name, adjust primary hues, or switch the type from process to spot, from Pantone to tint, and so on.

Use any of the following techniques to display the COLORS dialog box for a specific color:

- Select a color in the COLORS palette and choose "Edit…" from the ▶ pop-up menu.

- Double-click a color in the COLORS palette.

- Press OPTION and choose a color name option from the "Color" pop-up menu in the FILL AND LINE, FILL AND STROKE, INLINE, or ZOOM TEXT dialog box.

If you display the COLORS dialog box by some other means, you may still edit an existing color simply by choosing the corresponding color name option from the "Color" pop-up menu. After making the desired alterations, click OK or press RETURN to close the dialog box and implement your changes. Note that altering a color will change the appearance of all objects filled or stroked with that color.

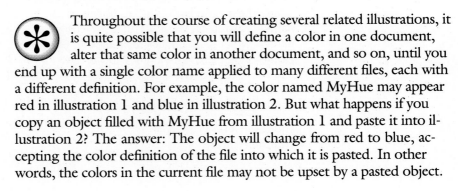

Throughout the course of creating several related illustrations, it is quite possible that you will define a color in one document, alter that same color in another document, and so on, until you end up with a single color name applied to many different files, each with a different definition. For example, the color named MyHue may appear red in illustration 1 and blue in illustration 2. But what happens if you copy an object filled with MyHue from illustration 1 and paste it into illustration 2? The answer: The object will change from red to blue, accepting the color definition of the file into which it is pasted. In other words, the colors in the current file may not be upset by a pasted object.

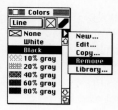

Deleting an existing color

You may delete any existing color that is not currently used in the illustration by selecting the color in the COLORS palette and choosing the "Remove" option from the ▶ pop-up menu. If the color is not being used in the current illustration, the color name will disappear from the scrolling list. If the color is being used, either in the fill or stroke of an object, as the basis of a tint, or in an attributes style, the alert box shown in Figure 11.13 will appear, preventing you from deleting the needed color.

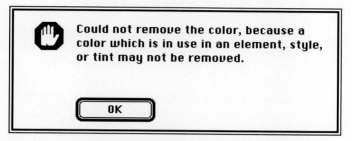

Figure 11.13: This alert box will display if you try to delete a color that is currently in use.

Using attribute styles

One of FreeHand's most inspired and useful new features is the STYLES palette, which contains a list of named *attribute styles* that may be used to control all aspects concerning the fills and strokes of graphic objects (not text). These styles allow you to apply a complex set of attributes with a single click of the mouse button, and then change these attributes globally at any time, affecting all objects to which the style is applied in the current illustration.

The purpose of attribute styles

Attribute styles automate the process of filling and stroking graphic objects. They make it possible to define a set of fill and stroke attributes only once, then use those attributes an unlimited number of times. Not only does this save time and reduce effort—since without styles, you must assign attributes again and again during the creation of a drawing, managing several

---

trips to the menu bar and through FreeHand's vast network of dialog boxes—but it also ensures consistency throughout an illustration. Every object to which a single style is applied will be colored identically.

 Alas, you may not apply a style to a text block. This would be extremely useful, not only for fill and stroke, but also for typeface, size, style, and so on. If you want to apply a style to type, you must first convert the type to paths.

Assigning attribute styles

Like the COLORS palette, the STYLES palette is an independent palette that appears in front of the foremost window. It is displayed by choosing "Styles" from the WINDOWS pop-up under the VIEW menu (⌘-3). All existing attribute styles in the current illustration are displayed as options in a scrolling list inside the STYLES palette. These options may be defined and manipulated using another set of options, which are made available by clicking and holding on the right-pointing arrowhead icon. The ▶ pop-up menu will display, as shown in Figure 11.14.

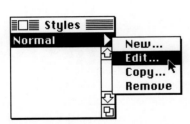

Figure 11.14: Choosing an option from the Styles palette pop-up menu.

The only style included by default in all FreeHand illustrations is "Normal," which includes a transparent fill, a 1-point black stroke, and no special halftone setting.

When you select an object in the illustration window, the corresponding attribute style becomes highlighted. If the attributes of a selected object are based on a specific attribute style, but the fill, stroke, and/or halftone screen settings do not exactly match those of the style definition, a plus sign will appear before the style name, showing that some additional attributes are in effect. If you select multiple objects that have different attribute styles, no style name will be highlighted. If no object is selected, the highlighted style name is the default attribute style, which affects the fills and strokes of any object created in the future.

To change the style of one or more selected objects, simply click a style name in the scrolling list. If the attributes of selected object are based on a style but differ slightly, clicking the highlighted style name will reapply the style so that the object matches the style definition exactly. Any plus sign preceding the style name will disappear.

Defining new styles

Only named attribute styles may be assigned to type and graphic objects in FreeHand 3.0. There are two ways to define or introduce an attribute style to the list of named styles in the STYLES palette:

* Choose the STYLES... command from the ATTRIBUTES menu.

* Choose the "New..." or "Copy..." option from the ▶ pop-up menu in the STYLES palette.

Either of these actions will display the STYLES dialog box, shown in Figure 11.15. The following sections describe how to use this dialog box to define an attribute style.

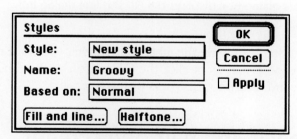

Figure 11.15: The Styles dialog box allows you to store fill, stroke, and halftone screen information as a named attribute style.

Specifying fills and strokes

After the STYLES dialog box displays, click the FILL AND LINE... button to display the FILL AND LINE dialog box, shown in Figure 11.16. This is the same dialog box that displays when you choose FILL AND LINE... from the ATTRIBUTES menu (⌘-E). Use the "Fill" and "Line" pop-up menus to determine the fill and stroke attributes that will be associated with the current style. For complete information about using the "Fill" options, refer to the *Assigning the fill* section of Chapter 9. All "Line" options are discussed in the section *Assigning the stroke* in Chapter 10.

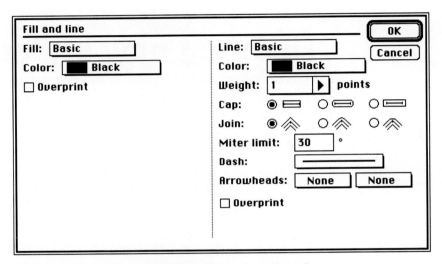

Figure 11.16: Clicking the Fill and line... button in the Styles dialog box displays the Fill and line dialog box.

After specifying the fill and stroke that you want to store with the style, press RETURN or click the OK button to close the FILL AND LINE dialog box and return to the STYLES dialog box.

Specifying halftone screens

Click the HALFTONE... button in the STYLES dialog box to display the HALFTONE SCREEN dialog box, shown in Figure 11.17. This is the same dialog box that displays when you choose the HALFTONE SCREEN... command from the ATTRIBUTES menu.

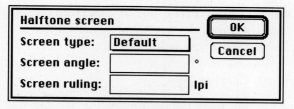

Figure 11.17: Clicking the Halftone... button in the Styles dialog box displays the Halftone screen dialog box.

The options in the HALFTONE SCREEN dialog box control the appearance of *halftone cells*, which are the tiny dots used to represent gray values and tints in the printing process. The "Screen type" pop-up menu determines the *screen function*, which is the pattern with which FreeHand simulates gray values and tints. You may choose from three options:

- **Default**. Accepts the default screen function produced by the current output device. Most printers rely on squarish black dots against a white background to simulate light tints, squarish white dots against a black background to simulate dark tints, and a checkerboard effect to simulate medium tint levels.

- **Line**. Represents gray values and tints using a series of parallel straight lines.

- **Round dot**. Represents gray values and tints using a pattern of perfectly circular dots.

The value in the "Screen angle" option box determines the *screen angle*, which is the orientation of the current pattern of halftone cells. Halftone cells are organized into a grid of rows and columns, like the squares on a checkerboard. By default, this grid is rotated 45° with respect to the printed page. To rotate the grid to some other angle, enter a value between 0 and 360 into the "Screen angle" option box.

The value in the "Screen ruling" option box determines the *screen frequency*, which is the number of halftone cells that print per linear inch. Frequency is measured in *lines per inch*, or lpi. If no value appears in this option box, FreeHand accepts the default screen frequency for the current output device. Examples include 60 lpi for the Apple LaserWriter and 120 lpi for the Linotronic 300. Any value from 4 to 300 lpi is permitted by FreeHand.

Manipulations performed in the HALFTONE SCREEN dialog box affect printing only; they do *not* in any way affect the manner in which objects display in the preview or keyline mode. For complete information about the options in the HALFTONE SCREEN dialog box, see the *Halftone screens* section of Chapter 14.

After specifying the halftone screen settings that you want to store with the style, press RETURN or click the OK button to close the HALFTONE SCREEN dialog box and return to the STYLES dialog box.

When you are satisfied with your attribute style specifications, enter a style name into the "Name" option, up to 32 characters in length. (Note that FreeHand does *not* allow you to replace an existing style by creating a new style with the same name.) Then press RETURN or click the OK button. If you want to apply the new style to a selected object, select the "Apply" check box before pressing RETURN. Your new attribute style will display in the STYLES palette.

New style defaults

The manner in which you access the STYLES dialog will have an effect on the default settings contained in the STYLES, FILL AND LINE, and HALFTONE SCREEN dialog boxes, as described below:

- **Choose** STYLES… from the ATTRIBUTES menu or "New…" from the ▶ pop-up menu when *no* object in the drawing area is selected. *Result*: The default attribute style appears in the "Based on" pop-up menu. The FILL AND LINE and HALFTONE SCREEN dialog boxes contain settings that exactly match the default style. If you choose a new style from the "Based on" pop-up menu, the contents of the FILL AND LINE and HALFTONE SCREEN dialog boxes will change to match the definition of this style.

- **Choose** STYLES… from the ATTRIBUTES menu or "New…" from the ▶ pop-up menu after having selected an object in the drawing area. *Result*: The default attribute style appears in the "Based on" pop-up menu. The FILL AND LINE and HALFTONE SCREEN dialog boxes contain settings that exactly match the selected object. Choosing a new style from the "Based on" pop-up menu will have no effect on the contents of the FILL AND LINE and HALFTONE SCREEN dialog boxes.

• **Choose** "Copy…" from the ▶ pop-up menu. *Result*: The highlighted attribute style appears in the "Based on" pop-up menu. The FILL AND LINE and HALFTONE SCREEN dialog boxes contain settings that exactly match the highlighted style. Choosing a new style from the "Based on" pop-up menu will have no effect on the contents of the FILL AND LINE and HALFTONE SCREEN dialog boxes.

These are the default settings only. You may, of course, choose different options and alter values as you see fit.

Note that although choosing the "Copy…" option from the STYLES palette ▶ pop-up menu copies all settings relevant to the current attribute style, the "Name" option in the STYLES dialog box will remain blank, allowing you to create a duplicate or similar style under a different name.

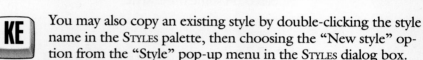

You may also copy an existing style by double-clicking the style name in the STYLES palette, then choosing the "New style" option from the "Style" pop-up menu in the STYLES dialog box. As when choosing "Copy…," the FILL AND LINE and HALFTONE SCREEN dialog boxes will contain all settings relevant to the selected attribute style and the "Name" option will be empty.

Parent/child styles

The "Based on" pop-up menu in the STYLES dialog box contains the name of every attribute style in the current illustration. As described above, this option may sometimes be used to alter the default contents of the FILL AND LINE and HALFTONE SCREEN dialog boxes. But its real purpose is to create a parent/child link between an existing style and a new style. Any fill, stroke, or halftone settings shared between the *parent style* (chosen from the "Based on" option) and the *child style* are controlled by the parent style. If any shared setting is altered for the parent style, FreeHand will automatically revise that setting for the child style as well.

For example, suppose that new Style B is based on existing Style A. Style A has a black stroke with a 1-point line weight. Style B also has a 1-point line weight, but it is colored 40% gray. Later you change the stroke for Style A to 80% gray with a 3-point line weight. The setting shared between Style B and Style A—the line weight—is automatically altered in Style B. However, Style B's stroke color is not affected, since this setting was not shared. Therefore, as a result of your changes to Style A, Style B now has a 40% gray, 3-point stroke.

You may choose a different parent style for an option at any time by choosing another option from the "Based on" pop-up menu. If you do so, however, every setting that was shared between the current style and its previous parent style will be altered to match the corresponding setting included in the new parent style. For example, suppose Style A is based on Style B and both styles include 3-point line weights. Another style, Style C, has a 6-point line weight. If you change Style B's parent style by choosing "Style C" from the "Based on" pop-up menu, Style B will now include a 6-point line weight.

 Although you may change links between styles, you may not break a link; that is, you may not create a style that has no parent or that is based on itself. Every style except "Normal" must be based on some other style.

Editing existing styles

Any attribute style displayed in the STYLES palette may be altered or deleted (except "Normal," which may not be deleted). You may change its name, adjust fill and stroke options, change halftone settings, or switch the parent style.

Use one of the following techniques to display the STYLES dialog box for a specific attribute style:

- Select a style name in the STYLES palette and choose "Edit…" from the ▶ pop-up menu.

- Double-click a style name in the STYLES palette.

If you display the STYLES dialog box by some other means, you may still edit an existing style simply by choosing the corresponding style name option from the "Style" pop-up menu. After making the desired alterations, click OK or press RETURN to close the dialog box and implement your changes. Note that altering a style will change the appearance of all objects filled and stroked according to that style. If an object differs slightly from its style (a plus sign displays in front of the style name in the STYLES palette when the object is selected), changing the style will affect only those attributes of the object that exactly match the style.

Throughout the course of creating several related illustrations, it is quite possible that you will define a style in one document, alter that same style in another document, and so on, until you end up with a single style name applied to many different files, each with a different definition. For example, the attribute style named MyStyle may have a red stroke in illustration 1 and a blue stroke in illustration 2. If you copy an object filled with MyStyle from illustration 1 and paste it into illustration 2, the stroke of the object will change from red to blue, accepting the style definition of the file into which it is pasted. In other words, the styles in the current file may not be altered by a pasted object.

Deleting an existing style

You may delete any existing attribute style—even if it is currently in use—by selecting the style name in the STYLES palette and choosing the "Remove" option from the ▶ pop-up menu. If the deleted style is used in the current illustration, all objects associated with that style become associated with the parent style (although their fill, stroke, and halftone attributes will remain unchanged). Only "Normal" may not be deleted.

Transforming
and Duplicating
Objects

In Chapter 7, we discussed several manipulation techniques that change the form of a path. These reshaping techniques are applicable to various elements, including points, segments, and entire paths, but in our discussion their scope is limited to graphic objects; type cannot be reshaped.

In this chapter we discuss two categories of manipulation techniques—*transforming* and *duplicating*—that do not necessarily alter the form of a path and are applicable to either type or graphic objects. We will also examine FreeHand's extensive collection of precision drawing features and how these features can be used to control the transformation and duplication of objects.

We end the chapter with a detailed discussion of *blending*, a special feature that both transforms and duplicates objects at the same time. This is the only feature covered in this chapter which cannot be applied to type, unless the type is first converted to paths using the CONVERT TO PATHS command.

Grouping

Generally, you will want to transform whole paths rather than individual points or segments. You may even want to transform multiple objects at a time. So imagine that instead of thinking in terms of paths and objects, you could manipulate whole images. This is the beauty of *grouping*, which allows you to assemble throngs of elements into a single object.

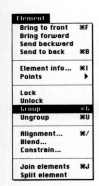

Suppose, for example, that you have created an image made up of several paths. You want to rotate the image, but you're afraid of upsetting the fragile relationship between the paths during the transformation. To safeguard the basic appearance of the image, select all objects in the image and choose GROUP from the ELEMENT menu (⌘-G) and then rotate the group. The rotation will affect the whole image, as shown in Figure 12.01.

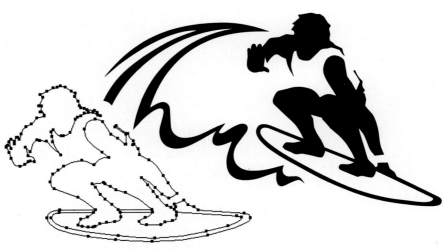

Figure 12.01: Before transforming a collection of complex paths, group the paths into a single object.

When you choose the GROUP command, you accomplish the same goal whether only a single point or segment is selected or a whole path is selected. All objects that are even partially selected become grouped in their entirety.

The GROUP command may be applied to a single path to safeguard the relationship between points and segments. You may even group multiple groups, and groups of groups. In fact, the GROUP command may be applied to any type or graphic object that you can create or import into FreeHand.

After grouping one or more objects, all points within the group disappear. When the group is selected, four *corner handles* define the perimeter of the group, much like those that surround a geometric path. Using the arrow tool, you may drag at any of these corner handles to scale a group, as discussed in the *Using handles* section of Chapter 7. Press SHIFT and drag a handle to scale the group proportionally.

 Groups offer less scaling flexibility than geometric paths or imported bitmaps and EPS graphics. For example, you may not scale a group with respect to its center by pressing OPTION, nor may you scale a group horizontally or vertically by pressing SHIFT and CONTROL.

Choosing ELEMENT INFO... from the ELEMENT menu (⌘-I, ⬺-🖰🖰) when a group is selected will display the GROUP dialog box, shown in Figure 12.02. The two "Position" option boxes display the location of the lower left corner handle of the group in relation to the ruler origin (discussed in the *Using the rulers* section, later in this chapter). Enter new values for these options to relocate the entire group according to the lower left handle.

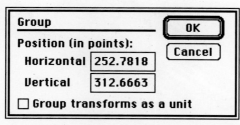

Figure 12.02: Press option and double-click a group to display the Group dialog box.

At the bottom of the Group dialog box is the "Group transforms as a unit" check box, which allows you to predetermine how a transformation will affect attributes of the selected group. If you want certain aspects of a group, such as type orientation, fill, and stroke, to remain constant throughout a transformation, as demonstrated by the right-hand object in Figure 12.03, leave this option deselected. However, if you want attributes of a group to be transformed along with the group, as shown in Figure 12.04, select the "Group transforms as a unit" check box before performing the transformation.

Figure 12.03: After grouping several objects (left), we skew the group (right). By default, the stroke remains constant and the type simply rotates around its transformed ellipse. Also notice that the relationship between paths in the cartoon has become jumbled.

Figure 12.04: Select the "Group transforms as a unit" check box to distort attributes of a group with respect to a transformation.

Selecting elements within groups

To select a whole group, click any path in the group with the arrow tool. You may also select an individual object in a group by OPTION-clicking it with the arrow tool. This displays individual points in the path, allowing you to fill, stroke, reshape, or transform a single path within a group without affecting other objects in the group.

After selecting a single path in a group, you may select groups within groups by pressing the TILDE key (~). Each time you press TILDE, you select the group that includes the current group.

The following exercise demonstrates how this works:

1. Draw four separate paths with the freehand tool. After drawing each path, choose GROUP from the ELEMENT menu (⌘-G).

2. Select two of the grouped paths and again choose GROUP. Select the other pair of paths and group them as well.

3. Select both grouped pairs and choose GROUP. The result is four groups (the original free-form paths) within two groups (the pairs) within a single group.

4. Using the arrow tool, OPTION-click one of the paths. This selects the entire path and displays its points.

5. Press the TILDE key. The points disappear and four corner handles appear around the selected path, indicating that you have now selected the grouped path.

6. Press the TILDE key a second time. The larger group, containing two grouped paths, becomes selected.

7. Press TILDE a third time. The highest-level group becomes selected, including all four free-form paths.

You may also OPTION-click with the arrow tool to select individual elements in a composite path or the first and last paths in a blend. However, you may *not* select elements within a geometric path, such as a rectangle or ellipse, without first ungrouping the object, as described in section.

Element

Bring to front	⌘F
Bring forward	
Send backward	
Send to back	⌘B
Element info...	⌘I
Points	▶
Lock	
Unlock	
Group	⌘G
Ungroup	⌘U
Alignment...	⌘/
Blend...	
Constrain...	
Join elements	⌘J
Split element	

Ungrouping

Any group may be ungrouped by choosing the UNGROUP command from the ELEMENT menu (⌘-U). Multiple groups may be ungrouped simultaneously, but only one level at a time. In other words, if a group contains groups, then the most recently created group must be ungrouped first. The member groups may then be ungrouped by again choosing UNGROUP while all groups are still selected. A geometric path created with the rectangle or oval tool may also be ungrouped.

Ungrouping can sometimes be an essential part of the reshaping process. Most notably, you may not join two elements contained in different groups. For example, if one endpoint in an open path is part of a group and another endpoint belongs to an ungrouped path, the two endpoints may not be joined. You must first ungroup the path before choosing the JOIN ELEMENTS command (⌘-J).

Distinguishing groups
from composite paths

What if ungrouping a path doesn't produce the desired effect? Perhaps the object wasn't a group in the first place. Rather, it might be a composite path that was created using the JOIN ELEMENTS or CONVERT TO PATHS command (as discussed in the *Making holes* section of Chapter 9). To determine whether a combined object is a group or a composite path, choose the ELEMENT INFO... command from the ELEMENT menu (⌘-I, ⌥-↖↑). If the COMPOSITE PATH dialog box displays, the selection is a composite path and may be broken apart using the SPLIT ELEMENT command in the ELEMENT menu. If the GROUP, RECTANGLE, ELLIPSE, or BLEND dialog box displays, the selection is a group and may be ungrouped.

Controlling movements

FreeHand allows you to move objects in the same way that you move elements, as described in the *Moving elements* section of Chapter 7. In fact, moving is the primary and most common means of transforming objects in Aldus FreeHand.

An entirely selected object may be moved in any of the following ways:

- Using the arrow tool, drag the object by any of its segments. To move a text block, or to move a filled object in the preview mode, drag anywhere inside the object.

- Press SHIFT and drag the object to move it along the constraint axis.

- Drag the object over the point of a stationary object to snap the object into place (provided the SNAP TO POINT command under the VIEW menu—⌘-', COMMAND-QUOTE—is active).

- Press an arrow key (↑, →, ↓, or ←) to move the object by the amount specified in the "Cursor key distance" option box in the MORE PREFERENCES dialog box (introduced in the *Setting preferences* section of Chapter 3).

- Choose the MOVE... command from the EDIT menu (⌘-M) to display the MOVE ELEMENTS dialog box. Enter the desired movement values and press RETURN.

Pressing the SHIFT key, snapping, using arrow keys, and the MOVE ELEMENTS dialog box all provide means for making precise, controlled movements in an illustration. FreeHand 3.0 provides several additional control features that we have not discussed previously, including *rulers, grids, guides*, the *information bar*, and the ALIGNMENT... command, all of which are discussed in the following sections.

Using the rulers

FreeHand provides access to one vertical and one horizontal ruler that may be used to track the movement of your cursor or of an object. Choose the RULERS command from the VIEW menu (⌘-R) to display these rulers, which appear at the top and left-hand edges of the current illustration window. Once the rulers are visible, a check mark precedes the RULERS command in the VIEW menu. Choose RULERS again to hide the rulers.

The unit of measure used by both rulers may be picas, inches, decimal inches, or millimeters. These units are displayed in Figures 12.05, 12.06, 12.07, and 12.08, respectively. To change the current unit of measure, choose DOCUMENT SETUP... from the FILE menu. The "Unit of measure" pop-up menu in the DOCUMENT SETUP dialog offers five options: "Points," Picas," "Inches," "Decimal inches," and "Millimeters." The first option is selected by default. Select the desired option and press RETURN.

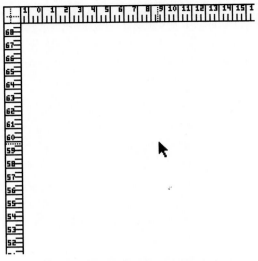

Figure 12.05: The horizontal and vertical rulers as they appear when the current unit of measure is picas. The rulers also display in picas when the current unit of measure is points.

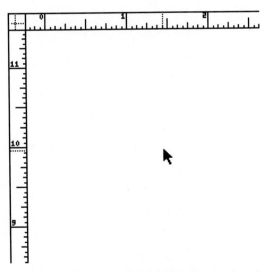

Figure 12.06: The horizontal and vertical rulers as they appear when the current unit of measure is inches. An inch is subdivided into 16 increments at actual view size.

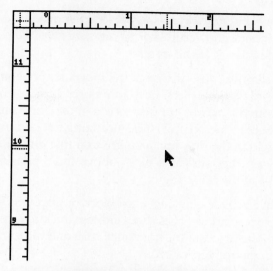

Figure 12.07: When the unit of measure is decimal inches, the rulers display standard inches divided into tenths.

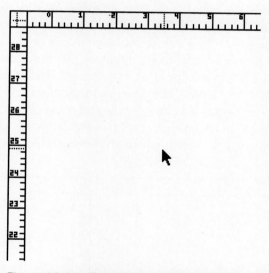

Figure 12.08: The rulers as they appear when the current unit of measure is millimeters.

Whole picas, inches, or millimeters are indicated by long tick marks; fractions are indicated by short tick marks. As you magnify the view size, the units on the rulers become larger and more detailed. As you zoom out, units become smaller and less detailed. Numbers on each ruler indicate the distance from the *ruler origin*, the location on your drawing area at which the horizontal and vertical coordinates are zero. All ruler measurements are made relative to this origin.

At all times, you may track the movement of your cursor on the horizontal and vertical rulers. Each of Figures 12.05 through 12.08 shows a small dotted *tracking line* that moves in the horizontal ruler and another that moves in the vertical ruler, indicating the current location of your cursor within the drawing area. For example, the cursor in Figure 12.05 is 59 picas 10 points (59⅚ picas) above and 8 picas 6 points (8½ picas) to the right of the ruler origin.

While you are dragging a text block or graphic object, two tracking lines display on each ruler. These lines indicate the locations of the left and right edges of the object in the horizontal ruler and the top and bottom edges of the object in the vertical ruler.

Changing the ruler origin

By default, the ruler origin for an illustration is located at the bottom left corner of the page size. You may relocate the ruler origin by dragging from the *ruler origin box*, the square created by the intersection of the horizontal and vertical rulers. Figure 12.09 demonstrates this relocation process. The dotted lines that extend from the arrow cursor indicate the prospective position of the new origin. Notice that even the movement of the ruler origin is tracked by the rulers. At the end of the drag, the ruler origin moves to the location occupied by the cursor. All ruler measurements will now be made from this new ruler origin.

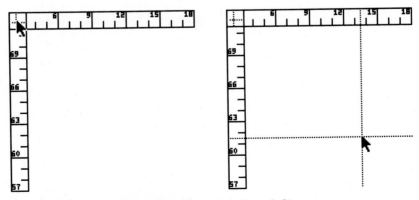

Figure 12.09: Drag from the ruler origin box (left)
to relocate the ruler origin (right).

Using grids

FreeHand 3.0 provides two systems of *grids* to aid in the precise positioning of elements within the drawing area:

- The *snap-to grid* controls the positioning and manipulation of elements within the drawing area. However, this grid is never visible.

- The *visible grid* is displayed as a network of dots in the drawing area. This grid does not print, and it has no effect on the movements of your cursor.

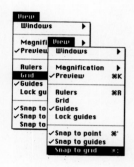

Turn the snap-to grid on and off by choosing the SNAP TO GRID command from the VIEW menu (⌘-;, COMMAND-SEMICOLON). Display and hide the visible grid by choosing the GRID command from the VIEW menu. In each case, a check mark appears before the command when it is active; no check mark appears when the respective grid is turned off or hidden.

To specify the size of the snap-to and visible grids, enter values into the "Snap-to grid" and "Visible grid" option boxes in the DOCUMENT SETUP dialog box, displayed by choosing the DOCUMENT SETUP... command from the FILE menu. Generally, the visible grid value should be greater than or equal to, as well as a multiple of, the snap-to grid. For example, if the "Snap-to grid" value is 3, the "Visible grid" value might be 3, 6, 9, 12, or some other multiple of 3.

The snap-to grid affects the creation of objects slightly differently than it affects the manipulation of objects. When turned on, the grid constrains the creation of all points and handles in an object. As an example, suppose that the snap-to grid is turned on and set to ½ inch. Every time you move your cursor, the tracking lines in the horizontal and vertical rulers will jump in ½-inch increments. As a result, you will not be able to create a rectangle that is ¾-inch wide; it must measure ½ inch or 1 inch.

When manipulating a point or handle in an existing object, your cursor will snap to the nearest grid intersection. Figure 12.10 on the next page shows an *M*-shaped path created while the ½-inch grid was inactive. (In Figure 12.10 and in those that follow, we have traced the invisible snap-to grid as a network of dotted horizontal and vertical lines so that you may follow along with the example.) Now suppose that you turn the grid on and drag at a point in the shape, as shown in Figure 12.11. The selected point will snap to the nearest intersection in the grid and, subsequently, will move in ½-inch increments as you continue to drag.

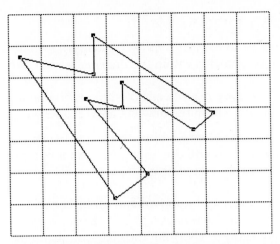

Figure 12.10: This shape was created when the snap-to grid was turned off. (In FreeHand, the snap-to grid is always invisible. We have drawn it as a network of dotted lines to clarify the figure.)

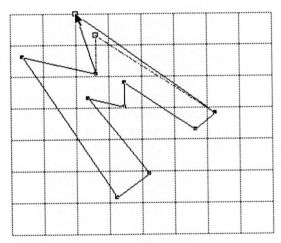

Figure 12.11: When the snap-to grid is on, dragging a point snaps the point to the nearest grid intersection.

If you drag at a segment in the selected path, FreeHand does not force your cursor to an intersection, but rather allows you to move the shape in snap-to grid increments only, as shown in Figure 12.12. This means that when dragging a segment, the relative distance from cursor to grid increment is maintained during the drag.

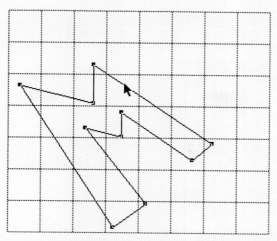

Figure 12.12: Drag a path by one of its segments to move the entire path in snap-to grid increments.

To snap some portion of a path to a grid intersection while not disrupting the form of the path, use the ALIGNMENT dialog box, as explained in the *Alignment and distribution* section later in this chapter.

Creating ruler guides

FreeHand 3.0 allows you to create *ruler guides* to assist in the positioning and alignment of objects within the drawing area. Guides appear as dotted black lines in the keyline mode and as solid colored lines in the preview mode. They do not print.

You may create a guide in one of two ways:

- Drag downward from the horizontal ruler to create a horizontal ruler guide the width of the entire drawing area, as demonstrated in Figure 12.13 on the next page.

- Drag to the right from the vertical ruler to create a vertical ruler guide the height of the entire drawing area.

Ruler guides are used to mark a specific horizontal or vertical location inside the drawing area. You may then align points or segments in an object to the ruler guide to create perfect rows or columns of objects.

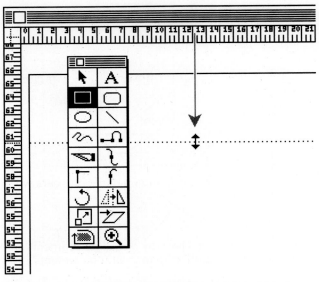

Figure 12.13: Drag downward from the horizontal rulers to create a horizontal ruler guide.

When the SNAP TO GUIDES command is active in the VIEW menu, your cursor will snap to a guide line. A check mark precedes the SNAP TO GUIDES command when it is active.

The interval at which a dragged element will snap toward a guide line may be altered by entering a new value into the "Snap-to distance" option in the MORE PREFERENCES dialog box (introduced in the *Setting preferences* section of Chapter 3). Any value from 1 to 5 is permitted, as measured in screen pixels. The default value is 3.

To move an existing ruler guide, use the arrow tool to drag it to a new location in the drawing area. To delete a guide, drag it back to the horizontal or vertical ruler. Choose the LOCK GUIDES command from the VIEW menu to protect existing guides from being moved or deleted. A check mark precedes the LOCK GUIDES command when it is active.

You may determine whether guide lines display in the keyline and preview modes by turning on and off the GUIDES command in the VIEW menu. When the guides are hidden, you cannot create new guides. Also, hidden guides will not affect the creation or manipulation of objects. A check mark precedes the GUIDES command when guides are displayed in the drawing area.

Using the information bar

Directly under the menu bar is the *information bar*, a thin horizontal strip that lists information about the current operation. The information bar constantly tracks the movement of your cursor in the drawing area and analyzes all changes that occur as a result of clicking or dragging with a tool.

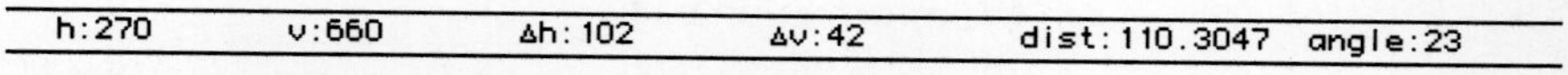

h:270	v:660	Δh: 102	Δv:42	dist:110.3047	angle:23

Figure 12.14: The information bar as it appears when moving an object.

For example, Figure 12.14 shows the information bar as it appears when dragging an object with the arrow tool. The first and second items in the figure ("h" and "v") represent the horizontal and vertical coordinates of the cursor with respect to the ruler origin. The third and fourth items ("Δh" and "Δv") list the horizontal and vertical components of the move, as demonstrated in Figure 12.15. The fifth and sixth items ("dist" and "angle") tell the distance and direction of the move. The distance may be gauged by measuring the length of an imaginary line that follows the movement of any point in the current selection. The direction is measured as the angle, in degrees, between the mean horizontal and the imaginary distance line, as shown in the figure below.

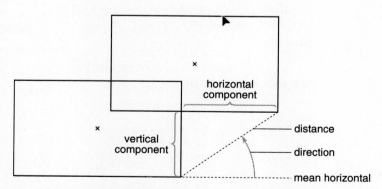

Figure 12.15: A diagram showing the distance and direction (angle) of a move.

The information bar will also display items concerning the creation of a geometric path; the creation of a free-form path drawn with the line tool or one of the point tools; the transformation of a selection using the arrow, scale, reflect, rotate, or skew tool; or the creation or manipulation of a text block. Table 12.01 lists all items that may display in the information bar and describes their meanings:

Table 12.01: A description of all items that may display
in the information bar

ITEM	CURRENT ACTION	MEANING
🔒	Any	Current selection is locked
h	None; moving selection with arrow; using any other tool except a transformation tool	Horizontal distance between cursor and ruler origin
v	None; moving selection with arrow; using any other tool except a transformation tool	Vertical distance between cursor and ruler origin
Δh	Moving selection with arrow; dragging with line or point tool	Horizontal component of distance dragged
Δv	Moving selection with arrow; dragging with line or point tool	Vertical component of distance dragged
dist	Moving selection with arrow; dragging with line or point tool	Direct measurement of distance dragged
angle	Moving selection with arrow; dragging with line or point tool	Direction of drag
	Reflecting or rotating selection	Angle of transformation
width	Dragging with rectangle, rounded-rectangle, or ellipse tool	Width of geometric path
height	Dragging with rectangle, rounded-rectangle, or ellipse tool	Height of geometric path
ch	Scaling, reflecting, rotating, or skewing selection	Horizontal location of transformation origin
cv	Scaling, reflecting, rotating, or skewing selection	Vertical location of transformation origin
sh	Scaling or skewing selection; scaling text block with arrow	Horizontal percentage (1=100%) scaled or skewed
sv	Scaling or skewing selection; scaling text block with arrow	Vertical percentage (1=100%) scaled or skewed

Table 12.01: A description of all items that may display
in the information bar (cont.)

ITEM	CURRENT ACTION	MEANING
Δleading	Dragging top/bottom handle of text block with arrow	Change in leading, measured in points
Δletter space	Dragging side handle of text block with arrow	Change in letter spacing, measured in points
Δword space	Option-dragging side handle of text block with arrow	Change in letter spacing, measured in points
kerning	Pressing ⌘-←, ⌘-→, ⌘-⇧-←, or ⌘-⇧-→ in TEXT dialog box	Change in pair kerning, measured in em spaces

Unless otherwise indicated, all position and distance items are listed in the current unit of measure, as set inside the DOCUMENT SETUP dialog box.

Alignment and distribution

We end our discussion of FreeHand's array of precision features with the concepts of *alignment* and *distribution*. Both techniques allow you to adjust the location of an object with respect to the grid or to one or more other objects. They are most useful within the context of schematic drawings, where objects line up in rows, columns, or other visual patterns.

To align or distribute one or more objects, select the objects, then choose ALIGNMENT... from the ELEMENT menu (⌘-/, COMMAND-SLASH). The ALIGNMENT dialog box will display, offering both alignment and distribution options, as shown in Figure 12.16.

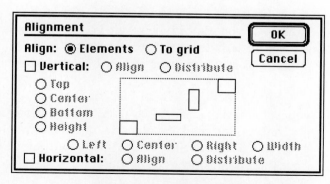

Figure 12.16: The Alignment dialog box allows you to align and distribute selected objects with respect to each other or to the grid.

The ALIGNMENT dialog box provides means for aligning objects to the snap-to grid, aligning object with respect to each other, and distributing objects with respect to each other. Each of these unique operations is discussed in the following pages.

● **Operation 1**: *Aligning the current selection to the snap-to-grid.*

To align the selection to the snap-to grid, select "To grid" from the "Align" radio buttons. Select the "Horizontal" check box to adjust the horizontal positioning of the selection with respect to the grid; select "Vertical" to adjust the vertical positioning of the selection. The "Top," "Center," and "Bottom" radio buttons below the "Vertical" check box, as well as the "Left," "Center," and "Right" radio button next to the "Horizontal" check box determine the portions of the current selection that will snap to the nearest snap-to grid intersection. For example, suppose that you have selected the *M*-shaped path from Figure 12.10, as shown on page 416. If you select the "Top" radio button from the "Vertical" options, the shape will be moved so that its topmost point resides on the nearest horizontal grid line. If you also select "Right" from the "Horizontal" radio buttons, the rightmost point in the shape will rest on a vertical grid line. The result is shown in Figure 12.17. (Again, we have traced the invisible snap-to grid to better demonstrate FreeHand's alignment capabilities. We have also emphasized the particular horizontal and vertical grid lines to which the shape has been aligned.) Notice that the form of the path remains unchanged; every point is the same distance and direction from its neighboring points as it was before we initiated the ALIGNMENT... command. This is always the case, since selecting the "To grid" radio button serves only to move an entire selection flush with the snap-to grid.

 If you want to align every point in an object to a grid intersection, you must drag each and every point by hand with the arrow tool, as discussed in the section *Using grids* earlier in this chapter.

When either the "Horizontal" or "Vertical" check box is selected, you will notice that the "Distribute" radio button associated with that option remains dimmed. An object cannot be distributed with respect to a grid. The "Height" and "Width" radio buttons will also be dimmed, since these apply only to distribution.

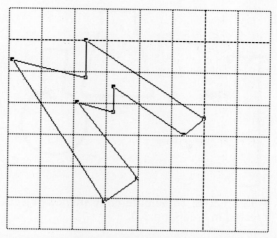

Figure 12.17: Select the "To grid" radio button to align a selection flush with the nearest snap-to grid lines without altering the form of the selection.

The size of the snap-to grid is defined by entering a value into the "Snap-to grid" option box in the DOCUMENT SETUP dialog box.

● **Operation 2**: *Aligning multiple selected objects to each other.*

You may also align and distribute objects in relation to each other. To do this, however, you must select at least two objects prior to choosing the ALIGNMENT... command.

Accessed by selecting the "Elements" and "Align" radio buttons inside the ALIGNMENT dialog box, the object-alignment feature allows you to create perfect rows and columns of selected objects. Because this feature requires the use of several interdependent options, we will use an example to demonstrate how it work. The following exercise begins with the three differently shaped paths shown in Figure 12.18 on the next page.

1. Select all three objects and choose the ALIGNMENT... command from the ELEMENT menu (⌘-/).

2. Select the "Elements" option from the "Align" radio buttons.

Figure 12.18: Three differently shaped objects created in FreeHand 3.0.

3. Select the "Horizontal " check box. Next, select "Align" and "Left" from the two rows of radio buttons next to the check box.

4. Click OK or press RETURN to instruct FreeHand to perform a two-step operation: First, determine the point that is the farthest to the left within each of the three selected shapes. We will call these key points A, B, and C. FreeHand notes that point A is farther to the left than B or C. The shape to which point A belongs will therefore remain stationary. In the second step, FreeHand moves the shapes containing points B and C until all points—A, B, and C—line up in a vertical formation, as shown in Figure 12.19.

Figure 12.19: The same objects horizontally aligned by their left edges.

4. Choose UNDO ALIGNMENT... from the EDIT menu (⌘-Z) to restore the objects to their original locations.

5. Choose the ALIGNMENT... command again. Deselect the "Horizontal" check box and select "Vertical." Next, select "Align" and "Top" from the row and column of radio buttons associated with the "Vertical" check box.

6. Press RETURN to produce the result shown in Figure 12.20. The topmost point from each shape is aligned in a horizontal formation. This configuration produces a better looking effect than Figure 12.19, since the chemical containers were positioned in a vaguely horizontal formation to begin with.

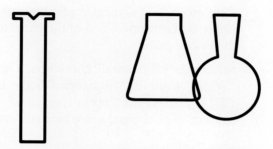

Figure 12.20: The shapes aligned vertically by their top edges.

As demonstrated in the preceding exercise, the "Top" and "Left" options work by moving key points in the selected paths into alignment with a model key point that remains stationary. This is also true for the "Bottom" and "Right" options. However, the two "Center" options work a little differently. They first determine the exact center of each selected path. These centers are then averaged to determine an average horizontal or vertical coordinate. Each path is moved so that its center is located at this coordinate.

Objects that are aligned horizontally fall into a linear column; objects that are aligned vertically fall into a straight row. Note that aligning objects both horizontally and vertically rarely produces satisfactory results, since it lumps all selected objects one in front of the other. To remedy this problem, and to provide additional more control, FreeHand includes the "Distribute" option, discussed on the next page.

- **Operation 3**: *Distributing multiple selected objects.*

To *distribute* objects is to place them so that the distance between each object and its neighbors is equal. For example, if a series of objects is distributed to the left, the leftmost point in each object is an equal distance from the leftmost point in each of its neighbors.

Suppose that you have selected the same three objects shown in Figure 12.18. The following exercise describes how you might distribute them:

1. Choose the ALIGNMENT... command and select the "Elements" radio button from the ALIGNMENT dialog box.

2. Select the "Vertical" check box. Then select "Align" and "Bottom" from the "Vertical" radio buttons. This, we know, will reposition the bottoms of two of the paths to align with the bottom of the lowest path.

3. Select the "Horizontal" check box. Then select "Distribute" and "Width" from the "Horizontal" radio buttons, as shown in Figure 12.21. The "Width" option instructs FreeHand to make the amount of horizontal space between each object equal.

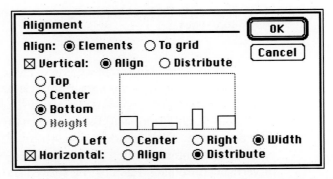

Figure 12.21: Select "Align" from the "Vertical" radio buttons and "Distribute" from the "Horizontal" radio buttons.

4. Press RETURN. Figure 12.22 shows the result. FreeHand's distribution feature automatically spreads the paths in an aesthetically pleasing formation.

Figure 12.22: Three objects aligned vertically by their bottom edges and distributed horizontally according to width.

If you are ever unsure of the results that your alignment or distribution settings will produce, simply refer to the small icons inside the dotted rectangle at the center of the ALIGNMENT dialog box. These icons move to represent the effects of your current selections. Keep in mind, however, that these icons can be used only to predict the results of aligning objects. Also, they in no way represent the effects of aligning objects to the snap-to grid.

✳ To gain additional control when aligning objects, try locking one (and only one) of the objects prior to choosing the ALIGN- MENT… command. The locked object will remain stationary, while other selected objects are aligned to it. (The LOCK command is discussed in the following section.)

Protecting objects

While working on a complicated illustration, you will probably create several objects that overlap. In the process of reshaping and transforming some of these objects, you may inadvertantly select and alter an overlapping object that was previously positioned exactly where you wanted it to be. Fixing an object that was previously correct can be exceedingly frustrating. Unfortunately, the more complicated your drawing becomes, the greater the likelihood of disturbing one or more perfectly positioned objects.

To protect text blocks and graphic objects from being upset or altered, FreeHand provides the LOCK and UNLOCK commands, which are the subjects of the following pages.

Locking objects

Locking a path prevents it or any of its points from being moved—you can neither drag nor transform a locked object in any way. A locked object, however, is not entirely unalterable. You may still select it and change its fill or stroke attributes.

To lock an object, select it and choose the LOCK command from the ELEMENT menu. You may not lock a single point independently of other points in a path. If you specifically select one point in a path and choose the LOCK command, the entire path will become locked.

The first example in Figure 12.23 displays two paths, one of which is selected. The following exercise demonstrates how the LOCK command may be used to protect this path:

1. Lock the selected path by choosing the LOCK command.

2. Marquee both shapes with the arrow tool. All points in both paths are now selected.

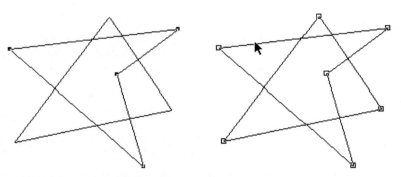

Figure 12.23: After locking the selected path (left), marquee both paths and drag at a segment in the locked path.

3. Drag at a segment in the locked path, as shown in the second example of Figure 12.23. As you drag, only the unlocked shape will move. Figure 12.24 shows that the unlocked path moves despite the fact that your cursor is not positioned on any element in the path. When an object in the current selection is locked, FreeHand treats the manipulation just as it would normally, except that it does not allow any point in the locked object to be moved.

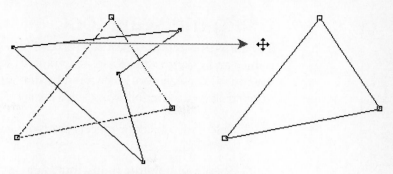

Figure 12.24: If you drag at a locked object, all unlocked objects in the current selection will move and the locked object will remain stationary.

If all objects in the current selection are locked, a small lock icon (🔒) will display in the information bar. If any object in the selection is unlocked, the lock icon will not display.

Unlocking objects

To unlock an object, select the object and choose the UNLOCK command from the ELEMENT menu. If the selected object is not locked, the UNLOCK command will be dimmed.

Locking is saved with the illustration. Therefore, when you open an existing file, all objects that were locked during the previous session will still be locked.

Scaling objects

A *transformation* is any manipulation that permanently alters the appearance of an object without affecting its basic form. In FreeHand, transformations include moving an object—as discussed in the *Controlling movements* section of this chapter—as well as scaling, flipping, rotating, and slanting an object. These latter transformations are accomplished in FreeHand using special tools, each of which is discussed in this chapter. The first tool we will discuss is the scale tool.

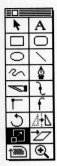

Using the scale tool

The *scale tool*, second-to-last tool on the left side of the palette, is used to reduce and enlarge text blocks and graphic objects. Like all transformation tools, the scale tool is operated by dragging relative to one or more selected objects. The following steps explain how to use this tool:

1. Select the object or objects that you wish to scale. Then select the scale tool. Your cursor will appear as a small star (✳).

2. Press and hold the mouse button at some location in the drawing area relative to the selection. This location will act as the *scale origin*, the core of a reduction or enlargement, as demonstrated in Figure 12.25.

3. Prior to releasing the mouse button, drag away from the origin to alter the size of the current selection:

   ↑ Drag up to enlarge the selection vertically.
   → Drag to the right to enlarge the selection horizontally.
   ↓ Drag down to reduce the selection vertically.
   ← Drag to the left to reduce the selection horizontally.

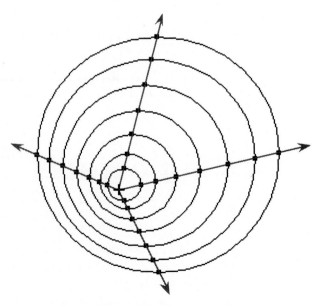

Figure 12.25: Enlarging a circle several times about a single scale origin.

To better understand the concept of the scale origin, consider the example shown in Figure 12.25—a series of circles enlarged one about the other. All circles have been enlarged about a single scale origin, shown in the figure as a small cross from which the four directional lines emanate. These lines follow the progression of the points in the enlarged paths. The fact that these progressions follow straight lines demonstrates that the scale origin marks the center of any reduction or enlargement.

Figure 12.26 displays two paths representing a telephone. The path of the receiver is selected. Suppose that you want to scale the receiver without affecting the telephone carriage. The following exercise demonstrates how:

1. Select the scale tool and press and hold the mouse button at the location displayed as a small star in Figure 12.26. This establishes the scale origin.

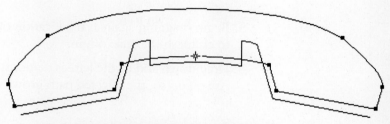

Figure 12.26: Begin dragging with the scale tool near the middle of the selected shape to establish a scale origin.

2. Drag up and to the right, as demonstrated in Figure 12.27 on the following page. Notice that the scale origin is marked by an ×. As you drag away from the scale origin, the path of the receiver grows larger and larger. Both the previous and current size of the selected path are displayed throughout your drag, allowing you to gauge the effect of the enlargement.

4. Release your mouse button to complete the enlargement. Choose the UNDO SCALE command from the EDIT menu (⌘-Z) to return the path to its original size.

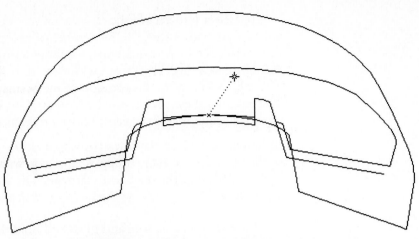

Figure 12.27: Drag up and to the right from the scale origin to enlarge the selected object. (We have added a dotted line to demonstrate the direction of the drag.)

5. Begin dragging again at the location of the × in Figure 12.27 to establish the scale origin.

6. Drag down and to the left, as demonstrated in Figure 12.28. As you do so, the selected path grows smaller and smaller.

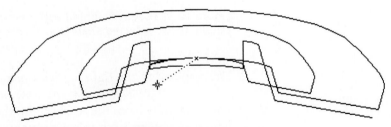

Figure 12.28: Drag down and to the left to reduce the selected object.

7. Release your mouse button to complete the reduction. Choose UNDO SCALE (⌘-Z) to return the path to its original size.

8. In the previous steps, the horizontal and vertical proportions of your drags have been nearly equal. Thus, the height and width of the selected object were affected similarly, resulting in one proportional enlargement and one proportional reduction. This time, however, you will stretch the height of the path but barely change its width. With the scale tool selected, press and hold the mouse button on the lower left-hand corner of the object to establish the origin.

9. Drag directly upward from the scale origin to increase the height of the shape while barely altering its width, as demonstrated by the dotted line in Figure 12.29.

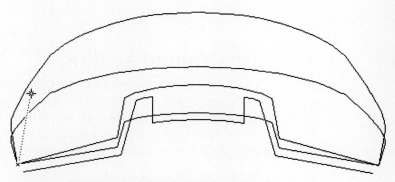

Figure 1229: Drag directly upward to stretch the object vertically while barely affecting its width.

There is no maximum size beyond which you can no longer enlarge a selected object, except that the object may not exceed the confines of the pasteboard,. You may also reduce an object into virtual invisibility. If you drag *past* the point at which a selection is reduced into nothingness, you will flip the selected object, as shown in Figure 12.30 on the following page. This little known feature of the scale tool allows you to reflect and scale objects at the same time.

You may flip objects only vertically (by dragging down) or horizontally (by dragging to the left) with the scale tool. To flip an object across an angled axis, use the reflect tool as described in the next section, *Flipping objects.*

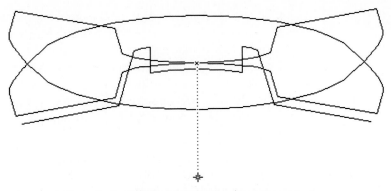

Figure 12.30: Drag very far down or to the left with the scale tool to flip the selected object.

Constrained scaling

To constrain an enlargement or reduction so that the height and width of the selected object are affected equally, press the SHIFT key while dragging diagonally with the scale tool. Press SHIFT and drag up and to the right with the scale tool to enlarge a selection proportionally; SHIFT-drag down and to the left to reduce a selection proportionally.

Scaling partial paths

FreeHand allows you to scale whole selected objects. But with version 3.0, you may also scale specific elements within objects independently of their deselected neighbors. Simply select the points that you wish to scale, and use the scale tool as directed in the previous sections.

For example, only six points are selected in the skyline path shown in Figure 12.31. The segments that border each of these points are the only segments that will be affected by the scale tool:

1. Begin dragging with the scale tool at the location indicated by the star cursor in Figure 12.31.

2. Drag downward and to the left, as shown in Figure 12.32. Only the selected points and the segments associated with those points are affected. Release when you are satisfied with the scaling.

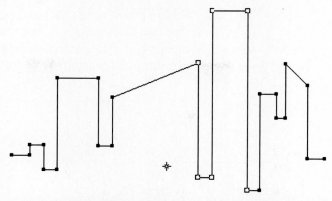

Figure 12.31: Position the scale origin below the partially selected object.

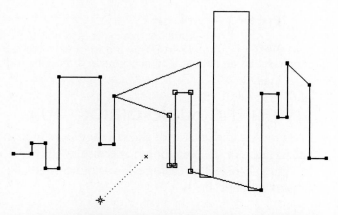

Figure 12.32: Drag down and to the left to reduce the size of the selected elements while leaving deselected elements unchanged.

Dragging points with the scale tool can be very much like dragging them with an arrow tool. The only difference is that each selected point is moved slightly differently, depending on its proximity to the scale origin. If you look closely at Figure 12.32, you'll notice that points close to the scale origin move much less than those farther away. The reduction in the length of each segment is unique, a result of the orientation of the segment relative to the drag.

The scale tool can prove very useful for moving specific points in ways the arrow tool does not allow. For example, to move two selected segments equal distances in opposite directions about a central point, drag from this point with the scale tool, as shown below.

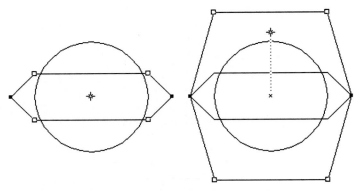

Figure 12.33: After establishing a scale origin at the center of the circle (left), drag directly upward to move both selected segments an equal distance in opposite directions (right).

Using the Scale dialog box

Press OPTION and click with the scale tool to simultaneously determine the location of the scale origin and display the SCALE dialog box, shown in Figure 12.34. This dialog allows you to scale one or more selected objects numerically.

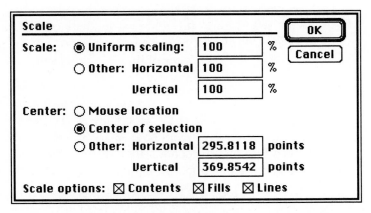

Figure 12.34: The Scale dialog box allows you to specify the percentage by which to enlarge or reduce a selected object.

To scale the width and height of an object proportionally, select the "Uniform scaling" value and enter a value in the option box. Values less than 100% will reduce the size of any selected object; values greater than 100% will enlarge the object; a 100% value will leave the size of an object unaltered.

To scale the width and height of an object independently, select the "Other" radio button. Then enter values into the "Horizontal" and "Vertical" option boxes as follows:

- A "Horizontal" value less than 100% makes the selection thinner.
- A "Horizontal" value greater than 100% makes the selection wider.
- A "Vertical" value less than 100% makes the selection shorter.
- A "Vertical" value greater than 100% makes the selection taller.

Below the "Scale" options are three "Center" radio buttons, which are used to specify the exact location of the scale origin. Select the "Mouse location" radio button to confirm the scale origin at the location where you OPTION-clicked with the scale tool. Selected by default, the "Center of selection" option allows you to assign the exact center of the selection as the scale origin. Select "Other" to set any origin location that you desire by entering custom values in the "Horizontal" and "Vertical" option boxes.

To the right of the "Other" radio button, the "Horizontal" and "Vertical" values represent the coordinates of the scale origin, in the current unit of measure and with respect to the ruler origin. If the "Mouse location" option is selected, the "Horizontal" and "Vertical" values list the exact coordinates of the location at which you OPTION-clicked. If the "Center of selection" is selected, the "Horizontal" and "Vertical" values represent the exact center of the current selection. If you enter your own numbers for these values, the "Other" radio button automatically becomes selected.

If any of the selected objects is a clipping path, select the "Contents" check box to scale the masked elements along with the selection. If an object in the selection is filled with a tile pattern, select the "Fills" check box to transform the tiles.

Select the "Lines" check box to scale the thickness of the line weights of the selected objects. For example, if you reduce a path stroked with a 4-point line weight to 25% of its original size, select "Lines" to reduce the stroke to a 1-point line weight. If the scale is not proportional, FreeHand averages the "Horizontal" and "Vertical" percentage values and applies the averaged percentage to all selected line weights. For example, if the "Horizontal" value is 200% and the "Vertical" value is 50%, FreeHand scales the line weight by $(200 + 50) \div 2 = 125\%$.

Flipping objects

In the previous section, we mentioned that dragging past the scale origin with the scale tool will flip a selected object. FreeHand also provides a dedicated *reflect tool* for those times when you want to flip an object without scaling it. The reflect tool flips an object around a *reflection axis*, which acts like a pivoting mirror. The selected object looks into this mirror; the result of the flip is the image that the mirror projects.

Using the reflect tool

The reflect tool, third-to-last tool on the right side of the palette, is used to flip text blocks and graphic objects. It is operated by dragging relative to one or more selected objects. The following steps explain how to use this tool:

1. Select the object or objects that you wish to flip. Then select the reflect tool. Your cursor will appear as a small star (✳).

2. Press and hold the mouse button at some location in the drawing area relative to the selection. This location will act as the first point in the reflection axis.

3. Prior to releasing the mouse button, drag away from the first point to determine the angle of the reflection axis, about which the selection will flip.

Figure 12.35 on the next page displays two paths representing a telephone. They are identical to those in Figure 12.26 except that a cord has been added to the selected path. This addition makes the path unsymmetrical, to better demonstrate the reflection operation. Suppose that you want to flip the path around an angled axis. The following exercise explains how to do this:

1. Select the reflect tool and press and hold the mouse button at the location displayed as a small star in Figure 12.35, establishing the first point in the reflection axis. This first point is sometimes called the *reflection origin*.

2. Drag with the tool. As you drag, the invisible reflection axis continually rotates so that it forms a straight line between the cursor and the origin.

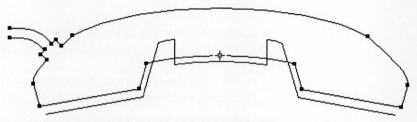

Figure 12.35: Begin dragging with the reflect tool near the middle of the selected path to establish a reflection origin.

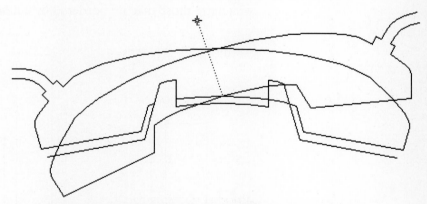

Figure 12.36: Drag up and to the left to tilt the reflection axis approximately 15° from vertical.

3. Drag above and to the left of the origin, as shown in Figure 12.36. FreeHand displays both original and current positions on screen. In the figure, a dotted line has been added to indicate the angle of the reflection axis.

Constrained flipping

To constrain a reflection so that the selected object is flipped about a vertical, horizontal, or diagonal axis, press the SHIFT key while dragging with the reflect tool. Constraining limits the angle of the reflection axis to some multiple of 45°.

Flipping partial paths

Just as you may flip whole objects, you may flip selected elements within objects independently of their deselected neighbors. Simply select the points that you wish to flip, and use the reflect tool as directed in the previous sections.

For example, suppose that you want to flip the selected elements in the skyline path shown in Figure 12.31 back on page 435:

1. Click with the reflect tool to the right of the path, at the location indicated by the small star cursor in Figure 12.37.

2. Drag up and to the left with the reflect tool arrowhead cursor. Figure 12.38 shows how all selected points pivot to the opposite side of the invisible reflection axis, rotating many selected segments and stretching those that are bordered by a deselected point.

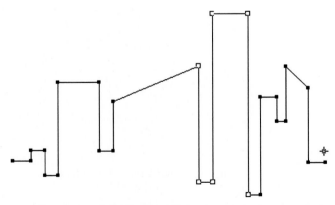

Figure 12.37: Position the scale origin to the right of the partially selected object.

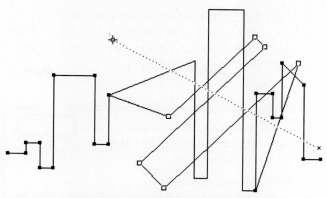

Figure 12.38: Drag up and to the left with the reflect tool to flip the selected elements across an angled axis.

Using the Reflect dialog box

Press OPTION and click with the reflect tool to simultaneously determine the location of the reflection origin and display the REFLECT dialog box, shown in Figure 12.39 on the following page. This dialog allows you to flip one or more selected objects around a numerically angled axis.

The REFLECT dialog box offers three "Axis" radio buttons, any one of which may be selected to determine the angle of the reflection axis. These options produce the following results:

- Select "Horizontal" to flip an object onto its head.
- Select "Vertical" to flip an object onto its side.
- Select "Angled" and enter a value between −360 and 360 in the corresponding option box to flip an object around an angled axis.

The value in the "Angled" option box is measured in degrees from the mean horizontal (0°). Because the axis extends to either side of the reflection origin, values over 180° are repetitious. (For an explanation of degrees, see the *Constrained movements* section of Chapter 7.)

Below the "Axis" options are three "Point" radio buttons, which are used to specify the exact location of the reflection origin. Select the "Mouse location" radio button to confirm the reflection origin at the location where you OPTION-clicked with the reflect tool. Selected by default, the "Center of selection" option allows you to assign the exact center of the selection as the reflection origin. Select "Other" to set any origin location that you desire by entering custom values in the "Horizontal" and "Vertical" option boxes.

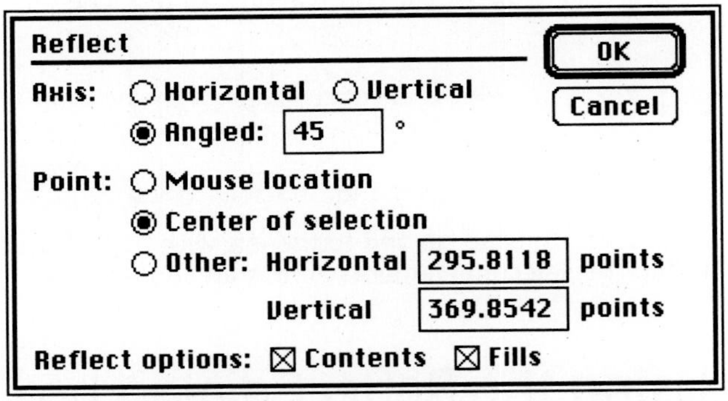

Figure 12.39: The Reflect dialog box allows you to specify the angle of the reflection axis.

To the right of the "Other" radio button, the "Horizontal" and "Vertical" values represent the coordinates of the reflection origin, in the current unit of measure and with respect to the ruler origin. If the "Mouse location" option is selected, the "Horizontal" and "Vertical" values list the exact coordinates of the location at which you OPTION-clicked. If the "Center of selection" is selected, the "Horizontal" and "Vertical" values represent the exact center of the current selection. If you enter your own numbers for these values, the "Other" radio button automatically becomes selected.

If any of the selected objects is a clipping path, select the "Contents" check box to flip the masked elements along with the selection. If some object in the selection is filled with a tile pattern, select the "Fills" check box to transform the tiles.

Rotating objects

In FreeHand, any text block or graphic object may be rotated to any degree imaginable. This allows you to create angled type and other tilted images. Rotations are accomplished with the rotate tool.

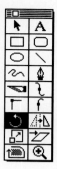

Using the rotate tool

The *rotate tool*, the third-to-last tool on right side of the palette, is operated by dragging relative to one or more selected objects. The following steps explain how to use this tool:

1. Select the object you wish to rotate. Then select the rotate tool. Your cursor will appear as a small star (✳).

2. Press and hold at some location in the drawing area to establish the *rotation origin*, the center of the rotation.

3. Prior to releasing the mouse button, drag the selected object about the origin to rotate it.

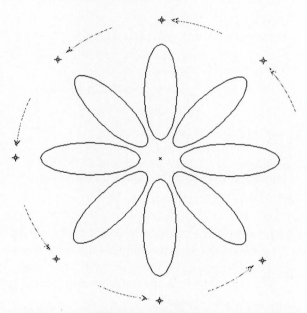

Figure 12.40: Rotating a single ellipse in 45° increments around a single rotation origin.

In principle, the rotation origin is much like the scale origin. Figure 12.40 shows an ellipse in various stages of rotating around a single origin, displayed as a small ×. The original location of the ellipse is the rightmost shape in the figure. All other ellipses are the results of seven drags, each of which has rotated the shape by 45°. During the drags, all points in the ellipse maintain their original distances from the rotation origin. A gray arrow demonstrates the course of each drag. Together, these arrows form a large circle whose center is the rotation origin.

 The rotate tool offers the most control when the distance of your drag from the rotation origin is greater than or equal to the length of the selected object.

We will demonstrate this tip in the following exercise, which offers various ways to approach the rotation of the selected path shown in Figure 12.41:

1. Select the rotate tool and press and hold on the lower left-hand corner point of the selected path, indicated by the small star in Figure 12.41. This establishes the rotation origin.

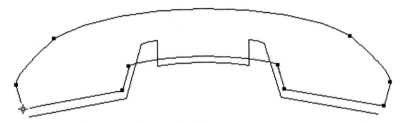

Figure 12.41: Begin dragging with the rotate tool at the lower left point in the selected shape to establish a rotation origin.

2. Drag with the star cursor to a location about ⅓ inch to the right of the origin and drag slightly upward, as shown in Figure 12.42. The distance of the drag in the figure is only 10 points (less than ⅙ inch), but the shape rotates dramatically, approximately 24° counterclockwise.

3. Release your mouse button to complete the rotation. Choose UNDO ROTATE from the EDIT menu (⌘-Z) to return the receiver to its original position.

4. As in step 2, begin dragging at the location of the small star in Figure 12.41 to establish the origin. However, this time drag to the lower right-hand corner point on the opposite side of the selected path, approximately 16 times the distance from the origin as the previous drag.

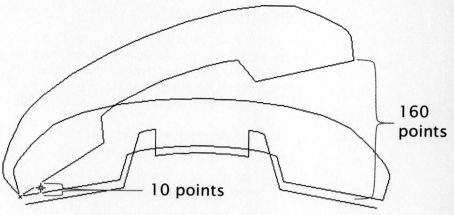

160
points

10 points

Figure 12.42: If you begin dragging close to the rotation origin, small movements will produce dramatic results.

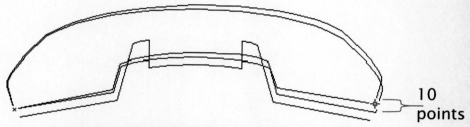

10
points

Figure 12.43: Begin dragging far from the rotation origin to better control the result.

5. As shown in Figure 12.42, you have to drag 160 points from this location to achieve the same result as your previous 10-point drag. If you drag upward only 10 points from the new location, as shown in Figure 12.43, the selected shape rotates less than 2°. Thus, dragging far from the rotation origin provides you with more refined control.

Constraining rotations

To constrain a rotation so that the selected object is rotated by a multiple of 45° from its original position, press the SHIFT key while dragging with the rotate tool.

Rotating partial paths

Just as you may rotate whole objects, you may rotate selected elements within objects independently of their deselected neighbors. Simply select the points that you wish to rotate and use the rotate tool as directed in the previous sections. For example, suppose that you want to rotate the selected elements in the skyline path shown in Figure 12.44:

1. Begin dragging with the rotate tool on the lower right selected point, as indicated by the small star cursor in Figure 12.44.

2. Drag up and to the right, as shown in Figure 12.45. All selected points maintain their original distances from the origin during their moves, causing the rotation of all segments surrounded by selected points.

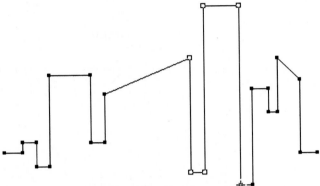

Figure 12.44: Position the rotation origin at the lower right selected point in the path.

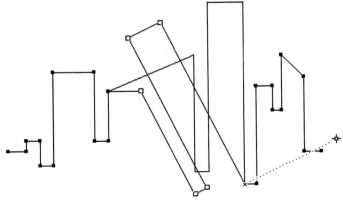

Figure 12.45: Drag up and to the right to rotate the selected elements counterclockwise around the origin.

Using the Rotate dialog box

Press OPTION and click with the rotate tool to simultaneously determine the location of the rotation origin and display the ROTATE dialog box, shown in Figure 12.46. This dialog allows you to rotate one or more selected objects numerically.

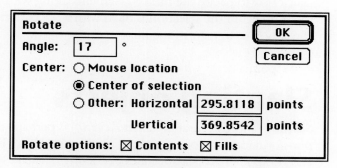

Figure 12.46: The Rotate dialog box allows you to specify the number of degrees by which to rotate a selected object.

Enter any value between –360 and 360 in the "Angle" option box. The value is measured in degrees and is accurate to 0.01 degree. A negative value rotates an object clockwise; a positive value rotates an object counterclockwise.

Below the "Angle" option box are three "Center" radio buttons, which are used to specify the exact location of the rotation origin. Select the "Mouse location" option to confirm the rotation origin at the location where you OPTION-clicked with the rotate tool. Selected by default, the "Center of selection" option allows you to assign the exact center of the selection as the rotation origin. Select "Other" to set any origin location that you desire by entering custom values in the "Horizontal" and "Vertical" option boxes.

To the right of the "Other" radio button, the "Horizontal" and "Vertical" values represent the coordinates of the rotation origin, in the current unit of measure and with respect to the ruler origin. If the "Mouse location" option is selected, the "Horizontal" and "Vertical" values list the exact coordinates of the location at which you OPTION-clicked. If the "Center of selection" is selected, the "Horizontal" and "Vertical" values represent the exact center of the current selection. If you enter your own numbers for these values, the "Other" radio button automatically becomes selected.

If any of the selected objects is a clipping path, select the "Contents" check box to rotate the masked elements along with the selection. If some object in the selection is filled with a tile pattern, select the "Fills" check box to transform the tiles.

Slanting objects

Slanting (more accurately called *skewing*) is perhaps the most difficult transformation to conceptualize. To skew an object is to slant its vertical and horizontal proportions independently of each other. For example, a standard kite shape is a skewed version of a perfect square. As shown in Figure 12.47, the vertical lines in the square are slanted backward and the horizontal lines are slanted upward.

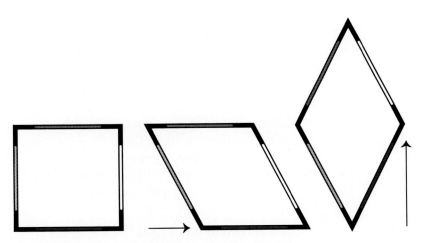

Figure 12.47: Transforming a square into a kite by skewing the shape in two steps, once horizontally and once vertically.

Using the skew tool

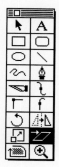

The *skew tool*, second-to-last tool on the right side of the palette, is used to skew text blocks and graphic objects. It is operated by dragging relative to one or more selected objects. The following steps explain how to use this tool:

1. Select the object you wish to skew. Then select the skew tool. Your cursor will appear as a small star (✳).

2. Press and hold at some location in the drawing area relative to the selection to establish the *skew origin*, the center of the skewing operation. Elements in the selection that appear on opposite sides of the origin will be skewed in opposite directions.

3. Prior to releasing the mouse button, drag away from the skew origin to skew the selected object as follows:

   ↑ Drag up to slant the right portion of the selection upward and the left portion downward.

   → Drag to the right to slant the top portion of the selection to the right and the bottom portion to the left.

   ↓ Drag down to slant the right portion of the selection downward and the left portion upward.

   ← Drag to the left to slant the top portion of the selection to the left and the bottom portion to the right.

   In other words, regardless of the angle of your drag, all portions of the selection that are above and to right of the skew origin will slant in the direction of the drag.

In general, the skew tool functions like any other transformation tool. However, it may take some experimenting before you're able to accurately predict the results of your actions. In the following exercise, you may experiment by skewing the telephone shape from Figure 12.26 (back on page 431):

1. Select the skew tool and begin dragging near the middle of the selected shape to establish the skew origin.

2. Drag upward, as shown in Figure 12.48 on the next page. The right half of the phone will shrug upward with your drag, because it is located on the right side of the skew origin. The left half of the phone shrugs downward.

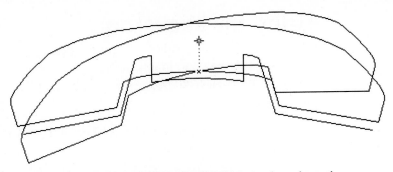

Figure 12.48: Drag upward with the skew tool to skew the right half of the selected shape up and the left half of the shape down.

If you find that the skew tool usually behaves erratically for you, try constraining the performance of the tool by SHIFT-dragging, as described in the following section. This generally makes the tool more manageable.

Constrained skewing

Press SHIFT while dragging with the skew tool to slant an object exclusively horizontally (forward and backward) or vertically (up and down).

Skewing partial paths

Selected elements may be slanted independently of their deselected neighbors in the same path. Simply select the points and segments that you wish to skew, and use the skew tool as directed in the previous sections.

For example, suppose you want to skew the selected elements in the skyline path shown in Figure 12.44 (on page 446):

1. Begin dragging with the skew tool on the lower right selected point, as indicated by the small star cursor in Figure 12.44.

2. Drag leftward with the skew tool as shown in Figure 12.49. As you drag, press the SHIFT key to constrain the transformation to a horizontal slant. All selected points move with the skew tool based on their proximity to the skew origin; points close to the origin move less than points farther away. All selected vertical segments are slanted backward; all selected horizontal segments are unaffected.

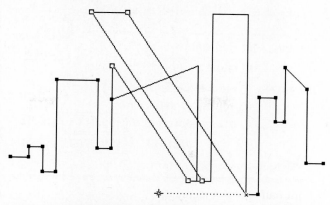

Figure 12.49: Shift-drag to the left with the skew tool to slant the selected elements so they lean backward.

Using the Skew dialog box

Press OPTION and click with the skew tool to simultaneously determine the location of the skew origin and display the SKEW dialog box, shown in Figure 12.50 on the following page. This dialog box allows you to skew one or more selected objects numerically.

Enter values between −360 and 360 in the "Angle" option boxes at the top of the dialog. Both values are measured in degrees and are accurate to 0.01 degree. FreeHand interprets both values in a counterclockwise direction as follows:

- A positive horizontal value slants a selected object backward.

- A negative horizontal value slants a selected object forward.

- A positive vertical value slants anything to the right of the origin up and anything to the left of the origin downward.

- A negative vertical value slants anything to the right of the origin down and anything to the left of the origin upward.

Below the two "Angle" option boxes are three "Center" radio buttons. Select the "Mouse location" radio button to confirm the skew origin at the location where you OPTION-clicked with the skew tool. Selected by default, the "Center of selection" option allows you to assign the exact center of the selection as the skew origin. Select "Other" to set any origin location that you desire by entering custom values in the "Horizontal" and "Vertical" option boxes.

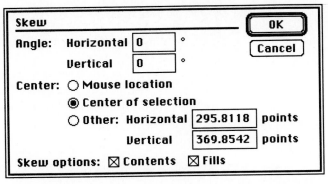

Figure 12.50: The Skew dialog box allows you to specify the angle of the skew axis and determine the angle of the slant.

To the right of the "Other" radio button, the "Horizontal" and "Vertical" values represent the coordinates of the skew origin, in the current unit of measure and with respect to the ruler origin. If the "Mouse location" option is selected, the "Horizontal" and "Vertical" values list the exact coordinates of the location at which you OPTION-clicked. If the "Center of selection" is selected, the "Horizontal" and "Vertical" values represent the exact center of the current selection. If you enter your own numbers for these values, the "Other" radio button automatically becomes selected.

If any of the selected objects is a clipping path, select the "Contents" check box to slant the masked elements along with the selection. If some object in the selection is filled with a tile pattern, select the "Fills" check box to transform the tiles.

Duplicating objects

To *duplicate* an object is to create and control one or more copies of an existing object. Some of these techniques utilize the Macintosh Clipboard, where objects may be stored for future retrieval. Others work without the Clipboard or in combination with manipulation techniques, including the transformation tools. All repeat the composition, movement, or transformation of an object.

Cut, copy, and paste

The CUT, COPY, and PASTE commands under the EDIT menu are available in any Macintosh application. CUT or COPY stores one or more selected objects for possible reuse later in the current session. The PASTE command retrieves the stored objects and displays them in the drawing area. Each command works with Apple's built-in *Clipboard*, which can hold only one object or one selection of objects at a time.

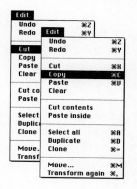

To *cut* an object is to remove the object from the current illustration and place it inside the Clipboard. This is done by selecting an object and choosing the CUT command from the EDIT menu (⌘-X). The COPY command (⌘-C) works very similarly. But rather than removing the selected object, this command makes a copy of the selection and puts it in the Clipboard.

Both CUT and COPY put something into the Clipboard. Since the Clipboard can hold only one selection at a time, each command disposes of the current occupant in the Clipboard and replaces it with the newly cut or copied selection. If no object in the drawing area is selected, the CUT and COPY commands will appear dimmed.

The PASTE command (⌘-V) works exactly opposite the COPY command. To *paste* an object is to copy the contents of the Clipboard and place them inside the current drawing area. The object still exists in the Clipboard and may be pasted into your illustration over and over again. You must have cut or copied an object into the Clipboard sometime previously during the current session in order to use the PASTE command. Otherwise, the command will be dimmed.

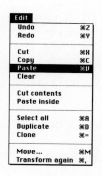

The PASTE command pastes the contents of the Clipboard at the exact center of the current window and in front of all other objects in the current layer. Pasted objects remain selected in the illustration window. In this way, you can easily find an object and move it to its proper location.

KE You may paste an object at the exact horizontal and vertical location at which it was cut or copied as well as in back of the current selection by pressing SHIFT when choosing the PASTE command (⌘-⇧-V). For more information, see the section *Layering objects*, later in this chapter.

Duplicating type

Characters, words, and paragraphs of type may also be duplicated. Double-click the desired text block to display the TEXT dialog box and highlight the type that you want to use later. Choose CUT to remove the highlighted type from the text block and store it in the Clipboard. Choose COPY to copy the highlighted type to the Clipboard. Choose PASTE to replace the highlighted type with type from the Clipboard or paste the type after the insertion marker.

 Pasted type does not retain its original character formatting. Instead, it assumes the formatting of the text immediately preceding the point at which it is pasted.

Cut or copied objects (selected with the arrow tool) may not be pasted into a text block. Cut or copied type (selected with the type tool) may not be pasted outside a text block.

Cloning objects

Cloning functions much like the COPY command with two important exceptions: First, cloning bypasses the Clipboard. It neither displaces the current occupant in the Clipboard nor does it replace that object with the cloned object. Second, cloning acts like a combined COPY-and-PASTE command. The cloned object immediately appears in your illustration, in front of all other objects in the current layer.

Cloning may be accomplished by selecting one or more objects and choosing the CLONE command from the EDIT menu (⌘-=, COMMAND-EQUAL). After choosing the command, your illustration may appear unchanged. This is because all clones appear in the same horizontal and vertical positions as their originals and at the front of the layer containing the original objects. If the originals are spread about onto more than one layer, each clone will appear at the front of the layer that contains its original. Only the cloned objects are selected immediately after choosing CLONE.

Duplicating a transformation

You may duplicate the effects of a recent transformation by choosing TRANSFORM AGAIN from the EDIT menu (⌘-, , COMMAND-COMMA). This command repeats the latest transformation, including a movement.

The first example of Figure 12.51 shows two rectangles: the deselected rectangle represents the original location of an object, and the selected rectangle demonstrates the location to which it has been dragged. After moving the shape, we choose the TRANSFORM AGAIN command to duplicate the distance and direction of the movement, as shown in the second example of the figure. The third example shows the results of choosing the TRANSFORM AGAIN command a second time.

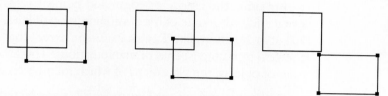

Figure 12.51: After dragging the selected rectangle from its original deselected position (left), the Transform again command is applied two consecutive times (middle and right) to twice repeat the transformation movement.

Each application of TRANSFORM AGAIN repeats the last transformation, regardless of how many other operations have been implemented since the transformation or whether the transformation was originally applied to the current selection.

The TRANSFORM AGAIN command may be used repeatedly after applying a slight transformation to fine-tune the transformation of an object. When the eventual transformation exceeds your requirements, choose UNDO TRANSFORM AGAIN (⌘-Z) to return the object to the exact position or size required.

Suppose you have created a complicated object that is too small to match the size of another object in your illustration. Rather than going back and forth, scaling the object by guess and by golly, you may perform a slight enlargement—about a quarter of what you think is required—and repeat the transformation several times using TRANSFORM AGAIN. With each application of the command, the selected object will grow by the specified percentage. When the size of the object surpasses the desired size, choose UNDO TRANSFORM AGAIN from the EDIT menu to reduce it to the size that most accurately matches your requirements.

Duplicating transformation and object

In one sense, the DUPLICATE command under the EDIT menu (⌘-D) operates much like the CLONE command. It makes an exact duplicate of a selection at the front of the layer containing the original and bypassing the Clipboard. However, rather the appearing at the same location as the original, a clone created with the DUPLICATE command is offset slightly, 10 pixels down and to the right of the original (independent of view size).

But using the DUPLICATE command simply to create offset clones does not take full advantage of the command's capabilities. When used properly, DUPLICATE functions like TRANSFORM AGAIN, except that it also considers cloning when repeating a series of manipulations. This allows you to create a string of objects, the placement of which follow a constant pattern.

In the first example in Figure 12.52, the selected rectangle has been both cloned and moved from the location represented by the deselected shape. The second example shows the result of choosing the DUPLICATE command. Notice that, like the second example of Figure 12.51, the movement of the rectangle has been repeated. But this time, the shape is also recloned, resulting in three rectangles instead of two. If DUPLICATE is chosen a second time, there will be four rectangles, each offset from the others a consistent distance and direction, as shown in the last example.

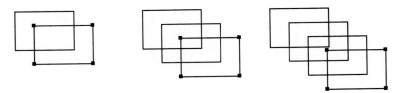

Figure 12.52: After cloning and moving the selected rectangle (left), the Duplicate command is applied two consecutive times (middle and right) to twice repeat the transformation and twice duplicate the rectangle.

By duplicating both transformation and object, you may achieve interesting effects. The following exercise demonstrates how to use the DUPLICATE command to create a perspective gridwork of objects. This exercise makes use of the three paths shown in Figure 12.53. The bottom segment of the outermost path is longer than the top segment, giving it an illusion of depth. The inner ellipses are positioned slightly closer to the top segment of the outer shape, enhancing the illusion.

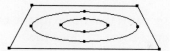

Figure 12.53: The following exercise explains how to transform and duplicate this grouped object to create a perspective effect.

1. Select the paths and choose CLONE (⌘-=, COMMAND-EQUAL). Three cloned paths will appear directly in front of their originals.

2. Select the skew tool. Begin dragging above the paths at the location indicated by the small star cursor at the top of Figure 12.53 to establish the skew origin.

3. Press SHIFT and drag to the right, skewing the cloned paths horizontally, as shown in Figure 12.54. Notice that the cloned object appears to lean into the original, extending back into the same visual horizon. This is a result of experimenting with the position of the shear origin.

Figure 12.54: Shift-drag to the right with the skew tool to skew the cloned paths to the left.

4. Choose the DUPLICATE command (⌘-D), which creates another clone and repeats the horizontal skew. Figure 12.55 on the next page shows the result, which enhances the illusion of perspective.

Figure 12.55: Choose Duplicate to repeat the skew and clone operations.

5. Select the six paths that make up the two leftmost images. Then press COMMAND-EQUAL to clone them.

6. In this step, you will flip a clone of these objects about the center of the original paths, resulting in five symmetrical images. Press OPTION and click with the reflect tool in the center of the deselected image to display the REFLECT dialog. Select the "Vertical" radio button at the top of the dialog box. Also select the "Mouse location" radio button and press RETURN. The result is shown in Figure 12.56: five symmetrical images emerging from the surface of the page.

Figure 12.56: Select the two left images, clone them, and flip the clones about the center of the deselected image.

7. You have now managed to impart a sense of perspective through the use of cloning, skewing, and flipping. But the illustration lacks drama. What's needed are additional rows of slanting tiles, which are most easily created by scaling clones of the existing row over and over. To begin, choose SELECT ALL from the EDIT menu (⌘-A). Then choose CLONE again.

8. Select the scale tool and OPTION-click above the images at the location indicated by the small star cursor at the top of Figure 12.57. This establishes a scale origin at the same location previously occupied by the skew origin. The SCALE dialog box also displays.

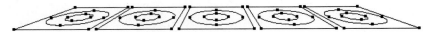

Figure 12.57: Clone the entire row of images and option-click with the scale tool to display the Scale dialog box.

9. Enter 150% into the "Uniform scaling" option box, select the "Mouse location" radio button, and press RETURN. Figure 12.58 shows how a second, larger row of shapes is created. Again, because of the placement of the transformation origin, the second row lines up perfectly with the first. By scaling the cloned shapes to 150% of original size, you enlarge both the size of the shapes and the distance between the shapes and the scale origin.

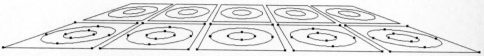

Figure 12.58: Scale clones of the top row of groups to 150% to create two perfectly aligned rows.

10. Choose the DUPLICATE command (⌘-D) to create a third row of larger clones directly beneath the second row.

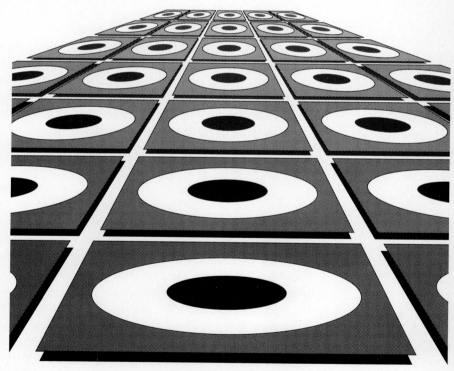

Figure 12.59: The result of choosing Duplicate several times and filling and stroking the resulting paths.

To create the illustration shown in Figure 12.59 on the preceding page, press COMMAND-D several more times. Each series of paths increases in size and distance from the paths above it, thereby creating an even and continuous sense of perspective. Figure 12.59 is shown as it appears when printed. All shapes are filled and stroked. Foreground images are filled with darker shades of gray than background images, heightening the sense of depth. A layer of shadows has also been added.

Layering objects

When you preview or print an illustration, FreeHand describes it one object at a time, starting with the first object in the drawing area and working up to the last. The order in which the objects are described is called the *layering order*. The first object described is behind all other objects in the drawing area. The last object is in front of all other objects. All other objects exist on some unique tier between the first object and the last.

Left to its own device, layering would be a function of the order in which you draw. The oldest object would be in back; the most recent object would be in front. But FreeHand provides a number of commands that allow you to adjust the layering order of existing text blocks and graphic objects. Using the LAYERS palette, you may create self-contained *drawing layers* (or simply *layers*), which act like transparent pieces of acetate. An image may be drawn on any layer and seen clearly through all layers in front of it. An illustration may contain any number of layers, each layer may contain any number of objects, and you may name layers and alter their order as you see fit.

Assigning layers

Like the COLORS and STYLES palette discussed in Chapter 11, the LAYERS palette is an independent palette that appears in front of the foremost FreeHand window. It is displayed by choosing "Layers" from the WINDOWS pop-up under the VIEW menu (⌘-6). All existing drawing layers in the current illustration are displayed as options in a scrolling list inside the LAYERS palette. These options may be defined and manipulated using another set of options, which are made available by clicking and holding on the right-pointing arrowhead icon. The ▶ pop-up menu will display, as shown in Figure 12.60.

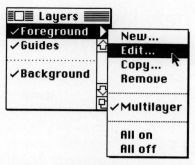

Figure 12.60: Choosing an option from
the Layers palette pop-up menu.

Three layers are included by default in all FreeHand illustrations:

● **Foreground**. Contains printing objects in the current illustration.

● **Guides**. Contains the nonprinting ruler guides in the current illustration. This layer is located in back of the "Foreground" layer.

● **Background**. Contains nonprinting objects in the current illustration. This layer is located in back of both the "Foreground" and "Guides" layers.

When you select an object in the illustration window, the corresponding drawing layer becomes highlighted in the scrolling list. If you select multiple objects from different layers, no layer name will be highlighted. If no object is selected, the highlighted layer name is the default drawing layer, on which all future objects will be created.

To send one or more selected objects to a different layer, simply click a layer name in the scrolling list. Only whole objects may be sent to a different layer. If a path is only partially selected when you click a layer name, the entire path is moved to the selected layer. You may not send objects to the "Guides" layer. Objects sent to the "Background" layer will appear grayed and will not print.

You may find that every time you send an object to a different layer, you also change the default layer. This is because the "Changing elements changes defaults" check box in the MORE PREFERENCES dialog box is selected. To send a selection to a layer without affecting the default layer, you must deselect this option. (Settings for other defaults will also be affected.)

Creating a new layer

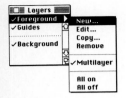

Only named layers may be assigned to type and graphic objects in Free-Hand 3.0. To introduce a drawing layer to the list of named layers in the LAYERS palette, choose the "New…" option from the ▶ pop-up menu in the LAYERS palette. The LAYER dialog box will display, as shown in Figure 12.61. Enter a layer name up to 32 characters long into the "Name" option box. (Note that FreeHand does *not* allow you to replace an existing drawing layer by creating a new layer with the same name.) If you want objects that are transferred to the new layer to display in the drawing area, select the "Visible" check box. Then press RETURN or click the OK button.

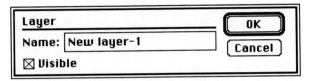

Figure 12.61: The Layers dialog box allows you to store fill, stroke, and halftone screen information as a named drawing layer.

Your new layer name will display at the top of the LAYERS palette. By default, the new drawing layer is a foreground layer that is positioned in front of all other layers in the current illustration.

Copying a layer

Choose the "Copy…" option from the ▶ pop-up menu in the LAYERS palette to copy all objects on the current layer to a new layer. The "Name" option box in the LAYER dialog box will remain empty, allowing you to assign a different name to the copied layer.

Copy a layer when you want to experiment with changing an image without upsetting the existing version of the image.

Renaming a layer

Any drawing layer displayed in the LAYERS palette may be renamed, re-ordered, displayed, hidden, protected, or deleted (except "Guides," which may not be deleted).

To rename a drawing layer in the current illustration, use one of the following techniques to display the LAYER dialog box for the layer:

- Select the layer name in the LAYERS palette and choose "Edit..." from the ▶ pop-up menu.

- Double-click the layer name in the LAYERS palette.

The LAYERS dialog box will appear, displaying the name of the selected layer. After making the desired alterations, click OK or press RETURN to close the dialog box and implement your name change.

Reordering a layer

The order in which layer names appear in the LAYERS palette determines the layering order in the current illustration. The first name in the list represents the foremost layer; the last name is the rearmost layer.

To change the order of layers in the current illustration, simply drag a layer name to a different position in the LAYERS palette scrolling list. Objects in the drawing area assigned to that layer will be repositioned behind or in front of objects in other layers.

Drag a layer name below the dotted line in the LAYERS palette scrolling list to make the layer a nonprinting background layer. All objects on that layer will appear grayed. Drag a layer above the dotted line to make it a printing foreground layer.

By default, the "Guides" layer is in front of all background layers but in back of all foreground layers. You may reorder it in any way you see fit. However, whether foreground or background, guides do not print.

Displaying/hiding layers

A check mark in front of a layer name indicates that all objects on that layer will be displayed on screen and printed. Click on the check mark to hide the check mark and, by so doing, hide all objects on that layer in the drawing area. This technique enables you to isolate a detail on another layer so you may examine it more closely or make corrections to it.

To specify whether objects on hidden layers are printed, select one of the two "Layers" radio buttons in the PRINT OPTIONS dialog box, as discussed in Chapter 14, *Printing Your Illustrations*.

To display objects on a hidden layer, click in front of the layer name in the LAYERS palette to display the check mark.

To hide all layers in the current illustration, choose the "All off" option from the ▶ pop-up menu. Then click in front of specific layer names to check the layers you wish to display. To display all layers, in the current illustration, choose the "All on" option.

Protecting layers

Just as you can protect a selected object from being altered by choosing the LOCK command from the ELEMENT menu, you can protect entire layers of objects in Aldus FreeHand. One way to protect a layer is to hide it as described in the previous section. Objects on a hidden layer may not be manipulated.

You may also protect all layers except the default layer by choosing the "Multilayer" option from the ▶ pop-up menu. If a check mark displays in front of "Multilayer," you may manipulate objects on all layers of the current illustration. If no check mark displays, you may manipulate only those objects that exist on the default layer.

When "Multilayer" is inactive, you may alter objects on a different layer by changing the default layer. To change the default layer, click on the desired layer name when no object is selected.

Incidentally, the "Multilayer" option does not affect the "Guides" layer. The only way to protect guidelines is to choose the LOCK GUIDES command from the VIEW menu. Also note that the "Multilayer" option does not affect whether objects (or whole layers) display or print.

Deleting an existing layer

You may delete any existing drawing layer—even if it's chock-full of text and graphic objects—by selecting the layer name in the LAYERS palette and choosing the "Remove" option from the ▶ pop-up menu. The alert box shown in Figure 12.62 will display, warning you that all objects on the current layer will be deleted from your illustration. Press RETURN to cancel the operation and retain the objects on the current layer. Click the OK button to confirm the deletion, in which case all objects associated with that layer will also be removed.

Figure 12.62: This alert box displays when you choose
the "Remove..." option from the Layers palette.

Before deleting a layer, hide all layers except the layer you want
to delete, then choose the "Fit in window" option from the
MAGNIFICATION pop-up under the VIEW menu (⌘-W). From this
vantage, you may view all objects that you intend to delete, including those
on the pasteboard.

If you delete a layer by mistake, choose the UNDO REMOVE LAYER command from the EDIT menu (⌘-Z) to restore the layer and all its objects to
the current illustration.

Only the "Guides" layer may not be deleted.

Reordering within layers

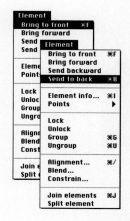

FreeHand also allows you to reorder objects on a single layer. Among the
commands provided for this purpose are the BRING TO FRONT (⌘-F) and
SEND TO BACK commands (⌘- B) under the ELEMENT menu. If you select an
object and choose BRING TO FRONT, the object is brought to the front of
the current layer (the layer that contains the selected object). This object
will be treated exactly as if it were the most recently created path in the
current layer and will therefore be described last in this layer when previewing or printing. By choosing SEND TO BACK, a selected object is treated
as if it were the first path in the current layer and is described first in this
layer when previewing or printing.

BRING TO FRONT and SEND TO BACK may be applied only to whole objects. If a path is only partially selected when choosing either command,
the entire path is moved to the front or back of the current layer.

If you select more than one object when choosing BRING TO FRONT or SEND TO BACK, the relative layering of each selected object is retained. For example, select two objects and choose BRING TO FRONT. The frontmost of the two objects becomes the frontmost object on the current layer, the backmost of the two objects becomes the second-to-frontmost object.

Forward and backward

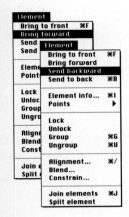

When creating complicated illustrations, it is not enough to be able to send objects to the absolute front or back of a layer. Even a simple illustration may contain over a hundred objects. Adjusting the layering of a single object from, say, 14th-to-front back to 46th-to-front would take days using BRING TO FRONT and SEND TO BACK.

Fortunately, FreeHand provides two commands that make relative layering manipulations possible: these are BRING FORWARD and SEND BACKWARD, also under the ELEMENT menu. Each command scoots a selected object one object forward or one object backward within the current layer.

Figure 12.63 demonstrates the BRING FORWARD command. The first example shows four layered shapes. If you select the black shape and choose BRING FORWARD, the selected path will be moved one step forward, as shown in the second example. The third example shows the results of choosing the BRING FORWARD command a second time.

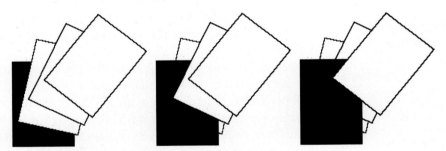

Figure 12.63: The effects of selecting the rearmost path
(left) and choosing Bring forward twice (center and right).

Regardless of layering order, you may select the object directly behind the current selection by CONTROL-clicking on it with the arrow tool. If you CONTROL-click a second time, you select the next object back, and so on. Eventually, you will cycle through all overlapping objects and again select the frontmost object.

Paste in back

FreeHand 3.0 now allows you to send one object, A, directly in back of another, B. To accomplish this, select object A, choose Cut (⌘-X), select object B, and press SHIFT while choosing PASTE (⌘-⇧-V). FreeHand places object A at the exact horizontal and vertical location from which it was cut, and directly in back of object B.

If multiple objects are selected when SHIFT-choosing the PASTE command, the contents of the Clipboard are placed in back of the backmost selected object. If no object is selected, the Clipboard contents are pasted into the center of the window, just as if the SHIFT key were not pressed.

Layering in combined objects

Any command that combines selected objects may also affect the layering of objects in an illustration. These include GROUP (⌘-G) and JOIN ELEMENTS (⌘-J). All objects in a group or composite path must be layered consecutively. To accomplish this, FreeHand sends all selected objects to the front of the default layer when you choose GROUP or JOIN ELEMENTS, regardless of the layer or layers that originally contained all the objects in the selection. (Choosing UNGROUP or SPLIT ELEMENT neither restores an object to its original layer nor otherwise affects its layering.)

You may also adjust the relative layering of objects inside groups or composite paths. Press OPTION and click an object with the arrow tool. Then choose the BRING TO FRONT (⌘-F), BRING FORWARD, SEND BACKWARD, or SEND TO BACK (⌘-B) command.

Blending objects

The last feature we discuss in this chapter is a combination transformation/duplication feature called *blending*. To blend two selected paths is to create a series of intermediate paths between them. For example, suppose that we have created two paths, one that represents a caterpillar and one that represents a butterfly. By blending these two paths, you may create several additional paths that represent metamorphic stages between the two life forms, as shown in Figure 12.64 on the next page. The first intermediate path is formed much like the caterpillar. Each intermediate path after that becomes less like the caterpillar and more like the butterfly.

Figure 12.64: Blending a caterpillar and a butterfly creates a
series of transformed duplicates between the two objects.

Using the Blend dialog box

In any blend, two paths must be selected. Of the two, the rear path acts as
the *source path* and the forward path acts as the *concluding path*. Each
path may contain any number of points. Only free-form paths—not
groups, composite paths, or text blocks—may be blended in FreeHand.

To blend two paths, select a specific point in each path. Then choose
the BLEND... command under the ELEMENT menu. The BLEND dialog box
shown in Figure 12.65 will display.

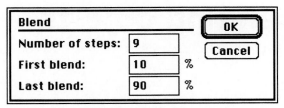

Figure 12.65: The Blend dialog box allows you to
determine the number of intermediate paths to create
between two selected paths.

The BLEND dialog box contains three options that allow you to control the nature of the intermediate paths, called *steps*, in a blend:

- **Number of steps**. Enter the number of intermediate paths that you want FreeHand to create in this option. Any number from 1 to 32,767 is acceptable. The "First blend" and "Last blend" values will update accordingly.

- **First blend**. The value in this option determines the location of each point in the first step as a percentage of the total distance between each selected pair of points in the source and concluding paths. This value also affects how the first step is painted as a percentage of the difference between the fills and strokes of the source and concluding paths.

- **Last blend**. The value in this option determines the location of each point in the last step as a percentage of the total distance between each selected pair of points in the source and concluding paths. This value also affects how the last step is painted as a percentage of the difference between the fills and strokes of the source and concluding paths.

If you can make sense of all of that, you've probably used the BLEND... command before. If not, don't keep reading it over and over; you'll just turn your brain to mush. These options are better demonstrated by example: Suppose that you specify 9 steps between your source and concluding paths. FreeHand determines the positioning of each step as a percentage of the distance between both paths. The source path occupies the 0% position and the concluding path occupies the 100% position. To space the steps evenly, FreeHand automatically assigns the nine steps to positions 10% through 90%. Therefore, the "First blend" option updates to display 10%, and the "Last blend" option displays 90%.

You may change the "First blend" and "Last blend" values to alter the percentage placement of the first and last steps. The second through eighth steps are automatically spaced evenly between them. If you change the "First blend" value to 30% and the "Last blend" value to 70%, you compress the steps closer together while leaving some breathing room between the intermediate steps and the source and concluding paths.

The "First blend" and "Last blend" values also control the fill and stroke of the intermediate paths. Suppose the source path is filled with white and stroked with a 100% black, 11-point line weight; the concluding path is filled with 100% black and stroked with a 50% black, 1-point line weight. The painting attributes of the steps are averaged incrementally as a function of the number of steps specified. To determine this average, FreeHand divides the difference for each painting attribute by the number of steps. In this case, the differences between source and concluding paths are as follows:

- The difference in fill color = 100% black – 0% black (white) = 100%.

- The difference in stroke color = 100% black – 50% black = 50%.

- The difference in line weight = (11-point) – (1-point) = 10-point.

With 9 steps, a "First blend" value of 10%, and a "Last blend" value of 90%, your blend will appear as shown in Figure 12.66. Each step is painted as follows:

Step	% change	Fill color	Stroke color	Line weight
1	10%	10% black	95% black	10-point
2	20%	20% black	90% black	9-point
3	30%	30% black	85% black	8-point
4	40%	40% black	80% black	7-point
5	50%	50% black	75% black	6-point
6	60%	60% black	70% black	5-point
7	70%	70% black	65% black	4-point
8	80%	80% black	60% black	3-point
9	90%	90% black	55% black	2-point

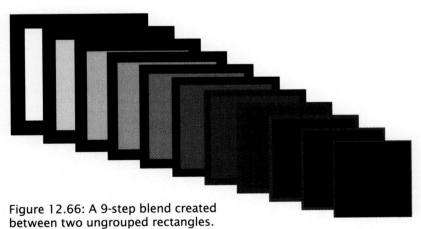

Figure 12.66: A 9-step blend created between two ungrouped rectangles.

Press RETURN to exit the BLEND dialog box and create the specified number of steps, beginning and ending at the prescribed locations. Free-Hand creates the steps as a grouped object, layered between the source and concluding paths. Within the group, the steps ascend in layering order as they approach the concluding (frontmost) path.

If either the source path or concluding path lacks a fill or stroke, Free-Hand will not allow you to blend the paths. If either the source or concluding path is stroked with a dash pattern, half of the steps will be stroked with that dash pattern and half will not.

Selecting points in a blend

Your mastery of the blend tool depends upon your ability to control the appearance of intermediate paths rather than simply relying on FreeHand's automation. The quantity and location of points in the steps, as well as the form of the segments between points, is based on two criteria:

* The number of points in the source and concluding paths.

* The specific point selected in each path when you choose the BLEND... command.

The BLEND... command relies on points as guidelines. It tries to match each point in the source path with a point in the concluding path. The blend tool then determines the form and number of segments required between each consecutive pair of points. For the most predictable results, your source and concluding paths should contain an identical number of points.

The points that you select before choosing BLEND... also control the appearance of the steps in a blend. The BLEND... command uses the selected points as origin points in creating intermediate steps. It then progresses around the paths in a consistent direction, from one pair of points to the next.

Try to select a similarly positioned point in each path. If possible, each selected point should occupy a central position in its path (unless the paths are open, in which case you *must* select an endpoint in each path).

To create the blend shown in Figure 12.67 on the next page, we selected the lowest curve point in the path of each eyeball. After displaying the BLEND dialog box, we specified 5 steps and changed the "First blend" option to 40% to create a large gap between the source path and the first step. The fills of the steps in this figure have been made transparent after the fact to make them easier to see. The distance is greater between the source path and the first step than between the last step and the concluding path, because we changed the "First blend" value to 40%. The shade and line weight of the stroke in the first step is also affected by this change.

Figure 12.67: The result of specifying five steps and changing the "First blend" value to 40%.

If you click on points that occupy different positions in the source and concluding paths, FreeHand will create distorted steps. Figure 12.68 shows three examples: In each, we create four blends by selecting different pairs of points in the two triangles. Each point in one triangle blends toward a point in the other triangle based on its proximity to the selected point, as demonstrated by the arrows.

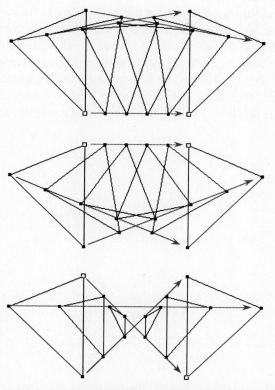

Figure 12.68: Selecting three different pairs of points (shown as hollow) affects the appearance of the steps, even though the source and concluding paths are identical.

 When blending, both the source and concluding paths must be closed or both must be open. If the paths are open, you must select an endpoint in each path.

Blending multiple paths

Although you may blend only two paths at a time, you may blend as many pairs of paths as you desire within a single illustration. The first image and the last image in Figure 12.69 each contain five open paths. These two images were specifically designed so that for each path in the man's face, a path performs a similar function in the werewolf's face. We carefully selected like points in each pair of like paths and entered identical values every time the Blend dialog box displayed. The result is a series of 30 blends that overlap to form six metamorphic images. With the exception of a slight stroking alteration (changing the stroke of the source path to black), the final images appear exactly as they were created with the Blend... command. It is natural when creating such a difficult series of blends that some paths will suffer from a variety of aesthetic imperfections, as do those in the figure. Such paths will require reshaping.

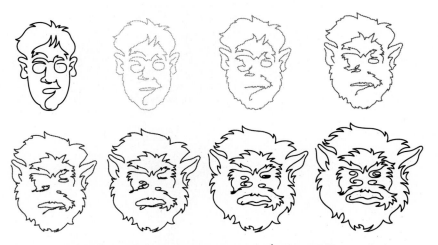

Figure 12.69: Blending five separate open paths to create a late-show metamorphosis.

Creating custom gradations

Despite the amazing visual metamorphoses that may be produced using this technique, you will probably find the Blend... command most helpful in creating a *gradation*, a special effect in which colors gradually change inside the fill of an object. For example, if the upper portion of a rectangle is filled with blue and the lower portion is filled with yellow, a gradient fill will traverse the chromatic spectrum between these two colors.

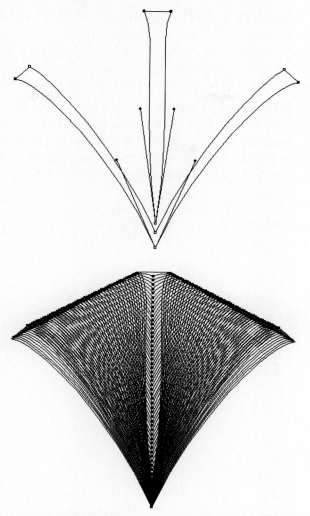

Figure 12.70: After selecting a white path (top, central) and a black path (top, V-shaped), we blend the paths to create a gradation containing 49 steps (bottom).

When creating a gradation with the BLEND... command, you will probably be more concerned with the color values of the source and concluding paths than with the shapes themselves. The top example of Figure 12.70 shows two paths: the central path is filled with white and the V-shaped path is filled with black. Neither path is stroked, since a repeating stroke would interrupt a continuous gradation. Also, the central path is in front, making it the concluding path.

After selecting the two paths, we select the bottom point in each path and choose the BLEND… command. We enter 49 into the "Number of steps" option in the BLEND dialog box. This means that each step will be 2% lighter than the step behind it. The second example of Figure 12.70 displays the 49 evenly spaced steps created with the BLEND… command.

After creating a gradation, you may incorporate it into a clipping path. In Figure 12.71, we have cut the gradation from Figure 12.70 and pasted it into a masking object to create a glistening charm. To create the outlines around the charm, we add two copies of the mask, each stroked with different line weights and with transparent fills.

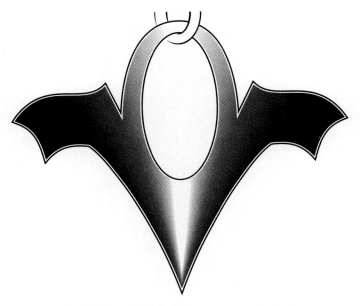

Figure 12.71: The result of incorporating the gradation from the previous figure into a clipping path.

If the source and concluding paths are filled and/or stroked with tints of an identical spot color—100% and 40% red—or with any color and white, FreeHand will fill and/or stroke the steps with tints of the spot color. If the source and concluding paths are filled and/or stroked with process colors or unlike spot colors, FreeHand will fill and/or stroke the steps with process colors. These incremental colors are not named, nor are they added to the COLORS palette or to any "Colors" pop-up menus.

If you'll be printing your final illustration to a 300 dot-per-inch laser printer, you won't need more than 24 steps, since a device of this type can produce only 26 gray values. However, if you'll be printing to a device with a higher resolution, such as a Linotronic, Varityper, or Compugraphic imagesetter, such a small number of steps may result in *banding*—an effect in which each step in a gradation appears clearly distinguishable from its neighbor. To determine the optimal number of steps for a specific imagesetter, use the following formula:

$$[(\text{dpi} \div \text{lpi})^2 + 1] \times \% \Delta c - 2$$

in which *dpi* is the resolution of the printer in dots per inch, *lpi* is the screen frequency in lines per inch, and $\% \Delta c$ is the percentage change in color. For example, the percentage change in color between a 40% tint source path and a 70% tint concluding path is 30%. If you intend to print this gradation to an Linotronic 100 with a resolution of 1270 dots per inch and a default frequency of 90 lines per inch, the optimal blends will contain $[(1270 \div 90)^2 + 1] \times 0.3 - 2 = 58$ steps.

For small blends, divide the result by an integer, such as 2, 3, or 4.

Editing a blend

Our favorite new FreeHand feature is the editable blend. In version 3.0, a blend is treated as a unique kind of grouped object. You may change the number of steps or alter the colors or shapes of the source and concluding paths. FreeHand adjusts the steps to your new specifications automatically.

To change the number of steps in a blend, select a existing blend with the arrow tool and choose the ELEMENT INFO... command from the ELEMENT menu (⌘-I, ⬿-⭦⭦). This will bring up the same BLEND dialog box that displays when you choose the BLEND... command. The dialog box will contain the settings for the selected blend. Enter any new values into the "Number of steps," "First blend," and "Last blend" option boxes and press RETURN. FreeHand will implement your changes.

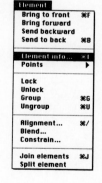

To reshape or recolor a blend, OPTION-click with the arrow tool on the source or concluding path to select this path separately from the rest of the blend. (You may *not* select an individual step in a blend; OPTION-clicking on a step selects the entire blend.) You may even select both the source and concluding paths by OPTION-clicking on one and SHIFT-OPTION-clicking on the other.

After selecting the source or concluding path, you may reshape it by dragging one or more points, adding or deleting points, and so on. You may also apply a different fill, stroke, or style to the path. FreeHand will immediately update the steps to meet the demands of the new path.

Ungrouping a blend

If you want to adjust one or more of the steps manually, or if you simply want to eliminate a blend, select the blend and choose UNGROUP from the ELEMENT menu (⌘-U). Ungrouping frees the source and concluding paths from the grouped steps. To separate the steps, choose UNGROUP again. However, once you ungroup a blend, you may not access the BLEND dialog box again—unless you choose UNDO UNGROUP (⌘-Z) immediately after ungrouping the path—except by reblending the paths; that is, selecting new points in the source and concluding paths and choosing the BLEND... command.

Element	
Bring to front	⌘F
Bring forward	
Send backward	
Send to back	⌘B
Element info...	⌘I
Points	▶
Lock	
Unlock	
Group	⌘G
Ungroup	⌘U
Alignment...	⌘/
Blend...	
Constrain...	
Join elements	⌘J
Split element	

Importing
and Exporting
Graphics

FreeHand allows you to use documents from
other applications in the creation of artwork. In
Chapter 6, we saw that MacPaint, PICT, TIFF,
and Encapsulated PostScript files created in
other drawing and painting programs can be introduced for use as tracing templates. We will
now see how any of these kinds of graphics may
be introduced and manipulated as printable portions of your artwork. You may also save a Free-
Hand file as an EPS document and import it to

any page-composition application that runs on the Macintosh or on an IBM PC compatible. We will also examine the effects of opening Illustrator 1.1 and object-oriented PICT files inside Aldus FreeHand 3.0.

Importing graphics

FreeHand is capable of importing any bitmapped or object-oriented image saved in one of the following standardized graphic formats:

- MacPaint
- PICT (QuickDraw picture)
- TIFF (Tag Image File Format)
- EPS (Encapsulated PostScript)

MacPaint-format documents may originate not only from MacPaint itself but also from other popular painting programs, like DeskPaint, SuperPaint, PixelPaint, and Studio/1, as well as from scanning applications like ThunderWare. The MacPaint format is one of the most widely supported graphics formats for the Macintosh computer. Unfortunately, it is also the most limited. MacPaint files are exclusively *monochrome* (black and white—no colors or gray values), no larger than 8 inches by 10 inches, vertically oriented, and always bitmapped at a resolution of 72 dots per inch. In FreeHand, you may increase the resolution of an imported MacPaint file by reducing it with the arrow tool or scale tool.

The *PICT format*, on the other hand, provides much more flexibility. The PICT format is most commonly associated with moderately powerful drawing applications such as MacDraw, Canvas, and MacDraft. But, in fact, PICT goes much farther. It is the original file-swapping format developed by Apple for the purpose of transferring both bitmapped and object-oriented pictures from one graphics application to another. PICT can accommodate any size graphic, resolutions exceeding 300 dots per inch, and over 16 million colors. For this reason, many scanning and image-editing applications, such as ImageStudio, PixelPaint, Studio/32, and Photoshop, support this format. In addition to converting object-oriented PICT files into FreeHand drawings using the OPEN... command (as described in *Opening files inside FreeHand 3.0* in Chapter 3) FreeHand allows you to import both bitmapped and object-oriented PICT files.

Don't be surprised if you encounter an out-of-memory error when importing a color bitmap saved in the PICT format. Since FreeHand provides much more reliable support for TIFF (some argue the format itself is more efficient), you may avoid most memory problems by saving your color scans and paintings as TIFF documents.

Like MacPaint, the *TIFF format* is exclusively a bitmapped format. But, like PICT, it is otherwise unrestricted, accommodating graphics of any size, resolutions exceeding 300 dots per inch, and over 16 million colors. TIFF was developed by Aldus in an attempt to standardize images created by various scanners. Most painting and image-editing programs support the TIFF format.

The *EPS format* combines a pure PostScript-language description of a graphic with a PICT-format screen representation. The EPS format was designed by Altsys (the developers of FreeHand) in cooperation with Aldus and Adobe for the swapping of high-resolution images from one PostScript-compatible application to another. It is possibly the best format for storing object-oriented drawings. It is not, however, an efficient format for saving bitmaps. A color EPS bitmap, for example, is typically twice to three times as large as the same bitmap saved in the TIFF format.

Because of the constraints FreeHand puts onto various file formats, we recommend that you save graphics that you intend to import into FreeHand according to the following rules:

- Save a small (less than 8 by 10 inches) monochrome bitmap in the MacPaint format.

- Save any other bitmapped file, including a gray-scale or color scan or painting, in the TIFF format.

- Save an object-oriented graphic created in MacDraw or other low-end drawing or graphing program in the PICT format. Then try to open it directly using the OPEN... command in the FILE menu (⌘-O). If that doesn't work adequately, import the file using the PLACE... command, as described in the next section.

- Save an object-oriented graphic created in Adobe Illustrator or other high-end drawing application such as Corel Draw on the PC in the Illustrator 1.1 format. Then try to open it directly using the OPEN... command (⌘-O). If that doesn't work, save the graphic as an EPS file and import the file using the PLACE... command, as described in the next section.

A graphic saved in any of these file formats may be imported into an illustration as an actual portion of the artwork. It may be transformed, duplicated, layered, and printed. However, even though an imported graphic may have been constructed as a series of points and segments, just like a FreeHand drawing, those points and segments may not be altered (unless the imported graphic was stored as a PICT file, as described in the section *Ungrouping PICT graphics* later in this chapter).

Placing a graphic file

To import a bitmapped or object-oriented graphic—regardless of format—into an open FreeHand illustration, follow these steps:

1. Choose the PLACE... command from the FILE menu. The PLACE DOCUMENT dialog box will display, as shown in Figure 13.01.

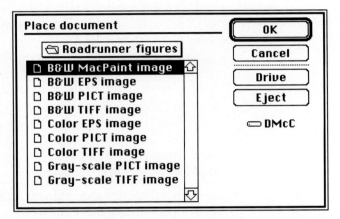

Figure 13.01: The Place document dialog box allows you to import a tracing template saved in one of four graphic formats.

2. Select a graphic file from the scrolling list and press RETURN. FreeHand will read the file from disk and display the *graphic placement cursor* that corresponds to the graphic format for the selected file. Each of these cursors is displayed in Figure 13.02.

3. Position the graphic placement cursor at the upper left corner of the prospective location of the template, then click. The selected graphic image will display in the illustration window, and all previously selected objects will become deselected, as shown in Figure 13.03.

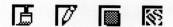

Figure 13.02: The graphic placement icons for (from left to right) a MacPaint graphic, a PICT graphic, a TIFF graphic, and an EPS graphic.

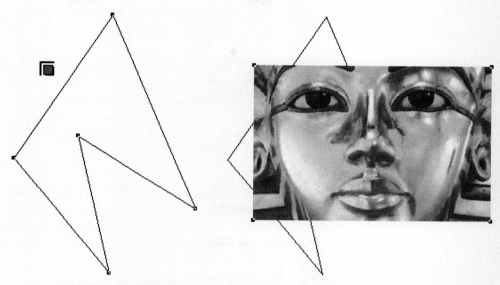

Figure 13.03: The graphic placement icon (left) represents the position of the upper left corner of an imported graphic (right).

Pasting a graphic file

You may also import a graphic via the Macintosh Clipboard, using the CUT, COPY, and PASTE commands common to the EDIT menus of all Macintosh applications. The following procedure explains how:

1. While inside a painting, drawing, or graphing program—such MacPaint, MacDraw, or Microsoft Excel—select the portion of the picture that you wish to import into Freehand and choose COPY from the EDIT menu (⌘-C).

2. Switch to the FreeHand application.

   a. If you are using the standard Macintosh Finder, choose QUIT from the paint program FILE menu (⌘-Q). If the copied image is sufficiently large, an alert box will display, like the one shown in Figure 13.04, requesting that you convert the contents of the

Clipboard. Press RETURN or click the YES button to approve the conversion. Then launch FreeHand, as described in the section *Starting FreeHand* in Chapter 3, and open an existing Free-Hand illustration or create a new one.

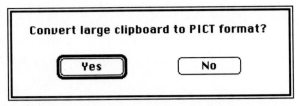

Figure 13.04: This alert box confirms the conversion of a Clipboard image to a format readable by other Macintosh applications.

b. If you are working under MultiFinder and FreeHand is currently running, click the application icon in the far right corner of the menu bar until the FreeHand toolbox comes to front, or choose the Aldus FreeHand 3.0 icon (🐢) from the list of running applications in the APPLE menu.

3. Choose PASTE from the FreeHand EDIT menu (⌘-V). The selected template image will display in the center of the illustration window.

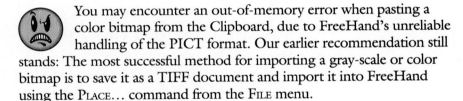 You may encounter an out-of-memory error when pasting a color bitmap from the Clipboard, due to FreeHand's unreliable handling of the PICT format. Our earlier recommendation still stands: The most successful method for importing a gray-scale or color bitmap is to save it as a TIFF document and import it into FreeHand using the PLACE... command from the FILE menu.

Manipulating imported graphics

At first glance, FreeHand treats an imported graphic much like a geometric path. After placing a graphic, four corner handles define the perimeter of the image. These handles show that the graphic is selected and may be used to scale the image.

Scaling a graphic

Using the arrow tool, you may drag any corner handle to scale an imported graphic. Press SHIFT while dragging the corner handle to scale the graphic proportionally.

KE After beginning to SHIFT-drag a corner handle, but before releasing the mouse button, press CONTROL to scale an imported bitmap or EPS graphic exclusively horizontally or vertically. (This technique does not work when scaling an imported PICT graphic unless it is first ungrouped.)

Scaling a bitmap

All imported graphics are not created equally. Because bitmapped graphics have a fixed resolution (generally 72 pixels per inch), FreeHand provides special means for scaling bitmaps to make them compatible with high-resolution output devices.

For example, suppose that you are printing a 72-dpi bitmap to a 300-dpi laser printer. Each pixel in your bitmap is $1/72$ inch square, while each pixel in the laser printer is $1/300$ inch square. Therefore, each pixel in the bitmap wants to take up $1/72$ divided by $1/300$, or $4\frac{1}{6}$ laser-printed pixels. Since pixels by definition can't be divvied into pieces, each bitmap pixel must be represented by a whole number of printed pixels. But your laser printer can't just round down each pixel to 4 dots square or it would shrink the imported graphic. Thus, to maintain the size of the graphic, five pixels in a row are 4 printed dots square; every sixth pixel is 5 printed dots square. These occasional larger pixels give your bitmapped artwork a throbbing appearance, known generically as a *moiré pattern*.

To eliminate moiré patterns, you must scale the imported bitmap so that the resolution of the printer divides evenly into the resolution of the bitmap. One way to accomplish this is to option-click the selected bitmap with the scale tool to display the SCALE dialog box. If you plan to print your finished illustration to a 300-dpi laser printer, enter a multiple of 24% (72 ÷ 300) into the "Uniform scaling" option box—48%, 72%, 96%, and so on. If you plan to print the illustration to a Linotronic typesetter, enter a multiple of 5.67% (72 ÷ 1270), which include such percentages as 17%, 34%, 51%, 68%, 85%, 102%, and so on.

Hate math? Then let FreeHand figure it out for you. Choose DOCUMENT SETUP... from the FILE menu and enter the resolution of your final output device in the "Target printer resolution" option box. Press RETURN to exit the DOCUMENT SETUP dialog box. Then OPTION-drag a corner handle of an imported TIFF or MacPaint-format graphic using the arrow tool. FreeHand will automatically scale the image to an increment compatible with the resolution of your printer. To proportionally scale a bitmap to a compatible size, SHIFT-OPTION-drag a corner handle.

Gray-scale bitmap info

In FreeHand, a selected TIFF or MacPaint-format graphic may be edited by choosing ELEMENT INFO... from the ELEMENT menu (⌘-I, ⌥-↖↖). If the selected bitmap contains no color—only gray values or black and white—the IMAGE dialog box will display, as shown in Figure 13.05. Here you may control the location and scale of the graphic, as well as the contrast between gray values and the manner in which gray values print.

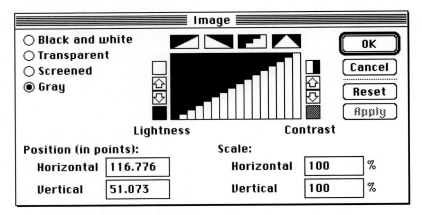

Figure 13.05: Option-double-click a monochrome or gray-scale bitmap to display the Image dialog box.

Along the bottom of the IMAGE dialog box, two "Position" option boxes display the location of the lower left corner handle of the selected bitmap in relation to the ruler origin (discussed in the *Using the rulers* section of Chapter 12). Enter new values for these options to relocate the selected bitmap according to the lower left handle.

The two "Scale" option boxes list the extent to which the selected bitmap has been reduced or enlarged, measured as a percentage of its original size. Enter any value below 100% in one of these options to reduce the width or height; enter a value greater than 100% to increase the width or height. Note that these option boxes will record the results of scaling the bitmap, whether by OPTION-dragging a corner handle with the arrow tool or by some other means. Enter 100% into both the "Horizontal" and "Vertical" option boxes to restore the bitmap to its original size.

Four mutually exclusive radio buttons display in the upper left corner of the IMAGE dialog box. These operate as follows:

- **Black and white**. If the selected bitmap was placed as a MacPaint or monochrome TIFF graphic, this option will be selected by default. Selecting this option for a gray-scale bitmap changes all dark gray values to black and all light grays to white. Use the *gray-value bars* in the center of the dialog box to determine which specific gray values will appear black and which will appear white.

- **Transparent**. Like the "Black and white" option, "Transparent" allows for only two gray values. However, in this case, the two values are black and transparent. Selecting this option for a monochrome bitmap makes all white pixels transparent, allowing you to see through white portions of a bitmap to view objects behind the graphic in the drawing area. Selecting this option for a gray-scale bitmap changes all dark gray values to black and all light grays to transparent. Use the gray-value bars to determine which specific gray values appear black and which become transparent.

- **Screened**. This option displays gray values as patterns of black and white dots, as on a monochrome monitor. If you use a color monitor, you may use this option to speed up the screen refresh speed. If you use a monochrome monitor, this option is most useful when substituting black and white pixels in a MacPaint graphic with gray values. In either case, "Screened" allows you to display 16 gray values, which may be adjusted using the gray-value bars.

If you're familiar with previous versions of FreeHand, you may wonder what happened to the options that accompanied the "Screened" radio button, which allowed you to adjust the halftone function, angle, and frequency for the current bitmap. In version 3.0, these attributes are controlled using the HALFTONE SCREEN... command under the ATTRIBUTES menu, as described in *Halftone screens* in Chapter 14.

- **Gray**. If the selected bitmap was placed as a gray-scale TIFF graphic, this option will be selected by default (although it will appear dimmed if you use a monochrome monitor). This option displays gray values as patterns of black and white dots on a monochrome monitor, and as true gray values on a color monitor. If you use a color monitor, you may use this option to substitute gray values for black and white pixels in a MacPaint graphic. The "Gray" radio button allows you to display 16 gray values, which may be adjusted using the gray-value bars.

Image mapping

The remaining options in the IMAGE dialog control the *mapping* of actual gray values to printed gray values. The *gray-value bars* in the center of the dialog box represent the current mapping specifications. Each bar represents a single gray value. If the selected bitmap is a gray-value TIFF graphic, 16 bars will display. If a MacPaint or monochrome TIFF graphic is selected, only two bars will display, one completely white and the other completely black. Regardless of quantity, the horizontal position of each bar represents the actual gray values, black being on the left and white being on the right, as demonstrated in Figure 13.06. The height of each bar represents the printed appearance of the gray value, black being toward the bottom and white being toward the top. When an image is first selected, a *linear mapping* is in force, so that the height of each bar increases in even increments relative to the bar's position in the chart. A black pixel will print as black, a dark gray pixel will print as dark gray, and so on.

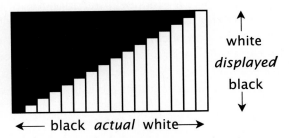

Figure 13.06: The gray value bars map each of 16 gray values in a selected bitmap to any level of brightness from black to white.

There are four different ways to control gray-value mapping in the IMAGE dialog box. You may use any one or all of them:

- Use the "Lightness" scroll bar to uniformly lighten or darken pixels in the selected bitmap.

- Use the "Contrast" scroll bar to adjust the contrast between pixels in the selected bitmap.

- Select one of the *mapping icons* above the gray-value bars to perform one of four special graphic effects.

- Drag an individual bar up or down to lighten or darken a single gray value.

The "Lightness" scroll bar allows you to lighten or darken all gray values in the current bitmap at the same time. Pressing on the up arrow lightens all values (except those already at 0%, or white); pressing on the down arrow darkens all values (except those already at 100%, or black). As these changes occur, they are reflected by the gray-value bars.

The "Contrast" scroll bar allows you increase or decrease the contrast between gray values in the current bitmap. Pressing on the up arrow darkens values darker than 50% (medium gray) and lightens values lighter than 50%, thus increasing the contrast toward a black and white image. Pressing on the down arrow lightens values darker than 50% and darkens values lighter than 50%, decreasing the contrast toward solid gray. As these changes occur, they are reflected by the gray-value bars.

When adjusting a scanned image that you intend to output to paper (rather than film), you may want to slightly decrease the contrast and increase the lightness. (Click twice on the "Contrast" down arrow and twice on the "Lightness" up arrow.) This gives the halftone dots room to spread when the illustration is commercially reproduced without making the image appear overly dark or muddy.

The four mapping icons displayed above the bar chart allow you to quickly access four common imaging effects:

- **Normal** (▬). Click this icon to return the gray-value bars to their original linear configuration. An example of normal mapping is shown in Figure 13.07 on the next page.

Figure 13.07: Tut with normal mapping.

- **Negative** (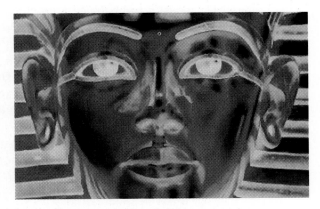). Click this icon to invert the light and dark pixels in a selected bitmap. White pixels become black, black becomes white, and so on. An example of negative mapping is shown in Figure 13.08.

Figure 13.08: Tut with negative mapping.

- **Posterize** (). Click this icon to employ a stair-stepped map that groups a range of values into one of four clusters. Printed values jump from black to 66% gray to 33% gray to white. Transitions between gray values are abrupt rather than smooth, ideal for artwork that you later intend to photocopy or submit to some other low-quality printing process. An example of posterized mapping is shown in Figure 13.09.

Figure 13.09: Tut with posterized mapping.

● **Solarize** (■). Click this icon to double the darkness of all values between white and medium gray and invert and double the darkness of all values darker than medium gray. In this way, both white and black pixels become white, light and dark gray pixels become medium gray, and medium gray pixels become black. The result is a unique glowing effect, as shown in Figure 13.10.

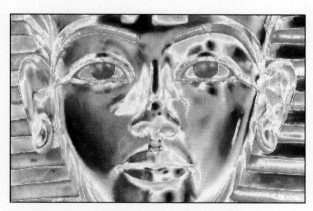

Figure 13.10: Tut with solarized mapping.

You may also drag individual gray-value bars up and down with your cursor inside the IMAGE dialog box. Drag up to lighten a gray value; drag down to darken a gray value. Click at a point inside the bar chart to move the height of the corresponding bar to that location. If you drag in a roughly horizontal direction inside the chart, several bars will adjust to follow the path of your drag.

Click the APPLY button to display the results of your changes in the drawing area without leaving the IMAGE dialog box. If you cannot see the drawing area because the dialog box is in the way, drag its title bar to move the box partially off screen. This allows you to make additional changes if the current settings are not satisfactory.

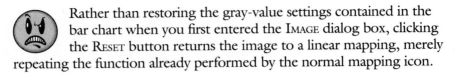

Rather than restoring the gray-value settings contained in the bar chart when you first entered the IMAGE dialog box, clicking the RESET button returns the image to a linear mapping, merely repeating the function already performed by the normal mapping icon.

Both the OK and CANCEL buttons function as they do in any other dialog boxes. You may undo your changes after clicking OK or pressing RETURN by choosing UNDO ELEMENT INFO… from the EDIT menu (⌘-Z).

As we mentioned earlier, the IMAGE dialog box will display only if the selected image was stored in the TIFF or MacPaint format. If an imported PICT image contains a bitmapped image (or is entirely bitmapped), select the PICT image and choose UNGROUP (⌘-U). Press TAB to deselect all elements, then select the bitmapped portion of the imported graphic and choose ELEMENT INFO… (⌘-I, ⬔-↖↖). If the bitmap is gray-scale or monochrome, the IMAGE dialog box will display. If the bitmap is colored, the COLOR IMAGE dialog box will display, as described in the next section.

Color bitmap info

If a selected TIFF (or ungrouped PICT) bitmap contains any colors other than black, white, and shades of gray, choosing ELEMENT INFO… from the ELEMENT menu (⌘-I, ⬔-↖↖) will display the COLOR IMAGE dialog box, as shown in Figure 13.11. Unlike the full-featured IMAGE dialog, this dialog box offers no image-editing options. Here, you may control only the location and size of the graphic.

Two "Position" option boxes display the location of the lower left corner handle of the selected bitmap in relation to the ruler origin. Enter new values for these options to relocate the selected bitmap according to the lower left handle.

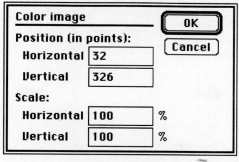

Figure 13.11: Option-double-click a color bitmap to display the Color image dialog box.

The two "Scale" option boxes list the extent to which the selected bitmap has been reduced or enlarged, measured as a percentage of its original size. Enter any value below 100% in one of these options to reduce the width or height; enter a value greater than 100% to increase the width or height. Note that these option boxes will record the results of scaling the bitmap, whether by OPTION-dragging a corner handle with the arrow tool or by some other means. Enter 100% into both the "Horizontal" and "Vertical" option boxes to restore the bitmap to its original size.

FreeHand will print a color graphic as a gray-scale image to a monochrome printer. However, it provides no means for converting a color bitmap to gray-scale so that you can edit the gray values. This may be accomplished only by using a color paint program, such as Studio/32 or PixelPaint Professional, or an image editor, such as Adobe Photoshop or ColorStudio.

EPS info

If you choose ELEMENT INFO... (⌘-I, ⬙-❧❧) when an Encapsulated Post-Script graphic is selected, the EPS ELEMENT dialog box will display, as shown in Figure 13.12 on the next page. Again, you may control the location and size of the graphic only.

Two "Position" option boxes display the location of the lower left corner handle of the selected graphic in relation to the ruler origin. Enter new values for these options to relocate the selected graphic according to the lower left handle.

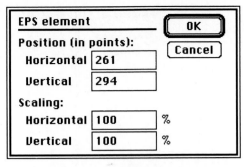

Figure 13.12: Option-double-click an imported
EPS graphic to display the EPS element dialog box.

The two "Scale" option boxes list the extent to which the selected graphic has been reduced or enlarged, measured as a percentage of its original size. Enter any value below 100% in one of these options to reduce the width or height; enter a value greater than 100% to increase the width or height. Note that these option boxes will also record the results of scaling the EPS graphic by dragging a corner handle with the arrow tool. Enter 100% into both the "Horizontal" and "Vertical" option boxes to restore the graphic to its original size.

Cropping imported graphics

Normally, when an application allows you to import graphics, you expect some kind of *cropping* feature, for deleting unwanted portions of the graphic. For example, after importing a scanned snapshot of your family, you might want to crop the photo tightly around their faces, as demonstrated in Figures 13.13 and 13.14.

FreeHand provides no specific cropping feature. However, you may crop imported images by creating a mask. Draw a rectangle or other path to represent the outline of the cropped image. Then position the imported image relative to the path, transfer it to the Clipboard using the CUT command (⌘-X), select the path, and choose PASTE INSIDE from the EDIT menu. The stroke of the path will act as the outline of the cropped graphic. For more information about masking, see the *Clipping paths* section of Chapter 9.

Figure 13.13: Great family, but too much picture. It might be more effective if we focused more attention on the faces and less on the background.

Figure 13.14: By pasting the image inside a rectangle, we can crop out undesirable portions of the photograph, leaving those gorgeous faces intact.

For more information about enhancing scanned images in FreeHand, check out the book *Drawing on the Macintosh*, also published by Business One Irwin, (800) 634-3966.

 This page is extremely self serving. First the author plugs his family, then he plugs one of his other books. If you're totally disgusted, feel free to rip this page out of the book.

Sorry, but we couldn't let an opportunity like that go by. There's so few times when we can beat book reviewers to the punch.

Linking graphic files

An illustration that contains a TIFF or EPS image must always be able to reference its original TIFF or EPS file in order to preview or to print the placed image successfully. Therefore, when you save an illustration, Free-Hand remembers the location of the original imported graphic file on disk. If you try to open an existing illustration after having moved its imported TIFF or EPS file to a different disk or folder, FreeHand will produce the alert box shown in Figure 13.15. This dialog asks if you want to locate your graphic file on disk. If you click Yes or press RETURN, a standard OPEN DOCUMENT dialog box will appear. Select the original TIFF or EPS file in the scrolling list and press RETURN. If you click the No button in the alert box or cancel out of the OPEN DOCUMENT dialog, the illustration will not preview at full resolution. If FreeHand cannot reference the graphic file on disk during the printing process, an imported TIFF image will print at low resolution; an imported EPS image will not print at all.

Figure 13.15: This alert box displays when FreeHand cannot locate the original TIFF or EPS file for an imported graphic.

Ungrouping PICT graphics

FreeHand imports PICT graphics as standard grouped objects. To edit the graphic, choose UNGROUP from the ELEMENT menu (⌘-U), then re-shape or transform individual objects in the graphic as desired. The quantity and complexity of the ungrouped paths will depend on the method used to produce them. For example, circles and arcs will convert as fluid Bézier curves, while free-form paths may convert as hundreds of tiny straight lines.

Exporting an illustration

Images created in FreeHand 3.0 may be used in any Macintosh or PC application that supports the EPS format. In this way, an illustration may become part of a full-fledged document, such as a newsletter, flyer, or catalog, or part of a video or on-screen presentation.

Exporting an EPS file

To store an illustration in the Encapsulated PostScript format, choose the EXPORT… command from the FILE menu. The EXPORT dialog box shown in Figure 13.16 will display.

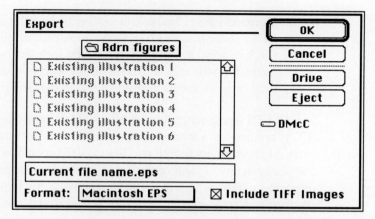

Figure 13.16: The Export dialog box allows you to export the current illustration as an EPS document for use in another Macintosh or PC application.

The file name for the current illustration will appear in the option box directly below the scrolling list, followed by the extension ".eps." Edit the file name as you wish, using up to 32 characters.

At the bottom of the dialog box, the "Format" pop-up menu allows you determine the PICT preview to be included with the current EPS file. It includes the following options:

- **Macintosh EPS**. Choose this option to save the illustration as an EPS file with a PICT screen preview for use in any Macintosh program that supports the EPS format. These include PageMaker, QuarkXPress, Adobe Illustrator, and FreeHand itself.

- **MS-DOS EPS**. Choose this option to save the illustration as an EPS file with a TIFF PC preview for use in any PC program that supports the EPS format. These include PC PageMaker, Ventura Publisher, Corel Draw, and several others. You may not place an image into a FreeHand 3.0 illustration if the image was exported in this format.

- **Generic EPS**. Choose this option to save the illustration with an EPS header in order to import it into any application that supports the EPS format. No preview will be included with the illustration; instead, it will appear as a box inset with two diagonal lines or a gray box on screen. However, the image will print correctly.

All EPS documents created by FreeHand contain *Open Press Interface* (OPI) comments. Developed by Aldus for outputting to ultra-high-end prepress systems, such Hell and Scitex, OPI specifications communicate the size, placement, and cropping of an illustration, as well as that of imported graphics. You may then manipulate the illustration using a prepress system to create four-color, professional-quality output.

Exporting illustrations with placed TIFF graphics

If the illustration that you are exporting contains one or more TIFF images that have been imported using the PLACE… command, be sure to select the "Include TIFF Images" check box in the EXPORT dialog box. This option directs FreeHand to include a PostScript description of all imported TIFF graphics as part of the exported EPS file.

Note that selecting the "Include TIFF Images" option does not free FreeHand from requiring access to the original TIFF file when you open the illustration at some later time. However, it does ensure that an exported EPS file which contains one or more TIFF graphics will preview and print correctly from within another application, such as a page-composition or presentation program. If this option is *not* selected when exporting an EPS file, any placed TIFF graphic will appear on screen but will not print at full resolution.

Use the DRIVE and EJECT buttons and the folder bar to determine a location for the exported file. Click OK or press RETURN to complete the export operation.

FreeHand will allow you to place EPS files that were previously created in FreeHand, but you may not open them or perform detailed manipulations such as reshaping. Also, Freehand will not prompt you to update as EPS file when closing the illustration or quitting FreeHand. Therefore, always be sure to also save your illustrations to disk using the SAVE command (⌘-S).

Drawing an export boundary

When FreeHand creates an EPS file, it automatically shrinks the size of the image to the exact boundaries of the objects in the illustration. For example, suppose that you create a 3-inch-by-4-inch image on a letter-sized page. When you save the illustration, FreeHand saves the page size information. But when you export the image for use in another application, FreeHand is interested only in the image itself. After all, you don't want to import an 8½-by-11-inch drawing into PageMaker when the graphic consumes only one-quarter of the drawing area. Therefore, the exported image will measure 3 inches by 4 inches, exactly matching the size of the exported image.

More often than not, FreeHand determines the size of an EPS file correctly. Sometimes, however, FreeHand may crop a graphic a bit too drastically. The casualties are usually strokes. The edges of heavy outlines may be sliced off or a mitered join may disappear.

To prevent the loss of strokes around the edges of an exported image, or simply to create a margin around an image, draw a rectangle that completely surrounds your artwork. While the rectangle remains selected, choose both REMOVE FILL and REMOVE LINE from the ATTRIBUTES menu. The rectangle will neither preview nor print, but it will affect the size of the exported EPS file.

Exporting a PICT file

FreeHand also allows you to create a PICT representation of an illustration via the Macintosh Clipboard, for use in programs, such as Microsoft Word and WriteNow, that do not support the EPS format. The following procedure explains how to export a PICT file:

1. Select the portion of the current illustration that you wish to transfer to another application.

2. Press the OPTION key and choose the COPY command from the EDIT menu (⌘-⌥-C). Pressing OPTION while choosing COPY writes a PostScript definition of the selection to the Clipboard along with the selected objects. The operation may take a few minutes to complete.

3. Switch to the other application.

   a. If you are using the standard Macintosh Finder, choose QUIT from the paint program FILE menu (⌘-Q). Then launch the desired application by double-clicking it at the Finder level. Open an existing document or create a new one.

   b. If you are working under MultiFinder and the other application is currently running, click the application icon in the far right corner of the menu bar until the other application comes to front, or choose its icon from the list of running applications in the APPLE menu.

3. Open a file or create a new file and choose PASTE from the EDIT menu (⌘-V). The selected template image will display in the current document window.

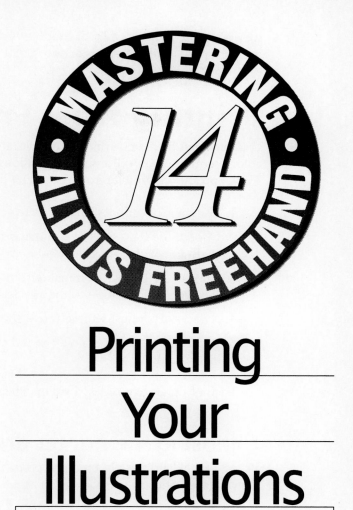

Printing Your Illustrations

FreeHand describes every text block and graphic object in an illustration as a combination of mathematically defined points and segments. This pure-math model allows FreeHand to translate the illustration to various hardware devices, regardless of device resolution. On a day-to-day basis, the primary display device is your monitor. However, finished illustrations are best displayed on a page printed from a high-resolution output device. In this chapter,

501

we discuss the printing of FreeHand 3.0 files, including black-and-white standard prints, color composite prints, and color separations.

Printing from FreeHand

You may print black-and-white, gray-scale, and color composites (using a color laser printer) as well as color separations directly from inside the Free-Hand application. Printing from Aldus FreeHand is a four-step process:

1. Use the Chooser desk accessory to select the desired printer driver.

2. Choose the PAGE SETUP... command from the FILE menu if directed to do so when closing the Chooser.

3. Choose the PRINT... command from the FILE menu (⌘-P) to print the current illustration to the selected output device.

4. If necessary, adjust settings inside the PRINT OPTIONS dialog box.

5. Return to the PRINT dialog box and click OK to initiate the printing operation.

Each of these steps is described in detail in the following sections.

Choosing the printer driver

Because FreeHand was programmed primarily as a PostScript-language drawing application, it provides the most reliable results when printing to a PostScript-compatible output device. Although you may print an illustration to a QuickDraw printer, such as the ImageWriter, LaserWriter SC, or HP LaserJet, many elements—most notably halftone screens and text effects—will print as low-resolution bitmaps, exactly as they appear on screen. Custom fills and strokes will not output at all to a non-PostScript device.

To select a printer, choose the CHOOSER from the list of desk accessories from the APPLE menu. The Chooser desk accessory will appear, as shown in Figure 14.01. One or more *printer drivers* display on the left side of the window. Printer drivers help the current application translate the contents of a printed file to a specific variety of output device. Click on the icon labeled "LaserWriter" if you intend to print to a PostScript-compatible printer. This allows you to prepare your illustration to be printed to a PostScript printer even if no such printer is currently hooked

up to your Mac. If your computer is networked to one or more Post-
Script output devices, select the desired printer from the "Select a Laser-
Writer" list on the right-hand side of the Chooser window. Then click the
close box to return to the FreeHand desktop.

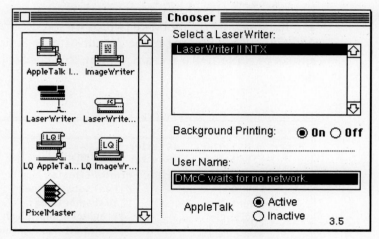

Figure 14.01: Use the Chooser desk accessory to select
the LaserWriter printer driver.

Setting up the page

If the LaserWriter driver was not selected the last time you accessed the
Chooser, an alert box will display upon selecting the driver icon, as shown
in Figure 14.02, directing you to confirm the new driver with FreeHand.

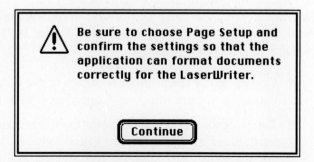

Figure 14.02: This alert box will display if you change
the printer driver.

If the alert box shown in Figure 14.02 displays, you will want to choose the Page Setup… command from the File menu when you return to the FreeHand illustration window. Otherwise, you can skip this step.

Choosing the Page Setup… command displays the LaserWriter Page Setup dialog box shown in Figure 14.03. Since every option in this dialog box that affects PostScript printing is duplicated in the LaserWriter Print and Print options dialog boxes (which we will describe shortly), there is no point in changing any of the default settings. Simply click OK or press return to confirm that you are printing to a PostScript-compatible output device.

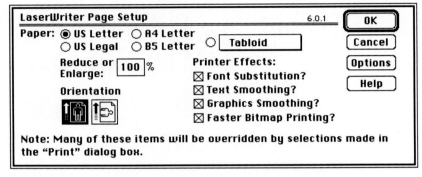

Figure 14.03: All options in the LaserWriter Page Setup dialog box that affect high-resolution printing are overridden by options in other printing-related dialog boxes.

Printing pages

To initiate the printing process, choose the Print… command from the File menu (⌘-P). An enhanced version of the standard LaserWriter Print dialog box will display, as shown in Figure 14.04. This dialog box contains the following options:

- **Copies**. Enter the number of copies of the current illustration that you want to print into the "Copies" option box.

- **Pages**. Since a FreeHand illustration is never more than one page long, FreeHand ignores the "Pages" options. We recommend that you leave the "All" radio button selected, as it is by default.

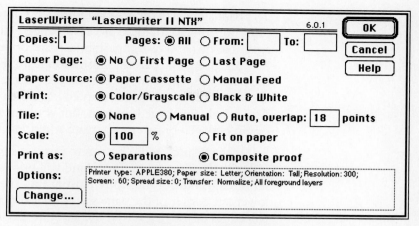

Figure 14.04: The LaserWriter Print dialog box allows you to print an illustration to a PostScript-compatible output device. It also provides access to the Print options dialog box.

- **Cover Page**. These radio buttons allow you to print an extra page that lists the user name, application, document name, date, time, and printer for the current job. The cover page may precede or follow the illustration page.

- **Paper Source**. If you want to print your illustration on a letterhead or other special piece of paper, select the "Manual Feed" radio button. Your laser printer will display a manual feed light directing you to insert the special paper. The "Paper Source" options are ignored when printing to a color laser printer or to an imagesetter or other film-based output device.

- **Print**. If you are using LaserWriter driver 6.0 (included in the Apple Color folder of the Macintosh Printing Tools disk for System 6.0.4 and later), two "Print" radio buttons appear in the middle of the LASERWRITER PRINT dialog box: "Color/Grayscale" and "Black & White." These options affect the printing of PICT images only and are ignored when printing PostScript illustrations from Aldus FreeHand.

- **Tile**. In the best of all possible worlds, the paper size listed in the dotted "Options" box at the bottom of the LASERWRITER PRINT dialog box should exactly match the current page size (specified using the "Page size" option in the DOCUMENT SETUP dialog box). However, since most laser printers cannot accommodate pages wider than 8½ inches, this is not always possible.

To proof large artwork to a laser printer, you may *tile* it; that is, print portions to multiple pieces of paper, which you may later reassemble by hand using traditional paste-up techniques. Selecting "None" prints the current illustration from the lower left corner of the page size. Only one page is output. Select "Manual" to align the lower left corner of the printed page with the ruler origin. Again, only one page is output, but you may reposition the ruler origin between printouts to create additional tiles.

Select the "Auto" radio button to instruct FreeHand to automatically tile the illustration. FreeHand will print as many pages as are required to output the entire illustration. The first tile begins at the lower left corner of the page size. Other tiles overlap the right and top edges of the first tile by the amount specified in the "Auto, overlap" option box.

- **Scale**. Enter a value into the percentage option box to enlarge or reduce the size at which the current illustration prints. Reductions may be as small as 10% and enlargements as large as 1000%. If you specify a percentage that expands the illustration beyond the current paper size, you will have to tile the illustration, as described above.

  If your illustration is larger than the current paper size, select the "Fit on paper" radio button to create a reduced version of your artwork. FreeHand will automatically calculate the exact reduction necessary to fit the entire illustration on a single sheet of paper. Because this option sacrifices resolution in favor of convenience, use it only when creating proofs or thumbnails.

- **Print as**. These options determine whether the colors in your illustration print separately—one color per page—or all on the same page. Selected by default, "Composite proof" prints the entire illustration on one page. If you are printing a color illustration to a monochrome output device, gray values will be used to represent colors, as on a black-and-white television. A color illustration output to a color printer will produce a *color composite*, a print that contains all colors used in the current illustration.

  Select "Separations" when you want to print each color on its own page. FreeHand outputs a page for each of the four process colors—cyan, magenta, yellow, and black—as well as each spot color used in the current illustration. Tints are printed on the same page as their parent color. Use the scrolling color list at the bottom of the PRINT OPTIONS dialog box (discussed in the next section) to specify which colors print and the screen angle of each color.

The dotted "Options" box at the bottom of the LASERWRITER PRINT dialog box lists a printer abbreviation, the current paper size and orientation, the resolution of the output device, the default screen frequency, and so on. All these settings may be altered by clicking the CHANGE... button, which will display the PRINT OPTIONS dialog box shown in Figure 14.05. This dialog box is described in the following section.

Adjusting print options

Click the CHANGE... button in the LASERWRITER PRINT dialog box to display the PRINT OPTIONS dialog box, shown in Figure 14.05. As you can see, this dialog box contains a ton of options, more than any other FreeHand dialog. However, all can be extremely useful when printing anything from proofs to final separations. The most simple options are duplicates of those normally associated with the LASERWRITER PAGE SETUP dialog box. Others control the printing of colors and layers.

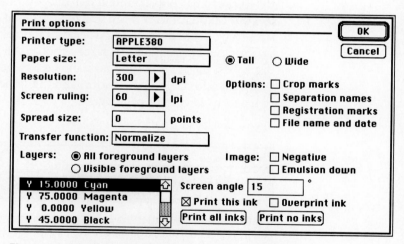

Figure 14.05: Click the Change... button to display the Print options dialog box, which allows you to adjust various options specific to printing in FreeHand.

To permanently alter the default settings inside the PRINT OPTIONS dialog box, adjust the options as desired, click OK, then click CANCEL in the LASERWRITER PRINT dialog box to return to the illustration window. Save the illustration over the existing Aldus FreeHand Defaults file, as described in the *Changing defaults* section of Chapter 3.

The options in the PRINT OPTIONS dialog box include the following:

- **Printer type**. Click and hold on the "Printer type" pop-up menu to choose the *PostScript printer description* (PPD) file that corresponds to the intended output device. PPD files reside in a PPD folder, which may reside in the folder containing the FreeHand application or in the Aldus folder inside the System folder. Each PPD file is named for the printer model it describes. For example, *LWNTX* is an abbreviation for the LaserWriter NTX. Some PPD files have numbers following the printer name. These numbers indicate the specific version of the PostScript ROM chips built into the output device. It is important to use the correct PPD file for your output device in order to properly output composite and color separations. If you do not have a PPD file corresponding to your printer ROM, contact Aldus or the printer manufacturer for information on obtaining the correct PPD file.

- **Paper size**. Based on information contained in the selected PPD file, the "Paper size" pop-up menu lists the page sizes that can be printed by your output device. If the selected printer allows custom page sizes to be defined—as in the case of a Linotronic, Compugraphic, or Varityper imagesetter—you may choose the "Other…" option to display the PAPER SIZE dialog box, shown in Figure 14.06. The default values for the "Size" (width) and "By" (height) options are the dimensions of current page size.

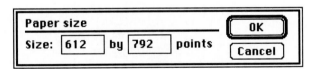

Figure 14.06: The Paper Size dialog box allows you to specify a custom page size.

If a "Transverse" suffix follows an option in the "Paper size" pop-up menu—"Letter.Transverse," for example—FreeHand rotates the page size relative to the paper or film on which it is to be printed. This is most commonly used when printing on imagesetters, which use long rolls of paper or film. The default positioning for any page on a PostScript printer places the long edge of the page parallel to the long edge of the paper. In most cases this is correct, but when printing to an imagesetter you can usually reduce paper or film waste by setting pages *transverse*; that is, with the short edges of the page parallel to the long edges of the paper.

An "Extra" suffix adds an inch to both the horizontal and vertical dimensions of the page size, allowing room for margin notes (discussed on page 511). For example, "Letter. Extra" measures 9½ by 12 inches.

The "Tall" and "Wide" radio buttons to the right of the "Paper size" pop-up menu control the orientation of the illustration inside the paper size. By default, this option will match the "Orientation" setting in the DOCUMENT SETUP dialog box.

● **Resolution.** Click and hold on the right-pointing arrowhead to display a pop-up menu offering options that control the *resolution* (the number of pixels printed per linear inch) of the output device. Resolution is measured in *dots per inch*, or *dpi*, with "dots" being device pixels. For example, the default resolution for an Apple LaserWriter is 300 dpi. If the "Screen ruling" value is not compatible with the current "Resolution" value, the arrowhead icon will appear dimmed. Choose another option from the "Screen ruling" pop-up menu to make the "Resolution" pop-up menu available again.

You may also enter any value from 72 to 5080 into the "Resolution" option box. Note that this value corresponds directly to the "Target printer resolution" option in the DOCUMENT SETUP dialog box. Changing the resolution setting here will change the setting in the DOCUMENT SETUP dialog box, and vice versa.

Don't ever use the "Resolution" option in the PRINT OPTIONS dialog box. (This may sound like strange advice, but you can end up doing more harm than good.) Instead, when you create a new illustration, enter a value into the "Target printer resolution" option in the DOCUMENT SETUP dialog box that matches the resolution of your *final* output device. When printing proofs to lower-resolution printers, choose the correct PPD file from the "Printer type" pop-up menu in the PRINT OPTIONS dialog box, but leave the "Resolution" value unaltered. Since the resolution of most laser printers and other proofing devices is fixed, the "Resolution" value will be ignored and the "Target printer resolution" value—which controls the scaling of imported bitmaps as well as the automatic path-breaking feature—will remain intact.

- **Screen ruling**. Click and hold on the right-pointing arrowhead to display a pop-up menu offering options that control the *screen frequency* (the number of *halftone cells* per linear inch) of the output device. Halftone cells are the dots used to represent gray values and tints. Frequency is measured in *lines per inch*, or *lpi*. For example, the default screen frequency for an Apple LaserWriter is 60 lpi. You may also enter any value from 4 to 300 in the "Screen ruling" option box. If the "Resolution" value is not compatible with the current "Screen ruling" value, the arrowhead icon will appear dimmed. Choose another option from the "Resolution" pop-up menu to make the "Screen ruling" pop-up menu available again.

  For more information about the relationship between resolution and screen frequency, refer to the *Halftone screens* section later in this chapter.

- **Spread size**. Applicable to spot-color separations only, this value controls the amount by which basic fills and strokes in the current illustration are thickened in order to prevent gaps between colors. Regardless of exactly how an illustration is output, spot colors on different separations may not meet with each other precisely, resulting in hairline gaps between colors. You can hide this problem using a technique called *trapping*, in which different spot colors are forced to slightly overlap each other.

  The cover of this book is a good example of the itsy-bitsy problems that may occur if you *don't* use trapping. Notice that many thin white lines occur between colors. Some of these gaps—those around the book title, for example—are intentional. However, the tiny gaps are not. Despite the fact that the cover was created and output using some of the best desktop technology available, trapping was not used. The result is minute gaps. (Remember the story of the *Princess and the Pea*? The test of a true, pure-blooded princess was whether she could feel a tiny pea under her mattress. Similarly, the test of a true, morbidly fastidious designer is whether you notice tiny gaps in registration in spot-color artwork. If you can't, you're just a normal, well-adjusted human being.)

  To compensate for slight variances in registration, enter a small value—0.01 to 2 points—into the "Spread size" option box. FreeHand will print an outline in the specified line weight around every object filled with a basic spot color. Thin outlines will also be added to both sides of every basic stroke.

The "Spread size" value does *not* affect patterned or custom fills or strokes, tiled or gradient fills, or objects filled or stroked with process colors or overprinting spot colors.

• **Transfer function.** Click and hold on the "Transfer function" pop-up menu to choose from three options—"Default," "Normalize," and "Posterize"—each of which controls the lightness and darkness of gray values and tints printed from FreeHand. Choose "Default" to bypass special instructions included in the current PPD file and rely on the default screen settings used by the current output device. Unfortunately, different printers render screens differently. A light tint printed from a typical laser printer, for example, is darker than the same tint printed from an imagesetter. To help eliminate this incongruity, choose the "Normalize" option, which accesses special instructions from the PPD file, making screens printed from a low-resolution output device more accurately match those printed from a high-end imagesetter.

Choose "Posterize" to remap tints to one of four screen values—100%, 67%, 33%, or 0% (white). Transitions between tints are abrupt rather than smooth, ideal for artwork that you later intend to photocopy or submit to some other low-quality printing process. For an example of a posterized image, see Figure 13.09 (back on page 491).

• **Options.** Each of the four "Options" check boxes that appear on the right-hand side of the Print options dialog box controls the printing of *margin notes* around the edges of your illustration.

Select "Crop marks" to print eight hairline *crop marks*, which mark the four corners of an illustration. When printing to a Linotronic 100 imagesetter, for example, all illustrations are printed on pages 12 inches wide, regardless of their actual size. When you have the illustration commercially reproduced, the printer will want to know the dimensions of the final paper size and how the illustration should be positioned on the final page. Crop marks specify the boundaries of the reproduced page and the position of your artwork relative to these boundaries.

Pantone 164 CV

Select "Separation names" to print the name of the current separation color in the lower left corner, just outside the page size. If you are printing a black-and-white or color composite, FreeHand outputs the word *Composite*.

Drawing No.1   4/1/90

Select "Registration marks" to print three *registration crosshairs*—one centered along the top of the illustration, one centered along the bottom, and a third along the lower right edge of the page—which are used to align separations. If the current print is a black-and-white or color composite, registration marks are not necessary. However, if you are printing separations, they are absolutely imperative, since they provide the only reliable means for ensuring exact registration of different process and spot colors during the commercial printing process.

Select "File name and date" to print the file name and the date on which you last saved the current illustration in the upper left corner, just outside the page size. Use this option to avoid the which-version-is-which confusion that often accompanies the creation of electronic documents.

All margin notes print outside the area consumed by the page size and bleed size, as specified in the DOCUMENT SETUP dialog box. Therefore, be sure to choose a "Paper size" option that is larger than the page size and bleed added together; otherwise, your margin notes will not print. The "Extra" paper sizes are especially useful for this purpose. For example, if the current illustration is set on a letter-sized page, choose "Letter.Extra" from the "Paper size" pop-up menu.

All margin notes will be used by the commercial printer reproducing your illustration, so be sure that they are not removed when trimming excess paper or film from your printed separation.

● **Image**. The two "Image" check boxes control the output of an illustration to film or plates.

Select "Negative" to change all blacks to white (or transparent) and whites to black. For example, 100% black becomes white, 40% black becomes 60% black, 20% black becomes 80% black. As a general rule, do *not* select this option when printing to paper; select "Negative" only when printing to film. Be sure to confirm your selection with your commercial printer.

Select "Emulsion down" to flip the objects in an illustration relative to photosensitive paper or film. The option name refers to the orientation of an image relative to the emulsion side of a piece of film. When printing film negatives, you will probably want to select "Emulsion down"; when printing on paper, deselect the option to print the emulsion side up.

- **Layers**. Use the "Layers" radio buttons to specify which layers in the current illustration will print. Select "All foreground layers" to print all layers in the LAYERS palette that appear above the dotted line (except "Guides," which never prints). Select "Visible foreground layers" to print only those layers above the dotted line that are preceded by check marks.

FreeHand does not allow you to output objects assigned to a background layer (any layer below the dotted line in the LAYERS palette). If you want to print a background image, drag the layer above the dotted line in the LAYERS palette, print the illustration, then drag the layer back to its original position. To print a single layer only, make sure the layer name appears above the dotted line, choose "All off" from the LAYERS pop-up menu, click in front of the layer name you want to print in order to display a check mark, then print the illustration after selecting the "Visible foreground layers" radio button in the PRINT OPTIONS dialog box.

- **Separation options**. All the options shown in Figure 14.07 work together to control the output of color separations. If you are printing a black-and-white or color composite, just click the PRINT ALL INKS button and press RETURN to close the dialog box.

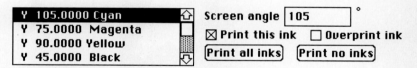

Figure 14.07: The scrolling color list contains the name of every process component and spot color contained in the current illustration. The options to the right of the list control the output of these colors.

Before discussing these options, we need to introduce a little color-separation theory: There are two ways in which a specific color can be professionally reproduced on a sheet of paper. Using the first method, *spot-color printing*, inks are pre-mixed to the desired color and then applied to the paper. A separation is printed for each spot color used in the illustration. Spot-color printing is usually used when only one or two colors (in addition to black) are used in an illustration. This printing method is neither exceedingly expensive nor technically demanding. Spot-color printing allows for precise colors to be selected and applied with perfect color consistency.

In the alternative printing method, *four-color process printing*, cyan, magenta, yellow, and black ink are blended in specific percentages to create a visual effect approximating a variety of desired colors. Four-color process printing is technically demanding and tends to be more expensive than spot-color printing.

Documents that are to be reproduced using the four-color process printing method require four color separations, one for each of the component inks that will be printed. Every colored object in an illustration is broken down into its component color separations, which conform to the original definition of the process color in FreeHand 3.0. For example, Figure 14.08 contains four color separations followed by a monochrome composite print of the image. The square field behind the star in the image is filled with a process color that is defined as 100% cyan, 60% magenta, 0% yellow, and 10% black. It therefore outputs as solid on the cyan separation, a 60% tint on the magenta separation, transparent on the yellow separation, and a 10% tint on the black separation. When these colors are printed in these percentages, the placement of the halftoned dots will visually simulate a deep blue.

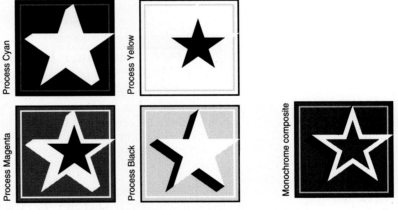

Figure 14.08: Four process-color separations (left) and a monochrome composite (right) of the same image.

It is possible in some cases to combine four-color process printing with spot-color printing. Although this option is more expensive than process printing alone and is subject to the capabilities of your commercial printer, it provides the advantages of both four-color process (many colors with few inks) and spot colors (precise colors) in one printed piece.

Many magazines, for example, are printed using four-color process colors for photos and artwork and spot colors for advertisements and logos.

Now to the options offered by FreeHand 3.0: The *scrolling color list* in the lower left corner of the PRINT OPTIONS dialog box contains the name of every spot color defined in the current illustration, including black. If any process color has been defined, the three non-black process colors—cyan, magenta, and yellow—will also display. No tint displays in the scrolling list. Rather, a tint is printed to the same separation as its parent color: 10% black prints to the black separation, 40% Pantone 164 prints to the Pantone 164 separation.

Each color name is preceded by a *Y* or *N* and a numeric value. The numeric value indicates the *screen angle*; that is, the angle at which halftone screens in the current separation will print. Traditionally, black screens are rotated 45°, magenta is printed at 75°, yellow is printed at 90°, and cyan is printed at 105°. However, the default angles in the scrolling color list may vary as determined by the selected PPD file. Screen angles are designed to prevent moiré patterns from occurring when primary colors overlap. All spot colors are printed at the same angle as black, since they are not intended to overlap. To change the screen angle for a color, click on the color to select it and enter a value between −360° and 360° in the "Screen angle" option box.

If an uppercase or lowercase *Y* (for *yes*) appears before a color name in the scrolling list, FreeHand will print a separation for this color when you select the "Separations" radio button in the LASER-WRITER PRINT dialog box. If a color name is preceded by an uppercase or lowercase *N* (for *no*), no separation will be printed for that color. To change whether or not a color is printed, select the color and then select or deselect the "Print this ink" check box.

If an uppercase *Y* or *N* appears before a color name, that color will *knock out* any colors that it overlaps, as described in the *Overprinting colors* section of Chapter 11. If a lowercase *y* or *n* precedes a color name, that color will overprint. To change whether or not a color overprints other colors that it may overlap in the current illustration, select the color and then select or deselect the "Overprint ink" check box. (Selecting the "Overprint" check box in the FILL AND LINE dialog box for a specific object overrides the deselection of the "Overprint ink" option for that object only.)

Click the PRINT ALL INKS button to display *Y*'s in front of all color names in the scrolling list. Click PRINT NO INKS to display *N*'s in front of all color names.

Click OK or press RETURN to close the PRINT OPTIONS dialog box and return to the LASERWRITER PRINT dialog box.

Initiating printing

Click the OK button or press RETURN in the LASERWRITER PRINT dialog box to initiate the printing process. The standard dialogs presented during any PostScript printing process will display. Press COMMAND-PERIOD to cancel the PRINT... command.

Printing to disk

When you print a FreeHand illustration to a PostScript printer, FreeHand *downloads* a PostScript-language text file to the printer. The printer reads the file and creates your illustration according to its instructions. Free-Hand also allows you to print an illustration to disk; that is, write the PostScript-language text file to your hard drive. You may then edit the file using a word processor or copy the file to a floppy disk. Printing to disk is used primarily when your artwork will be output to a PostScript printer from a Macintosh other than the one on which the illustration was created—at a service bureau, for example. The file is downloaded to the printer using a utility such as the Adobe Font Downloader, SendPS, or PSDownload, much as you would download a font file. This feature allows you to control the way in which an illustration is output, even if you don't own or have direct access to a PostScript printing device.

Printing to disk is easy. Prepare your artwork for printing as discussed in the previous sections of this chapter, defining all settings in the LASERWRITER PRINT and PRINT OPTIONS dialog boxes as desired. Immediately after clicking the OK button in the LASERWRITER PRINT dialog box, press and hold COM-MAND-F. Instead of the normal "Looking for LaserWriter" message, the print status dialog box will soon display the message "Creating PostScript0 file." This file will be saved as "PostScript0" to the same folder that contains the FreeHand application. You may then rename the file.

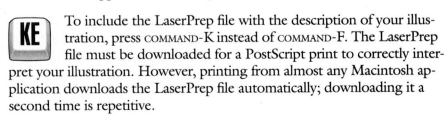 To include the LaserPrep file with the description of your illustration, press COMMAND-K instead of COMMAND-F. The LaserPrep file must be downloaded for a PostScript print to correctly interpret your illustration. However, printing from almost any Macintosh application downloads the LaserPrep file automatically; downloading it a second time is repetitive.

Note that the Apple PrintMonitor spooling utility will prevent the COMMAND-F or COMMAND-K operations from taking effect. Display the Chooser desk accessory, as described in the *Choosing the print driver* section at the beginning of this chapter. Then select "Off" from the "Background printing" radio buttons to deactivate the PrintMonitor utility. Other printer spoolers may also prevent the print-from-disk operation from taking place.

Special printing considerations

Every print job is not the same. Although the process itself is straightforward, your illustration may require special treatment not addressed by the PRINT... command. Alternatively, your illustration may seem fine, but complications may occur that prevent the printing process from completing successfully. In any of these cases, the following sections may be of assistance. They explain how to 1) alter settings for halftone screens, 2) use downloadable printer fonts, 3) avoid "limitcheck" errors, and 4) solve "out of memory" errors.

Halftone screens

In addition to allowing you to alter halftone screen frequencies from the PRINT OPTIONS dialog box, you may also control halftones on an object-by-object basis. However, to adjust the halftone settings for an object, it must be filled or stroked with a gray value, tint, or process color. This also includes all gradations and radial fills. Any 100% color—black, white, or a solid spot color—will not be affected, since such a color is printed as a solid ink; no halftoning is required.

To alter the halftone screen for a specific text block or graphic object, select the object you want to change and choose the HALFTONE SCREEN... command from the ATTRIBUTES menu. The HALFTONE SCREEN dialog box will display, as shown in Figure 14.09 on the following page. The options in this dialog box may be used to create special effects or to manipulate a document in preparation for some specific commercial printing process. Both the fill and stroke of the selected object will be affected by your settings.

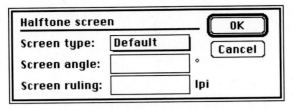

Figure 14.09: The Halftone screen dialog box allows you to alter the halftone settings for a selected text block or graphic object.

Time for some more background: The whole idea behind printing is to use as few inks as possible to create the appearance of a wide variety of colors. For example, suppose you want to print a picture of a pink flamingo wearing a red bow tie. Your printer could print the flamingos in one pass using pink ink, let that color dry, then load the red ink and print all the bow ties. But why go to all that trouble? After all, pink is just a lighter shade of red. Why not imitate the pink by lightening the red ink? Well, that's easy for you to say; but, unfortunately, printing devices don't do lighter shades of colors. They recognize only solid color (100%) and the absence of color (0%). So how do you print the 30% shade of red necessary to represent pink?

The answer is *halftoning*. Hundreds of tiny dots of ink are laid down on a page. Because the dots are so small, your eyes cannot quite focus on them. Instead, the dots appear to blend with the white background of the page to create a lighter shade of a color. Figure 14.10 shows a detail of the flamingo enlarged to display the individual dots.

The dots in a tint are arranged into a grid of *halftone cells*, much like a checkerboard. The dots grow and shrink inside their cells to emulate different shades of color. Large dots create dark tints; small dots create light tints. Each pixel in your PostScript printer belongs to one of the halftone cells and each halftone cell comprises some number of pixels. As an example, consider the Apple LaserWriter: By default, it prints 60 halftone cells per linear inch. Since the resolution of the LaserWriter is 300 pixels per linear inch, each halftone cell must measure five pixels wide by five pixels tall ($300 \div 60 = 5$), for a total of 25 pixels per cell. If all pixels in a cell are turned off, the cell appears white; all pixels turned on produces black; any number between 0 and 25 produces a particular shade of gray. A unique tint can be created by turning on each of 0 through 25 pixels, for a total of 26 gray values, as demonstrated in Figure 14.11.

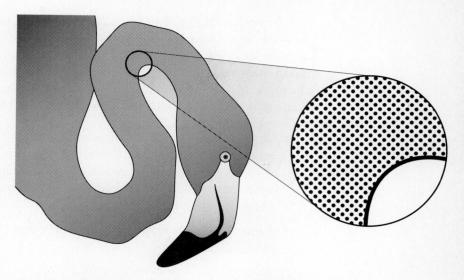

Figure 14.10: A tint or gray value is made up of hundreds of tiny dots called halftone cells, as demonstrated by the enlarged detail on the right.

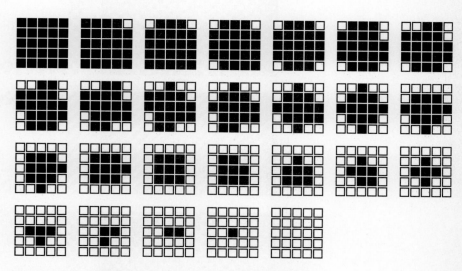

Figure 14.11: A five-by-five-pixel halftone cell with from 25 to 0 of its pixels activated. Each cell represents a unique gray value or tint from 100% to 0%.

The options in the HALFTONE SCREEN dialog box allow you to alter the shape, angle, and size of every halftone cell used to represent gray values, tints, and process colors in the current selection. The "Screen type" pop-up menu determines the *screen function*, which is the pattern with which FreeHand simulates gray values and tints. You may choose from three options, each of which is displayed in Figure 14.12:

- **Default**. Accepts the default screen function produced by the current output device. Most PostScript devices rely on squarish black dots against a white background to simulate light tints, squarish white dots against a black background to simulate dark tints, and a checkerboard effect to simulate medium tint levels.

- **Line**. Represents gray values and tints using a series of parallel straight lines.

- **Round dot**. Represents gray values and tints using a pattern of perfectly circular dots.

Figure 14.12: The default screen function (top), line function (middle), and round-dot function (bottom) applied to the fill and stroke of two objects. The frequency has been reduced to 12 lpi.

The value in the "Screen angle" option box determines the *screen angle*, which is the orientation of the current pattern of halftone cells. By default, this grid is rotated 45° with respect to the printed page. To rotate the grid to some other angle, enter a value between 0° and 360° into the "Screen angle" option box. Examples are shown in Figure 14.13.

Figure 14.13: Screens angled 0° (top), 30° (middle), and 60° (bottom) applied to the fill and stroke of two objects.

The value in the "Screen ruling" option box determines the *screen frequency*, which is the number of halftone cells that print per linear inch. Frequency is measured in *lines per inch*, or *lpi*. If no value appears in this option box, FreeHand accepts the default screen frequency for the current output device. Examples include 60 lpi for the Apple LaserWriter and 120 lpi for the Linotronic 300. Any value from 4 to 300 lpi is permitted by FreeHand.

As displayed in Figure 14.14, higher screen frequency values result in smoother-looking gray values and tints. However, raising the frequency also decreases the number of gray values a printer can render, because it decreases the size of each halftone cell, thus decreasing the number of pixels per cell. Therefore, when changing the "Screen ruling" value, consider how your change affects the number of gray values printable by the current output device.

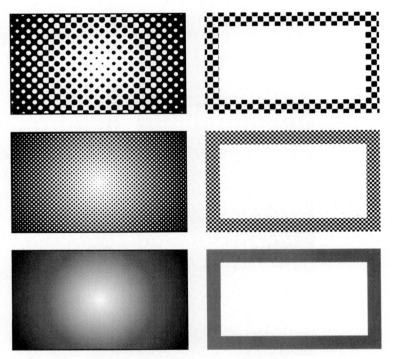

Figure 14.14: Screen frequencies of 12 lpi (top), 30 lpi (middle), and 90 lpi (bottom).

Manipulations performed in the HALFTONE SCREEN dialog box affect printing only; they do *not* in any way affect the manner in which objects display in the preview or keyline mode.

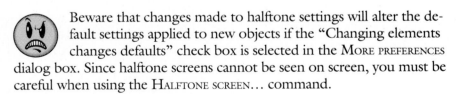 Beware that changes made to halftone settings will alter the default settings applied to new objects if the "Changing elements changes defaults" check box is selected in the MORE PREFERENCES dialog box. Since halftone screens cannot be seen on screen, you must be careful when using the HALFTONE SCREEN... command.

Using downloadable fonts

If you have used fonts in your artwork that are not resident in your printer or on the printer's hard disk, you must make sure that those fonts either are downloaded manually to the printer's RAM or its hard disk or are available for automatic downloading during printing.

If your printer has a hard disk, printer fonts should be kept on the disk as long as there is space for them. Depending on the size of your hard disk and the amount of disk space available, the disk should hold anywhere from 30 and 300 fonts. Fonts can be accessed very conveniently from the printer's hard disk and perform much faster than fonts downloaded automatically during printing.

When using fonts from the Adobe Type Library, be sure to use the Font Downloader from Adobe Systems, (415) 961-4400, to install the fonts on your hard disk. Due to Adobe's proprietary techniques, their fonts can be accessed and used much more quickly when installed in this way. The Adobe Font Downloader also allows you to check which fonts are currently stored on the hard disk and to manually download fonts to RAM for temporary use.

Fonts that will be used repeatedly should be downloaded manually into RAM if they are not already downloaded onto the printer's hard disk. While the process of downloading fonts manually is time consuming, any time spent will be offset by the increased printing speed if the downloaded fonts are used more than four or five times. Available printer RAM, however, is a major constraint in deciding how many fonts can be downloaded manually.

In general, printers that have only a few hundred kilobytes of available RAM, such as the Apple LaserWriter Plus, can hold only two or three manually downloaded fonts at a time. Printers having 2Mb of RAM, like the Apple LaserWriter II NTX, can hold six or more fonts, and printers having 3Mb of RAM can hold as many as a dozen fonts. When a printer is holding its maximum number of downloaded fonts, it cannot accept any more fonts, whether downloaded manually or automatically. Therefore, before downloading a font, consider not only how many times it will be used, but also how many other downloadable fonts will be used in the same printing session.

Suppose, for example that you intend to print a number of illustrations that contain different downloadable fonts within a few hours. You will save time by allowing the required fonts to download automatically rather than downloading the fonts manually and restarting the printer every time you print a different illustration. Of course, if your printer offers sufficient memory, you may be able to download all fonts at once.

When deciding on your strategy regarding printer fonts, do not forget the requirements of the other users of your laser printer. In a networked situation, fonts should not be downloaded manually unless your printer has adequate memory; a reasonable amount of working memory should be kept available for other users to print documents with automatically downloaded fonts.

If you do not have enough memory to manually download all the fonts that you expect to use repeatedly, or even all the fonts used in a particular illustration, a good strategy is to download the one or two fonts that you will be using most often.

Fonts should be allowed to automatically download whenever it is impossible or impractical to download them manually to hard disk or to RAM. Normally, printer fonts must reside in the System folder in order to be downloaded automatically, but several utilities—including the public-domain desk accessory Set Paths and the commercial applications Suitcase and MasterJuggler—instruct FreeHand to download fonts from any available disk or folder.

Splitting long paths

You may encounter several errors when printing an illustration. One of the most common is the "limitcheck" error, which results from a limitation in your printer's PostScript interpreter. If the number of points in the mathematical representation of a path exceeds this limitation, the illustration will not print successfully.

Unfortunately, the "points" used in this mathematical representation are not the points you used to define the object. Instead, they are calculated by the PostScript interpreter during the printing process. When presented with a curve, the PostScript interpreter has to plot hundreds of tiny straight lines to create the most accurate rendering possible. So rather than drawing a perfect curve, your printer creates a many-sided polygon whose exact number of sides is determined by a device-dependent variable known as *flatness*. The default flatness for the Apple LaserWriter is 1.0 device pixel, or $\frac{1}{300}$ inch. The center of any tiny side of the polygon rendering may be at most $\frac{1}{300}$ inch from the farthest X,Y-coordinate of the actual mathematical curve, as demonstrated by Figure 14.15.

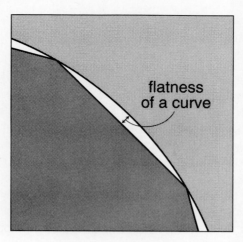

Figure 14.15: The flatness of a curve determines the greatest distance between any one of the tiny straight lines used to represent the curve and its true mathematical description.

Each tiny line in the polygon rendering is joined at a "point." If the number of "points" exceeds your printer's built-in "path" limit, an alert box will display, warning you that the printer has encountered a limit-check error, and the print job will be canceled. The "path" limit for the original LaserWriter was 1500, seemingly enough straight lines to imitate any curve. But every once in a while, you may create a curve that proves too much for the printer. For example, a standard signature contains several complex loops that might tax the limitations of the most advanced output device.

There are two ways to avoid limitcheck errors. The first and most preferred method is to enter the resolution for the *final* output device in the "Target printer resolution" option box in the DOCUMENT SETUP dialog box. The next time you print or export the current illustration, FreeHand will automatically break up every path that it considers to be at risk into several smaller paths. The integrity of your illustration will not be affected.

Unfortunately, FreeHand will continue to break up future paths unless you choose the DOCUMENT SETUP… command from the FILE menu and enter a new value for the "Target printer resolution" option. Also, there is no way to automatically reassemble paths that have been split. They must be joined back together manually if and when you decide to make alterations the illustration. And finally, FreeHand's automated path-splitting feature accounts only for the complexity of a path. It does not account for whether a path is filled with a complex tile pattern, which is the most likely cause of a "limitcheck" error.

If the automatic splitting technique does not solve your printing problem, you may use the "Flatness" value found in the RECTANGLE, ELLIPSE, PATH, and PATH/POINT dialog boxes. Select the geometric or free-form path that you think may be the culprit. Keep in mind that paths filled with tile patterns are the most likely candidates. Then choose the ELEMENT INFO... command from the ELEMENT menu (⌘-I, ⬚-↖↑) and enter a value between 0 and 100 in the "Flatness" option box. This value will increase the distance that a straight line may vary from the mathematical curve, as shown in Figure 14.15, thus reducing the risk of limitcheck errors. However, the affected path will also appear less smooth. Use the "Flatness" option only as a last resort.

Printing pattern tiles

As described in the previous section, tile patterns may cause limitcheck errors. But more often, they will cause "out of memory" errors, especially if several patterns are used in a single illustration. To accelerate the printing process, FreeHand downloads tiles to your printer's memory, much as if they were non-resident fonts. In this way, the printer may access tile definitions repeatedly throughout the printing of an illustration. However, if the current illustration contains too many tile patterns, or a single tile is too complex, the printer's memory may become full, in which case the print operation will be cancelled and an alert box will warn you that an out-of-memory error has occurred.

Out-of-memory errors are less common in high-resolution output devices, such as imagesetters, because these machines tend to include updated PostScript interpreters and have increased memory capacity. Therefore, you will most often encounter an out-of-memory error when proofing an illustration to an old-model LaserWriter or other low-memory device. Try any one of these techniques to remedy the problem:

- Change all typefaces in the current illustration to Times, Helvetica, or some other printer-resident font. In this way, FreeHand will not have to download both patterns and printer fonts.

- Print objects painted with dissimilar tile patterns in separate illustrations. Then use traditional paste-up techniques to combine the pages into a composite proof.

- Send all objects filled with pattern tiles to a separate layer, hide this layer by clicking its check mark in the LAYERS palette, then select the "Visible foreground layers" radio button in the PRINT OPTIONS dialog box during the printing process. This technique allows you to proof all portions of your illustration except objects filled with tile patterns.

When you print the final illustration to an imagesetter, it will probably print successfully because of the imagesetter's increased memory capacity. If the illustration still encounters an out-of-memory error, you will have to delete some patterns or resort to traditional paste-up techniques, as suggested in the second item of the list above.

Most service bureaus charge extra for printing a complex document that ties up an imagesetter for a long period of time. Tile patterns almost always complicate an illustration and increase printing time. Therefore, use masks and composite paths instead of patterns whenever possible.

Installing
Aldus
FreeHand

To use FreeHand 3.0, the on-line help system, Pantone colors, PostScript printer description files, and other related documents, you must *install* them onto your Macintosh computer's hard drive. The process is simple, and you have to install each file only once, not every time you want to operate the program. If FreeHand and its related files are already installed, you may begin using it as described in Chapter 3, *A Brief Tour of Aldus FreeHand 3.0.*

Taking stock

The Aldus FreeHand 3.0 package includes four 800K disks, which contain the FreeHand application and all accessory files. Each disk and its contents are listed below:

- **Disk 1**. The Aldus Installer/Utility program and controller file, as well as compressed versions of the Pantone colors, FreeHand filters, Aldus FreeHand defaults, and PPD files, along with several color template and tracing files.

- **Disk 2**. Part 1 of the FreeHand application file, compressed.

- **Disk 3**. Sample illustrations and tutorial files.

- **Disk 4**. Part 2 of the FreeHand application, the on-line help file, the CrayonLibrary clib, and the blend table and printer calibration files, all compressed. Also included are an electronic registration card and a keyboard equivalents file developed for use with the QuicKeys macros utility. If you own QuicKeys (not included with FreeHand), see the *Installing FreeHand macros* section later in this chapter for information on loading and using the Aldus FreeHand 3.0.KEYS file.

Hardware requirements

Before beginning any installation procedure, it is important that your Macintosh hardware configuration is complete and compatible with Aldus FreeHand 3.0. The following equipment is required:

- Macintosh Plus or later-model computer.

- 20 megabyte hard drive.

- 2 megabytes of RAM.

- Macintosh System version 6.0.3 or later.

- PostScript-compatible printer
  (optional, but highly recommended).

Keep in mind that this is the minimal configuration. A larger hard drive and more RAM will certainly work as well or better. If your computer lacks a hard drive or sufficient RAM, you will need to upgrade your hardware. Call your local computer dealer or discount house for more information. If your System Software is too old, you can obtain the newest System Software for a nominal fee from your Authorized Apple Dealer. If you do not own a PostScript printer, you can probably locate a service bureau in your area that will allow you to output your FreeHand files on their PostScript printer for a per-page charge.

The installation process

To use the Aldus Installer/Utility to install FreeHand onto your hard drive, power up your Macintosh as normal. If you use any anti-virus programs such as the Symantec Utilities' Shield Init or Symantec AntiVirus Macintosh (SAM) program, you may want to temporarily deactivate these, because the installation process will set them off. It is not required that you deactivate them, but it is a good idea.

Installing FreeHand

Insert Disk 1 and double-click on the Aldus Installer/Utility icon. After the startup screen displays and disappears, the ALDUS INSTALLER MAIN WINDOW dialog box will display, as shown in Figure A.01 on the following page. The dialog box contains three check boxes that allow you to select the files that you want to install:

- **Aldus FreeHand 3.0**. This option installs the FreeHand application, PPD files, and other related documents from Disks 1, 2, and 4.

- **Sample illustrations**. This option copies the contents of the Tracing Files folder from Disk 1 and the Sample Illustrations folder from Disk 3 to your hard drive. These documents include bit-mapped tracing files, sample clip art, and FreeHand illustrations.

- **Tutorial files**. This option copies the contents of the Tutorial Files folder from Disk 3 to your hard drive. These documents include illustrations used throughout tutorial exercises in the *Learning Aldus FreeHand 3.0* guide that accompanies the software.

To use Aldus FreeHand 3.0 and follow along with this book, select the "Aldus FreeHand 3.0" check box only. Sample illustrations and tutorial files are not required to learn or use FreeHand 3.0, and they take up much-needed disk space. (The sample illustrations alone require 1.7Mb.)

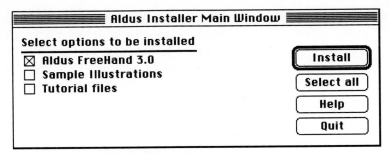

Figure A.01: The Aldus Installer Main Window dialog box
asks you to specify the files that you want to install.

After selecting the desired option(s) by clicking them or by using the
SELECT ALL button, click the INSTALL button or press RETURN to continue.
The PRINTER FILE INSTALLATION dialog box will next display, as shown in Figure A.02, asking you to select the printers that you will be using. Click on
the names of printers to which your artwork will be printed, including
those that are not attached directly to your Mac, such as the imagesetter
at the local service bureau. Each printer name corresponds to a *PostScript
printer description* (PPD) file, as described in Chapter 14. Press SHIFT and
then click to select multiple printer names or to deselect a selected printer.
Click the SELECT ALL button to select all PPD files.

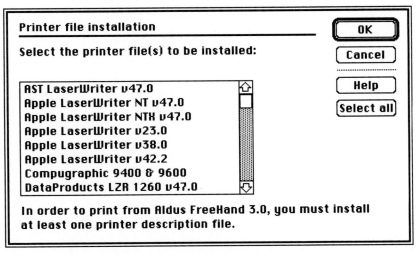

Figure A.02: The Printer file installation dialog box
displays a list of PostScript printer description files.

After selecting the desired PPD files, press RETURN to continue. If you are installing the FreeHand application, you will be presented with the PLEASE PERSONALIZE dialog box shown in Figure A.03. Here, you must personalize your copy of FreeHand by entering the appropriate information into the "Name," "Company," and "Serial number" option boxes. (It is not necessary to enter a company name in order to run the application.)

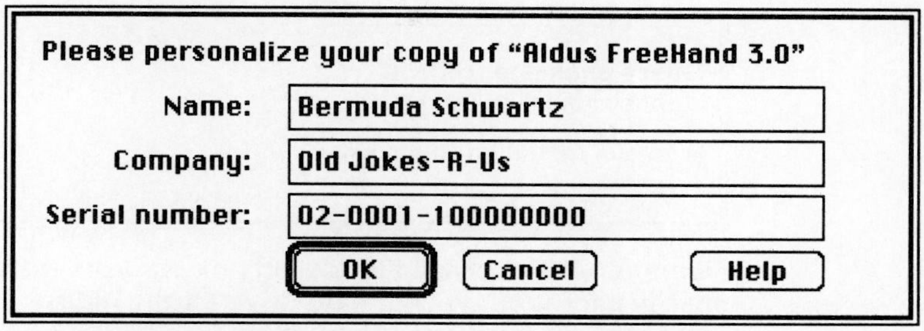

Please personalize your copy of "Aldus FreeHand 3.0"

Name: `Bermuda Schwartz`

Company: `Old Jokes-R-Us`

Serial number: `02-0001-100000000`

[OK] [Cancel] [Help]

Figure A.03: The Please personalize dialog box appears when installing the FreeHand application.

An alert box will display asking you to confirm the information just entered. Click OK to continue or click CHANGE to alter your name, company, or serial number. (All information is written to the installed version of the application. The contents of the original disks will not be personalized or altered in any way.)

The INSTALL FILES dialog box will display, asking you where you want to install the Aldus FreeHand 3.0 folder on your hard drive (see Figure A.04 on the next page). The folder name may be changed by entering a new name in the "Install in folder" option box. If your hard drive does not have enough free space to complete the installation, a message in the lower left corner will inform you of this problem. You will have to delete some other files from your hard disk before continuing. If the message "You can install on this disk" appears, you may continue.

After specifying a location and pressing RETURN, the *installation screen* will display, as shown in Figure A.05 on the next page. The horizontal bar fills with black to demonstrate how much of the installation process has been completed. Throughout the installation process, you may be requested to exchange disks. Do so as prompted.

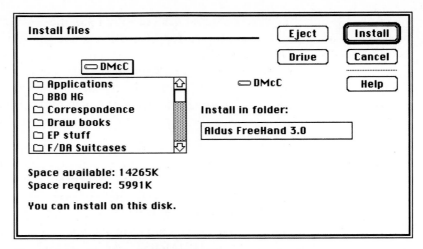

Figure A.04: The Install files dialog box requests that you specify a location on your hard drive for the Aldus FreeHand 3.0 folder and its contents.

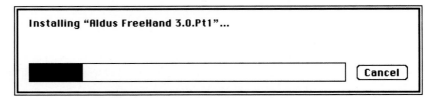

Figure A.05: The installation screen indicates how the installation process is progressing.

After FreeHand 3.0 has been installed successfully, the *assembly screen* will display, showing that the various files are being decompressed and assembled on your hard drive. Finally, an alert box will display, telling you that the installation procedure is complete. Press RETURN to close the alert box and return to the Finder. A new folder called *Aldus FreeHand 3.0* will exist at the location on your hard drive that you specified. This folder will contain the FreeHand 3.0 application as well as the several related files. The filters, defaults, and PPD files are copied to an Aldus folder in the System folder. If you can't locate a specific file, open the Aldus Installer History document inside a word processor or directly from the desktop using the TeachText utility (included with FreeHand). This document recounts all files copied during the installation process and lists their locations on your hard drive.

When you install FreeHand 3.0, the Aldus Install/Utility program copies itself to a Utility folder inside the Aldus folder in the System folder. This allows you to reinstall a specific file from an original FreeHand disk if the version on your hard drive goes bad or gets deleted. Simply double-click the compressed file on the original FreeHand disk. The installer utility will ask you to determine the location of the file, which is then decompressed and saved to the hard disk automatically.

Installing FreeHand macros

One of FreeHand's deficiencies when compared to other drawing programs is its lack of keyboard equivalents for common commands, such as PLACE..., SPLIT ELEMENT, ALIGN CENTER, and so on. Aldus has partially solved this problem by offering a set of external keyboard equivalents that may be used with QuicKeys 2, the popular macros utility distributed by CE Software, (515) 224-1995. A 30-day demonstration version of QuicKeys is included with FreeHand 3.0. If you like the program—we highly recommend it—it may be purchased for just under $100 through most mail order catalogs.

If you have already installed QuicKeys on your machine, skip to the next page. Otherwise, you may install the demo version of QuicKeys as follows: Insert the QuicKeys² Demo disk and double-click the Demo-QYInstall icon (the one that looks like a little truck). An installation screen will display. Click the INSTALL button or press RETURN to initiate to installation process. After the installation process has completed, restart your Mac to load the QuicKeys cdev. (If you use a init manager such as InitPicker or Aask, you may need to activate the QuicKeys cdev before restarting.) Having restarted, choose CONTROL PANEL from the APPLE (◉) menu. Scroll down to the QuicKeys icon and click on it. An alert box will display, telling you the date that the software will expire. After expiration, you may reinstall the QuicKeys demo utility without penalty using the DemoQKInstall program or, better yet, purchase a full-featured version.

QuicKeys is well worth the $100 investment. But if you were saving the money for something more important, like groceries, you can get around the 30-day expiration. Prior to launching DemoQKInstall, use the General cdev or the Alarm Clock DA to set the date ahead three or four years. Then follow the normal installation procedure described above. During installation, the QuicKeys demo records the current date and adds 30 days to determine the expiration date. After completing the installation, set the date back to the present day. Now QuicKeys won't expire for 30 days plus three or four years!

To use the special QuicKeys keyboard equivalents file provided with FreeHand, move the Aldus FreeHand 3.0.KEYS file (which is copied automatically to the Aldus FreeHand 3.0 folder when you install FreeHand) to the KeySets folder, which contains all macro files used by QuicKeys. The KeySets folder is located inside the QuicKeys folder, which is inside the Preferences folder, which is in the System folder.

QuicKeys will automatically load the keyboard equivalents file only if its name exactly matches the name of the application. Therefore, delete the *.KEYS* extension from the QuicKeys document so it reads simply *Aldus FreeHand 3.0*. Then launch the FreeHand application. Keyboard equivalents will take effect for the following menu commands:

⌘	command
⇧	shift
⌥	option
⌃	control
▥	on keypad
⎵	spacebar

Command or option	QuicKeys keystroke
Align center (ALIGNMENT pop-up)	⌘-⇧-C
Align left (ALIGNMENT pop-up)	⌘-⇧-L
Align right (ALIGNMENT pop-up)	⌘-⇧-R
Auto curvature (POINTS pop-up)	⌃-0 (CONTROL-ZERO)
Baseline shift…	⇧-⌃-B
Blend…	⌃-B
Bold (TYPE STYLE pop-up)	⌘-⇧-B
BoldItalic (TYPE STYLE pop-up)	⌘-⇧-⌥-B
Bring forward	⌘-⌥-F
Colors…	⌘-H
Connector point (POINTS pop-up)	⌃-▥4
Convert to paths	⌘-⇧-P
Corner point (POINTS pop-up)	⌃-▥7
Curve point (POINTS pop-up)	⌃-▥1
Cut contents	⌘-⌥-X
Document setup…	⌥-D
Export…	⌃-E
Guides	⌘-⇧-G
Halftone screen…	⌃-H
Horizontal scaling…	⌘-⇧-H
Italic (TYPE STYLE pop-up)	⌘-⇧-I
Justify (ALIGNMENT pop-up)	⌘-⇧-J
Lock	⌘-⇧-K

Command or option	QuicKeys keystroke
Paste inside	⌘-⌥-V
Place…	⌃-D
Plain (Type style pop-up)	⌘-⇧-␣
Send backward	⌘-⌥-B
Set note…	⌃-N
Spacing…	⇧-⌃-␣
Split element	⌘-⇧-X
Styles…	⌃-3
Toolbox	⌃-T
Unlock	⌘-⇧-U

⌘	command
⇧	shift
⌥	option
⌃	control
▣	on keypad
␣	spacebar

You may want to modify some keyboard equivalents. For example, the fact that pressing OPTION-D displays the DOCUMENT SETUP dialog box will prevent you from accessing the partial differential symbol (∂). Also, you will probably want to create keyboard equivalents of your own. The following exercise demonstrates how to create keyboard equivalents that access the PREFERENCES and MORE PREFERENCES dialog boxes:

1. Launch FreeHand if is not currently running.

2. Display the QuicKeys panel by choosing the "QuicKeys 2…" option from the QUICKEYS 2 pop-up under the APPLE menu or by pressing the keyboard equivalent (COMMAND-OPTION-RETURN, unless you've changed it). If an alert box displays, press RETURN to close it.

3. Choose "Aldus FreeHand 3.0" from the pop-up menu in the lower right corner of the panel. The QuicKeys keyboard equivalents provided with FreeHand 3.0 will display.

4. Choose the MENU/DA… command from the DEFINE menu along the top of the panel. Your cursor will change to a small menu (▭) and the message "Select an item from the menu" will display.

5. Use the menu cursor to choose the PREFERENCES… command from the FreeHand FILE menu. The QuicKeys MENU dialog box will display, requesting that you enter a keystroke. Press CONTROL-P or some other available keystroke, then click the OK button.

6. Now choose BUTTONS... from the QuicKeys DEFINE menu. The BUTTON dialog box will display. Enter *More...* (including ellipsis, which is accessed by pressing OPTION-SEMICOLON) into the "Name" option box. Then press TAB to enter the "Keystroke" option box and press CONTROL-M or some other available keystroke. Click the OK button to return to the QuicKeys panel.

7. You have now defined a keyboard equivalent for the PREFERENCES... command and for the MORE... button. To combine the two so that you may display the MORE PREFERENCES dialog box with one keystroke, choose SEQUENCE... from the QuicKeys DEFINE menu. The SEQUENCE dialog box will display. Here you may assign multiple operations to a single keyboard equivalent. Click the IMPORT button on the right side of the dialog box. A scrolling list of existing macros will appear in its place. Scroll down to the "Preferences..." menu item in the list and double-click it to copy the macro to the left-hand list, which contains items belonging to the current sequence. Next, scroll up to the "Move..." button item in the right-hand list and double-click it. Enter *More preferences* into the "Name" option box, press TAB, and press SHIFT-CONTROL-P for the "Keystroke" option. Click OK to return to the QuicKeys panel.

8. Click the OK button in the QuicKeys panel to return to the Free-Hand window.

9. Press SHIFT-CONTROL-P. First the PREFERENCES, then the MORE PREFER-ENCES dialog boxes will display.

If you make changes or additions to the Aldus FreeHand 3.0 macros file, you will want to output the list of macros using the PRINT... command under the QuicKeys FILE menu (⌘-P). Then photocopy pages 50 through 57 of this book and combine the copies with your printouts to create a comprehensive list of FreeHand keyboard equivalents.

The two QK2 Demo Doc documents—one in the MacWrite II format and the other in the Microsoft Word 4.0 format—provide more detailed explanations about how to use the QuicKeys demonstration utility.

FreeHand and the PostScript Language

In this appendix we take a close look at the relationship between Aldus FreeHand and the PostScript language, focusing on manipulations you can make to FreeHand files using routines included in the PostScript language. Some manipulations are made using the "Post-Script" and "Custom" options in the FILL AND LINE dialog box. Others are made by altering the PostScript-language version of a FreeHand illustration.

Access to the PostScript language extends the range of text and graphics you may create with your computer. This chapter is only the briefest introduction to the PostScript language. We encourage you to explore these potentials more fully by studying other sources dedicated to such information.

Learning the PostScript language

For some of the manipulations described in this chapter, no previous knowledge of the PostScript language is required. Other discussions assume a familiarity with and proficiency in PostScript programming. If you are not yet familiar with PostScript programming, several books on the subject are available. Foremost are three books from Adobe Systems, the creators of the PostScript language: *The PostScript Language Reference Manual*, *The PostScript Language Tutorial and Cookbook*, and *PostScript Language Program Design*, all published by Addison-Wesley, are available at most major bookstores. Also available are *Understanding PostScript Programming* by David Holzgang, published by Sybex, and *Learning PostScript: A Visual Approach* by Ross Smith, published by Peachpit Press.

The PostScript language and the Macintosh

One Adobe brochure states: "Although you cannot see, taste, or touch PostScript, it is the magic behind desktop publishing." Before PostScript, each software developer had to program its software to be specifically compatible with a diverse range of printers. PostScript provides printer manufacturers with a easy-to-use method for creating printed pages described by a myriad of software. Combined with page-layout software, such as PageMaker and QuarkXPress, and laser printers, such as the Apple LaserWriter, PostScript sparked the desktop publishing revolution.

The wealth of routines and commands contained in the PostScript language can be used to describe text, graphic, and scanned images as elements of a page. These routines also provide powerful positioning abilities so that these elements may be placed, rotated, and skewed virtually without limit. PostScript routines are assembled into a simple ASCII text file, which can be transported easily from the computer to the printer, or even from one computing environment to another.

Unfortunately, because the PostScript language is a true programming language, direct access to all its power requires the same amount of effort and ability that is required to program in any computer language. For this reason, most users will never program directly in PostScript.

Then how do *you* use PostScript? Right now, your Macintosh software and your laser printer are taking care of that for you. After you create your document in an application such as Microsoft Word, PageMaker, or Free-Hand, a PostScript file is created when you execute the PRINT... command. This document is downloaded to your PostScript-equipped output device, which executes the PostScript routines and prints your page.

Although software has become increasingly sophisticated, you continue to miss a subset of PostScript's full abilities when you rely entirely on your software's capabilities. The menus and commands do not allow you to access all of PostScript's power, nor all of its convenience. Thankfully, FreeHand allows you to add PostScript commands to your document, thereby taking advantage of as much of PostScript's power and convenience as you wish.

The routines that you enter into the FILL AND LINE dialog box using the "PostScript" options are passed directly to the PostScript interpreter inside your printer without being altered in any way. This ability can be used to create custom fills and strokes and to create many other advanced effects.

Another way to utilize the full range of the PostScript language is to capture the PostScript created by FreeHand and modify the document. Later in this chapter, we look briefly—in fact, very briefly—at this powerful method of modifying PostScript files created by FreeHand.

How PostScript works

Before we look at methods for using PostScript to manipulate a Free-Hand illustration, we must first explain the basic role that PostScript plays in the high resolution output of images. As an environmental factor, Post-Script has a tremendous influence on the way FreeHand works. It has influenced both the features that are available and the manner in which they are implemented. Understanding the relationship between FreeHand and PostScript will help you to understand FreeHand and its potential.

The PostScript computer language was designed primarily to describe elements on printed pages. Like any language, PostScript contains words (known as *commands* or *operators*) and rules governing the ways in which these words can be combined (*syntax* or *structure*). Since PostScript was designed specifically for describing elements on a printed page, its command set is rich enough to describe virtually any page element you may require. PostScript's structure allows for the infinite manipulation and combination of its elements.

To achieve its goals, PostScript uses an *imaging model* to describe and define pages. Three basic types of elements make up the possible images that PostScript can place on a page being described—*text*, *graphics*, and *sampled images*. Using only these three elements, but allowing them to be manipulated in many sophisticated ways, PostScript is able to describe an incredible, perhaps limitless, range of images.

Text

Text in PostScript actually consists of graphic representations of the various characters in the type styles supported by PostScript. Every font contains a detailed PostScript-language description of the shape of each of its characters. By describing characters as graphic objects, PostScript is able to manipulate text in any way it can manipulate graphics. Letters may be filled and stroked with patterns, halftone screens, colors, or even with other text.

Graphics

Graphic elements in PostScript consist of paths that can be open or closed. When closed, a path can be filled with any shade of gray (including black or white), color (if the output device is color-equipped), or pattern. It may also serve as an irregularly shaped canvas on which more complex graphics can be drawn. PostScript allows control of the thickness of any line or curve segment and of the bevel placed on any corner.

Sampled images

PostScript's ability to utilize sampled images (also known as *scanned images*) supports the electronic description of a graphic captured by a scanner or video-input device. The use of photographs in desktop publishing is one example of sampled images.

Manipulating PostScript images

Each of the elements in the PostScript imaging model may be subjected to a variety of manipulations. The first set of manipulations controls the basic placement of elements. PostScript defines a grid system for every page. It is possible to place any element at any coordinates in this grid. PostScript also allows any element or group of elements to be rotated, scaled proportionally or nonproportionally, or otherwise transformed.

FreeHand's use of PostScript

When you use FreeHand, the software masks the complexities of PostScript programming by providing you with familiar mouse and menu-based commands to specify the objects in your document. Using these commands, you can describe the document or elements you want to produce. Free-Hand then converts these descriptions into the specific operators and syntax required by the PostScript language. As in other programs, this translation takes place when you choose the PRINT... command.

The difference between FreeHand and lesser graphic applications, such as MacDraw, is the breadth of its PostScript-based drawing abilities. You may also add PostScript commands to native FreeHand files, which considerably extends the power FreeHand provides to users familiar with the PostScript language. We'll now look at the ways in which the Post-Script language can be used to alter images created using FreeHand.

Fills and strokes

The first and most common use for PostScript routines in FreeHand is to create custom fills and strokes. The FILL AND LINE dialog box provides access to two sets of "Custom" and "PostScript" options—one for the fill of a selection and one for its stroke. These options make available an infinite number of fill and stroke patterns. For example, you can fill your shapes with randomly spaced, sized, and rotated shapes, with any of a dozen cross-hatch varieties, with simulated textures, or with virtually anything else that can be created on a printed page. Custom PostScript strokes can be used to create a string of hearts, a string of irregularly shaped dots, or to have virtually any other series of shapes follow a path to create a line.

When a custom PostScript fill or stroke is applied to an object, Free-Hand is unable to provide an on-screen preview, because PostScript commands do not possess the information to portray themselves on the QuickDraw-driven Macintosh screen. But when printed on a PostScript-equipped output device, the custom PostScript code will be executed exactly as described.

Three basic methods can be used to access custom PostScript fills and strokes inside FreeHand's FILL AND LINE dialog box:

- Choose "PostScript" from the "Fill" or "Line" pop-up menu and enter complete routines into the "PostScript code" text-entry area.

- Choose "Custom" from the "Fill" or "Line" pop-up menu, then choose one of the many predefined PostScript effects from the "Effects" pop-up menu.

- Choose "PostScript" from the "Fill" or "Line" pop-up menu and, in the "PostScript code" text-entry area, enter routines that access predefined procedures from a special UserPrep file stored on disk.

Each of these methods is described in the following sections.

Entering raw PostScript routines

To fill or stroke a selection with a special PostScript-language routine, choose FILL AND LINE… from the ATTRIBUTES menu (⌘-E) to display the FILL AND LINE dialog box. Then choose "PostScript" from the "Fill" or "Line" pop-up menu. A "PostScript code" text-entry area will display, in which you may enter your routine.

Here's an easy example. Suppose you want to fill the current selection with a 50% gray value. The PostScript routine for such a fill is *.5 setgray fill*. If you enter this routine into the "PostScript code" entry area, press RETURN to close the dialog box, and print the illustration, you will find that the current selection is indeed filled with 50% gray.

Unfortunately, this method has its problems. Most notably, it forces you to enter your PostScript-language routines separately in every illustration. Because a PostScript routine can vary in length from a few lines to a few pages and because PostScript, like other computing languages, requires perfect syntax, this method is both time consuming and difficult. Luckily, FreeHand provides a better way to implement custom PostScript lines and fills.

Predefined custom effects

If you're familiar with previous versions of FreeHand, you may be interested to learn that version 3.0 no longer requires a UserPrep file. Every PostScript effect previously contained in the UserPrep and Advanced UserPrep files is now included as a resource in the FreeHand application.

If you *really* know what you're doing, you may edit the PostScript definitions for custom fills and strokes using Apple's ResEdit utility. All custom attribute definitions are found in the *Post* resource, IDs 10,000 and up. Adjust the definitions only if you have an advanced understanding of both PostScript and resource editing.

To fill or stroke a selection with a predefined PostScript-language routine included with Aldus FreeHand 3.0, choose FILL AND LINE... from the ATTRIBUTES menu (⌘-E) and choose "Custom" from the "Fill" or "Line" pop-up menu. Next, choose the desired custom PostScript routine from the "Effect" pop-up menu. A specialized dialog box will display, requesting additional information.

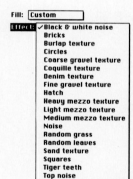

Each of the 19 "Custom" fill options and the 23 "Custom" stroke options is discussed in this section in the order in which it appears in the "Effect" pop-up menu. We begin with the fill effects.

PS Black-and-white noise

The *black-and-white noise* effect fills the selection with a random pattern of black and white 1-point squares. Since this effect may not be manipulated, no dialog box displays when you choose "Black & white noise" from the "Effect" pop-up menu. An example of black-and-white noise is shown in Figure B.01.

Figure B.01: The black-and-white noise effect.

PS Bricks

The *bricks* effect fills the selection with rows of offset rectangles that resemble a brick pattern. Choosing "Bricks" from the "Effect" pop-up menu displays the BRICKS dialog box, as shown in Figure B.02. The dialog box contains these options:

- **Brick color.** Use this pop-up menu to determine the color of the background bricks.

- **Mortar color.** This pop-up menu controls the color of the 1-point lines between bricks.

- **Brick width**. Enter a value into this option box to determine the width of each rectangle, in points.

- **Brick height**. Enter a value into this option box to determine the height of each rectangle, in points.

- **Brick angle**. The value in this option box controls the angle of each row of rectangles, in degrees.

An example of the bricks pattern is shown in Figure B.03.

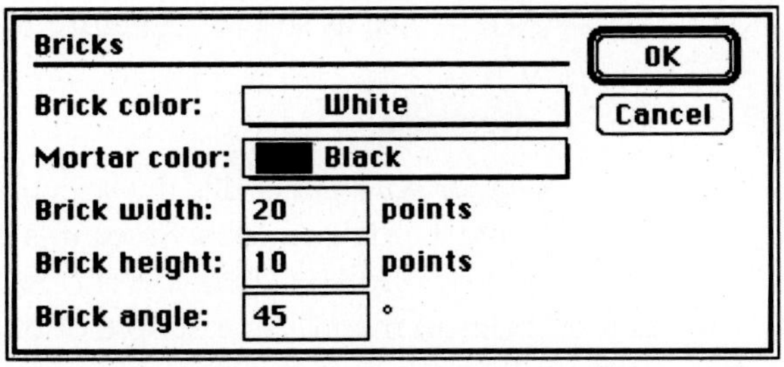

Bricks	OK
Brick color: White	Cancel
Mortar color: ■ Black	
Brick width: 20 points	
Brick height: 10 points	
Brick angle: 45 °	

Figure B.02: The Bricks dialog box displays these default settings when you choose the "Bricks" option.

Figure B.03: The bricks effect with 20% gray bricks, 60% gray mortar, 20-point brick width, 10-point brick height, and 45° angle.

PS Burlap texture

The *burlap texture* effect fills the selection with a pattern that resembles burlap fabric. Choosing "Burlap texture" from the "Effect" pop-up menu displays the BURLAP TEXTURE dialog box, which contains a single option, "Texture color." Use this pop-up menu to determine the color of the burlap pattern. An example of the burlap texture colored with 60% gray is shown in Figure B.04.

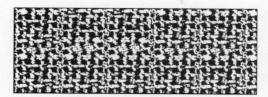

Figure B.04: The burlap texture effect colored with 60% gray.

PS Circles

The *circles* effect fills the selection with rows and columns of evenly spaced circles. Choosing "Circles" from the "Effect" pop-up menu displays the CIRCLES dialog box, as shown in Figure B.05 on the next page. This dialog contains these options:

- **Circle color**. Use this pop-up menu to determine the color of the outline of each circle. The interior of each circle is transparent.

- **Circle radius**. Enter a value into this option box to determine the radius of each circle, in points.

- **Spacing**. The value in this option box controls the distance between the center of a circle and the center of each of its neighbors, in points.

- **Angle**. The value in this option box controls the angle of each row of circles, in degrees.

- **Line width**. Enter a value into this option box to determine the thickness of the outline of each circle, in points.

An example of the circles pattern is shown in Figure B.06.

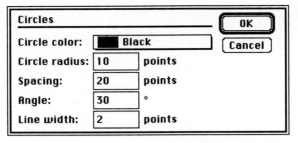

Figure B.05: The Circles dialog box displays these default settings when you choose the "Circles" option.

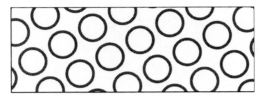

Figure B.06: The circles effect colored with 60% gray, 2-point outlines, 10-point circle radius, 26-point spacing, and 30° angle.

PS Coarse gravel texture

The *coarse gravel texture* effect fills the selection with a pattern that mixes rock shapes with random specks. Choosing "Coarse gravel texture" from the "Effect" pop-up menu displays the COARSE GRAVEL TEXTURE dialog box, which contains a single option, "Texture color." Use this pop-up menu to determine the color of the gravel pattern. An example of the gravel texture colored with 60% gray is shown in Figure B.07.

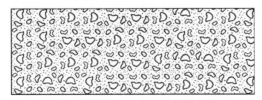

Figure B.07: The coarse gravel texture effect colored with 60% gray.

PS Coquille texture

The *coquille texture* effect fills the selection with a raised, shell-like pattern, much like the pattern associated with traditional etching. Choosing "Coquille texture" from the "Effect" pop-up menu displays the COQUILLE TEXTURE dialog box, which contains a single option, "Texture color." Use this pop-up menu to determine the color of the coquille pattern. An example of the coquille texture colored with 60% gray is shown in Figure B.08.

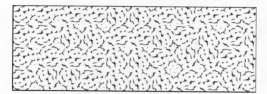

Figure B.08: The coquille texture effect colored with 60% gray.

PS Denim texture

The *denim texture* effect fills the selection with a cross-hatch pattern that resembles denim fabric. Choosing "Denim texture" from the "Effect" pop-up menu displays the DENIM TEXTURE dialog box, which contains a single option, "Texture color." Use this pop-up menu to determine the color of the denim pattern. An example of the denim texture colored with 60% gray is shown in Figure B.09.

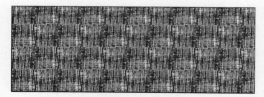

Figure B.09: The denim texture effect colored with 60% gray.

PS Fine gravel texture

The *fine gravel texture* effect fills the selection with a pattern that mixes random specks that vary in size. Choosing "Fine gravel texture" from the "Effect" pop-up menu displays the FINE GRAVEL TEXTURE dialog box, which contains a single option, "Texture color." Use this pop-up menu to determine the color of the gravel pattern. An example of the gravel texture colored with 60% gray is shown in Figure B.10.

Figure B.10: The fine gravel texture effect colored with 60% gray.

PS Hatch

The *hatch* effect fills the selection with hatch marks created by overlapping two sets of parallel lines. Choosing "Hatch" from the "Effect" pop-up menu displays the HATCH dialog box, as shown in Figure B.11. This dialog box contains these options:

- **Line color**. Use this pop-up menu to determine the color of the hatch lines. The background of the pattern is transparent.

- **Angle 1**. Enter a value into this option box to determine the angle of the first set of parallel lines, in degrees.

- **Angle 2**. The value in this option box controls the angle of the second set of parallel lines, in degrees.

- **Spacing**. The value in this option box controls the distance between parallel lines in each set, in points.

- **Hatch line width**. Enter a value into this option box to determine the line weight of all lines, in points.

- **Dashed lines**. Select this check box to create dashed hatch lines; deselect the option to create solid lines.

An example of the bricks pattern is shown in Figure B.12.

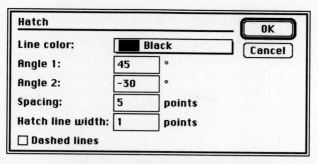

Figure B.11: The Hatch dialog box displays these default settings when you choose the "Hatch" option.

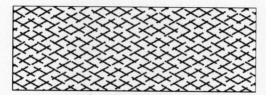

Figure B.12: The hatch effect composed of two sets of 60% gray, 1-point parallel lines, angled at 30° and –30°, spaced 6 points apart, and dashed.

PS Heavy mezzo texture

The *heavy mezzo texture* effect fills the selection with a dark *mezzotint* pattern, a special kind of screen used in traditional halftone photography. Choosing "Heavy mezzo texture" from the "Effect" pop-up menu displays the HEAVY MEZZO TEXTURE dialog box, which contains a single option, "Texture color." Use this pop-up menu to determine the color of the mezzotint pattern. An example of the heavy mezzo texture colored with 60% gray is shown in Figure B.13.

Figure B.13: The heavy mezzo texture effect colored with 60% gray.

PS   Light mezzo texture

The *light mezzo texture* effect fills the selection with a light mezzotint pattern. Choosing "Light mezzo texture" from the "Effect" pop-up menu displays the LIGHT MEZZO TEXTURE dialog box, which contains a single option, "Texture color." Use this pop-up menu to determine the color of the mezzotint pattern. An example of the light mezzo texture colored with 60% gray is shown in Figure B.14.

Figure B.14: The light mezzo texture effect colored with 60% gray.

PS   Medium mezzo texture

The *medium mezzo texture* effect fills the selection with a medium mezzotint pattern. Choosing "Medium mezzo texture" from the "Effect" pop-up menu displays the MEDIUM MEZZO TEXTURE dialog box, which contains a single option, "Texture color." Use this pop-up menu to determine the color of the mezzotint pattern. An example of the medium mezzo texture colored with 60% gray is shown in Figure B.15.

Figure B.15: The medium mezzo texture effect colored with 60% gray.

PS   Noise

The *noise* effect fills the selection with a random pattern of 1-point squares, randomly colored with a range of gray values. Choosing "Noise" from the "Effect" pop-up menu displays the NOISE dialog box, as shown in Figure B.16. In this dialog box, you may define the range of gray values.

The Noise dialog box contains these options:

- **Minimum white**. Enter a value into this option box to determine the color of the lightest gray value with which a square may be filled.

- **Maximum white**. The value in this option box determines the color of the darkest gray value with which a square may be filled.

An example of the noise pattern is shown in Figure B.17.

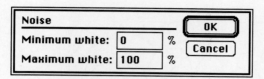

Figure B.16: The Noise dialog box displays these default settings when you choose the "Noise" option.

Figure B.17: The noise effect with a minimum gray value of 20% and a maximum gray value of 60%.

PS Random grass

The *random grass* effect fills the selection with a specified number of randomly placed, black-stroked curves. Choosing "Random grass" from the "Effect" pop-up menu displays the RANDOM GRASS dialog box, which contains a single option, "Number of blades." Enter any value from 0 to 32,000 into this option box to determine the number of curves spread over the selected area. An example containing 50 curves is shown in Figure B.18.

Figure B.18: The random grass effect filled with 50 blades.

PS Random leaves

The *random leaves* effect fills the selection with a specified number of black-stroked, white-filled leaf shapes, randomly sized and placed. Choosing "Random leaves" from the "Effect" pop-up menu displays the RANDOM LEAVES dialog box, which contains a single option, "Number of leaves." Enter any value from 0 to 32,000 into this option box to determine the number of leaf shapes spread over the selected area. An example containing 50 leaves is shown in Figure B.19.

Figure B.19: The random leaves effect filled with 50 leaves.

PS Sand texture

The *sand texture* effect fills the selection with a pattern of random specks, more closely knit than the fine gravel texture. Choosing "Sand texture" from the "Effect" pop-up menu displays the SAND TEXTURE dialog box, which contains a single option, "Texture color." Use this pop-up menu to determine the color of the sand pattern. An example of the sand texture colored with 60% gray is shown in Figure B.20.

Figure B.20: The sand texture effect colored with 60% gray.

PS Squares

The *squares* effect fills the selection with rows and columns of evenly spaced squares. Choosing "Squares" from the "Effect" pop-up menu displays the SQUARES dialog box, as shown in Figure B.21.

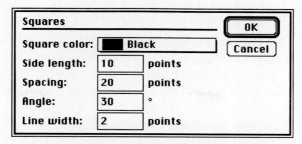

Figure B.21: The Squares dialog box displays these default settings when you choose the "Squares" option.

The options in the SQUARES dialog box operate as follows:

- **Square color**. Use this pop-up menu to determine the color of the outline of each square. The interior of each square is transparent.

- **Side length**. Enter a value into this option box to determine the length of any side of each square, in points.

- **Spacing**. The value in this option box controls the distance between the center of each square and the center of any of its neighbors, in points.

- **Angle**. The value in this option box controls the angle of each row of squares, in degrees.

- **Line width**. Enter a value into this option box to determine the thickness of the outline of each square, in points.

An example of the squares pattern is shown in Figure B.22.

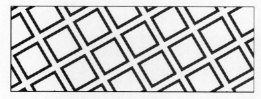

Figure B.22: The squares effect with 60% gray, 2-point outlines, 20-point sides, 26-point spacing, and 30° angle.

PS Tiger teeth

The *tiger teeth* effect fills the selection with two sets of dovetailed triangles that resemble a closed mouth of sharp teeth. Choosing "Tiger teeth" from the "Effect" pop-up menu displays the TIGER TEETH dialog box, as shown in Figure B.23. The dialog box contains these options:

- **Tooth color**. At 0° angle, the right-pointing triangles are considered to be the teeth and the left-pointing triangles are the background. Choose an option from this pop-up menu to determine the color of the teeth.

- **Background color**. Use this pop-up menu to determine the color of the background (left-pointing triangles at 0°).

- **Number of teeth**. The value in this option box controls the number of teeth triangles (right-pointing at 0°) that fill the selection.

- **Tooth angle**. Enter a value into this option box to determine the angle of the triangles, in degrees.

An example of the tiger teeth pattern is shown in Figure B.24.

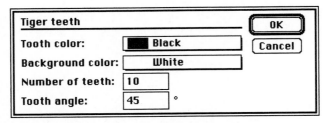

Figure B.23: The Tiger teeth dialog box displays these default settings when you choose the "Tiger teeth" option.

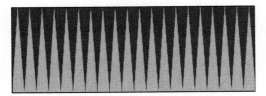

Figure B.24: The tiger teeth effect containing 20 teeth filled with 20% gray against a 60% gray background, angled at 90°.

PS Top noise

The *top noise* effect fills the selection with a random pattern of 1-point squares, filled according to your specifications against a transparent background. Choosing "Top noise" from the "Effect" pop-up menu displays the TOP NOISE dialog box, which contains a single option, "Gray value." Enter a value into this option box to determine the gray value assigned to the 1-point squares. An example of the top noise pattern colored with 60% gray is shown in Figure B.25.

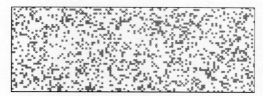

Figure B.25: The top noise effect with a gray value of 60%.

Five custom fill patterns have transparent backgrounds. These include circles, hatch, random grass, squares, and top noise. A sixth pattern, random leaves, is partially transparent. Any of these custom patterns may be layered over an object, allowing the background object to partially show through, as demonstrated in Figure B.26.

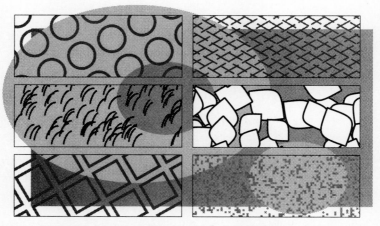

Figure B.26: The five transparent custom fill patterns in front of several shapes with basic fills. The sixth pattern, random leaves (second pattern on the right), is partially transparent.

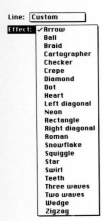

Unlike the "Custom" fill effects, 22 of the 23 "Custom" stroke effects are remarkably similar, so much so, in fact, that if you know how to use one, you know how to use them all. The only exception is the neon effect, which is described at the end of this section.

For the majority of the stroking effects, we will use the *arrow* effect as an example. Like the others, the arrow effect repeats a series of objects along the length of a selected path. Choosing "Arrow" from the "Effect" pop-up menu displays the ARROW dialog box, as shown in Figure B.27.

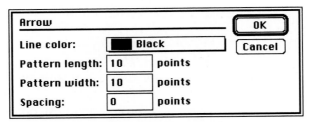

Figure B.27: The Arrow dialog box displays these default settings when you choose the "Arrow" option.

Like most other custom stroke dialog boxes, the ARROW dialog box contains these options:

- **Line color**. Use this pop-up menu to determine the color of the outlines of the arrowheads. The interior of each arrowhead is transparent.

- **Pattern length**. Enter a value into this option box to determine the length of each arrowhead, in points.

- **Pattern width**. Enter a value into this option box to determine the thickness of the custom stroke, in points.

- **Spacing**. The value in this option box controls the distance between the end of one arrowhead and the beginning of another, in points.

An example of the arrow stroke is shown in Figure B.28.

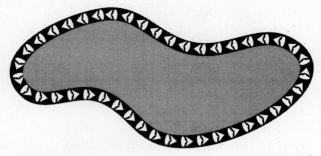

Figure B.28: A path stroked with the arrow effect. The effect includes 60% gray line color, 10-point pattern height, 10-point pattern width, and 2-point spacing.

Among the stroking effects that use the same options as the arrow effect are *ball, braid, cartographer, checker, crepe, diamond, dot, heart, left diagonal, rectangle, right diagonal, roman, snowflake, squiggle, star, swirl, teeth, three waves, two waves, wedge,* and *zigzag*. Each of these effects is displayed in Figures B.29 through B.49. All options for these strokes are set as described in Figure B.28.

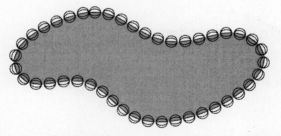

Figure B.29: A path stroked with the ball effect.

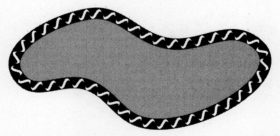

Figure B.30: A path stroked with the braid effect.

Figure B.31: A path stroked with the cartographer effect.

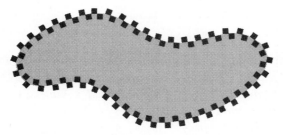

Figure B.32: A path stroked with the checker effect.

Figure B.33: A path stroked with the crepe effect.

Figure B.34: A path stroked with the diamond effect.

BUSINESS REPLY MAIL

FIRST CLASS MAIL   PERMIT NO. 99   HOMEWOOD, IL

POSTAGE WILL BE PAID BY ADDRESSEE

BUSINESS ONE IRWIN

1818 Ridge Road
Homewood, IL 60430-9924

ATTENTION
Joan Zagone

BUSINESS ONE IRWIN is dedicated to providing you with the most timely, authoritative, and comprehensive computer guides to meet your personal and professional needs. Our goal is to offer you excellent reference tools written by experienced, highly-qualified authors. Please take a moment to answer the following questions so that we can continue to develop our products based on your needs.

Thank you.
BUSINESS ONE IRWIN

Current Computer Hardware:
- ☐ IBM or compatible
- ☐ Apple or Macintosh
- ☐ Commodore
- ☐ Atari

Disk Density:
- ☐ High
- ☐ Low

Disk Size:
- ☐ 5.25"   ☐ 3.5"

Is It Portable?
- ☐ Yes   ☐ No

Printer Type:
- ☐ LaserJet
- ☐ PostScript
- ☐ Dot Matrix
- ☐ Other

Peripherals:
- ☐ Modem
- ☐ Scanner
- ☐ Mouse
- ☐ Networking
- ☐ FAX
- ☐ Other (please specify)

_____
_____
_____

Operating System:
- ☐ MS-DOS
- ☐ OS/2
- ☐ Macintosh
- ☐ UNIX

Programming Languages:
- ☐ BASIC
- ☐ C
- ☐ Pascal
- ☐ Prolog
- ☐ Assembly
- ☐ HyperTalk

The Most Recent Software Program I Purchased Is: _____

Software I Use Most Often:
(please check all that apply and state name of product)
- ☐ Word Processing_____
- ☐ Spreadsheet_____
- ☐ Database/File Mgmt_____
- ☐ Desktop Publishing_____
- ☐ Presentation Graphics_____
- ☐ Accounting_____
- ☐ Statistical Analysis_____
- ☐ Financial/Tax Planning_____
- ☐ Integrated _____
- ☐ Business Form Design _____
- ☐ Utilities_____

Additional Comments: _____
_____
_____
_____
_____
_____

Name_____
Title _____
Organization_____
Address _____
City/State/Zip_____
Telephone_____
☐ Please send a catalog of Business One Irwin books.

businessOne
IRWIN
1818 Ridge Road, Homewood, IL 60430

QUALITY PUBLISHING FOR WORLDWIDE BUSINESS MARKETS

J15-3403-01-02

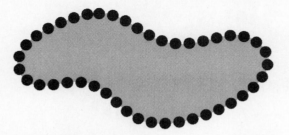

Figure B.35: A path stroked with the dot effect.

Figure B.36: A path stroked with the heart effect.

Figure B.37: A path stroked with the left diagonal effect.

Figure B.38: A path stroked with the rectangle effect.

B—FreeHand and the PostScript Language 561

Figure B.39: A path stroked with the right diagonal effect.

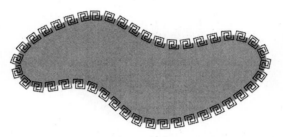

Figure B.40: A path stroked with the roman effect.

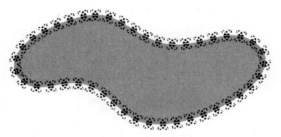

Figure B.41: A path stroked with the snowflake effect.

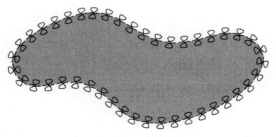

Figure B.42: A path stroked with the squiggle effect.

Figure B.43: A path stroked with the star effect.

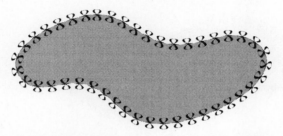

Figure B.44: A path stroked with the swirl effect.

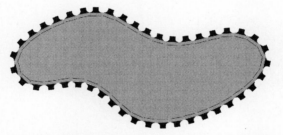

Figure B.45: A path stroked with the teeth effect.

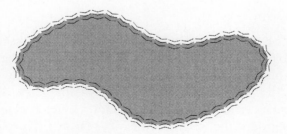

Figure B.46: A path stroked with the three waves effect.

Figure B.47: A path stroked with the two waves effect.

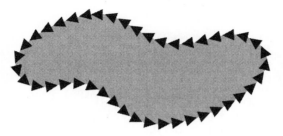

Figure B.48: A path stroked with the wedge effect.

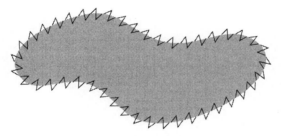

Figure B.49: A path stroked with the zigzag effect.

PS Neon

The only unusual "Custom" stroking effect is the *neon* effect, which combines three lines: one stroked with white, in front of another stroked with black, in front of a third stroked with 50% gray. Choosing "Neon" from the "Effect" pop-up menu displays the NEON dialog box, which contains a single option, "Line width." Enter a value into this option box to determine the weight of the 50% gray line. The black line will be half this weight. The foremost white line is always 1 point thick. An example of the neon stroke is shown in Figure B.50.

Figure B.50: A path stroke with a 10-point version of the neon effect.

Creating and using a UserPrep file

The third method for accessing custom PostScript-language fills and strokes is to enter routines in the "PostScript code" text-entry area in the FILL AND LINE dialog box. Such routines call up predefined PostScript procedures from an on-disk UserPrep file. This method allows you to avoid retyping a procedure each time you want to apply it. It also overcomes the 255-character limit imposed by the "PostScript code" text-entry area, as well as the limitations regarding comments and carriage returns.

In PostScript, a *procedure* is a sequence of commands assigned to a particular name. To execute the commands in the procedure, you simply type the procedure's name into the "PostScript code" text-entry area. When this name is received by the PostScript interpreter, it references the full command sequence in the UserPrep file.

Suppose, for example, that we want to create a custom PostScript routine that strokes the current path with a double line. You might enter the following PostScript code to accomplish this:

```
gsave 4 setlinewidth 0 setgray stroke grestore
1 setlinewidth 1 setgray stroke
```

The following code creates a PostScript procedure named *double* that produces the same result:

```
/double {
gsave 4 setlinewidth 0 setgray stroke grestore
1 setlinewidth 1 setgray stroke
} def
```

This procedure strokes the current path with a 4-point black line and then strokes that same path with a 1-point white line. Both of these lines are centered exactly on the same path, so you are really creating what looks like a double black line by drawing a thin white line on top of a thicker black line. Having downloaded this procedure to a PostScript printer, you simply have to enter the word *double* into the "PostScript code" text-entry area to execute it. A path stroked with the double effect is shown in Figure B.51.

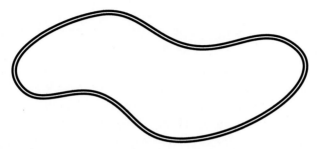

Figure B.51: A path stroked with the double effect, a custom PostScript procedure.

FreeHand implements PostScript procedures by automatically downloading a text-only file named UserPrep to the current PostScript-compatible output device before an illustration is printed. The UserPrep file traditionally contains predefined PostScript procedures. When downloaded, these procedures become available for use by the current illustration. For example, suppose that you have created a UserPrep file that contains a procedure to fill a path with stars. The procedure is named *stars*. To use the procedure, you simply select a path, choose the FILL AND LINE... command from the ATTRIBUTES menu (⌘-E), choose the "Post-Script" option from the "Fill" pop-up menu, enter the word *stars* in the "PostScript code" text-entry area, and press RETURN. When printed, the complete stars procedure will execute and the object will be filled with stars.

UserPrep is a standard text file that can be edited using any standard word processor. UserPrep contains PostScript commands grouped to form procedures. FreeHand will automatically download the UserPrep file if it is located in the folder that contains the FreeHand application or in the Aldus folder in the System folder.

Unlike in previous versions of FreeHand, Aldus no longer provides a UserPrep file with your FreeHand application. In fact, unless you have added procedures of your own, you may delete any previous versions of UserPrep and Advanced UserPrep, since all of these procedures may be accessed using the "Custom" pop-up menus. If you have modified the UserPrep file, don't throw it away; instead, delete all routines originally included in the file, leaving only your own intact.

To add procedures to an existing UserPrep file, open the file in any word processor. To create a new UserPrep file, create a new ASCII (text-only) file in any word processor and name it *UserPrep*. Then enter your procedures in any order you desire.

Although you are probably beginning to see the powerful potential of a UserPrep file, you may have also noticed a limitation. For example, if you want to alter the double procedure by changing the thickness of the line from 4 points to 10 points, or by changing the gray value of the thick or thin lines, you must return to your word processor and edit the procedure contained in the UserPrep file. To avoid this problem, you may define several different procedures—double1, double2, and so on—each with slightly different parameters.

An even better solution is to exploit an attribute of the PostScript language that provides additional power and functionality to any procedure. The PostScript language uses what some programmers call a "reverse Polish notation." Instead of saying "add 4 to 3," as you would in English, PostScript requires that you enter *4 3 add*. The fact that PostScript uses this notation, combined with PostScript's stack orientation, allows you to pass parameters to a PostScript procedure, customizing them on a case-by-case basis.

For example, suppose that you want to be able to change the line width of the stroke created by the double procedure. By leaving the settings for line thickness as a variable, it is possible to enjoy all the benefits of a procedure and still customize the line each time you use it. The modified PostScript procedure for a variable-width double stroke is:

```
/double {
/width exch def
gsave width setlinewidth 0 setgray stroke grestore
width 4 div setlinewidth 1 setgray stroke
} def
```

Notice how the procedure has been modified. First, a definition for the word *width* has been added, which assumes that a width value precedes the word *double* when the procedure is called. Second, the literal values of 4 and 1 before the *setlinewidth* commands have been substituted with *width* and *width 4 div* (the width value divided by 4). To use the variable-thickness double stroke, you simply enter a line weight value before the word double into the "PostScript code" text-entry area. For example, 8 double will produce a line with an 8-point black line and a 2-point white line, as displayed in Figure B.52. Compare this figure with the double effect shown in Figure B.51.

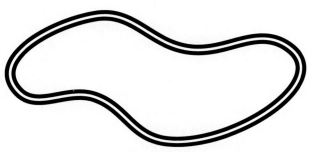

Figure B.52: A path stroked with the 8 double effect.

If you aren't a programmer, but you still want to be able to take advantage of some fantastic PostScript effects, you can purchase a collection of PostScript procedures from some small, third-party distributors. One example of such a collection is PSpatterns from Parallax Productions, (206) 633-4030. This fine collection includes 28 procedures, with as many as six variables apiece. Figure B.53 shows an example of a procedure that fills a selection with a series of concentric circles. This procedure includes 3 variables: The first controls the line weights; the second controls the radius of the innermost circle; and the third determines the number of circles. The figure below shows the result of entering 6 10 6 circle into the "PostScript code" text-entry area.

Figure B.53: A sample third-party PostScript effect.

Several additional effects from the PSpatterns library are displayed in Figure B.54.

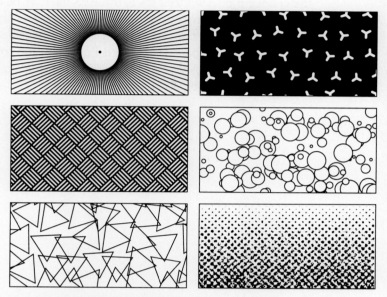

Figure B.54: Examples of the ray, sticks, weave, bubbles, triangles, and airbrush effects included in the PSpatterns UserPrep file (not included with FreeHand 3.0).

Working with PostScript and EPS documents

If you really super-dooper know what you're doing, it is possible to modify FreeHand files that have been printed to disk or saved in the Encapsulated PostScript format.

As described in Chapter 14, *Printing Your Illustrations*, standard PostScript files are captured by pressing COMMAND-F immediately after clicking the OK button in the LASERWRITER PRINT dialog box. Encapsulated PostScript files are created using the EXPORT… command. Both standard PostScript and EPS files can be opened in a word processor. Any modifications that you make must use the exact commands and syntax provided within the PostScript language.

Note that before modifying an EPS file, you must change the creator type from EPSF to TEXT. This can be accomplished using any one of a variety of utilities, including Disktop, SetFileType, and MacTools. Once the creator type is set to TEXT, the EPS file may be opened in a word processor and you may alter the PostScript code. Modification of EPS format files should be undertaken only with a complete understanding of the Altsys/Aldus/Adobe Encapsulated PostScript file conventions. To use this file as an Encapsulated PostScript format file after modifying it, change the creator type back to EPSF.

Index

Symbols

L

M

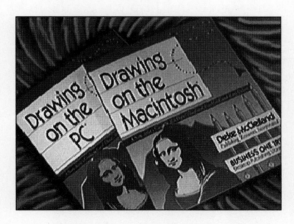

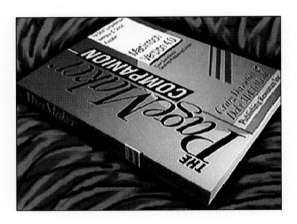